PRAISE FOR GR

'Engagingly written
portra
The

'Vivid, detailed and well written'
Daily Telegraph

'A staggering accomplishment that can't be missed by
history buffs and story lovers alike'
Betterreading.com.au

'A free-flowing biography of a great Australian figure'
John Howard

'Clear and accessible ... well-crafted and extensively
documented'
Weekend Australian

'Kieza has added hugely to the depth of knowledge about
our greatest military general in a book that is timely'
Tim Fischer, Courier-Mail

'The author writes with the immediacy of a fine
documentary ... an easy, informative read, bringing
historic personalities to life'
Ballarat Courier

ALSO BY GRANTLEE KIEZA

Mr and Mrs Gould

Sister Viv

Flinders

Knockout: Great Australian Boxing Stories

The Remarkable Mrs Reibey

Hudson Fysh

The Kelly Hunters

Lawson

Banks

Macquarie

Banjo

The Hornet (with Jeff Horn)

Boxing in Australia

Mrs Kelly: The Astonishing Life of Ned Kelly's Mother

Monash: The Soldier Who Shaped Australia

Sons of the Southern Cross

Bert Hinkler: The Most Daring Man in the World

The Retriever (with Keith Schafferius)

A Year to Remember (with Mark Waugh)

Stopping the Clock: Health and Fitness the George Daldry Way
(with George Daldry)

Fast and Furious: A Celebration of Cricket's Pace Bowlers

Mark My Words: The Mark Graham Story
(with Alan Clarkson and Brian Mossop)

Australian Boxing: The Illustrated History

Fenech: The Official Biography (with Peter Muszkat)

GRANTLEE KIEZA

Bestselling author of *Sister Viv*, *The Remarkable Mrs Reibey*,
Hudson Fysh, *Banjo*, *Banks* and *Mrs Kelly*

Annette Kellerman
Australian Mermaid

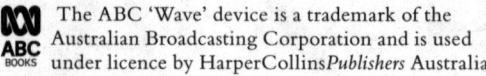 The ABC 'Wave' device is a trademark of the Australian Broadcasting Corporation and is used under licence by HarperCollins*Publishers* Australia.

HarperCollins*Publishers*
Australia • Brazil • Canada • France • Germany • Holland • India
Italy • Japan • Mexico • New Zealand • Poland • Spain • Sweden
Switzerland • United Kingdom • United States of America

HarperCollins acknowledges the Traditional Custodians of the lands upon which we live and work, and pays respect to Elders past and present.

First published on Gadigal Country in Australia in 2025
by HarperCollins*Publishers* Australia Pty Limited
ABN 36 009 913 517
harpercollins.com.au

Copyright © Grantlee Kieza 2025

The right of Grantlee Kieza to be identified as the author of this work has been asserted by him in accordance with the *Copyright Amendment (Moral Rights) Act 2000*.

This work is copyright. Apart from any use as permitted under the *Copyright Act 1968*, no part may be reproduced, copied, scanned, stored in a retrieval system, recorded, or transmitted, in any form or by any means, without the prior written permission of the publisher. Without limiting the author's and publisher's exclusive rights, any unauthorised use of this publication to train generative artificial intelligence (AI) technologies is expressly prohibited. HarperCollins also exercises its rights under Article 4(3) of the Digital Single Market Directive 2019/790 and expressly reserves this publication from the text and data-mining exception.

A catalogue record for this book is available from the National Library of Australia

ISBN 978 0 7333 4330 8 (paperback)
ISBN 978 1 4607 1702 8 (ebook)

Cover design by Michelle Zaiter, HarperCollins Design Studio
Front cover image: National Film and Sound Archive of Australia
Back cover image: Los Angeles Times Photographic Archive, UCLA Library Special Collections
Author photograph by Steve Pohlner
Typeset in Bembo Std by Kirby Jones
Printed and bound in Australia by McPherson's Printing Group

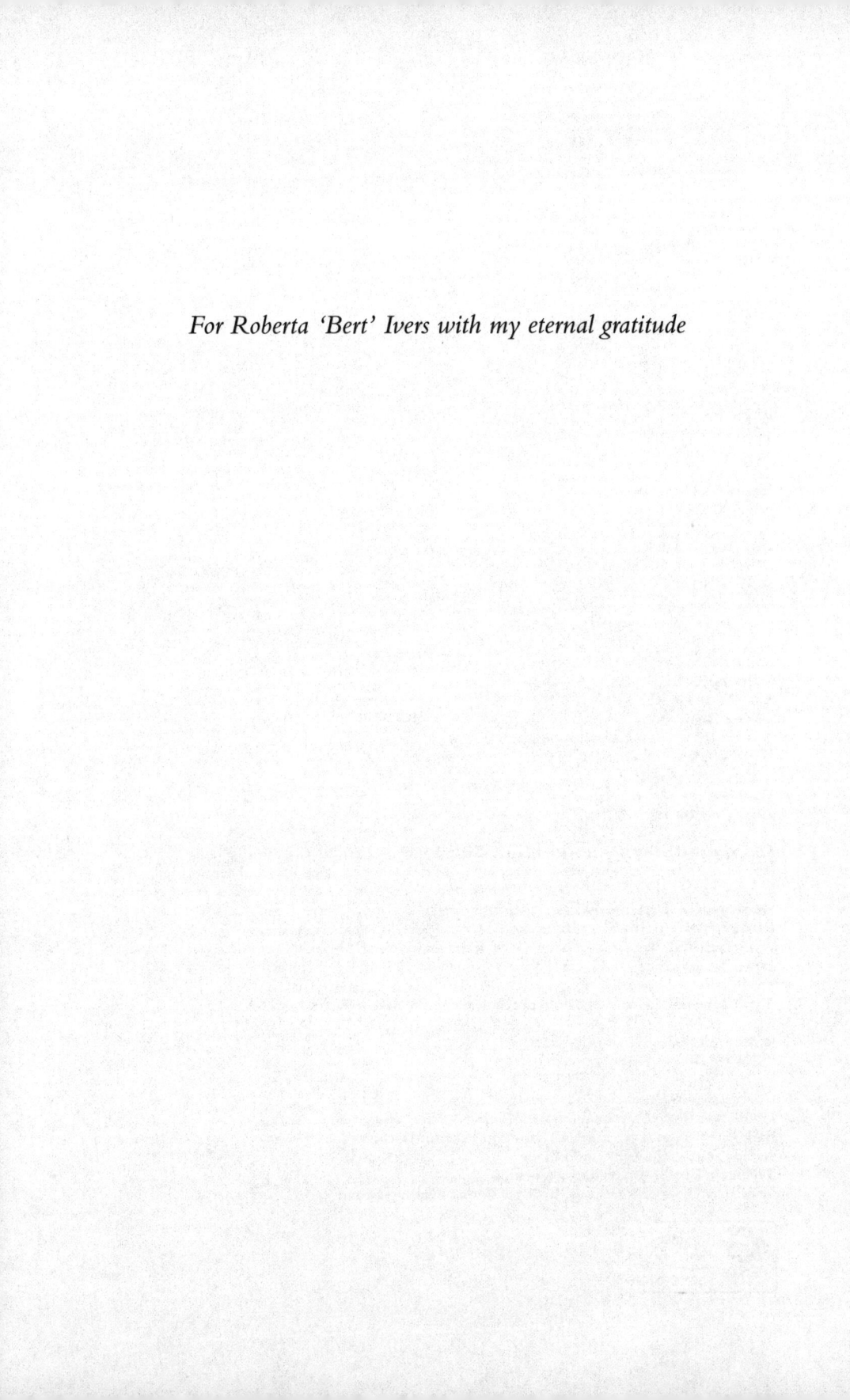

For Roberta 'Bert' Ivers with my eternal gratitude

Prologue

ANNETTE KELLERMAN strode into the Hollywood studios of Metro-Goldwyn-Mayer with shoulders back, her spine ramrod straight and her head held regally high.

She was dressed immaculately, in a smartly cut suit that reached just below her knees and exquisite high-heeled shoes befitting the status she once held as a global fashion icon.

It was a bright, clear winter's day in 1952.[1]

Dwight D. Eisenhower was President of the United States; Princess Elizabeth, Duchess of Edinburgh, had just been made Queen of Great Britain and her Dominions; and Hollywood was filming the story of Annette Kellerman's life in an epic extravaganza.

All around Annette there was the buzz of excitement that only the creation of a big budget motion picture can produce: hundreds of exotically dressed extras clad in glittering swimsuits and shining swimming caps were rushing to their positions, lighting men were busily setting up and testing their equipment, and set directors were making last minute adjustments.

Annette had embraced vegetarianism for much of her adult life, so at sixty-five she was still wickedly fit and about 20 kilograms lighter than she was half a century earlier when she set world swimming records as a curvy teenager known around the world for bucking conventions and wearing what at the time were considered skimpy swimming costumes.

She was now on the MGM lot for her first day as technical director for the celluloid depiction of her struggles and triumphs, *Million Dollar Mermaid*.

Annette was greeted by the movie's director, Mervyn LeRoy,[2] who had high hopes that his new movie would be a success akin to his 1939 production, *The Wizard of Oz*. LeRoy was sparing no expense to make this much-ballyhooed Technicolor wonder the must-see movie of the year. It was to be an aqua extravaganza, recreating the great water ballet stage shows of Annette's career.

LeRoy introduced Annette to the movie's fabled choreographer, Busby Berkeley,[3] who was tasked with turning hundreds of dancers into a dazzling kaleidoscope of long limbs moving with jaw-dropping precision.

LeRoy took Annette by the arm and escorted her further into the film's engine room, promising that he would faithfully recreate the story of a crippled Australian girl who became the most daring and celebrated entertainer of her time, a woman the British press once called 'a little Colonial girl with a veritable lion's heart'.[4]

It was almost sixty years since Annette had been all but frozen with fear as she first dipped her toe into the cool waters of Sydney Harbour, her father believing that swimming might help her weak and withered legs that had been blighted by childhood disease.

She had first loved the ocean as a child because it made her curious. It told her a different story every time she dived in. She wondered whether it really went down and down and down, and if it would really hold her up as she moved about in it. She wanted to know what made it so blue and to feel the white of a wave.[5]

Annette would later claim that her early physical misfortune had turned out to be her greatest blessing. Without it, she said, she would have missed the grim struggle upward and the enormous reward waiting at the end of it all.[6]

Now, six decades later, striding through a movie lot where her life was to be immortalised by the most important filmmakers in the world, she could look back on her extraordinary success. Annette had gone on from a childhood mired in disability and despair to claim world swimming records for women from 100 yards (90 m) to 36 kilometres.[7] She had made headlines around the world with marathon swims in the Yarra River, the Thames, the Seine, the Danube, Boston Harbour and the English Channel. To a generation of women constrained by tight corsets and long heavy skirts, she was a real-life superhero, swimming for mile after mile, often singing as she went. At other times she performed diving routines from dangerous, dizzying heights, flying through the air in daring, skin-tight costumes while shouting the Australian cry 'Cooee'.

From her handicapped childhood, Annette had developed a kind of spiritual connection with life-giving water. It had cured her of a severe disability, and her ardent and unbroken pursuit of swimming success created worldwide fame and made her a shining example of vigour and beauty to inspire others.[8]

While still a teenager she became the most celebrated female sports star in the world and a symbol of high fashion, equally at home strolling the boulevards of the Champs-Élysée near the Paris home she bought her mother, or the salons of Fifth Avenue in New York, where she had once been hailed the queen of American vaudeville, working alongside lesser-known performers on the rise such as Buster Keaton, Charlie Chaplin, Al Jolson and Mae West.

Now, on the MGM lot almost a lifetime after her sporting career took off at the turn of the century, Annette still moved with the easy grace she had shown as a ballerina at the Metropolitan Opera House on Broadway, or as a vivacious, irreverent convent schoolgirl running up Sydney's Church Hill to class, long before Australia was even a nation.

In the years before World War I, a newspaper columnist was moved to write that to see Annette Kellerman 'is to increase one's faith in the human form divine. Unaided by corsets and high heels, in trustful reliance on daily exercise, clean cold water, and all the open air that a busy life will permit, she has made herself into the likeness of Greek sculpture.'[9]

Now, at sixty-five, Annette still looked a picture of the supreme fitness and glowing health that had once earned her

Annette Kellerman (left) with Hollywood choreographer Busby Berkeley and movie star Esther Williams on the set of *Million Dollar Mermaid* in 1952. National Film and Sound Archive 1586677

the title of 'The Perfect Woman' from no less an authority than the physical training department of Harvard University, which had studied 10,000 women and girls and declared the young Australian the most magnificent of them all.[10] Though she had laughed off that accolade by saying that no one was really perfect, Harvard's endorsement had been Annette's calling card, and she became one of the first and most successful social influencers to use mass media.

Annette had pioneered the one-piece bathing suit for women, and figure-hugging dresses that became the talk of the fashion world. From the early years of the twentieth century, she gave lectures and published books and mail-order fitness manuals to empower women around the world with the message that fitness was beautiful and a beautiful body could be the key to a beautiful life. With her guidance, she told her adoring audiences, women could throw off their domestic shackles, toss out their corsets and embrace strength and fitness as the keys to health and beauty.

In the early 1900s, when women's roles were largely defined by the men they married and the domestic chores they were expected to perform, Annette helped to fashion a new ideal of womanhood by modelling an athletic, energetic femininity.[11] The new woman for a new age, she said, was not buried under layers of corsets and heavy clothing but was instead kissed by the sun, caressed by the water, lithe, and always on the move.

Her famous figure made her a movie star, and she became a friend and favourite of Bill Fox and his Fox Film Corporation.

To her movie audiences she was a real-life Wonder Woman: doing her own death-defying stunts, diving off huge towers into the ocean and even plunging into a pool of crocodiles to get the perfect footage. Her 1916 epic, *A Daughter of the Gods,* filmed on location in Jamaica, was the most expensive film made up until that time. It featured a cast of more than 20,000 extras, and she became the first big name actor to appear naked on screen.

In later life she composed songs and organised dance routines to help the Red Cross during World War II. She also raised money to help female students at the Queensland University in Brisbane, and for the charity founded by the Queensland nurse Elizabeth Kenny to combat polio.

For a time, Annette lived in the southern Whitsunday Islands off the Queensland town of Mackay, where she championed the Great Barrier Reef as one of the natural wonders of the world, something that had to be preserved at all costs for future generations.

By 1952, she and her husband of forty years were back in California, living in semi-retirement in the upmarket suburb of Pacific Palisades in the Westside region of Los Angeles. There, Annette indulged her love of healthy life by running a health food store at Long Beach.[12] Metro-Goldwyn-Mayer had cast one of the most beautiful actresses on their books, Esther Williams,[13] herself a former swimming champion, to play Annette in *Million Dollar Mermaid*.

Now Mervyn LeRoy ushered Annette onto Stage 30, which would be used for the swimming scenes. The cast and crew called it 'Pneumonia Alley'[14] because it was so cold in there, but when Annette met Esther on set, the young actress, who was preparing for an elaborate water scene, seemed to be sunlight itself. Annette had met the glamorous star months earlier to discuss the movie but now shimmering all over in a sequined head-to-toe gold leotard that clung to her like glue, Esther's every curve was exaggerated.

Taken aback by the young, glowing woman, Annette declared modestly that Esther was just about the most beautiful woman she'd ever seen and that she was far too pretty to play her.

Esther smiled a million-megawatt Hollywood smile and told Annette that it was an honour to portray a living legend. She said she had craved the role ever since the movie's producer showed her a photograph from the 1920s of Annette waving a parasol above her head as she negotiated a tightrope wire strung between the bluffs of the Pacific Palisades, across the beach towards the Santa Monica pier.[15]

There was more banter about how Esther would tackle the Australian accent and how she would handle some of the dangerous dives that had helped make Annette a household name long before Esther was born.

Over the next few days Annette came to the studio to watch the story of her life take shape. But soon she had concerns about the final product.

Esther was twenty-nine and she and her second husband had two children, but she had already started a torrid affair with her *Million Dollar Mermaid* co-star, Victor Mature, a sword-and-sandal mainstay fresh from Cecil B. DeMille's Biblical epic *Samson and Delilah*. Annette didn't think that augured well for a harmonious production.

She got talking to a newspaper columnist and screenwriter named Vince Flaherty,[16] who was on the set reporting on the splendour of the new film. He told Annette that it was the thrill of a lifetime to meet her; how millions of women around the world forty years earlier had applauded her because they had grown weary of their old-fashioned clothes, the bloomers and sailor jackets that were standard beachwear; and how her swimsuits had been all the rage among his young female friends back then.

He recounted how, as a boy on holiday in Atlantic City, New Jersey, he had watched transfixed as Annette performed at the famous Steel Pier amusement park.

Now, Flaherty was impressed by the way Annette could still bound up flights of stairs two at a time, and he told her that she looked as fit as he remembered her in a one-piece swimsuit decades earlier, standing high above the crowd as what seemed like 1000 musicians played silvery instruments and banged drums, building the tension for her diving routine.

When the show had ended and Flaherty returned home, he told his friends that he had seen Annette Kellerman – 'honestly I had' – and he had seen her dive off a platform that must have been 'five hunnerd feet high!' He'd amend that to 'maybe a hunnerd feet high', but it was still a mighty something.[17]

Annette smiled and told Flaherty that she still swam every day and walked miles to stay fit.

Privately, she wondered about the decision to cast big burly sourpuss Victor Mature to play the love interest in the movie, and she worried about some of the liberties being taken with her story. Annette had always been a champion for empowering women and helping the underdogs rise. She hoped the movie would reflect that.

She wanted people everywhere to be inspired by the story of Annette Kellerman – the Australian Mermaid.

Chapter 1

WATER, WAVES AND CHEERING crowds were in Annette Kellerman's DNA. Both of her parents had backgrounds in entertainment, and as a girl Annette's mother had lived amid the golden beaches and swaying palms of the French South Pacific.

Annette was born in 1886[1] in a terrace house[2] in Darlinghurst, a tree-lined suburb of narrow lanes and avenues on the edge of Sydney's harbour, one of the most majestic waterways in the world. All around the newborn there was sand and surf, energy and excitement. And there was music – warm, passionate, uplifting music on the piano and violin, which had jangled her limbs even while she was still in her mother's womb and which now stirred this wrinkled, wide-eyed new soul.

Annette was the second child of American-born, Paris-educated Alice Charbonnet[3] and her Australian-born husband, Fred Kellermann.[4] (The family gradually dropped the second 'n' from their surname.)

Both parents were talented young musicians, and Annette's mother had been making news in Sydney since her first visit to the city as a child. But in keeping with the male-centric mores of her time, Alice received scant public recognition for her role in Annette's birth – only a brief acknowledgement as a no-name ancillary to her husband in the Family Notices section of Sydney's two leading newspapers.

KELLERMANN.—July 6, at her residence, 101, Victoria-street, the wife of Fred. Kellermann, of a daughter.[5]

The newborn was named Annette Marie Sarah Kellermann[6] – Marie after some relatives and Sarah after the acclaimed queen of the Paris stage, Sarah Bernhardt, one of her mother's friends. As a child, Annette was fascinated by a portrait of the actor that hung in the family's drawing room, complete with an autographed dedication in French that translated as: 'to the charming Alice Charbonnet with great affection Sarah Bernhardt'.[7]

Three months after Annette's birth, the Statue of Liberty was erected in New York, symbolising freedom and the deep friendship between France and America. The chubby, happy baby with big bright blue-grey eyes and seemingly boundless energy had deep roots in both countries.

In the 1880s, the brash young city of Sydney buzzed with the endless possibilities of growth. Long before Annette's birth, however, her mother had already laid the foundation for her child to have a life of daring adventure while defying deeply entrenched social taboos. Like her mother, Annette would be a precocious and vivacious risk taker who steadfastly defied the stodgy conventions of her time.

Alice Charbonnet had been raised in Paris and the French South Pacific, and she came from a bold, globetrotting family with American, French and English branches. Alice would tell her children that their ancestor, James Jackson,[8] was born in the north of England in 1771, the same year that the giant Yorkshireman James Cook returned in his ship, *Endeavour*, from mapping the east coast of what is now called Australia.

Jackson began work as a clerk with a firm of bankers and merchants in Lancaster but was soon managing a fleet of transport ships sailing around the globe. While still a young man he was given oversight of a foundry that produced iron from the ores of Lancashire and Cumberland.[9]

Towards the end of the Napoleonic Wars he could see that steel mills in a devastated France might make his fortune, and he established forges in Saint-Étienne, in the heart of the Loire coal basin. Jackson's sons, all naturalised Frenchmen, expanded the family's steelmaking enterprises, and two of Jackson's children married into the Peugeot family of French industrialists.

The Jacksons expanded their trade to the United States. It was in Baltimore that Annette Kellerman's great-grandfather Joe Jackson, who would become a 'professor of languages',[10] was born in 1816.

Joe's daughter, seventeen-year-old Ellen Jackson,[11] married ambitious young American-born lawyer Amable Charbonnet[12] in Paris in 1854.

Many of Amable's family had died by the guillotine during the French revolution, but the American branch of the family had flourished. Amable had been born in New Orleans, Louisiana, once a French territory in America's deep south, and the young couple's daughter Alice, Annette Kellerman's mother, was born in 1858 in the American city of Cincinnati, though she would soon become as familiar with the boulevards of Paris and the beaches of the South Pacific as she would be with the big cities in America.

Annette's London-born grandmother Madame Ellen Charbonnet, nee Jackson, pictured in 1850, four years before her marriage to Amable Charbonnet. SLNSW, MIN 385

Annette's French-educated grandfather Amable Charbonnet as an infant in New Orleans, USA. *State Library of NSW, MIN 386*

Despite his youth, Amable held a judicial position with the French government in Paris and also spent time in a posting to French Indochina. Back in Paris, when his small daughter showed a rare talent for music, he was able to shower her with piano lessons from the best teachers in France.

French families, especially those aspiring to high society, considered proficiency on the keyboard vital for a young lady's education, and from the age of four Mademoiselle Alice Charbonnet took lessons from Paule Gayrard, a young woman who would later cross the English Channel to tutor the children of the future King George V.[13]

At four and a half, Alice played piano for the Empress Eugenie, wife of Napoleon III, at the Château de Saint-Cloud just west of Paris.[14] She also studied with the celebrated French composer Félix Le Couppey,[15] who, in addition to conducting classes at the Paris Conservatoire, oversaw music lessons at the best French schools for young women.[16]

The girl who would become Annette Kellerman's mother was nine years old and under the instruction of piano instructor Mademoiselle Buchey, 'known in Parisian circles as one of the best independent teachers',[17] when her father was appointed 'Judge President du Tribunal Supérieur'[18] of New Caledonia, effectively the roving chief justice for the French colonies in the South Pacific.[19]

Amable, Ellen and their little curly-haired daughter had already spent time in the French territory of Algeria,[20] and they sailed for Noumea at the end of 1867 on a ship that also carried a group of French convicts exiled to the South Pacific. Alice spent much of the voyage embroidering the family's new linen from Alsace.[21] For the next decade the world would be her playground.

Amid the blue skies and rolling waves of the South Pacific, Alice Charbonnet spent some of her happiest years. Her father was a popular official, treated in Noumea and Tahiti with 'the liveliest demonstrations of respect and goodwill'.[22] Life might have been entirely delightful for young Alice in the French South Pacific but for her father's periodic bouts of ill health.

During the three years Alice spent in the South Pacific, her piano teacher and taskmaster was her mother, Ellen, whose energy in keeping her daughter at the keyboard for several hours every day laid the foundation for even more rigid musical training later.[23]

The Charbonnet family returned to Paris in 1870, stopping off in Sydney and sailing from there on the giant three-masted timber passenger ship *Kosciusko*.[24] Alice was able to resume her musical studies in France and at the age of thirteen won three medals – one for composition, another for harmony and the third for proficiency as a player.[25]

The Charbonnets returned to Noumea in 1873 via Sydney, where every diplomatic courtesy was extended to them. Amable attended a function to inspect the French ironclad war steamer *Atalante* in Sydney Harbour, along with New South Wales Premier Henry Parkes and elderly Sydney judge Sir Alfred Stephen.[26]

Alice gave a couple of piano concerts in Noumea in 1873 and 1874,[27] but her father's time in New Caledonia was again blighted by ill health. In 1875, the family sailed for France via the United States, but Amable, aged just forty-two, died during a stopover in Chicago.[28] Ellen and Alice returned to Paris with his body, for burial in the Charbonnet family vault.[29]

Times quickly became desperate for the madam and mademoiselle, who were left with little more than a meagre pension from the French government. After a short time at a convent on the French coast at Brest,[30] Alice entertained the idea of supporting her mother and herself as a musician. She applied herself to further study under Mademoiselle Buchey and Felix Le Couppey, who eventually presented her for admission to the Paris Conservatoire in 1876.[31] Monsieur Le Couppey said Alice was the most proficient of 190 candidates vying for just fourteen places. Every day, Alice practised rigorously for six or seven hours, and she studied harmony with another Parisian composer and music teacher, a man named Marie Savard.[32] One of Alice's classmates was the brilliant prodigy Cécile Chaminade,[33] who would become the first female composer to be awarded the Légion d'honneur.[34]

Work was needed to tidy up Amable's finances in New Caledonia, and Alice and her mother were soon back in Sydney,[35] bound for meetings with lawyers in Noumea.[36] But three months after they arrived in the French colony, a bank collapse[37] took what little money remained.

Alice would later tell Annette that, at the age of nineteen and a half, she hit upon the idea of giving a concert tour of Australia, working the contacts in Sydney that her father had made on previous visits. So, on 13 April 1878, the precocious youngster placed a small display advertisement in *The Sydney Morning Herald*:

MADEMOISELLE ALICE CHARBONNET
(of the Conservatoire of Paris)
has much pleasure to announce that her first CONCERT,
under the patronage and in presence of his Excellency the
Governor and Lady Robinson, will take place on
TUESDAY, APRIL 30th,
at the
MASONIC HALL.[38]

Then the lively, determined teenager got busy drumming up publicity.

Annette remembered her mother as barely five feet tall (150 cm) and 'extremely pretty',[39] with a mass of long, curly auburn hair. Alice spoke perfect English with a soft, alluring French accent.[40]

An audience of a few hundred, described as 'crowded and fashionable',[41] took their seats. The petite teenager 'arranged her skirts, gave them a fond pat'[42] and played, exquisitely, pieces by Frédéric Chopin, Johann Hummel and Hans Liszt.

The Sydney Morning Herald reported that it had been a long time since Sydney had the pleasure of listening to a better concert.[43]

The rave reviews continued a week and a half later, with a second concert at the same venue before another large and enthusiastic audience that included members of the governor's family. Alice received a number of bouquets and many encores.[44]

Alice began teaching advanced piano technique to the most promising pupils in Sydney at the house she shared with her mother in Darlinghurst.[45]

A dozen more concerts followed every two or three weeks, including some with the choirs of local Catholic churches[46] and some to raise money for various charities, including St Vincent's Hospital,[47] Sydney's School of Industry and the European victims of a New Caledonia uprising.[48]

Some of Sydney's leading arts patrons met at the Royal Hotel in George Street to organise a thank-you concert for Alice, 'in recognition of her generosity to the charities of Sydney, and in appreciation of her abilities as a pianiste'.[49]

Among the organising committee for this tribute show was a middle-aged, German-born merchant, Frederick Kellermann, a foundation committee member of the Sydney Philharmonic Society. His teenage son, Fred, a talented violinist, was about Alice's age.[50]

A draftsman,[51] young Fred was athletic and liked to row. He indulged his passion for sailing on Sydney's magnificent harbour most weekends, often riding the wind in his skiff with his baby brother, Emile.[52] He was 'a very good-looking man', 'his sartorial appearance ... always impeccable'.[53] He cut a dashing figure, favouring top hats, double-breasted Prince Albert coats and pinstriped trousers.[54] With his sharp features and neatly cut moustache, Fred was perfectly in tune with the pert and elegant Alice, and the more time they spent together the more it seemed they were in harmony.

Alice hoped that they might be able to make beautiful music together some time. But first, the young pianist wanted to create her own slice of fame across the sea.

Chapter 2

AFTER SIX MONTHS and fourteen concerts in Sydney, Alice and her mother tried to repeat their success across the Tasman. Packed halls in New Zealand followed and students there rushed to Alice's piano classes.[1]

Alice would later tell Annette that newspapers across New Zealand's North Island vied with each other to bathe Alice in extraordinary praise. Wherever she went she charmed the public. In Auckland, she staged seven concerts in 'a musical festival almost unparalleled of its kind in that city'.[2]

Her tour manager insisted she play at what could be remote and rough venues. At a goldfield, Alice and her mother were lowered down a steep cliff to the concert venue in bucket trays as they wailed, holding on to their male guide for dear life.[3]

Alice then based herself in the New Zealand capital of Wellington and became a great favourite of the New Zealand governor, George Phipps, the Marquess of Normanby.[4] At just twenty, Alice was already a hard-driving businesswomen who knew the value of powerful friends. Annette Kellerman would inherit her mother's audacity.

Having been invited to Government House in Wellington once, there was no keeping Alice out, and soon the gossip columnists were reporting that 'morning, noon, and night did the vivacious little pianiste flutter round the "Markiss".'[5]

Whenever the 'Markiss' went to the theatre, Mademoiselle and her mother went also. From box to box in the Opera House they would flit, at all periods of the entertainment, whatever it was, so that they might gaze upon the 'Markiss' from all points, and bring themselves under his and everybody else's notice. On one occasion when the 'Markiss' patronised her benefit, [Mademoiselle] had no sooner finished the performance of her first selection when to the astonishment of the audience, she rushed up from the stage and sat herself down alongside of his Excellency, shaking hands, and chattering so that she might be heard all over the theatre.[6]

Alice's attachment to the vice-regal continued in Melbourne when the Marquess was appointed Governor of Victoria, and Alice and her mother sailed there for another series of concerts starting at Melbourne Town Hall in 1879.[7]

Alice made her first appearance in the Melbourne arts scene, though, in the audience at the Theatre Royal to watch the Irish Shakespearean actress Augusta Dargon, then one of the leading tragic actresses of the American stage,[8] playing Queen Mary in the title role of Tennyson's play.

Alice had little regard for the formal conventions of a male-dominated world, and she would later teach Annette that she shouldn't live by rules made by men. Watching from a distant box at the theatre, Alice became visibly agitated not so much by Dargon's interpretation of the role but by the sight of the new Victorian governor in the audience. As the curtain dropped on the second act, Alice made her way to the royal box before banging on the door and shouting loudly: 'Markiss! Markiss!'

Not even the orchestra playing full bore could drown her out, and the audience turned their attention to the commotion. Before long, Alice gained admittance to the box, where she plonked herself down beside a somewhat embarrassed governor, wrapped her hands around his arm and carried on a lively one-sided chatter. 'His Excellency's share was ... restricted to monosyllables.'[9]

The incident began 'to assume a ridiculous aspect',[10] with the eyes of the entire dress circle fixed on the little mademoiselle and the uncomfortable governor. There were titters and giggles all about.

The governor's secretary reddened and bit his lip, the aide-de-camp reddened and bit his lip also, and then both retired to the back of the box, leaving audacious little Alice in full possession of the colony's most powerful man.

Alice also set the gossip pages ablaze with her close friendship with the much older British actor 'Handsome' George Rignold,[11] who was in Melbourne performing Shakespeare's *Henry V*. At one performance Alice threw Rignold a large wreath from the audience. Tongues were again wagging when, a few days later, Rignold took a prominent place in the audience for a recital Alice was giving at Glen's Music Store in Collins Street, going so far as to hand the 'little French–American lady ... a huge bouquet' at the end of one piece.[12]

MELBOURNE CROWDS SWOONED at Alice's concerts and recitals. She blew kisses to audiences 'in her accustomed bewitching manner and the bouquets ... rained down upon her'.[13] She made heavenly music in concert with another French–American virtuoso, the violinist[14] Camilla Urso.[15] The Australian press hailed Alice as 'indisputably ... in the front row of living pianistes',[16] and she signed agreements to endorse piano manufacturers,[17] gave music lessons from the home she shared with her mother in Avoca Street, South Yarra, and ran other piano classes at the huge Allan & Co.'s music warehouse in Collins Street,[18] owned by George Allan.[19]

Alice and Annette would delight in telling people in later years that Alice's first piano student[20] in Melbourne was a promising teenager named Helen Mitchell, who would become better known by her stage name, Dame Nellie Melba.[21]

Annette would learn that at just twenty-one Alice added another chapter to her burgeoning business portfolio when she published booklets on how to play the piano. The first, 'a piano study for the left hand only', was dedicated to the 'Markiss' and his wife, Laura,[22] and the second was a seven-chapter explanation of the methods of her Paris mentor Félix Le Couppey.[23]

Alice told Annette all about the months she spent in 1880[24] touring Australia with Italian operatic soprano Carlotta Patti.[25] The young Mademoiselle Charbonnet drove a hard bargain whenever she performed, and developed a reputation as a 'charming but pugnacious artiste'.[26] Her belligerence bubbled over later in 1880 at the Melbourne International Exhibition, regarded as the first world's fair in the Southern Hemisphere.

At a time when almost every Australian household aspired to own a piano, Alice gave demonstrations on those made by the Austrian firm Playel,[27] which had provided instruments for Chopin.

In August 1880, Alice was contracted for a six-month assignment in which she would be paid a total of fifty pounds to perform once a week on behalf of George Allan, who was marketing the French-made Erard grand pianos.

It was a time when the bushranger Ned Kelly dominated the news in Melbourne, having just arrived in the city under heavy police guard from the Victorian town of Glenrowan, where he had been captured in his suit of armour. Kelly would hang, despite pleas for mercy made to Alice's friend the 'Markiss' by his supporters.

Five months into Alice's contract, George Allan demanded she perform a waltz called 'Mon Amour' by the young Melbourne composer Alfred Moul.[28] Begrudgingly, Alice agreed to play the piece, even though it was not part of the original arrangement and she thought the composition beneath her.

She claimed George Allan had 'behaved very nasty to her mother',[29] and was angry at Moul for a less than flattering newspaper review of her performance, in which he wrote that if Mademoiselle Charbonnet really wanted to be regarded as a high-class performer she should stop playing to the crowd with 'peculiarities of manner' more suited to 'the pet of the ballet'.[30]

Allan was also not happy with the way Alice played Moul's waltz. He said her performance was full of hostility, and that she

Annette's father Fred Kellerman managed the early stages of her rise to world fame. SLNSW, MLMSS 6270

Annette's mother, Alice Charbonnet, was one of the finest pianists in Australia in the late 1800s. SLNSW, MLMSS 6270

had sought to damage him and the composer by 'bad and careless playing',[31] 'banging' and 'thumping' the piano 'in the 'most disgraceful manner'.[32] He refused to honour the contract.

At the age of just twenty-one, Alice took Allan to Melbourne's County Court and won.[33] However, she knew that making powerful enemies among the leading lights of Melbourne music would not bode well for her, and before long she was back living with her mother in Darlinghurst.[34]

Not far away, Alice's grandparents - Baltimore-born Joe Jackson, the retired 'professor of languages', and his French-born wife, Laurentine,[35] both in their late sixties - were living out their sunset days in Silver Street, Marrickville.[36]

Alice wasted no time getting back to business. Soon she was advertising that 'having determined to establish herself in Sydney', she welcomed 'Pupils for Pianoforte'.[37]

She started her classes at Orwell Cottage, 126 Victoria Street, Darlinghurst, near her mother's home,[38] and at the Palings music store in Sydney's central business district.

At the same time, the musical Kellermann family were also competing for pupils.

Alice's great supporter, Frederick Kellermann Snr,[39] and his older brother William,[40] had been in Sydney for almost thirty years and were pillars of the city's arts community. Born in Germany in the 1820s, they had arrived in Australia from Britain on the ship *Panthea* in 1853[41] as part of the gold rush immigration. Their Sydney import business, Kellermann Brothers, competed with other ambitious Sydney traders such as Anthony Hordern and David Jones, and they branched out with a depot north of Sydney at Maitland on the Hunter River, selling, among other items, concertinas, accordions, flutes, violins, looking glasses and German music boxes.[42]

But William Kellermann, who billed himself as a 'Professor of Music'[43] and a pupil of Viennese opera singer Joseph Staudigi,[44] decided to concentrate on his music as a teacher and concert promoter, first in Maitland and other country towns and then in Sydney.

By the early 1880s, William was teaching instruments and singing in Darlinghurst Road, just around the corner from Alice's home.[45]

Alice got to know the Kellermanns better, and soon she was playing duets with young Fred, the talented violinist who had started a business selling musical instruments.

Their blossoming young love helped Alice overcome her sorrow when her mother, Ellen, died aged just forty-five.[46]

Six months later, on 18 December 1882, 24-year-old Alice Charbonnet married 22-year-old Fred Kellermann in two ceremonies – a Catholic ceremony at the Sacred Heart Church in Darlinghurst and, later in the day, an Anglican wedding at St John's in Ashfield to please the groom's father, who lived nearby.

The couple were very much in love, and they established a music school in Phillip Street, Sydney. A few doors along lived feminist Louisa Lawson and her teenage son Henry, a budding poet and short story writer who was then working as a painter at a railway carriage works.

Young Fred Kellermann took out a patent so that he could have the monogram 'The Alice' embossed above the keyboard of every piano he sold.[47] Alice continued to appear on the concert scene as Alice Charbonnet-Kellermann, but she took a break from early 1885 because she was now heavily pregnant.

The couple's first child, Maurice Charbonnet Kellermann,[48] was born at their home music school at 149 Phillip Street on 7 April 1885. The Kellermanns soon moved into a bigger home at 101 Victoria Street.

Fifteen months later, on 6 July 1886, after a morning dip to help her relax — a dip she would later bitterly regret[49] — Alice gave birth to her first daughter, Annette.

Alice had already opened the way for her striking daughter to be a born entertainer. At home the pretty little mother spoke to her children in French, so Annette was bilingual from an early age.[50]

But before long Alice was exclaiming 'Mon Dieu, Mon Dieu' and collapsing with grief as she and Fred despaired for their baby's life.[51]

Chapter 3

ANNETTE'S HOMETOWN was a vibrant city on the move. As Sydney prepared to mark a century of European settlement, its population swelled from a quarter of a million people to almost 400,000 in the ten years from 1880. Long rows of cheaper, high-density terrace houses sprouted like mushrooms in inner-city areas such as Darlinghurst.

The Kellermanns were on the move, too. Alice had fallen pregnant again not long after Annette's birth, and another daughter, Marcelle,[1] known as 'Mipps' by the family, was born in 1887.

To help with the children, the Kellermanns lived for a time with Alice's grandparents in Marrickville and became closely associated with St Brigid's Catholic Church there, Alice playing the organ and arranging performances of the choir, and Fred conducting.[2]

Their passion for producing soul-stirring hymns may have helped them endure some tough times, including a burglary at the house not long after they'd moved in. The shock that the young parents felt after thieves made off with cash, a gold watch worth a whopping sixty pounds and a gold medal,[3] was nothing, though, compared with the rising fears they had about Annette's health.

Alice and Fred doted on all their children, and Annette always felt that she was special. But she also knew she was different from other children.

With the arrival of Mipps, who needed to be carried, it was time for Annette to start walking.[4] But while older brother Maurice, now three, scampered about their temporary home,

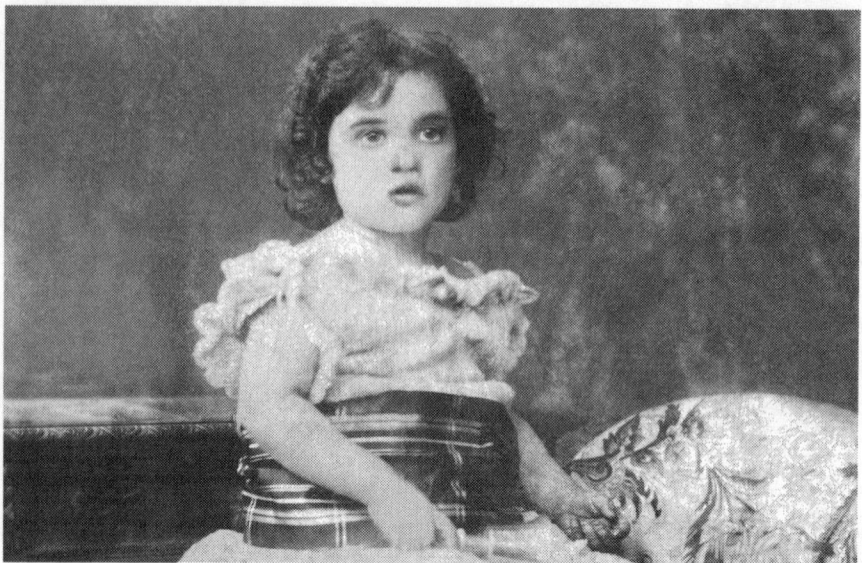
Annette as an infant growing up in Sydney. *SLNSW, MLMSS 6270*

Annette was still immobile at the age of two, unable to stand upright, let alone walk. Her stumpy little legs were bowed and there was a thickening of the ankles, wrists and knees.

Doctors gave Alice and Fred the grim news that Annette was suffering from rickets, which, in its most severe forms, can lead to seizures and death. One doctor told the Kellermanns there was chalk in the child's bones.[5]

Annette would endure many years of pain and despair. So did Fred and Alice, as they fretted over what would become of their darling child, whose deformed limbs were becoming more swollen and painful by the day.

Annette would later learn that Alice fell down with grief at the news of her daughter's illness, blaming herself for Annette's condition because she had gone for a swim on the morning of her daughter's birth. She could only be consoled when the doctor explained that rickets had nothing to do with that pre-natal dip but was due 'to chemicals in Annette's body'.[6] Rickets is in fact associated with a lack of vitamin D, and while that might have seemed implausible in sunny Sydney, Alice may have been harbouring untreated conditions such as coeliac disease during her pregnancy.

To straighten her bones, Annette's legs were strapped into hard, unforgiving braces made of iron and leather. 'Mother had grand plans for her children,' Annette wrote years later, 'but as I hobbled about, a frail and sickly child, no one thought I would ever amount to anything, and even my fondest relations believed that I was not very long for this world.'[7]

Annette wailed and railed at becoming a prisoner in irons,[8] and even though her father gave Annette the pet nickname 'Toots', it was hard to ever make the toddler smile. The braces were excruciatingly painful, especially the left brace, which dug hard into the little girl's plump flesh. Annette soon learned how to remove the left brace when her parents weren't looking, and Fred and Alice would often find their daughter sound asleep in a closet with the left brace lying by her side.[9]

THE KELLERMANNS WORKED hard to build up their music school. By the time Annette was five she had a baby brother, Freddie Kellermann Jnr,[10] who was born in the home of his great-grandparents in Silver Street, Marrickville.[11]

All the Kellermann children were put to the piano at an early age, and each morning the three oldest were in the music rooms practising their scales. Annette found the constant music lessons and forced practice torturous.

Later in the day, students would come from all over Sydney to learn from Mister and Madame Kellermann, who had built their home music academy, Sydney's Conservatoire de Musique, into a profitable business at different rented properties, including one in Macleay Street, Potts Point.[12]

At their longest-serving Conservatoire de Musique at 43 Phillip Street, Alice and Fred attracted as many as 115 pupils[13] for each twelve-week term.

Annette remembered that the Kellermann Conservatoire in Phillip Street was a three-storey terrace house with almost every room given over to instruction in every kind of music. There were six pianos in the house, and the 'drawing room' was really a salon in which a small stage was built. On the stage were two grand pianos, which were the centrepiece for concerts by the students every month.[14]

Annette was four when she saw older brother Maurice presented with the academy's 'beginner's prize' for piano recital.[15] Before long Maurice was being featured in the press for showing 'marvellous skill, both with piano and violin, for so young a performer'.[16]

Annette recalled that, already miserable in the invasive braces squeezing and cutting her flesh, 'the continual din all day long of pianos, singing, violins, cellos all going at full blast' nearly drove her crazy.

'I hate music, Mum,' she told Alice, who just patted her on the head and replied softly in French: '*Tu l'aimeras plus tard, petite*' – 'You'll get to like it later, little one.'[17]

Often, as well as the Kellermann children practising their scales, there would be twenty music students in the house. Some played sublimely, but others would jag the wrong notes or hit the keyboard like they hated it, while some of the violin players were so off-key they sounded like cats yowling.

Sometimes Annette would shuffle, stiff-legged in her iron braces, into the room furthest from the music classes to escape into a world of fantasy, a book of fairytales in one hand while practising her piano scales with the other. The fairytales would inspire a lifelong love of pantomime.[18]

But what really became the focus of her childhood were three large portraits that dominated the recital room of the house. One was a portrait of her mother's classmate in Paris, Cécile Chaminade; one was of her mother's student, Nellie Melba; while the biggest and grandest, which dominated the room and always held Annette's attention, was of Sarah Bernhardt. Music may have been a constant in the Kellermann house, but there was something about being an actress that the little girl found far more mesmerising.[19] For much of her early childhood, Annette would retreat into a fantasy world in which she would be both the beautiful heroine and the all-action hero riding to the rescue.

Because Alice blamed herself for her daughter's infirmity, she was less strict with Annette than the other children. Annette's sister Mipps later said, 'My mother could never say no to Annette', and Annette soon worked out that being different resulted in a lot more attention.

Fortunately, there were always plenty of guests in her family home to satisfy her need to be noticed.[20] Fred and Alice socialised with Sydney's elite arts set, and in 1892 they helped organise the Sydney Orchestral Society.[21] Annette, who longed to be an actress, would often be allowed to stay up late and meet the guests. Observing her mother in action, Annette learned how to work the room at an early age.

ANNETTE'S PAINFUL, uncomfortable and humiliating[22] childhood trapped in iron braces played out against a widespread national malaise. The Australian colonies were gripped in the worst financial crisis they had ever suffered as the 1880s property boom ended with the bubble bursting and a sudden collapse of investment in both Australia's urban development and pastoral industries.[23] Dependent on agricultural exports, drought brought the colonies to their knees.

Unemployment and poverty skyrocketed. A widespread maritime strike was supported by militant coal miners and transport and agricultural workers. A six-month shearers' strike turned violent, and troops were sent in as parts of Queensland and New South Wales slid towards civil war.

By June 1893, as Annette approached her seventh birthday, eleven major Australian banks had been forced to close their doors. Melbourne house prices soon fell more than 50 per cent and Sydney's by 36 per cent. Thousands of people had their homes repossessed and money for luxuries such as music lessons became scarce.

Despite the economic gloom all around them, there was at least some optimism in the Kellermann house regarding Annette's condition. The little girl still couldn't walk without the aid of braces, but one of her parents' friends, opera singer David Cope, suggested they take Annette to Sydney's glorious beaches as often as possible and 'let her splash her legs in the sea'.[24]

Free from the braces, with the shallow waves rolling over her and the white sand below, little by little Annette's bandy legs strengthened and straightened ever so slightly, until she began to believe that one day she would walk unaided.[25]

With salt water proving such an elixir, Fred and Alice consulted doctors again. They advised that Annette should learn to swim and practise swimming regularly to build up her legs and body.

Fred had an extra incentive for Annette to learn to swim. Once when out sailing with Emile, he had fallen overboard and needed rescuing.[26] He was sure that swimming could be the saving of Annette, too, and he took his little girl to nearby Cavill's Baths to meet Australia's first family of swimmers.[27]

FRED CAVILL,[28] WHO BILLED himself as a 'Professor of Swimming', was a British naval veteran in his mid-fifties. He had twice come close to completing his attempts to swim across the English Channel, and had given swimming lessons to the future Queen Mary. He had also coached his six sons – Ernest, Charles, Percy, Arthur, Syd and Dick – who, along with his three daughters – Madeline, Fredda and Alice – had all achieved great notoriety in the pool.

The burly, barrel-chested Cavill had opened a pool on the north shore of Sydney Harbour, but the site had been resumed for the construction of the North Shore railway.[29] He had mounted such a spirited protest over the resumption that New South Wales government gave him permission to set up new baths at Farm Cove, near the site of the First Fleet's landing a century earlier.

Just east of Bennelong Pont, the area that would one day be occupied by the Sydney Opera House, Cavill and his family built his famous 'natatorium', a floating pool made of light, wooden slats and iron tanks.[30]

Swimming clubs were springing up all around the harbour and on Sydney's glorious beaches, using natural rock pools or enclosures surrounded by shark netting.

Cavill's Baths was in an extraordinary location, situated so that swimmers could see the rolling lawns of the long-established Royal Botanic Garden behind them and, out across the harbour, the sandstone island of Fort Denison and the many boats plying the waters.

In 1893, Fred took little Annette there with her brother and sister for their first swimming lessons.

Fred Cavill, with his dark bushy beard, was a constant presence on the deck of his pool. Dressed in a straw boater, striped tunic and trousers cut off at the knees, he would bark out encouragement to his pupils, sometimes tossing them a rope for safety when they didn't or couldn't follow his instructions.

On her first day with the Cavills, Annette was more than reluctant to test the waters of Sydney Harbour. 'I loathed it. They had to drag me kicking and screaming to the lessons,'[31] she said. The water was much deeper than the shallows she was used to at the beach.

'I was awfully scared of the water and did not learn quickly.[32]

'Perhaps my fears were increased ... because of my dread of exposing my weak and ill-formed legs. But all pleading availed me nothing. Daddy had discussed the matter with the doctor and the doctor was very, very sure that swimming was the only thing that would help me.'[33]

Although Annette's braces had been removed, her legs were still withered and weak. Often she had to be carried in her parents' arms from the Conservatoire de Musique in Phillip Street, past majestic Government House with its stunning view of the harbour and down through Sydney's lush Royal Botanic Garden to Farm Cove.

Cavill told his nineteen-year-old son Percy[34] to look after the swimming school's most frail charge. Percy slowly and patiently helped Annette overcome her fear of the water,[35] coaxing her to let go as she held on to the side of the pool for dear life. Initially, she struggled even to dog paddle.[36] Percy's younger brother, Arthur Cavill,[37] who had the middle name 'Channel' in honour of his father's English Channel quest, coached Annette as well.[38]

Soon the Kellermann family were making a regular 7 a.m. daily procession down to the pool before Alice and Fred began their music classes and the children set off for school. Maurice and Mipps needed just four or five lessons before they were swimming like porpoises, but Annette reckoned she needed seventeen or eighteen to become competent in the water.

But, after a while, swimming came to equal freedom for Annette. Cavill's Baths was a place where her limbs could move about unfettered and painless for the first time she could remember, without the 'horrible steel braces'.[39] Mipps recalled that 'thus was born [Annette's] aptitude for swimming, and every day she swam. All through her school days, on every opportunity, she swam and swam and never seemed to tire.'[40]

Through persistence and perspiration, and with the encouragement of the Cavills and her parents, Annette felt her small, frail body transforming. Her weak, feeble legs became empowered, so that after a few weeks of classes she felt she was able to push her way through the water the way she imagined fish could.

Even at that young age, Annette developed a spiritual connection with the water. She became one with it and it became one with her.

She remarked years later that only someone who had experienced a severe disability, as she had done, could understand the intense joy she experienced when, little by little, she found that her legs were growing stronger and taking 'on the normal shape and the normal powers with which the legs of other youngsters were endowed'.[41]

'In Australia practically all children are taught to swim,' she wrote many years later, 'but in my case if my father had not been especially persistent, I am sure I never could have overcome my childish dread and fears.

'But for his wisdom I might have been hobbling about on crutches to-day. Of course, I had some other exercises in calisthenics, but it is to swimming that I feel I owe the great debt.'[42]

Chapter 4

ANNETTE'S CONFIDENCE grew at the same rate as her rejuvenated muscles.

Despite bemoaning the constant noise at the home music academy, she kept at her piano practice, and at about the same time she started her swimming lessons she received her first press notices as a seven-year-old entertainer.

Along with Maurice and Mipps, she played the piano in a large children's concert organised by her parents in an upper room at the YMCA Hall in Sydney's Pitt Street. The room was crowded with admirers of all ages, from grandmas down to babes in arms.

The Sydney Mail reported that 'Master Maurice Kellermann and his little sisters, Annette and Marcelle', were assisted by some of the junior pupils of Madame Charbonnet-Kellermann's Conservatoire de Musique.[1]

Maurice and Mipps opened the program with a piano duet, and being 'such tiny tots', their feet did not stretch even halfway down the music stool.[2] A year later, the three Kellermann children were in the press again for their marvellous fancy-dress outfits at an Elizabeth Bay society function. Maurice dressed as a French soldier and the two girls were *vivandiers* or 'canteen keepers'.[3]

Economic pressures continued to tighten in the Australian colonies, but Fred and Alice had never been busier. Their music academy was still drawing high-paying students and Alice was still headlining concerts and publishing her own compositions.[4] Fred was also teaching music to large classes of girls at various schools and colleges in Sydney and had gained a reputation as the finest teacher of harmony and counterpoint singing in Australia.[5] Under the patronage of the New South Wales Governor and other citizens of note, Fred and Alice had formed the Australian Musical Association 'for the purpose of raising and maintaining a high standard of music, both theory and instrumental, in the colony', with a board of examiners from Sydney's leading classical musicians assigned to grant diplomas.[6]

Meanwhile, Annette was performing new physical feats every day she hit the water at Cavill's Baths, going further and faster with each lesson.

BY NOW THE KELLERMANN children were all enrolled at St Patrick's Church Hill Primary School, a fifty-year-old building on Grosvenor Street about 800 metres up a steep rise from their home. Mipps always wondered, though, just what her sister actually learned at St Patrick's since 'school studies indoors were just a waste of beautiful time, to be doing something outside'. Annette preferred skylarking to use all her pent-up surplus energy after the removal of the braces.[7]

The Catholic sisters were so sweet, Annette told them that she wanted to be a nun, too, but that attitude was only for the schoolroom.

She was often the ringleader when good-natured pranks were played on the sisters. On one occasion, she came into the classroom early and, realising the nuns had not yet arrived, she organised all the small children already there to hide under a bank of seats against a classroom wall. As usual, all the children did as Annette said – 'she had that gift', according to Mipps.[8] Eventually two nuns arrived for classes, only to find there were no children. One of the nuns left to investigate while the other sat at the piano, perplexed.

The smallest children in hiding began to get restless. Hearing scratching and thinking the room had been invaded by rats, the sister who remained pulled out the bank of seats to uncover Annette surrounded by a group of giggling youngsters.

Seven-year-old Annette (right) with sister Mipps and brother Maurice at an 1894 fancy-dress party in Elizabeth Bay, Sydney. *SLNSW, MLMSS 6270*

'We didn't get the cane at that school,' Mipps recalled, 'but I suppose we were given an extra prayer to say – to absolve our sins.'[9]

Then came Annette's first communion and confirmation. She was now a 'skinny kid in a long white robe', with a few stray locks poking out from beneath her veil.

Annette was chosen to read the Act of Consecration at her confirmation ceremony in St Patrick's Church, with a full choir and organ. It seems that, despite her regular shenanigans, Annette had a way of winning friends and influencing people.

EIGHT-YEAR-OLD ANNETTE beamed like never before when, in November 1894, her mother was fêted by the French

Consul-General at a gala function for more than 400 guests[10] in Sydney's Hotel Australia, arguably the most elegant hotel that Sydney had ever seen.[11] Many in the audience were past and present students of the Kellermans, and even Alice's grandmother, the now widowed Laurentine Jackson of Marrickville, was there, a tiny woman in a black satin gown and lace cap, carrying a bouquet almost as large as herself.[12]

Consul-General Georges Biard d'Aunet, representing the French government, made Alice an 'Officier de l'Ordre des Palmes Académiques' for a career 'distinguished by devotion to her art, by perseverance and progress and tenacity'.[13]

Alice, dressed in a magnificent buttercup-coloured dress made of bengaline silk (a blend of rayon and cotton), addressed her audience in her soft French accent:

> Monsieur le Consul-General, my dear pupils, my brother musicians, ladies and gentlemen, I cannot refrain from telling you how grateful I feel for your kindness in having assembled tonight to welcome me upon my new distinction. I feel both proud and happy. Proud as a French woman to have been distinguished by the French Government ... but more than proud I am happy to be the first Australian woman having received this high distinction. I hope you will pardon me for calling myself an Australian. I arrived amongst you from Paris 16 years ago, then a mere girl, and ever since I have devoted most of my time to the teaching of the gifted children of Australia. Besides this, there is a nearer and dearer title which I have acquired by my marriage with one of you, that of Australian mother.[14]

Annette was only eight but she felt ten feet tall, and she was determined to one day be a star as dazzling and beautiful as her mother. Unfortunately for the Kellermanns, the cost of living was starting to bite as the economy tanked and fewer parents could afford music lessons for their children.

ANNETTE WAS NOW GLIDING through the Farm Cove waters faster than the other girls at the pool, using breaststroke, which she had thoroughly mastered.[15] The Cavills also taught her to dive into the water with precision and barely a ripple.

Annette had undergone an almost miraculous transformation in a short time. Unable to walk unassisted only a year or so earlier, she now walked 10 miles (16 km) a day, becoming stronger and fitter with each outing.

She took to ballet with gusto. A photograph of her at this time shows an enthusiastic, exuberant little girl in a tutu, balancing on one pointed ballet shoe and flashing a confident and mischievous grin, so at odds with her time in leg braces.

Swimming, walking and dancing made Annette strong. Diving – from greater and greater heights – made her fearless.

Having overcome rickets, Annette had come to realise she could train her new body to do anything. She never wanted to be that sickly little girl again.

However, for a long time, Annette's mother and father took very little interest in her swimming. In their minds, having ditched the leg braces and built her physical strength, she had extracted everything she needed from her hobby.

Alice wanted Annette to become an actress like Sarah Bernhardt, so she was enrolled in elocution and dancing classes with the Clitherows, a family who ran the Juvenile Dramatic Company in Sydney's William Street.[16] Annette could recite parts of plays she'd studied at the 'drop of a hat' and would often perform them in front of her mother's favourite painting, with Bernhardt herself gazing down on the young actor's histrionics.[17]

In November 1896, when Annette was ten, Alice's old admirer George Rignold arrived in Sydney to play Henry V at Sydney's Theatre Royal.[18] Alice invited George to dinner, seventeen long years after they had shared platitudes when they were both performing in Melbourne. Over dinner, Rignold congratulated his old friend on her decoration as an 'Officier d'Académie' and was told the Kellermann children had a treat for him.

Seizing the opportunity to perform for one of the world's great Shakespearean actors, Annette recited Lady Macbeth's impassioned soliloquy. Maurice played the doctor in the scene, and Mipps the nurse carrying a candle.

With 'all the fervour and gusto' Annette could command, she marched up and down before Rignold, wailing 'Out, damned spot! Out, I say!'

Rignold and the Kellermans clapped politely as Annette took her bows. She was already convinced that the stage would be her home.[19]

The children charged Rignold thruppence for the show, with a free biscuit included in the ticket price.[20]

AS SYDNEY BUZZED WITH the exciting prospect of the Australian colonies finally coming together in one federated nation, the Kellermanns' Conservatoire continued to be a fashionable place for Sydney's high society. But there were fewer and fewer patrons, and the family staged home concerts to stimulate more interest in their lessons.

When Annette was eleven, Emily Soldene,[21] who had been one of the most famous comic opera singers in England and America, attended one of the Kellermans' concerts and was startled by the quality of the performances and the crowds packing out their Phillip Street home. She wrote about the night for *The Evening News*, a journal that would soon hire the writer Banjo Paterson as editor.

> [Madame] Kellermann's 'at home' Tuesday afternoon was a crush. You couldn't get in at one door; but, having got in, you couldn't get out at the other. All the talk (pretty loud talk, too – the music couldn't get a word in edgeways) was of 'frocks' and 'federation.' We sat two together on chairs, or three together on stairs. We took our tea standing in the hall, or squeezed up with agreeable people in tiny corners. Everything was unconventional and delightful. Vive la Vie Bohème![22]

Annette had grown into a strong, fit, confident girl with a mischievous streak, who took every opportunity to entertain. Once, she borrowed without asking a pair of her mother's most stylish high-heeled shoes and an expensive feather for her hair. Then, having left home in her school clothes, she quickly discarded her shoes and tam o' Shanter cap for her mother's more stylish things.

For 800 metres she tottered in high-heeled shoes too big for her up the hill to St Patrick's, before striding into class as an incredulous Sister Agnes made a great effort not to laugh.[23]

This was not the only time Annette ditched her striped sailor's blouse for her mother's Government House regalia, to wear in her own wanderings through Sydney, often dragging little Mipps behind.[24]

Though her passion was now amateur theatrics, Annette played sport, and she won a tennis championship in the Blue Mountains.[25] Swimming still captivated her, too, and she visited the Cavills as often as she could. By the age of thirteen she reckoned she was like a fish in the water[26] and that her legs 'were practically normal, though for some years afterwards one of them was easily susceptible to strain, and I was compelled to wear tightly laced high shoes until the age of eighteen.'[27]

Her fearlessness was astonishing, and she vividly remembered when a brash, blond fifteen-year-old named Snowy Baker,[28] a star swimmer, diver, fighter and football player at Crown Street Public School, dared her to make a high dive.

> I will never forget my first high dive as long as I live. Snowy Baker, who was a wonderful diver, dared me to go off the high platform, so I went. I suppose it was about 30 feet high [about 9 m], but when I arrived on the top of the diving stand it looked 100. It's funny how distance always seems greater looking down than looking up. Anyhow my knees were quivering, but I made up my mind that I would not come down the ladder and be laughed at, so I swallowed hard and took the plunge. They told me afterwards that it

was not bad for the first effort, only I had allowed my head to drop forward ... It spoils a perfect entry into the water.[29]

Snowy's older brother Frank[30] remembered that the first time Annette tried to copy Snowy diving, she hit the water 'all wrong'. 'She lay there until she got her breath,' he said, 'and then she climbed the ladder again. Then she leapt out. It was perfect. She entered the water like an arrow, and from that time on, I don't think she ever made anything but clean dives.'[31]

Frank eventually had a long career as a Hollywood stuntman and actor, though not quite as storied as Snowy, who went on to play test matches for the Australian Wallabies rugby union team, won a silver medal at the 1908 London Olympics in boxing, became the owner of Australia's leading sports arenas, found success as a major Australian filmmaker and eventually followed Annette to Hollywood, performing stunts and teaching horsemanship to Douglas Fairbanks, Elizabeth Taylor, Shirley Temple, Greta Garbo and Rudolph Valentino among others.[32]

ON 20 JUNE 1900, VOTERS in New South Wales – and it was still only men who had a say at the time – overwhelmingly approved a resolution to join the proposed Federation of Australia. There was enthusiasm all around the city for the birth of a nation, but in the Kellermann household things had become increasingly grim.

Fred and Alice continued to boost their funds through small concerts and recitals, and all four children took to the stage to perform their musical instruments.

Alice travelled to Melbourne with fifteen-year-old Maurice to perform there, having had so much success twenty years earlier.[33] But even in a city where the gold rushes had financed many exquisite and ornate buildings, money was short for entertainment.

Annette continued with her drama classes in Sydney and performed in amateur productions for the Clitherows.[34] She played Madame Vine in *East Lynne,* Lady Macbeth, and then Prince Arthur in *King John,* displaying what one critic said was 'intelligence quite above her age'.[35] But professional opportunities were scarce, and in the cool, calming waters of Sydney Harbour Annette escaped from the family struggles.

Fred Cavill had moved his baths around the harbour to the suburb of Woolloomooloo. His son Percy, Annette's first coach, had gone to England, where he was the first Australian to win a major international swimming race, taking out two events: the 440 yards (400 m) and the long distance (5 miles – about 8 km) in the English Amateur Swimming Association Championships of 1897.

And so Annette, who was now attending St Vincent's College, the oldest Catholic girls school in the colony, began training at George Farmer's baths in the Domain on the western side of Woolloomooloo Bay.

George's star pupil was Freddie Lane,[36] a twenty-year-old who had just returned from Paris, where he had won Australia's first ever Olympic swimming medals – two golds dredged from the muddy waters of the Seine. Annette always said Freddie was the most graceful swimmer she ever saw.[37]

Annette had copied Percy Cavill's freestyle or 'Australian crawl' stroke, which had recently been pioneered in Australia by the Solomon Islander Alick Wickham,[38] but Farmer told Annette that she also perfectly imitated Freddie's popular 'trudgen' stroke, named after British swimmer John Trudgen,[39] and which had evolved from sidestroke, with the swimmer's head kept above water.[40]

In December 1900, George Read from the East Sydney Swimming Club had used the trudgen to defeat Fred Cavill's son Dick and claim the world record for 440 yards in 5 minutes, 42 seconds. The press of the time described his trudgen stroke in this way: 'As Read rolls on to his right side with his double-over-arm his left leg draws up from the hip to such an extent that with his face screwed back to the left shoulder for inhalation he conveys the idea that he resembles the domestic cat comfortably coiled up on the hearth.'[41]

As well as the trudgen stroke, Annette had now developed a very forthright personality and, like all confident kids, she thought she knew more than her parents.[42] It took every ounce of her willpower to stay on the path to St Vincent's rather than follow her sport. Sometimes the willpower would cave in and she would dive into the pool rather than her lessons, spending all day doing laps – much to the anger of her parents and teachers.[43]

THE AUSTRALIAN COLONIES came together to form a federated nation two months after Freddie Lane's return from Paris.

The first car to hit the streets of Sydney, a French-built De Dion Bouton, had trundled along Harris Street, Pyrmont, in April 1900, but the cost of automobiles was prohibitive, so when 60,000 Sydneysiders dressed in their Sunday best on New Year's Day 1901 and gathered in Centennial Park to witness the reading of Queen Victoria's proclamation creating the nation of Australia, most people walked there or travelled by horse.

The optimism radiating on that hot summer's afternoon was reflected around the new country. But in the Kellermann household, money was becoming so scarce that Fred and Alice were growing desperate. Alice had experienced a reversal of fortune following a bank crash after her father's death twenty-five years earlier, and the collapse of the Australian financial system meant that, for a second time, her 'once prosperous family was down on their uppers'.[44]

The Conservatoire de Musique, once an icon of the Sydney music scene, had to be closed.

Fred was pacing around town in his top hat and pin-striped trousers looking for work but the demand for teachers of counterpoint and harmony was non-existent. The couple had four children to feed and educate, and Alice became so troubled by their lack of funds she decided it was best to leave her husband for a time and take a job in Melbourne. Maurice, fifteen, Mipps, thirteen, and ten-year-old Freddie went with her, leaving Annette in Sydney with her father.

Chapter 5

IT WAS AT GEORGE FARMER'S baths that Annette said she caught 'mermaid fever',[1] a burning desire to become a champion swimmer and to make a name for herself in the sport, something that no Australian woman had ever done, let alone a girl of fifteen.

She was a formidable talent in both sprints and long-distance swimming, powering through lap after lap at Farmer's, building up tremendous strength in her shoulders, arms and legs, as well as astounding lung capacity. She became ever more daring with her high dives, too, and could hold her breath underwater for what seemed an eternity.

Annette's mother had told her that while swimming was a fine exercise for young ladies, she was dead against them competing in sporting contests; the cultured Parisienne matron certainly didn't want strangers gawking at her daughter's bare arms and legs in her skimpy swimming costume. But Annette's mother and all of Annette's siblings were now living in Melbourne, and what Alice didn't see couldn't possibly hurt her, could it?

There was just Annette's father to convince about the merits of having a daughter who was the best swimmer in Australia. But when Annette told her father of her ambition to enter one of the few swimming competitions open to Australian women, Fred – already wearied from family turmoil and the crash of his economic and social standing – laughed her off. Too busy trying to make a living, Fred had not seen Annette swim for six years. He thought it 'quite absurd' that Annette, now a student at Apsley House, a finishing school for girls in the suburb of Stanmore,[2] wanted to compete with well-known swimmers, one of whom was the champion of Australia. But Annette was spending more time at the baths than at school, to the point that her headmistress told Fred it might be a good idea if Annette and the school ended their relationship.[3]

Annette convinced Snowy Baker to ask Fred: 'Why don't you let her enter the championships? You ought to see Annette beat all the girls at swimming distances.'[4]

When Fred had recovered from this news, he flew off the handle. 'No daughter of mine will make a fool of herself in front of a lot of people,' he thundered.

Annette then used Freddie Lane to convince her father that she could be a champion.

'I don't think any girl in the world can beat her,' Lane told Annette's gobsmacked father. 'She has wonderful endurance. All she needs is a little coaching.'

And so, for the first time since Annette was nine years old, Fred Kellermann went to see her swim. He watched his little mermaid cruise through a mile with so much ease that he gave her permission to enter whatever races she chose.[5]

Annette's first official race was at Farmer's Baths, a 45-yard (about 40 m) event against Vera Buttel. Vera was regarded as the fastest female swimmer in Sydney, and was just a month older than Annette. Bathing was heavily scrutinised by police in 1901, and for the sake of the standards of modesty enforced upon them, women usually swam in loose dresses over bloomers, with shoes and hats. Annette favoured the outfits of the male swimmers she watched at the baths – a woollen, knee-length unitard that left her arms bare. Vera wore the same. It was deemed risqué by the more conservative sections of Sydney, but it allowed Annette to swim fast and she showed that in her first real contest:

> I came in winner by a couple of yards, very much to my father's astonishment ... My father's incredulity was immediately changed to a most enthusiastic and persevering

faith. To him had been due my childhood swimming which kept me from remaining a cripple, and to his revived interest I owe much of my success as a professional swimmer. Father took up my training in a systematic fashion and through thick and thin saw that I stuck to it. The rest of the family were doubtful that anything outside of a little local notoriety could ever come of my swimming. But I was certain that there was no hope for me in music, and equally determined to make my mark in something; hence, with father's more mature will to make smooth the road, I took up swimming with an earnestness that was bound to succeed.[6]

On 7 December 1901, the East Sydney Swimming Club staged its eighth annual carnival at Farmer's Baths, with a huge crowd 'in which the fair sex was strongly represented' lining the pool's surrounds on a glorious summer day.

Once again Annette was contesting a 45-yard race in a sport that still did not have an overabundance of female competitors. All comers of all ages were welcome.

Given Annette's earlier success, all the other swimmers were given head-starts of varying times against her. Vera Buttle was off a one-second head start.

Twelve-year-old Fanny Durack[7] was off 8 seconds, ten-year-old Mina Wylie[8] 10 seconds, and George Farmer's five-year-old daughter Doris got to start a whole 22 seconds ahead of Annette. Despite George Farmer leading the crowd to give their biggest cheers for little Doris, Annette surged through the water like an orca and won the race from Vera Buttle by 'a touch'.[9] Eleven years later, Fanny Durack and Mina Wylie would finish first and second in the 100-metres freestyle final at the Stockholm Olympics.

The feature event of the Eastern Suburbs carnival saw Freddie Lane, 'the 120-yards and 220-yards world's record holder' just miss out on the world 100-yards record, despite beating brilliant twenty-year-old Cecil Healy[10] in a thriller.

Not only did Annette win the 45-yard race at Farmer's Baths but she and Vera Buttel then gave the big crowd a breathtaking display of high diving from a platform estimated to be 50 feet (about 16 m) above the water.[11]

Annette reckoned no girls had ever made public displays of such stunning dives, and she credited her ballet training, which she still maintained, for her gracefulness and skill to perform so spectacularly.[12]

Photographs of the girls' dazzling diving appeared in the popular press. Young women, baring arms and some leg, making death-defying dives into water from dizzying heights was unheard of, and the pictorial display in the popular *Australian Town and Country Journal* was staggering for the publication's huge readership. Whatever was the world coming to?

Before she knew it, at just fifteen, Annette had become a major personality in the Australian sports world. The enormous

The diving feats of Annette (right) and Vera Buttel made a stunning pictorial display in the popular press just before Christmas 1901. *Australian Town and Country Journal*, 21 December 1901, p. 41.

publicity quickly convinced her that her star was only going to burn brighter and brighter.

AFTER MOVING TO MELBOURNE in 1901 without her husband, Alice began work as a music teacher at Simpson's School, Mentone, the forerunner of Mentone Girls' Grammar School. She and the three children with her gave concerts, too,[13] but life was a struggle in their rented accommodation.

If her reduced circumstances after having been fêted as one of the world's finest concert pianists were not bad enough, the newspapers gave Alice a shellacking after her ten-year-old, Freddie, accidently shot a young friend.

In September 1901, Freddie and his chum, Sydney Provis, were out rabbit shooting with 16-year-old Maurice near the new sea baths at Beaumaris on Port Phillip Bay.

It was not entirely uncommon in the early 1900s for ten-year-olds to go out shooting, and Freddie was carrying a pea-rifle — a thick-barrelled muzzle-loading weapon. The three lads were looking down a rabbit burrow, when Freddie, not noticing that the gun was half-cocked, bumped the trigger. A lead bullet the size of a pea ripped into Sydney's ankle.[14]

Maurice carried the wounded, crying boy 4 kilometres along the beach road to the Provis home in Mentone. A doctor was called and the bullet was eventually extracted.[15]

The press was scathing. 'The folly of parents allowing children to play with firearms was severely illustrated here on Thursday evening,' one newspaper opined. 'It is very common to hear gun shots in the ti-tree and even in some backyards. It should be a punishable offence to use any firearms within the township.'[16]

The stress of separation and anxiety over money had already played havoc with Alice's health, and not long after Freddie's mishap with the gun, Alice became gravely ill. She recovered, but it was slow, and perhaps wondering how long it would be before she had a personal audience with God, Alice began composing a mass for the little Catholic church at Mentone.[17]

In letters to Annette Alice wrote that she strongly disapproved of girls competing in sports,[18] but Annette was having the time of her life in the pool and the publicity could only help her career on the stage. In tough financial times, Annette saw swimming and diving as a means to make her own headway through the world as a strong and independent young woman.

FRED KELLERMANN WAS STILL trying to make a living teaching music and staging small theatrical shows in Sydney, but the publicity from Annette's swimming and the development of her physique and extraordinary endurance overshadowed everything he was doing.[19] Fred was coming to realise that Annette could make a huge splash in the world of entertainment, with swimming as the foundation.

At Farmer's Baths on Christmas Day 1901, Annette decided to have a crack at the women's world record for the mile (1600 m). While she had only been serious about swimming for a few months, she made her record attempt before a panel of accredited judges. To their great elation, and hers, she shaved almost five minutes off the record set by Englishwoman Edith Styer. Using the trudgen stroke, that combination of freestyle and sidestroke with her head out of the water,[20] Annette covered the distance in 34 minutes, 20 seconds. She defied the lactic acid burning in her shoulders and just about everywhere else by swimming the last quarter-mile 40 seconds faster than the first.[21]

The press notices were fulsome and generous. A few days later, Annette and Vera Buttel were making more spectacular dives from on high at the annual carnival of the Nautilus Swimming Club in Sans Souci on Botany Bay.[22]

Then, at the Wollongong Town Hall, 80 kilometres south of Sydney, Annette appeared in a supporting role in one of her father's productions, a farce called *Her Nurse*.[23] Wollongong's main newspaper pointed out that she was the very same young woman who held the world record for the mile swim and 'who made the sensational high dive of fifty feet, which brought her into all the illustrated papers in a new role'.[24]

A month later, Annette and her father were in Wollongong again for another show, but this time she had star billing as the 'chief attraction' at the first carnival of the new Wollongong Swimming Club. Annette's exhibition of 'fancy diving' drew gasps from the big crowd before she swam several laps of the pool using both the trudgen and freestyle strokes.[25]

Annette's brilliance in the pool had caused a huge increase in the number of women wanting to swim. There had also been a desire by the better female swimmers to have their own competition and to have the chance to improve and excel.[26]

With Annette's prompting, Fred announced to the press that his world-champion daughter was contemplating a visit to England to race the best of Britain, but in the interim he would be organising the first ever ladies' swimming carnival in New South Wales. It would be contested at the Redfern Baths in Cleveland Street, just on the outskirts of Sydney's central business district, on the night of 25 March 1902.

Fred was chuffed that he already had the support of the New South Wales Amateur Swimming Association, the Department of Education, the principals of (among others) Fort Street and Cleveland Street public schools, and the mayor and mayoress of Sydney. A large number of prominent women had also promised to be poolside.[27]

Fred would prevent male gawkers ogling the young ladies in their swimming costumes by limiting male attendance to invitation only.

Annette's father was now almost forty-two, but weighed down by financial stress and the absence of his wife and Annette's brother and sisters, he appeared older. He began to devise ways to make Annette's star shine brighter, and he hoped that, somehow, Annette's success would turn around the family fortunes.

THE FIRST NEW SOUTH WALES Ladies Swimming Championships were a roaring success, especially for the Kellermann family. A large, vocal and almost exclusively female audience turned up to cheer the finest female swimmers in the newly created state.

Two championships were decided and Annette was the undisputed star of the show. Alongside four other entrants for the 100 yards, including her arch rival Vera Buttel, Annette leapt into action at the sound of the starter's gun. Using the trudgen stroke, she drew away after 10 yards, and after four laps of the pool she won the state title from Vera, who was 10 yards behind. Three yards further back was Flo Riley, a promising youngster from Rockdale, who came in third.

'Miss Kellermann was expected to put up a remarkable time, but, as it was won without pressure, only one minute, 26 seconds was ticked,' wrote a reporter from *The Sydney Mail*.

Not long after her win, Annette lined up for the quarter-mile (440 yards) against Vera and Flo.

Again, it was no contest. After the first lap Annette drew away easily. Vera gave up chasing after two 25-yard laps and Flo wanted to quit several times as the crowd rallied her again and again. Eventually Annette won by two laps, 'some 50 odd yards' ahead of Flo.[28]

Annette's photograph appeared in the press with glowing reports of her prowess. 'The time was exceptional,' *The Sydney Mail* told readers, '[at 440 yards in] 7 minutes, 48 seconds, and it is claimed that it has never been approached by lady swimmers in England.'

The Sydney Sportsman newspaper pointed out that with the large audience who came to watch Annette 'there should be very little difficulty in making these gatherings a prominent feature of our swimming season'.[29] Sydney's venerable dames, it said, might throw up their hands 'in holy horror at the mere mention of ladies swimming in the presence of the trousered sex … but thank heaven, mock modesty is being sent to the right about, and the day is not far distant when ladies will have as little objection to doing a mermaid act as they have to attending a ball or the theatre in a low-necked dress.'[30]

The following month, on 12 April 1902, at the Domain Ladies Baths run by Harry Hellings, Annette broke what was claimed to be her own ladies' world record for 100 yards, this time covering the distance in 1 minute, 22 seconds.[31]

Then, just two days later at Hellings' Baths, Annette took on Vera Buttel and twelve-year-old Dorothy Hill for the ladies' mile state championship.

Annette won by 150 yards, beating her own world record with a time of 33 minutes, 49 seconds.[32]

Her performances made news right around Australia, with Melbourne's *Weekly Times* declaring she was 'without doubt the champion lady swimmer of Australia'.[33]

The weekly *Bulletin* magazine, with a readership in the hundreds of thousands, ran an artist's portrait of 'the graceful girl' and 'record swimmer' and declared that 'the daughter of those well-known musicians, Mr. Fred and Madame Charbonnet-Kellermann' was studying for a dramatic career away from the pool.

> Swimming is her favourite pastime, and Miss Kellermann is doubly lucky in having been gifted with a passion for a pastime that gives, in addition to pleasure, grace to the form and beauty to the complexion. Swimming is an ideal pastime for a lady studying for a dramatic future.[34]

Fred was now certain that Annette could draw bigger crowds to the pool than he could to the stage, and he saw a role for himself in managing her swimming performances.

Annette was practising at her ballet barre one day when her father entered the room 'a little abashed'. The hard slog of trying to make ends meet had made Fred haggard, and for a long time he had been short of breath. But he had sparked up in recent weeks and was germinating an idea. 'Toots,' he said, 'What would you say to making swimming and diving a profession?'

Annette was stunned and horrified at the same time. 'No, no,' she retorted. 'I want to be an actress and a dancer. Swimming is just fun. That's all.'[35]

Annette was well aware that professional athletes were not regarded highly in cultured society. But Fred predicted that with proper care, diving and swimming could be elevated above professional sports and crafted into an art form. 'Toots,' Fred continued, 'there are many women dancers and actresses. Later, perhaps you could take it up again. I really believe, darling, that you and I can help get this family back on our feet.'[36]

Annette was listening.

'Besides, you could show the world what a wonderful thing swimming and diving can be for a woman.'[37]

Fred convinced Annette to dive into a wonderful new chapter of her life.

But first she would face a firestorm at home.

Chapter 6

ANNETTE WAS SIXTEEN when her family was reunited in the Melbourne suburb of Mentone in January 1903. The prospects of employment in music for the ailing Fred were so poor in Sydney that he had taken Annette south so the Kellermanns could be one family again, even if it meant struggling together.

Alice was still teaching music at the Mentone high school, run by the Simpsons, and was giving concerts and recitals with Maurice, who earned his share of plaudits as a remarkable young violinist.

Maurice and Freddie were enrolled at McCristal's Mentone College near their home in Palermo Street, though the Kellermanns had been forced to move several times as it was hard to pay the rent out of income derived from music lessons.[1]

Annette was enrolled at the Simpson's school, where Mipps was already a student.

Initially, there was friction in the Kellermanns' rented Mentone home between mother, daughter and husband over Annette's swimming ambitions. Alice had seen all the press generated by Annette's record-breaking swims and breathtaking dives, but – *sacré bleu* – she remained aghast at the thought of her daughter becoming a professional athlete.[2]

Money was in desperately short supply, though, and two weeks after Annette had arrived at Mentone during the summer holidays, Melbourne's press reported that 'Miss Annette Kellermann, champion lady swimmer of New South Wales, now resident of

Mentone' had accepted the post of coach at the Mentone and Brighton Beach Baths to undertake the 'teaching of ladies, boys and children desirous of becoming proficient in the useful art, healthy exercise and glorious pastime of swimming'.[3] Her pupils included her eleven-year-old brother, Freddie, and she performed an exhibition of 'fancy diving', featuring the 'back header', the 'double header', and the 'splosh', a trick dive when she fell into the water like a bundle of rags. In company with her pupils, she also performed 'a very novel variety of combination dives' in a sort of aqua ballet.[4]

Brighton was one of the few locations in Melbourne to allow men and women to bathe together. Again, Annette favoured wearing a boy's swimming costume, brief for the times, with bare arms and legs from the mid-thigh down, in stark contrast to the pretty serge bathing gowns worn by most of Melbourne's female bathers. These gowns were often complemented by Russian blouses, braided or trimmed with machine stitching, and bloomers. Decorated oilskin caps completed the usual costume for female bathers there, though most women were cautious about putting their head underwater, especially if they had a dance on that night.

A week after Annette's first swimming display, she and her father invited about 300 men and women to watch her aquatic show at Brighton on an afternoon when the boisterous weather made the sea rough inside the enclosure of the baths.[5]

Men and women were dressed in their Sunday best, the men in dark suits, the women in long skirts and white ruffled blouses, most with hats adorned with feathers. The children had straw boaters or bonnets as protection against the summer sun.

Alice's attitude towards her daughter's ambitions had softened and she joined Fred and the other children poolside to watch Annette and her co-star, her little brother Freddie. There was a large press contingent too.

Shortly after 3.30 p.m. on a sunny but windy and cool summer day in January 1903, Annette presented herself to the crowd on the top platform at the sea end of the baths. She was wrapped in a large tartan woollen rug. A murmur of excitement came from the onlookers, which included a number of men and boys who cheered loudly.

The journal *Table Talk* reported that 'those among the fair sex who had expected to see something dressy and up to date in a bathing costume' must have been sadly disappointed, 'as when the rug was discarded it revealed the girl swimmer in the simplest of navy-blue gowns with a red stripe'.[6]

One reporter described Annette as a 'powerfully built young lady with pleasant features',[7] while another said that with her 'short, dark hair, and olive brown skin, she recalled paintings of Eastern beauties ... her tapering fingers and well-shaped feet adding to the likeness'.[8]

Without hesitation, Annette dived into the foaming waters and then 'struck out, arm-over-arm', for the opposite end. The heavy sea would have quickly knocked out a less robust swimmer, the *Herald* reported, but the champion was 'not at all annoyed by the rough caresses of Neptune', swimming backwards and forwards with all the dexterity of a seal in the water.[9] Though Annette was only sixteen, another reporter observed, she possessed 'enormous muscular power and development, enabling her in a few overhand strokes to cross the baths'.[10]

As Annette emerged from the water she was greeted with cheers and an enthusiastic round of applause. She said her demonstrations in such rough water were calculated to impress her audience with the belief that her swimming pupils would be well taught to face heavy seas.[11]

Annette next dived from the springboard with 'consummate grace', and her pose on entering the water was 'perfect'. The crowd was charmed and once more a hearty round of applause erupted, just as it did when she did more dives, including plunging into the water backwards off the springboard, somersault diving, diving without the help of the arms and diving from a height with brother Freddie upside down in her arms.[12]

Towards the close of the exhibition, which lasted an hour, Freddie was exhausted, and his father rubbed him with brandy when he came out of the water.[13]

Names of prospective pupils for Annette's summer swimming classes were taken at the end of the exhibition, but both Fred and Annette knew the real money would be made by selling tickets to thrilling aquatic extravaganzas.

Annette visited the Swiss photographic studios in Bourke Street to pose in her revealing men's swimming costume. Melbourne's *Punch* magazine ran two of the portraits: one looking demurely away from the camera; one looking wistfully towards it, her eyes languid and her head tilted to the side. For the times, Annette appeared to be a model of innocence and provocation all in one.[14]

Punch continued to support Annette's aquatic feats,[15] as did the mass-circulation *Weekly Times*, which ran a large pictorial display of Annette's performances.[16]

Already the best-known female sportsperson in Melbourne, Annette gave in-depth interviews, even though she was quick to point out that she was still really only a child. *Table Talk* reported:

> People are astonished when they hear that the splendid specimen of womanhood measuring 5 feet, 5¾ inches in height, and weighing 10 stone, is only sixteen years of age ... Born in sea girt Sydney, and encouraged by her father to indulge in sea bathing, aquatic exercise became a passion with her from an early age. She was a puny, weak and slender little mite of humanity when she was first tempted by the blue waters of the Beautiful Harbour. Now the champion swimmer of New South Wales is the possessor of a robust constitution and an enviable physique ... she attributes much of the suppleness of her limbs to dancing and other physical exercise.[17]

Annette stressed that while she was 'very fond of swimming', she also liked dancing and elocution, and her ambition was 'to appear on the dramatic stage'.[18]

One interviewer remarked that Annette 'certainly gives the idea that if she makes up her mind to achieve anything, from deep sea diving to star acting, she will succeed. In the short space of six weeks, which Miss Annette Kellermann has spent in Melbourne, she has already formed swimming classes in Mentone, Brighton, St Kilda and South Melbourne, but owing to the peculiar laws connected with swimming competitions in the Melbourne suburbs, [she] has been debarred from competing in matches. She is considered a "professional", and therefore disqualified.'[19]

The papers pointed out that Annette was the daughter of Madame Charbonnet-Kellermann 'the well-known pianist and teacher of music' who had taught Madame Melba when the singer was known as Miss Nellie Mitchell and aspired to be a pianist.[20]

More swimming and diving exhibitions followed. Annette stressed water safety at all times, saying that everyone should learn how to help a person having difficulties in the water, and learn how to be saved if they were in difficulty.[21]

At a private exhibition in South Melbourne in February 1903, Annette used Mipps and Maurice in her swimming display and performed a daring 50-foot [16-m] dive. She also held Freddie upside down again for a double dive before showing patrons what the press called 'every style of fancy swimming'.

'She does not know the meaning of the word "fear",' a reporter remarked. '... She presents a very sunburnt appearance, but after the swimming season she generally regains her natural colour, that of a fresh, healthy brunette, with large grey eyes. Her brown hair is worn short, so as not to impede her swimming exercises. She intends to keep up her aquatics, but the dramatic stage is her ruling passion.'[22]

Or it was her 'ruling passion' until the trustees of the Melbourne Exhibition Aquarium, boasting the largest glass tank in the world – 60 feet (almost 20 m) long and 20 feet wide – made Annette an offer she couldn't refuse. She was to play a real-life mermaid and swim among schools of fish before packed crowds.

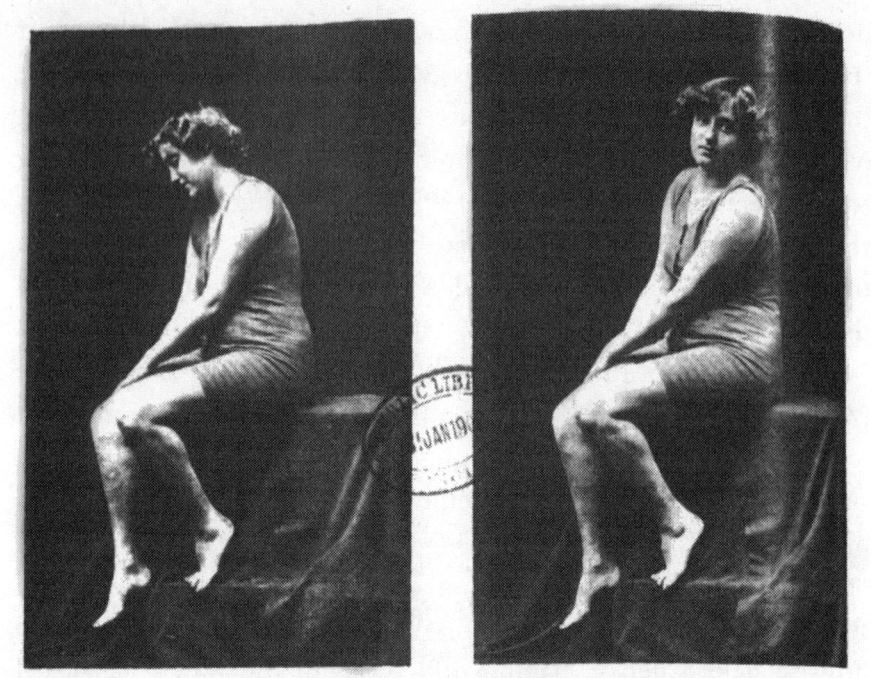

Sixteen-year-old Annette as she appeared in Melbourne's *Punch* magazine. *Punch*, 29 January 1903, p. 142.

SCHOOL ATTENDANCE WAS sporadic as Annette was hired for a six-week stint at the Aquarium – sometimes doing two shows a day. Under the direction of their father, she and brother Freddie gave the first of their swimming and diving exhibitions there on 24 March 1903.[23]

The Aquarium was in an annexe of the Exhibition Building, where Alice had played the piano more than twenty years earlier. It was surrounded by a maze in which visitors could easily lose themselves: a musty, dimly lit chamber of Egyptian mummies and mummy cases; plaster casts of naked Greek goddesses; a cool fernery; screeching peacocks; an aviary; slot-machines and a museum. The huge Aquarium itself was full of live marine creatures, from long-tailed Chinese carp to stately seahorses.[24] Seals glided through the water, leaping out to snatch a fish lunch offered by the keepers.

Melbourne *Punch* raved about Annette and her show because she sold thousands of copies of their paper.

> A finely-moulded woman she is, indeed ... The water is so deep that she can dive with the same freedom as at the baths. Yet more singular was her performance in the glass tank ... well stocked with eels and various kinds of fishes, amid which Miss Kellermann fearlessly gambolled ... Miss Kellermann is within a few inches of the spectators. A more beautiful object cannot be imagined than her form, as she swims along under water ... Her skin is all tanned a rich brown from frequent exposure to the healthy beams of Father Sol.[25]

Punch predicted that Annette's underwater act would become the rage of Melbourne. And it did, with Annette even peeling and eating a banana as she glided around the sea creatures.[26]

The Bulletin's correspondent had no idea that such a daring performance could be attempted, and wrote of Annette:

> A finely-developed woman, she disdains tights, except a very close-fitting black body shape. Miss K. is a rich mahogany brown, through her habit of classic sea-bathing. She is not as hard as nails, but all splendid muscle.[27]

At another performance, *The Bulletin*'s reporter arrived early and found 'the diving lady' in her dressing room, curled up in a corner reading a book. There were some minutes to spare, and Annette explained the water in the tank was not as pleasant as the sea, being much colder than she preferred. She didn't like having to swim in the tank with a gummy shark, either, so an attendant fished him out with a net before Annette dived in.

IN THE BRIEF TIMES SHE attended school between swimming and diving appearances, Annette immersed herself in sport. She took part in a once-only cricket game against the boys from McCristal's Mentone College. The match ended in chaos when a girl had some teeth knocked out while trying to stop a hefty slog from one of the McCristal's boys.[28] Annette had already overtaken her mother as the biggest celebrity at her Mentone school and was the driving force behind their amateur student productions. She also became a regular tennis player at the nearby Cheltenham Tennis Club.

Fred had taken to riding a bicycle all over Melbourne, dressed in his top hat, double-breasted coat and pin-striped trousers, visiting as many schools and colleges as he could in search for work. One day he overdid it, and he arrived home exhausted and distressed.

Alice sent for a doctor, who told the family that Fred's heart was in a bad way,[29] and that he would not only have to give up all thought of work but would have to avoid excitement and stress as a priority. The doctor prescribed digitalis tablets in the hope they would increase Fred's blood flow and reduce swelling in his hands and ankles. Alice and Annette were sure this would curtail Fred's role in managing Annette's swimming career.[30]

While her father was recuperating, Annette kept fit riding his bicycle five days a week. On three of those days she would ride 26 miles, and on the other two she would ease through a 14-mile spin.[31]

As Fred slowly regained his health, his zeal for Annette's swimming career resurfaced. He told his concerned doctor that he planned to take Annette to England to race against the best there.

The doctor was adamant. 'Mister Kellermann,' he said gravely, 'I don't think you'll ever reach England. I most certainly do not advise it.'[32]

Fred had other ideas.

BY JUNE 1903, ANNETTE was claiming that she had taken another 4 seconds off her 100-yard world record, making it one minute, 18 seconds,[33] and she was basking in the success of her six weeks swimming among the seals and fish in the big glass tank.

Annette gave swimming tips for women to the fledgling publication *New Idea,* using little sister Mipps to replicate the moves.

> The breast stroke, for the ordinary person, who merely swims for health and pleasure, is by far the most important stroke. Most people – ladies, at any rate – swim with the breast stroke; but it makes a great difference whether or not they learn it properly. A big percentage of people who swim with the breast stroke would get about twice as much speed, and three times as much good exercise, if they did the stroke thoroughly ... I make my pupils practise the strokes on land, before going into the water, and teach them to do all the movements thoroughly.

Annette and Mipps gave a demonstration of the sidestroke, but Annette said the speediest stroke was the trudgen, or 'what they call the double overarm'.

> You face the water as in the breast stroke; but instead of extending your arms under water, and bringing them back together, you bring, say, your right hand out of the water at your side, swing it forward in a circle close to the water, till it points straight in front of you; then force it downwards and backwards through the water as far as you can reach. By the time the right arm has reached the end of its stroke, the left arm should be extended in front of you, just ready to begin its stroke. The legs are kicked with each stroke, and the result is that you seem to go through the water in a succession of bounds ...[34]

The Sydney Mail told readers that Annette's 'graceful performances and personal attractions drew such large attendances and made swimming so popular for ladies that 'Miss Kellermann [had] found a lucrative field opened for her as a professional swimming teacher, and in that capacity has created quite a swimming boom among her sex in Melbourne.' She hoped to swim in England soon.[35]

Annette was one of the most talked about women in Australia, and she was in big demand. Now the leading theatrical impresario in the young nation offered her the chance of a lifetime. He was staging a bold new stage production and wanted Annette as his headline act.

It would prove to be the most dangerous thing she had ever done.

Chapter 7

BLAND HOLT[1] WAS THE biggest name in Australian theatre. A renowned actor and producer, he had a reputation for giving moving performances and staging innovative productions.

Holt had a novel idea for his drama, *The Breaking of the Drought* at the Theatre Royal in Melbourne, and he offered Annette her big chance in theatre: diving into a stage flooded with water.

Fred remained in poor health, but he was lifted by a job directing Annette and some assistants as they dived into a water tank on a stage that was 'artfully fitted into the painted representation of the blue waters of Coogee Bay'.[2] Water was pumped into the tank through large pipes before each performance and then pumped out each night after the final curtain.

Attired in a bright red, short-sleeved costume with braid trimmings that showed off most of her legs, Annette looked stunning.[3] The family had started dropping the 'double n' from Kellermann because the shorter version looked better on a marquee.

The play ran for two months at the Theatre Royal, but Annette's run was nearly over long before. One night, as the water was being emptied from the stage tank, Annette, still only sixteen but 'quite sure she knew more than others',[4] stayed in the water, despite repeated warnings. Before she realised it, the suction from the outlet pipe had her trapped in a whirlpool and she was being dragged under. One arm was already in the outlet pipe, but Annette had the presence of mind to catch the end of a beam that was projecting over the side, and with her head out of the water and screaming hard, she managed to attract the attention of a stage hand, who shut down the pumps with just seconds to spare.[5]

Mipps noted that this was 'occupational hazard No. 1 of which Annette had many with her surplus of self-confidence'. Annette would 'do stupid but courageous stunts … Nothing daunted her, if it were in the script,' Mipps recalled. 'Her willpower was built-in.'[6]

Despite the terrifying close call, Annette was back in a tank again in no time, the Exhibition trustees having hired her to perform her underwater ballet in the Aquarium for as long as she liked.[7]

For months on end, Annette followed a similar routine at the Aquarium. A bell was rung, Annette's father shouted out the order of the dips, and the 'complacent girl, with the fine eyes and the soft mouth, and the drawl' sauntered off to disrobe. Then she entered the tank, scattering eels, bream and pike, swimming forward and back and around the fish and seals. She'd eat her banana underwater, then climb out to raucous cheers, don a brief leopard-print gown, then run along a passage and up onto the springboard for a series of spectacular dives into an open pond.[8]

Steadily she built up a huge circle of admirers, not surprisingly among young men of a certain age. One report in February 1904, almost a year after Annette had first dived in Melbourne, noted:

The attraction of Miss Annette Kellerman at the Aquarium remains strong. I had a look in the other afternoon, expecting to see, as I did once before, an army of children and women. It was not so. There was a legion of Johnnies instead. The inexperienced, who could not get near enough for their satisfaction to absorb the dexterous diving and eel-like capers of this brown-hued nymph in the water, and who pressed round to the brink of the huge tank, were incontinently splashed. It is impossible for Annette to dip and plunge through the deeps of the tank without distributing a volume of water over the nearest spectators. So the most curious of the admiring sex get the lot ... Doctors, artists, and lovers of the beautiful were among the interested crowd of onlookers. A certain number of these go up regularly, the form of the diver so generously displayed by a brief guernsey being considered the most perfect in Melbourne. The diving feats take second place to the glory of the form.[9]

Now seventeen and with more than one hundred performances under her belt, Annette was flattered by the praise and publicity, though she wanted to be known for her athleticism rather than just as a 'nymph' to be ogled. She wanted to test her full potential as a swimmer.

Prompted by friends, she swam 2¼ miles (3.6 km) from Melbourne's Church Street Bridge to Prince's Bridge in 58 minutes, 30 seconds, averaging just over 23 minutes to the mile, a time regarded as extraordinary by swimming experts, even when assisted by the river currents. Annette had low blood pressure and a steady, slow, heartbeat that allowed the engine of her finely tuned body to tick over for hour on end.[10]

Annette and her father resolved that she should swim the same course of the Yarra again, this time with three accredited timekeepers to make her swim official.

The date was fixed for 23 April 1904, with a starting time between 11 a.m. and noon. The attempt was kept quiet, with only Annette's family and a few of her friends along with the timekeepers from the Amateur Swimming Association of Victoria aware of it.

Standing on the prow of a rowboat, readied for the start, Annette smiled and posed for photographs before waving to her parents and pals, who were on a little steamer that would follow her down the river.

On the word 'go', she dived into the dark waters of the Yarra, amid cheers and cries of 'Cooee'.

When she rose to the surface, she shook her hair out of her eyes and, with a bright smile to all and sundry, she set out with the trudgen stroke for the Princes Bridge. 'Shaking her head like a bright little mermaid,' *The Herald* reported, 'she smiled and kept plodding on.'

A crowd of cheering spectators grew to include a number of ladies on bicycles, who followed beside the Yarra.

Passing the Cremorne Gardens, Annette called out to her parents in the steamer, 'It's not a bit cold!' but at times she complained that the Yarra was full of dead water with no current.[11]

As the Prince's Bridge appeared in sight, Annette appeared to grow stronger amid cheers from a crowd that had now swelled to hundreds. She passed the finishing marker after a swim of 2¼ miles[12] in 46 minutes, 20 and ⅗ of a second, at an average of just over 20 minutes per mile.[13]

Annette at once seized hold of the rowboat and was towed to the landing-place at Edwards' boatshed, where she stepped ashore and was wrapped in a rug. She walked merrily up to the shed, not in the least tired or fatigued.

She told everyone that the world record for 2 miles was 54 minutes, 7 seconds, accomplished by T.E. Hitching, an American, in July 1878, and thus she was now claiming the world 2-mile record.[14] After that she said she was heading to the much colder waters of the Aquarium for her afternoon performance.[15]

IF THE MURKY WATERS of the Yarra had not been perilous enough for Annette, Melbourne's Bijou Theatre, where she was performing a diving routine a couple of weeks later, proved almost fatal.

She and Fred had made plans to visit America for the 1904 St Louis World's Fair, which ran until December, and they had organised a farewell fundraising show. Part of Annette's performance at the Bijou consisted of a dive from a springboard 12 feet high into a shallow tank with 4 feet of water. But just as she was about to make a daring backwards somersault plunge,[16] a cross piece supporting the platform collapsed. Instead of diving into the shallow water, Annette crashed heavily into it. Her head struck the bottom of the tank, and she suffered severe concussion and major damage to her neck.

Reports said that, given 'the nature of the fall her escape from very serious, if not fatal, injuries' was regarded as 'providential'. In an understatement it was announced that Annette would not be performing anymore that night.[17] She and Fred got into the back of a cab and headed home.

The accident did Fred's heart no good, and Annette spent three weeks in bed recovering, but she was still eyeing her trip to St Louis. She was offered a series of exhibitions in Sydney before her planned departure and had barely started back in the pool to prepare for them when a kettle of boiling water fell on her foot.

She was sidelined for several more weeks as a result, and her 1904 American visit was abandoned. She and her father now concentrated on their earlier plan to visit England and challenge the best swimmers there.

'In England there were more people, more theatres, and more money to be earned by professional swimmers,' Annette wrote later. 'Indeed, in Australia swimming is so much a sport for everyone, and amateur swimming contests and exhibitions so plentiful, that the very abundance of the sport makes it commonplace, and there is less opportunity for the professional swimmer.'[18]

Maurice was already making his way in the world as a musician, and Annette and Fred resolved that once they were sure Alice and the other children were provided for, they would raise enough money themselves to finance their English campaign.

First Annette undertook a week of performances in December 1904 as 'The Australian Mermaid'[19] for the big Christmas holiday crowds at the Adelaide City Baths. Her brother Freddie was again her offsider.[20] In the new year they performed together at Adelaide's seaside suburb of Glenelg[21] and then in the mining centre of Broken Hill on the edge of the Australian Outback.[22] The summer heat coming off the vast desert pushed the thermometer to 112 degrees Fahrenheit (45°C) in the shade, and made diving into the water to the cheers of the miners surrounding the Municipal Baths especially refreshing.[23] But the press noted 'Pa Kellerman' had to apologise that the water in the baths was so muddy that many in the crowd could not see his daughter's legs.[24]

Then it was on to Maryborough in Central Victoria for another show featuring Annette swimming with her hands tied behind her back and doing a spectacular 'torpedo dive' while holding on to an upside-down Freddie.[25]

Annette was earning hefty paydays for the time — ten pounds a week[26] — and it was vital money for her household, but she decided to set more milestones to bolster her reputation internationally.

On 2 February 1905, she set what was said to be the longest officially timed swim by an Australian woman. At 1.40 p.m. the steam-launch *Laura* left Princes Bridge carrying Annette and her family and friends, including a number of Australia's champion swimmers, among them Alick Wickham and Cecil Healy, as spectators.[27]

Forty minutes later, dressed in a thin, dark-blue swimming costume, Annette, with her legs and arms 'nut brown'[28] from the summer sun, entered the Yarra at the Hawthorn Bridge. She had swum the course in a trial run two days earlier and knew she had the stamina to put in a great time.

'It was not Miss Kellerman's intention to attempt to lower any records,' *The Argus* newspaper reported, 'but merely to give the interstate champions an idea of her staying and swimming powers.' But once in the water, Annette turned on the speed and power.

With her father beside her in a row boat with a friend rowing, Annette commenced with the trudgen, even though it was generally regarded as too tiring for long-distance swimming. She glided through the water with the ease of someone who knew she had a strong reserve of strength.[29]

After a few hundred metres she called out to her supporters that the water was 'absolutely lovely'.[30]

Her father told her to swim more in the centre of the river to avoid the shallows and dead areas with no current.

Annette covered the first mile in twenty-three minutes, and as she approached 'the big bend' of the Yarra at Richmond, the stopwatch showed forty-two minutes. At this stage, her father called for three cheers, which were heartily given.

At the Church Street bridge, 2¾ miles from the starting point, Annette had been in the water for 54 minutes, 30 seconds.

A large crowd had assembled at the Princes Bridge to witness the finish, and as Annette passed below they roared their encouragement. She had covered 5 miles in one hour, 48 minutes, 34 and ⅖ seconds.[31]

'She accomplished a feat which must be regarded as a record for a lady swimmer,' *The Argus* noted, 'keeping well within the standard time limit for each mile, which the various interstate amateur swimming associations have fixed at twenty-eight minutes.'[32]

After the event, the interstate swimmers on the steamboat presented Annette with an autographed group photo and a prize of five pounds.[33] The swim attracted the notice of the leading British newspapers, too, making Annette even more determined to visit London and take on the best swimmers there.[34]

A few days later, the Kellermans were giving shows over three days and nights at the City Baths in Ballarat, about 100 kilometres west of Melbourne. The 'most vivacious'[35] swimming star told a reporter there that she was now eighteen years old, stood 5 feet, 7 inches (170 cm) and that she weighed 10 stone, 8 pounds (67 kg).

Annette said she took a keen interest not only in swimming but 'also in every other kind of athletics', and that she wanted to encourage other women to take up all manner of sports. 'I like to see them engaging in rifle shooting, tennis, cricket, rowing or any other suitable exercise, but above all, in swimming; that is undoubtedly the finest exercise going for ladies.'

She said her father supervised her diet and it was mostly 'plain, well-cooked food'.

'I eschew anything of a rich nature,' she said. 'I don't do much training, my daily swimming practice gives me all the training I require, but if the water at Mentone, where we live, is too rough for swimming, I take a smart walk of three or four miles, and that serves me almost as well.'[36]

Annette's father, watching on, interjected. 'Look at her,' he said as he gazed proudly at his daughter. 'She is strong, healthy, and happy, and she can attribute it all to her swimming ... Indeed, there are very few male swimmers in Australia who could hope to equal her times over various distances.'[37]

Fred said that Annette had further shaved her 100-yards time and now claimed 74 seconds using the trudgen stroke, though she was now mastering Alick Wickham's Australian crawl, too, and expected to swim that distance much faster.

They were both sure that Annette could topple the finest swimmers in Britain and they were well advanced in their preparations to prove it.

ANNETTE STARTED PERFORMING in swimming and diving shows[38] at the new Princes Court amusement park in St Kilda Road, next to the Fitzgerald Brothers Circus building.[39] Princes Court was built on five acres (2 ha) and had a series of thrill rides, including a water chute 70 feet high (about 22 m) that emptied riders into a lake 220 feet wide (70 m).[40]

In Annette's first shows she dived from a springboard into a glass tank 24 feet (7 m) wide, 9 feet (3 m) long and 7 feet (2 m) deep.[41] The water was illuminated by electric lights under the tank. Annette would sometimes do three shows a day; the owners charged patrons sixpence to watch her, in addition to the entrance fee to the park.[42] Fred Kellerman put some of Annette's takings towards their voyage to London.

It was at the Princes Court that Annette gave her first display of what would become her trademark. Sitting high up on the water chute, she was adorned with a glittering green and silver mermaid tail.

Looking down to see an audience enthralled, she spotted her beaming mother in the front row. While Alice had once disapproved of her daughter's swimming career, she now embraced it. Annette was becoming one of Australia's great sporting and theatrical stars.

The teenager was so nervous at the top of the chute that she hardly heard the gasps and applause as she slid at astonishing speed down the 70-foot slide into a darkened lake.

To thrill the crowds, she stayed underwater for as long as possible before emerging triumphant.

But this time, after a minute and a half, some of the men in the crowd leapt up to save her. One took off his shirt and was preparing to dive in when Australia's mermaid leapt out of the water like a happy seal. She had been submerged for more than two minutes.

The crowd stood as one to clap. Above the rousing applause, Annette could hear a distinctly French voice: *'Bravo! Bravo, ma petite!'*[43]

HAVING TAMED 5 MILES of the Yarra, Annette fired another warning shot towards the best of Britain. Two months after her speedy effort on Melbourne's murky river, she made an attempt to double it in what she believed would be one of the longest swims ever by any female swimmer in the world. Two Brisbane swimmers, Mabel Mahoney and May Clarke, had beaten Annette's 5-mile swim by going 5¼ miles in the Bremer River at Ipswich, though their times didn't come close to Annette's.[44] Still, in response to the fact they had swum further than her longest swim, she decided to leave them and any other challengers in her wake.

At 10.50 a.m. on 11 April 1905, Annette entered the water in bright sunshine at the Dights Falls rapids just downstream from where Merri Creek joins the Yarra. As usual, she was lightly clad, her long hair loose, and she powered away with the trudgen stroke.

Again, a steam launch carrying family and friends followed her, while Fred was rowed in front of Annette as he guided her down a river that was muddier than usual after recent rains.

Annette covered the first 5 miles in just one hour, 33 minutes, 15 minutes faster than her great swim two months earlier. But then a strong head wind sprang up, and the choppy water made swimming much tougher.

Still, throughout her progress and especially at the bridges, large groups of people had collected to cheer Annette, and for the last couple of miles she was accompanied along the river banks by about 500 pedestrians and cyclists, who followed her to join an even bigger crowd along the Princes Bridge.

Fred kept the small boat just ahead of his daughter to minimise the effect of the wind and the churning water, but the difficulties were tremendous, and Annette spent nearly an hour covering a short stretch between the Royal Botanic Garden bridge and the Princes Bridge. But with half a dozen final vigorous strokes, Annette covered 10¼ miles amid great cheering from the steamer, both river banks and the parapet of Princes Bridge.[45] The swim had taken 4 hours, 52 minutes in total, with the last 5¼ miles taking 3 hours 19 minutes[46] due to the wind and the tide against her.[47]

Despite the gruelling swim, Annette showed no signs of distress, and after climbing out of the water she even skipped through the crowd as they cheered and patted her on the back. That night she delivered not one, but two stunning swimming and diving shows at the Princes Court.[48]

IN AN AGE WHEN A GLIMPSE of ankle from under a woman's long skirt was considered risqué, Annette was not only a sports star but a sex symbol. Photographs of her in seductive poses no doubt helped her sell her swimming and diving routine, and she built a huge following throughout Australia. She had a large fan base in the mining centres of Western Australia. *The Dryblower's Journal* of Kalgoorlie described Annette as 'the plump and pretty swimmist, whose "noodness" shocked Adelaide'.[49] Another Kalgoorlie paper told readers that after Annette's last swim in the Yarra she had sprinted up the bank to her dressing room as if she was just going to begin again.

> She's a big lump of a girl ... As she came out of the water wearing nothing particular in the way of [a] blue serge bathing dress the crowd admired her muscular legs,

broad hips, and well-developed bust. Her proportions are good ...[50]

On the night of 20 April 1905, Annette made the final appearance of her ten-week run at the Princes Court, swimming in the lake with her hands tied behind her back on a variety night that also included the Newman family of trick cyclists; Val Verno, a ventriloquist; and Jerry the fighting kangaroo.[51]

Annette and her father were gearing up for their trip to London, starting within a week, but first she had a three-day assignment of shows at the City Baths in Bendigo, about three hours north-west of Melbourne by train. She gave up to five half-hour performances each day in the celebrated gold-mining town, with the last show at 9 p.m. Fred collected a shilling for adults and sixpence for children.[52]

Annette played to packed crowds throughout her stay, coming out to perform with a 'bright, cheery face and brim full of humor', chatting with admirers and answering smartly any wisecracks from them.[53] She displayed a variety of strokes and all manner of springboard dives, making a perfect curve after take-off and entering the water silently with hardly a ripple.

She dived in all manner of ways: backwards, forwards, off her forearms, and even off her neck – first balancing on her head atop the springboard before flipping over to enter the water feet first.

Annette and her father returned to Melbourne by train on the morning of 26 April.[54] The Victorian capital was still buzzing with her marathon down the Yarra and the press was glowing in its praise. *The Argus* was just one newspaper to laud Annette's swim as perhaps the most monumental endurance feat ever made by a female athlete.

> The task accomplished by Australia's champion lady swimmer ... is one that very few men, even professionals of the champion class, have ever attempted. So unusually long is 10 miles as the distance of a swimming feat that there is no record of the best time chronicled. Several

historic swimmers have on rare occasions attempted longer distances as, for instance, Captain Webb, who crossed the English Channel [but] certainly no lady has ever before accomplished such a performance ... Had the weather continued fine, her record would unquestionably have been greatly reduced and even after overcoming the difficulties of wind and wave she was so little distressed that she could easily have covered a couple of miles more. For a man, such a swim would be a feat fit to rank with the best athletic achievements of the day. For a woman, it stands as probably the finest feat of athletic endurance yet recorded ...[55]

Annette was justifiably proud of her finest swim yet. But her joy was tinged with great sadness too. She and Fred were about to sail for England, leaving Alice and the other children behind.[56]

Fred's health was delicate. Annette feared that her family would never be the same.

Chapter 8

THERE WERE POOLS of tears when the world's greatest female swimmer, all of eighteen years of age, stood with her mother, father and siblings on the platform at Spencer Street Railway Station in Melbourne on the evening of 26 April 1905. It was cool and overcast as the sun went down,[1] but a biting chill went through all the family.

Fred and Annette were preparing to ride the Melbourne Express train through the night to Adelaide, where the British Royal Mail Steamship *Ophir* was anchored in Largs Bay.[2] Despite Annette's success over the past two years in Melbourne, the Kellermans were still battling financially. Nevertheless, Fred, Alice and Annette had gathered enough money together to buy two second-class passages on the ship. Fred had another forty pounds in his wallet as spending money to finance the great gamble he and Annette were about to undertake thousands of miles from home.[3]

Annette saw victory over the best British swimmers as her chance to 'swim back' the family fortune, and there was always the chance of finding roles on the London stage, too.

Alice saw only disaster ahead. She knew how sick her husband was and guessed at the amount of stress he would experience on the long ocean voyage and from the challenges he'd face making Annette's name in Britain. At forty-five, he was almost an invalid. Alice prayed to Jesus and the Virgin Mary that they, and the supply of digitalis tablets Fred had with him, would protect him. Annette promised her mother that she would take good care of her father, but as steam billowed from the engine of the locomotive Alice's face was a mask of dread.

The conductor made his final call of 'All aboard' and after more kisses, hugs and tears, Annette helped her father onto the train. As Fred and Annette leaned out of their window to wave their last goodbyes, their faces were grim. Alice was weeping.

And so into the dark night and a world of uncertainty they sped. Despite his ill health, Fred told Annette she would handle this great challenge with the same ease that she had conquered the Yarra. He was sure, ill as he was, that great things were in store for his daughter.[4]

A couple of hours after leaving Melbourne, the Express reached Ballarat,[5] then chugged on through Victoria's Western Districts before crossing the South Australian border as the sun rose. The train continued on, over the winding Murray River and through the Adelaide Hills.

It was still morning[6] when they reached the South Australian capital during light showers. From there they took another train right to the end of the seemingly endless Largs Bay jetty, 16 kilometres away, where the *Ophir* was anchored.[7]

More than 140 metres long, the steam-powered ocean liner was an imposing vessel that carried almost 1000 passengers. In 1901 it had been a royal yacht that carried the future King George V and Queen Mary on a tour of the British Empire. Now it was the first word in luxury sailing, and although Annette and her father only had second-class tickets, they were given first-class treatment as soon as they set foot on the ship.

The *Ophir* was also carrying Broken Hill's distance swimmer George Read to London,[8] but Annette was still the most famous passenger on the voyage, and her impending departure had been given great advance publicity. Even before she unpacked her trunk, she was the focus of just about everyone on board, especially the young men wanting to become better acquainted with this fit, suntanned young wonder woman whose brief swimming costumes famously left little to the imagination.

Fred gave all the potential suitors eyeing his daughter flinty looks and told Annette to ignore them because she had a big task ahead on the far side of the world. Young men circling like hungry sharks were of no use to them.

That night, the *Ophir*'s young English skipper, Fred Kershaw,[9] invited Annette and Fred to dine at his table as, under heavy skies, the ship set a course for Fremantle, its first scheduled stop before it crossed the Indian Ocean to Colombo. From there the *Ophir* would sail on to Bombay, Port Said, Naples and Marseilles before reaching London.

The next morning, as the *Ophir* passed the immense limestone cliffs along the Great Australian Bight, Fred began supervising Annette's on-board training. He spent much of his time on the ship sitting in the sun wrapped in a blanket, but he insisted Annette go through her stretches and calisthenics. Though she had no pool to practise her diving and strokes, Annette would embark each day on long walks of many laps of the main deck. She was always joined by a young man, sometimes many, ever keen to assist her in her training, despite Fred's angry stares from his deck chair.

Annette left most of her training partners gasping for breath as they stumbled to keep up, and at night, despite Fred waggling a warning finger, she would dance them off their feet.[10] He was not well and often had to retire to the cabin and take his medication.

Four days after leaving Adelaide, the *Ophir* arrived in Fremantle, where a reporter boarded the ship to interview Australia's greatest female sportswoman on her first visit to the west. Annette explained that she was going to England to give exhibitions, 'and, if possible, challenge, other lady swimmers ... I want to show them what an Australian girl can do. I will be the first Australian lady athlete to visit the old world,' she said, adding that she also had plans to conquer America.[11]

By the time the *Ophir* reached Colombo, the capital of what is now Sri Lanka, the heat and humidity were cloying, but Fred

Annette at her most provocative as she appeared before crowds in Britain in 1905. *State Library of Victoria H36145/65*

was also concerned that a young New Zealander was getting too hot and heavy with Annette. They had started walking together around the deck, and before long Annette's brisk pacesetting had slowed to a dawdle as the youngsters held hands and stopped often to look for what seemed an eternity into each other's eyes. Fred's pallid face almost turned purple when he spotted the impertinent Kiwi getting a good feel of his daughter's muscles on the dance floor.

Annett recalled this was her first experience of 'puppy love' and she was revelling in it. For her, the voyage was just magical, and though it had been a long time now since she'd been in the pool, she felt like she was floating on the moonlight shining across the vast grey sea.

Fred grew angrier and angrier, wolfing down the digitalis as his daughter's romance blossomed.

By the time the *Ophir* reached Bombay, Annette was besotted with her Kiwi beau. The ship travelled on to the Suez Canal, and in places it was so narrow Annette could throw pennies to the Egyptians waving to her on the desert sands.[12]

Fred told Annette that her boyfriend had become too close for comfort and was throwing a spanner in their preparations for the England campaign. They hadn't even reached London, he said, and Annette was putting herself many lengths behind in the greatest challenge of their lives. He told his daughter that she had to pack her bags and tell her boyfriend 'bon voyage' because they were getting off at the next port. 'Remember you have a lot to do before you settle down,' Fred told her.

When the *Ophir* reached Naples, Annette said 'a sad goodbye' to her first serious love. Father and daughter disembarked, leaving the ship to sail on for Marseille and then London without them. Then, using some of the forty pounds he had for expenses, Fred bought two tickets for them to cross Europe by train followed by a boat across the English Channel.

Annette was angry for a while, but in time she had to admit that it took only 'a very few weeks' for the 'Tropical Moonshine' of young love to wear off.[13]

AFTER THE THOUSANDS of miles of travel and months of anticipation, London was initially a bitter disappointment for Annette and her father. They arrived on a Sunday in the first week of June,[14] a summer day that was still dark and foggy with the streets 'as still as the dead'.[15] After the sunshine and 'she'll be right mate' bonhomie of Australia, Annette felt she'd dived into a dark and cheerless hole. She and Fred found a small, down-at-heel hotel in Gower Street,[16] a narrow lane where Charles Dickens once lived and which he might have used as a model for the sombre, soul-destroying slums of his time. The street was just down from the theatre district of the West End, but the atmosphere of the hotel and its surrounds was funereal rather than festive.

The mood of the two displaced Australians darkened further when the Kellermans realised that, to many in Britain's elite sporting circles, being a professional athlete was what they called an 'unpardonable sin'.[17]

For a few days, Fred made the rounds of the different newspapers and swimming clubs in London, spruiking the talents of his daughter and her extraordinary success in Australia as a 'Diving Venus'.

Doors were constantly slammed in his face, despite considerable advance publicity in England about the teenager's swims in the Yarra.

'We were utter strangers,' Annette recalled, 'and theatrical managers at that time were no more interested in a "Diving Venus" than they were in a "Flying Mercury".'[18]

At first, none of the newspapers seemed remotely interested in Annette or her fancy diving and long-distance feats. If she was an amateur athlete, well that would have been a different story, as one of the newspapermen told Fred, but then again, she was a woman, so what was she doing in sport anyway?[19]

Any hope that the storied British swimming clubs would let Annette perform her routines at their establishments seemed forlorn. British high society was not up for mermaids that season.[20]

The forty pounds in Fred's pocket was quickly disappearing, so he and Annette soon found themselves looking for rooms in Kings Cross, which at that time was the cheapest part of London.

In a narrow house with a window card marked 'rooms for rent', a little old Cockney lady showed them into a small parlour decorated with stuffed birds under glass, wax fruit and linen covers over the arm chairs.

Annette explained that they wanted to rent two rooms and asked if her father could have one on the ground floor as his heart was playing up something fierce and the stairs would be too much.

'Well,' said the little landlady, 'I could let your father have this room down here as a special favour, if you would take the small room on the top floor.'

Annette was so happy at having her father on the ground that she quickly followed the landlady to the upstairs quarters.

Her small room was actually a tiny windowless garret with a narrow, rickety cot and a little broken mirror so Annette could comb her hair. Annette would often bang her head on the low ceiling, but so as not to make her ailing father's condition worse, she did not tell him about her room whenever he asked, 'is everything all right Toots?'[21]

For the price of one guinea (one pound, one shilling) a week, the Kellermans now had uncomfortable beds and a stingy breakfast of bread and milk. Annette was able to add some dubious smelling eggs with Fred's remaining pennies.

Persistence paid off, and Fred eventually made some headway with the press and swimming clubs. He told Annette that the best way to get attention in England was for her to go ahead with her plan to replicate her final swim in the murky Yarra, but this time down the muddy Thames.

Annette started doing long training swims in the river from Kew, and newspapers announced she was training for another marathon effort.[22]

Australian test cricketer Victor Trumper was in blazing form on a particularly hot day before 25,000 fans at Lord's in London that week, but *The Daily Mirror* told readers that while the great batsman had shown he was 'hot stuff' against the Englishmen, 'Miss Annette Kellerman' promised to be a cool performer at the Westminster Baths in Great Smith Street on 19 June. 'Introduced by the Ravensbourne club, [she] will make her début in an exhibition of diving and swimming,' *The Mirror* told its readers. 'This exhibition is guaranteed to be better than a strawberry ice.'[23]

The Westminster exhibition was a great success, with *The Sportsman* and other journals referring to Annette as 'Australia's Mermaid'. There was a large audience of men and women, among them many Australians, including men's swimming champions George Read and Barney Kieran,[24] who were also competing in England.

The Aussies shouted 'cooee' when Annette went through her diving routine, including the 'splosh'.[25] Annette told reporters she had all sorts of ambitions and was even thinking about swimming the English Channel. The general feeling expressed among the media was that Annette had the pluck to do it, though no woman had ever swum from England to France and female swimmers were so rare that mixed bathing was still very much frowned on in England.[26]

But Annette was already breaking down barriers with the attention she was gaining. A week after her debut performance at Westminster, she was invited to perform her routine in the famous indoor pool at the prestigious Bath Club,[27] with the Duke of Connaught,[28] son of the late Queen Victoria, watching from the royal balcony.

The club was another level of luxury from anything Annette or Fred had seen in Sydney or Melbourne. Housed in a mansion at 34 Dover Street, Mayfair, it was a temple of marble and gilt balustrades, with a glass conservatory roof suspended on wrought-iron pillars. The ballroom had been turned into the club's ornately tiled 80-foot (25-m) pool with diving boards, and there were Turkish baths, a gymnasium, squash courts and fencing galleries.[29]

The club had admitted women from its opening day in 1894, a radical step for the times, but there were limits – women had their own entrance in Berkeley Street and could only use the sports facilities three afternoons a week.

On the day of Annette's scheduled exhibition, there was consternation about her performing with bare legs. A club official was sent to speak with Annette and her father. 'You understand that you can't possibly appear before their Royal Highnesses exhibiting bare limbs,' the official said.

Annette tried to explain that Australians did not find her outfits shocking, but the club official was adamant.

Annette decided to add stockings to her outfit. She donned her bathing suit and pulled on a pair of stockings. There was a gap of white thigh between the tops of her tights and the bathing costume. She showed her father.

'Oh dear, no. That will never do,' Fred tutted.

So Annette bought the longest pair of stockings she could find and sewed them on to her bathing suit. The entire length of the black costume from the neck to the feet accentuated the symmetry of a figure that was to become the most famous in all the world. Her one-piece bathing suit became her trademark.[30]

Annette saw herself as a game changer, and her spectacular performance in the pool where the future Queen Elizabeth II learned to swim made all the patrons think more about equal rights.

But as Annette's popularity in England grew, so did her anxiety over her father's worsening health. Fred put on a brave face as her manager and promoter, but he was often grey and lethargic, suffering frequent bouts of angina with its brutal chest pains.

'I never went to bed without wondering if he would be alive in the morning,' Annette recalled. 'At his bedside every night were his digitalis pills. Many were the times when I would have to crush one of these capsules and give it to him while tears of agony rained down his face. He would recuperate just as quickly and between spells it was an unwritten law that neither of us would mention the attack just passed.'[31]

BUOYED BY THE CHANGE in attitude of the British press and sporting institutions, Annette now prepared for the most important swim of her career. Having done very little long-distance preparation in the preceding weeks, and on a diet of mostly bread, milk and her landlady's suspect eggs, Annette dived into the Thames at the Putney Bridge in West London at 2.30 p.m. on 30 June 1905. Rain was falling, and experts on the river did not view the conditions favourably.[32] Fred had hired a small boat and a little old man to row it as he once again acted as Annette's pilot. As was the case on the Yarra, a small launch carried a few Australians to cheer on their hero. There were some pressmen, too, dubious about how long Annette could last in what many regarded as an environmental hazard full of London's rubbish and raw sewage.

Passengers on the London County Council steamers shouted encouragement as they passed by the bronzed, scantily clad young woman with her long hair flowing free in the grey-brown water.

Annette turned halfway on her side for the trudgen and, pushed along by a strong ebb tide, powered on stroke after stroke towards London Bridge and beyond. The same council steamers passed Annette again going the other way and found her still fighting the immense river 'with apparently indefinite reserves of strength and determination'.[33] There were ringing cheers, and now and then Fred gave Annette a sip of the latest thing in sports supplements, an egg and sherry mix.[34]

After one hour, 27 minutes, 43 seconds, Annette had swum 5 miles and passed Westminster Bridge. Thirty minutes later she swam under London Bridge. Here the tide and boat traffic threw up a considerable sea, but Annette took on the waves with supreme confidence, while the great incoming liners and fleets of barges kindly gave her a wide berth.

Crowds were now gathering along the banks of the Thames to watch her extraordinary show.

Annette dodged the boats, big and small, for almost two more hours, continuing a laughing conversation with her father throughout,[35] as she pushed her way through the flotsam and jetsam of London, dodging tugs and swallowing what seemed like pints of oil from the greasy surface of the river.[36] The reporters and swimming experts watching her effort were astounded. They were tired, but she was not.[37]

Annette had commenced her marathon with twenty-five strokes to the minute, and was still maintaining twenty-four when she reached her finish line at the shipbuilding yards of Blackwall Pier, in East London. She had completed 13 miles, 2½ furlongs (21.4 km), in 3 hours 54 minutes, 16 seconds.[38]

The following day, the British newspapers were glowing in their praise for what they termed 'a magnificent performance', calling Annette a 'handsome brunette' and 'a model of grace and proportion'.[39] But when she climbed out of the water just before 6.30 p.m. on Friday evening, Annette was not so much concerned about the milestone she'd just set. With matted hair and covered in muck from the river she looked anything but a 'glamour miss',[40] and all she wanted was something to eat.

'I was absolutely starving,' she admitted. 'Lunch had been forgotten and there was nothing to eat.'[41]

An elderly Cockney watchman on the wharf had some bread and cheese wrapped in the pages of a newspaper. 'It's not much, Miss,' he said as he offered it to Annette, 'but it's yours.'

Annette took the parcel gleefully and, still in her bathing costume, devoured the food right there on the wharf. Hunks of bread and cheese had never tasted so good.[42]

Chapter 9

ANNETTE HATED HER swim in the Thames and vowed she would never take on the river again because it was so dirty.[1]

After she finished her dinner of cheese and bread, she and Fred returned to the Kings Cross boarding house to find a large gathering of locals wanting to congratulate the Australian mermaid. Annette would never forget their cheers and hurrahs.[2]

News of the swim was telegraphed to the press in Australia and it thrilled Alice, who was preparing for a concert at the Mechanics Hall in Cheltenham.[3]

The next morning, when Annette banged her head on the low ceiling of her garret and went downstairs, the landlady came inside, excitedly holding aloft an envelope that she announced bore the stamp of *The Daily Mirror* newspaper.

Annette opened the envelope to find a note from the editor Hamilton Fyfe,[4] asking Fred – not Annette, because she was a woman, after all, and a young one at that – to call at his office in Bond Street, West London, as soon as possible. Fyfe wanted to discuss a sponsorship proposal.

Dressed in his best outfit – the pin-striped trousers, Prince Albert coat, gloves and top hat – Fred set off for the *Mirror* office. He planned to walk the 3 kilometres from Kings Cross, but given his recent heart palpitations, Annette insisted he spend what remained of the forty pounds on a hansom cab. She would wait at the boarding house with bated breath.[5]

The Daily Mirror's offices were imposing and impressive. The paper had only been in publication for eighteen months but was already the jewel in the crown of press baron Lord Northcliffe,[6] who had capitalised on the growing literacy in Britain by promoting journalism for the masses. He already owned major publications *The Evening News, The Edinburgh Daily Record* and *The Daily Mail* when he launched *The Daily Mirror* at the end of 1903 as a newspaper for women, run by women, intended to be 'a mirror of feminine life'.[7]

Britain wasn't quite ready for that and sales had flopped. So Northcliffe hired Hamilton Fyfe as editor, fired all the women journalists and relaunched the paper using bold pictorial spreads on the front page. Even the barely literate were attracted to the pictorial displays.

Under Fyfe, the circulation had risen to more than 300,000 copies a day and was still growing fast.[8]

The beautiful, curvy, suntanned Australian mermaid was the ideal subject for Fyfe's photojournalism – what he called 'reported by camera' – to push daily sales towards half a million.

A secretary ushered Fred in to see the editor and his sporting staff. Fyfe was an ambitious, sharp young man of thirty-six, with a neat moustache and a fresh, angular jawline like the one Fred had possessed before illness had aged him so.

'Well, I'll come to the point,' Fyfe told Fred. 'As you know, we have started the first picture paper in England, and Lord Northcliffe is anxious to push the publicity.'

Fred was all ears.

'I see your daughter has just made a very long swim in the Thames and she is talking about trying the Channel?'

'Well,' Fred replied, 'I don't see why not.'

'The summer is just about to start,' Fyfe went on, 'and the beaches from Dover to Margate will be thronged with thousands of holidaymakers. We would like to engage your daughter Annette for eight weeks.'

'What do you mean, "engage"?' Fred asked.

'She would make a swim from one seaside resort to another,' Fyfe said.

'Each day *The Daily Mirror* staff will photograph her. The press department will announce that Miss Kellerman will swim into one of the summer resorts at such and such an hour. You will have a rowboat and a pilot.'[9]

Fred asked how many days a week Annette would have to swim and how many miles.

'Five days a week,' Fyfe said, 'with a rest day after every couple of swims.'

He said the swims would cover resort towns such as Dover, Deal, Ramsgate and Margate.

Fyfe was very keen for Annette to challenge the Dover to Ramsgate record of Captain Matthew Webb,[10] a young steamship skipper who became the first recorded person to swim the English Channel.

'Dover to Ramsgate is how far?' Fred asked.

'A bit more than 24 miles [the actual swim is more like 20 miles (32 km)]. Nearly double what your girl just did in the Thames.'[11]

Webb had swum Dover to Ramsgate in 8 hours, 45 minutes in July 1875, and a month later, swimming breaststroke and covered in porpoise oil, he swam from Dover to a spot near Calais, covering the 33.5 kilometres across the English Channel in 21 hours, 45 minutes.

Fred knew that Webb had died trying to swim the Whirlpool Rapids below Niagara Falls, and that in the thirty years since he had crossed the Channel no one else had ever made it.

To say that Fred was flabbergasted by Fyfe's offer is putting it mildly. 'That's a frightful lot of swimming,' Fred ventured. 'Let's see now, that would make it an average of 45 miles a week, not including the 24-mile swim from Dover to Ramsgate during the period.'[12]

'Well, Mr Kellerman,' Fyfe replied, 'if the Northcliffe papers take your daughter up, her future would be assured. This would be the greatest press campaign ever launched about a young girl.'[13]

Fred knew it was the opportunity of a lifetime to make Annette a star. 'Mr Fyfe, what sort of compensation would you be willing to provide? Once again, that's a frightful lot of swimming.'

Fyfe was direct. 'I think we could manage eight guineas [eight pounds, eight shillings] a week for the eight weeks.'

Fred did some quick calculations. 'Well gentlemen,' he said, rising slowly to his feet. 'I'll have to discuss this with my daughter. She's the one who'll be doing all the swimming, after all. But I promise an answer in a couple of days.'[14]

Fred shook hands with *The Daily Mirror* men then took a hansom cab back to break the news. He was in two minds about the whole business. He and Annette could buy a lot of food with sixty-four guineas, and the gruelling schedule might be the making of Annette on the world stage. It might also be the breaking of her.

ANNETTE'S SWIM IN THE Thames had made news right around Australia, and it had received notice in the American press as well.

But Fred did not want to push his daughter to the outer limits of endurance with a workload beyond what she could bear. When he arrived back at the boarding house, Annette dashed out to meet him.

By the time they reached the front door, Fred had explained the scenario. It was a mammoth undertaking, he said, and 'you know, dear, you must swim through to the end, and everything must be done in a sportsmanlike fashion'. There would be no shortcuts and no helping hands once she was in the water.

'If any time you feel that you cannot complete the distance you must come out of the water and into the boat and just admit you will try again.'

'Well, Dad,' Annette replied, 'I never seem to get tired, and you've always said I swim like a clock. Besides, just imagine what eight guineas a week could be to us for eight weeks. I really think I can do this.'[15]

Fred finalised arrangements with *The Daily Mirror* and agreed that the first payment of eight guineas would be made in a week's time.

Fred was very much about keeping up appearances, and he would not admit to the *Mirror's* editor that he and his daughter were stone broke. Nor was he one to ever ask for a loan.

He had high hopes for Annette's success, and as they headed to the train station he had a spring in his step. But by the time he had paid the train fares to Dover, he had exactly one halfpenny left from his original forty pounds. *The Daily Mirror* money would not arrive for another seven days.

To make matters worse, Fred and Annette arrived in Dover only to discover that seaside accommodation there was always paid one week in advance. Soon they were sitting dejectedly on a bench above the white cliffs, wondering how far half a penny would go.

But Fred had a plan. Outwardly father and daughter looked well-to-do, and Fred decided to approach the finest of the terrace houses facing the water.

'Now Annette, when we go into the house be perfectly silent and let me do the talking and we will be all right,' he said.

'Righto, Dad,' she replied, 'but let me hold the halfpenny for luck.'[16]

Fred marched up to the front door and demanded – yes demanded mind you – to see some rooms.[17]

'Very well,' the landlady said, taken a little aback by his manner, and proceeded to show the visitors her best accommodation.

Fred asked Annette 'in a very dignified manner' whether she thought they would suit.

'I think so,' Annette replied, doing her best to not appear too eager.

Fred nodded. 'How much?' said Fred, turning to the landlady.

'Two guineas each per week.'[18]

Fred produced his best bluster, telling the landlady that he and Annette had just arrived from Australia and that Annette was the famous world champion swimmer. 'You must have read of Annette's exploits on the Thames?'

The landlady had.

'Lord Northcliffe has engaged my daughter to make a series of swims from one resort to the other. Of course, we will have the press here and a great deal of publicity, so we picked the nicest house on the street.'

The landlady was more than impressed and promised them 'splendid rooms' overlooking the sea.[19]

Annette spoke up and, clutching the halfpenny for luck, told her that Fred would need a room on the ground floor because of his heart.

The landlady readily agreed.

Then Fred gave his finest performance of the day. He was still a good-looking, charming man, impeccably dressed and with a very professional appearance.[20]

Fred thrust his hand into his coat pocket and in a grand manner said: 'Perhaps I had better give you a cheque. I suppose you require the usual week in advance payment?'

Annette went limp at the knees, knowing there was nothing in his pocket but lint.

But the landlady would have none of it.

'Oh dear, no,' she said. 'That will be quite all right. You pay when you feel like it. We will be very proud to have you and your daughter here as guests.'[21]

After the landlady left, Fred sank into a chair, wiping his sweaty brow. Annette feared another angina attack. But Fred just grinned. 'By Jove,' he whispered, 'that was a whopper.'[22]

FOR THE NEXT WEEK, until their eight guineas arrived, Fred and Annette couldn't write home because they didn't have the price of a stamp. They couldn't afford a newspaper either, not even *The Daily Mirror*, so wherever they could they would sit next to strangers and look over their shoulders in order to see what the sporting pages were saying about Annette's upcoming swims.

Then, on 18 July 1905, having just celebrated her nineteenth birthday, Annette had her first long practice swim in preparation for an assault on the English Channel. Over the next eight weeks, she would have what she called 'the greatest training period' of her career. While she still ate a little meat, Annette was experimenting with vegetarianism, something that was becoming popular at the time as the world embraced new ideas. It was a diet at odds with most athletes of the time, who trained on juicy steaks.[23]

Soon after 10 a.m. and with a *Daily Mirror* photographer following her, Annette set off from Dover with her father in a boat rowed by Skipper Cole, a veteran boatman who had recently helped British distance swimmer Monty Holbein[24] with his training. When, forty minutes later, the rowboat reached the mobile lighthouse, the New Pier Lightship, Annette threw off her wraps and, clad in a neat blue boy's swimming costume with a cap over her hair, dived into the English Channel.

On the way out, the sea had been very choppy, and Annette had complained of seasickness before she even entered the water.

She started with the trudgen and looked strong, but there was a big swell on, and sometimes she would appear far above the boat, poised on the crest of the wave, and in the next moment she would be lost to sight in a deep trough.

After swimming for twenty minutes, Annette asked her father for chocolate, which she ate while swimming with a graceful sidestroke. Soon she began to complain of seasickness again, but despite Fred's requests she refused to come out of the water.

The sea became rougher still. Annette struggled on until 11.40, when, after an hour's swim and having covered 4 miles (6.4 km), she finally gave in to her father's requests and climbed back into the boat.[25]

The next day *The Daily Mirror* announced that Annette would attempt to swim the English Channel towards the end of August, against a number of men.

'What chance has a woman of swimming the Channel?' the paper asked rhetorically. 'The Answer is to be found in the fact that all the best judges of swimming in this country and in Australia agree that Miss Kellerman is a phenomenal performer in the water.'[26]

There were five main reasons why she was such a talent, the paper said.

(1) She possesses great powers of resisting cold, having never yet been troubled by the temperature of the water.
(2) She has a buoyancy that lifts her head and shoulders well out of the water – her weight being close on 12 st [76 kg].
(3) Unlike all other Channel swimmers, she eats well during her long swims and digests her food without the slightest difficulty.
(4) She is faster over a distance than most of the men who will shortly attempt to swim the Channel.
(5) And, lastly, Miss Kellerman has a wonderful store of vitality and enthusiasm. She is fired with a desire to be the first woman to emulate the late Captain Webb, and at Dover, where she is now training, she is certainly doing everything possible to get fit for so great a task.[27]

Over the next two days, Annette did two-hour training sessions in the sea with fellow Australian George Read[28] and male swimmers who were planning to swim the Channel. Then, on Friday, 21 July, she powered through 9 miles (14.5 km) from Dover to the port of Deal. *The Daily Mirror* reported that their star representative did so 'with a very powerful stroke, and made rapid headway through the sea'.[29]

The following day, Annette gave her greatest performance yet. Captain Webb had taken almost nine hours to swim from Dover to Ramsgate in 1875, and only two swimmers had done it in the thirty years since.

The current record holder, 'Jabez' Wolffe,[30] the beefy son of a German-Polish Glasgow jeweller, had cut the time down to 4 hours, 30 minutes only a few days before Annette's attempt, and he agreed to pace Annette for the longest swim of her life.

Annette's training partner, the Scottish distance swimmer Jabez Wolffe, in front of the White Cliffs of Dover. *channelswimmingdover.org.uk*

The conditions were perfect when the pair entered the water at Dover soon after noon. Followed by her father and a party of boatmen, and going with a fast current, Annette set a cracking pace with the trudgen, even when she turned to use sidestroke while eating the sugar sandwiches Fred passed her from the boat. She assured her father that the water was warm and she felt as fresh as when she started, and quite ready for a 'square meal'.[31]

Annette reached Ramsgate with Wolffe still pacing her, and after a course that actually measured 20 miles (32 km), broke the record he'd set just four days earlier by two minutes.[32] Annette reckoned that good swimmers were 'never excessively thin', but they could be moderately fat, and that Jabez, who was 'pretty fat for athletic work' would hardly fit any other sort of athletic event except swimming, even though he had the huge lungs of a whale.[33]

The Daily Mirror said the record was further proof of Annette's 'extraordinary swimming powers'.[34]

Back in Australia, *The Sydney Daily Telegraph* noted that the swim was 'another feather in the cap for Australian womanhood' and that 'the daughter of Madame Charbonnet-Kellerman has evidently transferred her mother's musical rhythm to her own muscles. When muscular men succeed – or fail – with considerable, effort and exhaustion,' it noted, 'she arises from the waves as fresh as a mermaid, energetic, hungry, absolutely "fit", to use schoolboy slang, and eager for her next exploit.'[35]

Annette's gruelling training continued. Four days after her marathon to Ramsgate, she and Wolfe took off together from Dover at 7.30 a.m. in a choppy sea with great banks of fog rolling in. The fog lifted a little after two hours, and welcome sunshine appeared over the gleaming sails of the stately merchant vessels loaded with people watching this new sporting phenomenon.

But the sea was getting choppier and every inch of progress Annette and Wolffe made was a struggle.

After three and a half hours they had covered 7 miles (11.2 km).

Fred thought the conditions were doing Annette more harm than good. He picked up his tin megaphone and above the howling winds and waves bellowed: 'That's it, Toots. You've done as much as we want. More than we expected you to do. Don't overdo it.'

Annette turned sidestroke to argue with him, but realising that mutiny at sea was a serious crime, hauled herself aboard his little boat and wrapped herself in a blanket.[36]

Ted Heaton,[37] a burly Liverpool swimmer making an attempt on the Channel the same day, had to give up after six hours because of the dangerous fog. He had come close to being run down by a mail steamer.[38]

Back in Australia, Annette's training swim was misreported as a failed attempt on the Channel too, but she had news for her supporters that the real attempt was coming shortly and they wouldn't be disappointed.[39]

Undaunted, she had another long practice swim off Dover the next day, wearing a swimming cap, goggles, and grease all over. A large crowd turned out to watch. Annette was attracting far more interest than all the male entrants planning to swim the

Channel, and *The Daily Mirror* ran a whole page of photographs of her training.

Annette told the newspaper she was 'very optimistic' about her chances of swimming to France. 'The water in the Channel is warm enough for me to swim for many hours without feeling in the least cold,' she said.

'The cross tides in the Channel are often the greatest difficulty a swimmer has to overcome, but I didn't find they troubled me on my Ramsgate swim.

'There are so many risks of bad weather springing up during the swim that it would be foolish to say I was certain of getting through. But I shall do my level best, and I am very hopeful that with favourable conditions and good luck I shall reach the French coast.'[40]

Annette's swim would come amid a growing tide of female empowerment in Britain with Emmeline Pankhurst leading a long and frustrating fight for women to receive the vote. Annette was determined to show the strength and tenacity of Pankhurst's followers who *The Daily Mirror* would soon label the 'suffragettes'.

Chapter 10

THE EXPOSURE ANNETTE was receiving in the pages of *The Daily Mirror* and other newspapers and magazines was opening doors for her in Britain and across the Channel. Swimming clubs everywhere were inviting her to events scheduled to follow the Channel swim.

Five years earlier,[1] the first woman to attempt the Channel, Baroness Isacescu,[2] an Austrian widow who was pushing fifty at the time, ran into bad weather and worse tides after taking off from Calais and had to give up after ten hours, and 20 miles.[3] She had announced plans for another attempt in 1901 and 1903, but these never materialised.

Annette was sure she could make it, and she became adept at convincing the press as well, as she learned the art of selling herself and her dreams.

On 31 July 1905, it seemed that everyone in the port town of Deal – thousands of residents and holidaymakers – turned out to welcome her as she strode onto the beach just before 11 a.m., after a mighty swim through rough seas from Dover. The harsh weather had forced her to take a longer course than her previous swim from there. All morning, the crowds on the beach and pier had strained their eyes southward, watching for the little tossing boat that would proclaim her coming. Soon after 8 a.m., Skipper Cole, a Dover boatman who knew the adverse currents and tides of the Channel as well as any man living, had ordered a start. The *Mirror* reported:

The morning was glorious, with a light breeze rippling the water. Sunday's gale had left its mark in the long, slow-rolling billows, but Miss Kellerman only laughed as the boat rolled and tossed this way and that ... This little Colonial girl has a veritable lion's heart. Nothing daunts her, and her one trouble is that she cannot start off quickly by herself and swim to Calais without anybody knowing.[4]

Carried by the current, Annette covered 12 miles (19.2 km) in 2 hours, 40 minutes. She wrote later of those terrific long-distance swims that she was always moved by her father's insistence that she give her very best, so she always resisted the opportunity to hang on to the side of his rowboat for an occasional rest. She knew her father would have been horrified by any cheating.[5]

The next day, with Fred's bobbing boat beside her flying *The Daily Mirror* banner, Annette swam from Deal to Ramsgate, a distance of about 11 miles (17.6 km). She was not worried about the time, frolicking occasionally like a child during the swim and at times stopping to eat some chicken jelly and nibble at slices of bread.[6] However, when the Australian Mermaid came within a mile of Ramsgate Harbour, she was met with a rushing outgoing tide that halted her progress.

'I'm not moving,' she cried out to her father.

'You're all right,' he yelled back. 'Keep pushing.'

With the sea splashing in her eyes and mouth, slowly, slowly, she forged ahead.

Five minutes, ten minutes passed, and with people gathered on the pier and beach cheering her, she pressed on towards land.

A tremendous, enthusiastic crowd greeted her, so large that six stalwart police constables were needed to escort Annette safely through thousands of men, women and children as they enveloped the young Australian, eagerly holding out their hands to shake hers and pat her on the back. She found pushing through the crowd much more difficult than pushing through the sea.[7]

'Bravo, Miss,' they yelled, 'The Australian mermaid!'

MISS KELLERMAN'S SWIM ROUND THE COAST.

Huge crowds greeted Annette at Ramsgate in Kent after a marathon swim from the port of Deal. She needed a guard of police to get through the mass of fans. *The Daily Mirror*, 3 August 1905 p. 11.

The crowd joined in, giving her three cheers as she blushed and bowed to her admirers, right and left. When Annette emerged from her dressing shed, she looked picture perfect for a social outing in a long cream dress with a straw hat decorated with flowers. Then she went straight back to her lodgings with her father for some quiet time.

'The little Colonial lady is so great a figure at Ramsgate,' *The Daily Mirror* reported, 'that she may not venture out on foot.'[8]

Skipper Cole, a weather-beaten instructor who had plied those waters for years, sighed gratefully after the swim. 'It's wonderful,' he told *The Mirror*. 'There are very few men, let alone mere children, who could have met and crossed that tide.'[9]

Later, Annette wrote of the excitement she felt at 'being greeted at each resort by thousands upon thousands of holidaymakers crowded on the cliffs and beaches'.[10] The officials of the coastal towns were all waiting to welcome her, she said, and the 'pages upon pages of stories and photographs every day in *The Daily Mirror*' was like nothing she had experienced, even during her last few exhilarating months in Australia.

The British swimming clubs that had once ignored Annette and her father now proffered invitations for the coming season,[11] and the French swimming association invited her to compete against the world's best male swimmers in a 12-kilometre race on the River Seine in Paris in September.[12]

ON 2 AUGUST 1905, Annette prepared to swim 12 miles (20 km) from Ramsgate to Margate. It would be the hardest day's work of her life.[13]

All the old fishermen had solemnly shaken their heads and urged the teenager against attempting so tough a task on such a blustery day on a stretch of water where the currents and tides from the North Sea and the Channel merge.[14] They told pressmen that, with the way the currents were running, no swimmer alive could beat the elements on that day.

'Well, I'm going to try,' Annette declared, and no amount of persuasion or argument could change her mind. So at 11 a.m., with thousands of cheering holidaymakers watching, she dived into the sea from the steps of Ramsgate Beach and headed north.

A strong wind was blowing and big choppy waves smashed Annette in the face. Steadily, though, she swam on with her strong trudgen stroke, laughing at the spray, even though she had foregone her goggles and her eyes were red-rimmed and filled with salt.

Skipper Cole told Annette to swim deeper seawards, and the battle was on. She would need all her strength. After an hour or so Fred called out, 'Have some grub,' and with a little shriek of joy

Annette came closer to his boat to drink down some Cadbury's cocoa and eat some bread. She called for more, had her fill, and then went back to work.

Annette was the first person, man or woman, to make the swim,[15] the extremely strong tides running round the North Foreland having scared off all previous attempts.[16] She was, *The Daily Mirror* declared, 'the finest woman swimmer in the world'.[17]

In the space of three days, she had covered 35 miles (56 km) so, despite her protests, Fred ordered her to have a couple of days' rest.[18]

'This Colonial girl of nineteen summers, who is going to attempt the stupendous task of swimming the English Channel for *The Daily Mirror* trophy in a few days' time, does not like remaining out of the water very long,' the paper told its readers. 'The girl's physique is marvellous. She has felt not the slightest effect from the three days' hard work ... Each day she grows more and more fit. Eagerly she is looking forward to the minute when she will wade into the water at Dover for the great attempt.'[19]

Annette was back in the sea off Dover four days later to continue her training. With a strong westerly wind blowing and a heavy sea running, she dived from a boat about 50 metres from the beach and swam straight out to sea in the teeth of a strong incoming tide.[20]

For two hours she swam steadily towards France, using the trudgen in a way that delighted her father and Skipper Cole. After 3 miles (4.8 km) they told Annette she'd done enough for the day.

'I'm not coming in yet,' she replied immediately. Instead, she headed for St Margarets Bay, 4 miles north of Dover, powering on magnificently to arrive there in the best of condition.[21]

The following day, the sea was so angry off Dover that Fred refused to let her swim, despite her entreaties. So Annette spent the day in a careful study of tide-tables and Channel currents, closely examining the records of previous attempts to swim it.[22]

The next day, watched by an admiring crowd in Dover, Annette dived into the water and played for an hour until Fred appeared, ropeable.

Reported by Camera:

LADY CHAMPION'S SWIM FROM RAMSGATE TO MARGATE.

Fred was the driving force behind Annette's success in Britain and despite his ill health accompanied her in a pilot boat whenever she ventured into rivers or seas as on this occasion in her swim from Ramsgate to Margate. *The Daily Mirror*, 5 August 1905, p. 8.

He waved frantically for her to come ashore. 'I told you to rest,' he said sternly, in front of a big crowd. 'You are not to go into the water for three days.'[23]

At the same time, Annette began a series of endorsements for Cadbury's, praising their cocoa and chocolate in the pages of *The Daily Mirror*. She promised to use their products during the Channel swim.[24]

Then, on 9 August, as Annette waited for her chance to tackle the Channel, a burly, bearded Yorkshireman called Bill Burgess,[25] who ran a rubber company in France, made an attempt on the Channel, starting from Dover. He had previously tried to cross at the end of July, but the changing currents had thwarted him when he was just 6 kilometres off Calais. This time, he was overcome by the coldness of the water and forced to drift a great distance off course before giving up near Wissant, a small fishing port 18 kilometres south of Calais.

A week later, on 16 August, Annette made a 10-mile training swim from Dover to Folkestone[26] and shared her training tips with *Mirror* readers:

> Miss Kellerman's method is that of living a simple, natural, life, eating good, plain food, exercising moderately, and taking plenty of sleep ... Rising between six and seven o'clock she takes a dip before breakfast and a swim of a quarter of a mile, or a brisk half-mile walk. For breakfast she eats a couple of eggs and two or three slices of well-cooked bacon with plenty of bread and butter. She drinks coffee or cocoa, but never tea. About eleven she enters the water for a practice swim of three, four, or five hours, according to the conditions of the weather. On alternate days she spends an hour in the morning with a first-class masseuse. She finds massage the best means of keeping the limbs supple, and strongly advocates it.
>
> If she is ashore between one and two o'clock Miss Kellerman takes her midday meal, consisting of roast beef or mutton, with plenty of vegetables, followed by stewed fruit and custard or milk pudding. Between seven and eight o'clock Miss Kellerman takes a light evening meal, with plenty of fruit, vegetables, and milk pudding. There is another short walk afterwards, and at ten o'clock she retires for the night. In the water the swimmer pins her faith on Cadbury's cocoa, beef essence, and chicken jelly, and in some form or other has nourishment every twenty minutes to half an hour.[27]

Annette would need all the nourishment she could get.

THE SEA WAS RAGING OFF Dover as the greatest distance swimmers in the world assembled there for the most famous swim in the world: four burly British swimmers – Jabez Wolffe, Monty Holbein, Billy Burgess and Horace Mew – and one Australian teenager who was receiving more attention in Britain than the rest put together.[28]

Jabez Wolffe had arrived with six stars of the British Amateur Swimming Club to pace him on his Channel attempt, and English and French fishermen as his pilots to guide him on the best course through the waves. Wolffe had also hired musicians from the London Scottish Rifle Volunteers to follow him on his swim and play the bagpipes from a launch as he headed to France.[29] He told the press: 'You have no idea how the sound of the pipes cheers one on a job like this.'[30]

Annette's legion of supporters felt that, given the courage she was showing in taking on the best male swimmers in the world and the raging white-topped waves, she should have the full brass band of the Grenadier Guards playing for her.[31]

For a whole week, it blew a gale around Dover, thwarting Annette's hopes to get in more long swims before taking on the men and the 33 kilometres to Calais.

On Friday, 18 August, the wind continued roaring, pushing great waves, white topped, into Dover Beach. But the finest woman swimmer in the world refused to stay ashore no matter what her father, Skipper Cole or any of Dover's boatmen had to say.[32] She donned her brief dark costume, goggles and red rubber cap and plunged into the boisterous sea. Out she went until all that could be seen of her from the shore was the bright red cap, appearing now and then atop the mountainous waves.

For nearly an hour she taunted the fierce conditions and swam twice across Dover Bay.

Then, finally Fred had seen enough and sent a tossing boat out to bring her in.

Annette emerged from her dressing shed with glowing cheeks and sparkling eyes. 'It was a good swim,' she said enthusiastically, 'but I shall only paddle about now until Wednesday, when I take on the Channel.' She paused for a moment to gather her thoughts, then waved her hand towards the gleaming white Calais, 33 kilometres away. 'You see, I shall want all my energies to reach there.'[33]

'You sometimes have to wait for days before you can get a good time to start,' Annette wrote later of attempts to swim the Channel.

[You need] the right weather and tide. The Channel is most treacherous. The idea is to catch the tide running northerly, avail yourself of this for a certain time, and, though carried northeast, cut in when farther out in the Channel to the return tide, so to speak. You see, your course is not a straight but a zig-zag one. If it were only a matter of swimming the distance from Calais to Dover, the task would not be so difficult, even if the sea were a bit choppy. But having to zig-zag by reason of the tides, the actual swimming distance across the Channel is something more than 40 miles [65 km].[34]

On Sunday, 20 August, a strong south-easterly gale churned up the waters of the Channel, and the four men proposing to swim across it looked despondent. But Annette remained as cheerful and confident as ever. She was trimming down and putting on muscle with all the training and now weighed 72 kilograms.[35] Despite the roughness of the sea, she went out for a two-hour swim in the morning with a man in Dover who was Monty Holbein's pacesetter. Holbein, who was also one of Britain's leading cyclists, had failed in six previous Channel attempts,[36] once so affected by the salt water he couldn't see for four days, and at another time driven back by the relentless tides when he was within a mile of victory.

On the morning of Monday, 21 August, all the Channel hopefuls, with the exception of Jabez Wolffe, went for a dip. Annette was out as usual before breakfast, and looked a picture of health, her skin like satin and her eyes almost glowing, according to *The Daily Mirror*.[37] 'I have never been in better condition,' she told reporters, 'and I shall put forth all my powers of swimming and of endurance in order to get across.'[38]

Annette had a veritable ocean of admirers assembled in Dover, including Tom Reece,[39] a well-known Manchester billiards player and talented swimmer who had ambitions to tackle the Channel someday as well.

The following morning, Tuesday, 22 August, Jabez Wolffe and Horace Mew,[40] a professional photographer and fine oarsman used to rough seas, were due to start their attempt on the Channel at 2.30 a.m. But the cold south-westerly wind was blowing so hard through the darkness that they had to postpone their attempt. Wolffe decided to pack up his pipers and pacesetters and head home.[41]

When day finally broke, Annette walked the Dover beach. The shrieking wind tossed her long hair about her face, but she said that, more than ever, she was ready.[42] She posed for a front-page *Daily Mirror* photograph, looking through a telescope at the enormous waves rolling in,[43] while another full page of the newspaper was devoted to her endorsement of Cadbury's.[44]

Opinions in the press over Annette's chances were divided. *The Westminster Gazette* was dismissive, saying that while 'Miss Kellerman was remarkably powerful for a woman' and had gained plenty of attention with her new bathing costume, 'much advertised', she could 'hardly hope to succeed where so many fine athletes have failed.'[45] But other British papers gave her a great shot, Scotland's *Dundee Evening Telegraph*, for one, pointing out that while the endurance of Burgess was 'marvellous', Annette 'bids fair to rival the strongest men swimmers ... Miss Kellerman seems to regard swimming for an hour or two in the waves of the Channel as equivalent to a morning stroll, and a 12 hours' day in the sea does not wear her out.'[46]

The following night, Annette began her final preparations for the swim that would begin just after dawn on 24 August, the thirtieth anniversary of Captain Webb's 1875 triumph.

Father and daughter went over the course again, leaving nothing to chance. Annette would leave the Admiralty Pier outside Dover and on the first tide swim through the waves to a point 2.4 kilometres (1½ miles) south-west of the South Goodwin Lightship. On the second tide she would endeavour to reach a mark at the closest point in France within Cap Gris-nez (Cape Grey Nose), 26 kilometres south-east of Calais.[47]

Annette and her father prepared supplies – blocks of chocolate, chicken jelly sandwiches cut into bite-size pieces one-inch square, chicken soup and hot cocoa – for the trip of a lifetime.

Chapter 11

AT 2 A.M. ON THURSDAY, 24 August 1905, Annette and Fred rose for the biggest day of their lives and assembled on the beach with their team. Two other swimmers, Billy Burgess and Horace Mew, would also start with Annette but from different points below the White Cliffs of Dover.

Like Annette, Burgess and Mew had studied the coast and the tides and had calculated the route across the water they felt would be the most advantageous for them.[1]

All three swimmers that morning would be followed by rowboats containing their pilots. Each would also have a tugboat containing their supporters and back-up teams. In what she hoped was a portent for the day, Annette would be accompanied by the tug *Champion*, upon which would be her father, her masseuse Mrs Lewis, the debonair Tom Reece, and five young men from the Dover Swimming Club[2] who would act as pacesetters for her. There were also two people she hoped she wouldn't need on the journey: her doctor and a hospital nurse.[3] To the amazement of all the onlookers and the British press, the tug would also carry a gramophone to play some of Annette's favourite tunes. Skipper Cole would be beside her in a rowboat, acting as her pilot through the currents and flying *The Daily Mirror* and Cadbury's banners.

The sun had not yet risen when Mrs Lewis began limbering up Annette's body for the great task ahead. Annette recalled that Channel swimmers always liked to start early, 'in order to get the hardest three or four hours of the work done while they feel most fit. Then, when their strength and courage begin to wane, daylight comes and gives them new hope and vigour. The first two hours of a long-distance swim are very difficult. It takes one that long to settle down to steady work, to get one's pace, to feel confident that one is doing the regulation twenty-eight strokes to the minute.'[4]

Annette changed into her thin two-ounce black silk costume, and in an attempt to shield her from the cold of the water, Mrs Lewis covered her in a paste of porpoise oil[5] and resin. Her goggles and rubber cap were fastened.

A fine morning, with brilliant sunshine and a calm sea, gave her the promise of success.[6]

At 6.30 a.m. she dived off the Admiralty Pier and into history. The water was 60 degrees Fahrenheit (15.5°C) as Annette headed for France with her usual steady, strong trudgen stroke.

'You start out absolutely alone, so as to have everything authentic,' Annette wrote later. 'No one is allowed to give you the slightest assistance. If you so much as touch the boat or rest your fingers on the tip of an oar, you are declared "out".'[7]

For the first hour Annette made splendid progress to the merry strains from the gramophone aboard the tug *Champion*. The flood tide carried her along and in combination with her powerful trudgen stroke she advanced rapidly, leaving the English coastline behind. Now and again, in an occasional break, she sang a snatch of whatever song was playing on the tug.[8] In the early stages, she swam between the *Champion* and her pilot's rowboat, the steam vessel keeping about 90 metres away so that she would not be affected by its wash, and the rowboat about 45 metres away but always ready to come to her immediate aid should she need it.

Every half hour the tug slowed down and Annette would swim alongside.

Her father would pass down a long-snouted cup containing hot soup or chocolate, which she would snatch as he let go. Sometimes Fred would also hand down little chicken jelly sandwiches from the end of a long stick.

Members of the Dover Swimming Club took turns swimming beside her to help her maintain speed, and for a time the billiards whiz Tom Reece joined her in the water, too, the only one of her team who could keep up with her. He had more than swimming on his mind. Reece had been a close supporter of Annette's for some time and was keen to get even closer.

Annette remembered that Reece made himself 'extremely agreeable' and said many gallant things to her as they swam together. 'He interested me so much,' she confessed, 'that I forgot all about my task. The time seemed to fly, and I was making excellent progress. I asked him if he was tired, and he said, "No", that he just felt he could swim alongside me forever."[9]

Suddenly Reece blurted out, 'Annette, I'll propose to you.'

'I remembered that it was the usual thing to faint, but I knew that this wouldn't be a wise proceeding in 50 fathoms of water,' she recalled.[10] So with a laugh and a cheery grin she replied, 'I'll accept you.'

'No, no!' shouted Annette's father from the accompanying tug. Fred wasn't certain if Reece was serious, but he was taking no chances. 'I can't allow that. She's too young to marry,' he said.[11]

Reece dropped off both pacesetting and proposals, and Annette was left to battle on alone.

At about 9 a.m., Annette was off the South Foreland Lightship and was swimming very strongly. But then the ebb tide caught her, and carried her back again towards Dover.[12]

The fine sunny morning and calm sea vanished and the waves became big and cruel. The changed conditions altered Annette's prospects immediately.[13] The westward tide was retarding her progress, but the huge waves were causing her even more distress.

After four hours, Annette realised that hot chocolate may not have been the perfect fuel for ocean swimming and 'the chocolate and the chop of the water' began to make her 'very seasick'.[14] But she kept going, with France and the record books in her sights. *Dad and I are desperately poor*, she told herself. *We must have money.* Over and over she repeated a silent mantra: 'The longer you stick, the more you get!'[15]

Almost five hours into her swim, Annette was passed by Horace Mew, who had left Dover at 7.15 a.m. and seemed unstoppable.

SNAPSHOTS OF THE CHANNEL MERMAID.

Daily Mirror photographers followed Annette closely during her English Channel campaign and these shots from training show how much she revelled in the water and how easily she could take a meal in the middle of a marathon. *The Daily Mirror*, 3 August 1905, p. 9

An hour later, Annette was vomiting, and her distress became too much for Fred. He had his own health issues to burden him and watching Annette struggle so valiantly was almost breaking his weak heart. He called out to her that enough was enough and that they could try another day.

Wracked by seasickness, still Annette ploughed on, ignoring her agitated father's calls to come in.[16]

Not only was she desperately seasick, but her swimming costume had chafed her badly and the flesh under her arms was 'raw and hurt fearfully'.[17]

Fred was adamant that she must give up, so, at 12.35 pm, near the long sandbank called the Varne about halfway across the Channel, Annette was virtually dragged into the boat against her will. She had been in the water for six hours and had swum and drifted for 12 miles.[18]

An hour after Annette was pulled out of the event, Horace Mew hit a dead end when battered by surf and 'an ice-cold current'[19] on the Varne bank. He was also forced to surrender.[20]

Bill Burgess had left Dover's chalk headland known as the South Foreland at 8.35 a.m., 'his propeller-like action sending him through the water at a great pace',[21] but after eight hours of fighting the raging sea his internal motor cut out and he too was conquered by the Channel's mercurial tides.

At 4 p.m. that day, as Fred and Annette were working on ways to improve their chances in their next Channel assault, Monty Holbein entered the cold water near the Kent Coal Works 'full of confidence and in splendid fettle'.[22] At 11.20 that night,[23] after covering 26 kilometres (about 16 miles), he could not overcome the waves and had to retire as well.[24]

ANNETTE WAS SHATTERED by the experience, but that night, to lift her spirits, she went to the theatre with several friends. Tom Reece came along to comfort her, even when she told him she was feeling fine.

'He didn't look half-bad, either,' Annette said later, 'but he wasn't tall enough. Besides, I had too much to think about at the time, and I told him to try again when next I was attempting to swim the Channel.'[25]

The Daily Mirror told readers the next day that Annette had been 'defeated only by sickness, but from a swimming standpoint' she finished 'as strong as she started six hours before'.[26] There was no doubt about the fitness of this extraordinary young woman, it said, nor the power of her 'supple muscles'.[27]

Annette said she earned thirty pounds from her sponsors for the Channel attempt but lost 7 pounds (3.3 kg) in bodyweight from the gruelling experience.[28] Still, she was all smiles and seemed to have recovered well when she was interviewed not long after the attempt.

> Of course, I shall try again. It was a failure, I know, but, honestly it was not a physical failure, was it?
>
> When I was told I must come into the boat, in a sense it was a relief. I was feeling horribly bad – that sort of feeling when you just want to put up your hands and slide right down to the bottom. Seasickness is bad enough, but sickness when you are swimming is ever so much worse ... While the sick part of me was glad to leave the water, the whole part of me was intensely disappointed to come out ... until the sickness came I think, if you will forgive me saying so, I was doing pretty well ... I shall most certainly try again,

and now that I have made the acquaintance of the fickle Channel I shall perhaps do better things. *Au revoir*, old Channel, until next year.[29]

The English Channel wasn't the only great body of water in Europe, and soon Annette, who remained the darling of the sporting world despite the setback, was receiving offers of more challenges.

Chapter 12

TWO WEEKS AFTER COMING up short in her swim to France, Annette prepared to cross the Channel by boat with her father for what Annette remembered all her life as 'the *thrillingest* race I was ever in'.[1]

Bill Burgess and Monty Holbein, who had also come off second best in their battles with the Channel, were on their way to Paris too, finding a steamer much more convenient than their own power.

Father and daughter left London on the morning of Friday, 8 September,[2] so that Annette could take part in the first cross-Paris swimming race, a 12-kilometre battle on the Seine two days later. The race was being sponsored by Paris sporting magazine *L'Auto*, which, in the hopes of boosting circulation, had just started a bicycle race called the Tour de France.

The swim had attracted some of the best male distance swimmers in Europe, plus one bright-eyed, ever-smiling female hopeful.

Annette had spoken French since she was a toddler, and as soon as she arrived in Paris, she was fêted by the Parisians. One of the popular themes in newspapers at the time was a comparison between her brief bathing suit and the far more elaborate swimming costumes of the chic Frenchwomen of the time.[3] The subject of her bathing suit featured in many French stage skits and cartoons, and one of the leading fashion houses placed a model of her short boy's swimming outfit that she wore for racing in the window of his salon with a sign underneath that said, 'Will women ever wear this bathing suit?'[4]

Annette's enormous public profile, driven by the British and Australian newspapers, had created interest across the Atlantic as well, and Annette left London to the news that the brash New York teenage open-water star Elaine Golding[5] had challenged her to race over any distance, any time.[6]

For now, Annette's immediate concern was the 12-kilometre stretch of the Seine from the Pont National in the east of Paris to the Viaduct at Auteuil in the west.[7] Each of the twenty-four bridges along the course would be packed with crowds of sightseers, but the water was no more inviting than the Thames. It was cold and contained an infinite variety of dubious materials that Annette didn't like to think about.[8]

Eight hundred swimmers[9] from across Europe had applied to enter the event, but only a small field was selected. To their utter astonishment, two Manchester swimmers – Annette's flirtatious friend Tom Reece, and Channel aspirant 'Professor' William Stearne – had their entries cancelled. They had previously been given permission to swim and had been training for some weeks. But when they were packing their luggage and changing their English pounds into French francs, they had been informed that, for safety reasons, the Chief of Police in Paris would only allow eight swimmers to compete, and consequently they were beached.[10]

The eight starters would be led by three Frenchmen, including 44-year-old hat maker Emile Paulus.[11] Their rivals would be Annette and four distance experts who were the pride of British swimming: Bill Burgess, Monty Holbein, rising young star David 'Boy' Billington,[12] the relentless veteran Joey Nuttall.[13]

Thousands lined the banks of the Seine and the bridges to see the event, largely drawn by the fame of Annette and the Channel contestants. The spectators formed a continuous line along the entire course, while many followed the competitors on foot and in carriages.[14]

The English swimmers were heavily favoured by experts in

Paris, though reporters noted that 'in the spirit of gallantry which distinguishes the French, some had plumped for the lady'.[15]

Each swimmer would be accompanied by a rowboat. Annette's contained her father, a family friend and two oarsmen.

The event was staged as a pursuit race, with Annette the first starter into the dirty water at 8 a.m.[16] The baby-faced Billington took off 45 minutes later, whirling like the wind through the grey murk with a mix of freestyle and trudgen.[17] He overtook Annette after about 6 kilometres, but the water was very cold, and all the swimmers were suffering in the conditions.[18]

Annette recalled that for 12 kilometres the river was thronged with thousands of excited French folk, and the fact that a young Australian girl of French ancestry was competing made the race 'a highly spectacular event'.[19] As Annette swam under each of the twenty-four bridges, the French people threw flowers to her, shouting the encouraging words 'Allez, Miss, allez, Miss!'

The spectators became even more excited as, one by one, the men started to drop out of the race. David Billington, impressing with his youth and immense speed, had been leading for most of the event. But 3 kilometres from the finish, when he was almost opposite the Eiffel Tower, he hit a patch of particularly rough water. The wind had been in the teeth of the competitors most of the way, but now it rose in strong gusts. Passing steamers, who pressed the swimmers much too closely, were also creating waves. Billington's whirring arms slowed to a stop. Overcome with cramps, he had to abandon all hope of finishing. As he climbed into his support boat, the crowd gave him an enormous round of applause.[20]

French officials in motorboats would announce with megaphones when an entrant was overcome with fatigue and retired. One of the swimmers, a French army sergeant, was pulled out of the water – and arrested because he did not have permission from his commanding officer to compete.[21] Eventually, there were just four left in the race. Annette was holding her position at third, and despite her interest in vegetarianism she ate two chickens while in the water.[22]

'As I pushed my way through the dirty water of the Seine, the people would cry to me, "Come on, Mademoiselle, you've only one more kilometre, two more bridges, that's all,"' she recalled.

This was one of those kindly prevarications intended to cheer me up. But they shouldn't have done it, for I would make a dash or sprint trying to wind up with a flourish and would get out of my stroke and use up most of my reserve strength. Because the river was full of curves and I couldn't see ahead, they fooled me for a little while. At last, when I thought I'd reached the last bridge and they called out, 'Only two kilometres more!' I was so disappointed that I began to cry.[23]

Annette, who was stronger and fitter than ever after her eight weeks training under *The Daily Mirror* sponsorship, had felt the strain of the race like some of the men. But the surges she mounted towards the finish left her almost spent. She would never forget the crestfallen expression on her father's face when he saw her weeping, and she feared another angina attack.[24]

Annette was to receive forty pounds from *L'Auto* if she finished the race and, as usual, she and Fred needed the money.[25] The sixty-four guineas from *The Daily Mirror* was just about gone.

'Things looked pretty black,' Annette recalled, but then she heard the cheery Yorkshire accent of burly Bill Burgess, who emerged from the water with his head covered in white grease. His thick motorcycle goggles made him look like a giant fly. He had started half an hour after Annette in the race, but had now drawn level.

'Well, now, little girl, what's da matter?' Burgess asked.[26]

'They told me this was the finishing bridge,' Annette spluttered. 'I don't know how I can finish it now. I went all out on the last kilometre.'

Burgess threw a brawny arm around Annette's brown shoulders as they bobbed together in the Seine.

'Come on now, lass,' Burgess said, 'come on, we will finish the last two kilometres together.'[27]

While Annette became a global fashion icon, her friend and fellow Channel swimmer Bill Burgess did not. *Library of Congress, Bain News Service, LC-B2-2294-8 [P&P]*

Burgess paced Annette for the last leg of the race, giving up his chance to win. Together they glided towards the finish line, and with about 100 metres to go Burgess said, 'Let's race for it.' They both passed the finish line 'neck and neck'.[28] To the surprise of even the French experts, they had not been able to catch the veteran hometown hero and race winner, Emile Paulus. Monty Holbein crossed the line fourth.[29]

Annette and the other finishers were greeted with the sound of celebratory cannon fire and cheers from an immense crowd that lined the Seine's banks on both sides for a great distance.

Since Annette had started thirty minutes before Burgess on a staggered start system, he was awarded second place.[30]

The Paris correspondent for London's *Pall Mall Gazette* reported that Annette had 'captivated the susceptible heart of the Parisian by her grace and youthfulness and admitted good looks ... The day was a great triumph for French sport and also, since we are in France, for *Féminisme*.'[31]

Annette guessed there had been half a million people watching the event.[32] When she left the water, she was surrounded by well-wishers who made it hard for her to reach her dressing shed. Once dressed, she and Fred tried to get into a four-wheel fiacre cab to return to their hotel. But to their amazement, some of the spectators unhitched the horses from the cab and a group of young men volunteered to tow Annette and her father through a streets of Paris to their hotel as a tribute.[33]

At the hotel, Annette found telegrams from her mother's esteemed musical friends Nellie Melba and Cécile Chaminade.

L'Auto pulled out all stops to thank Annette for what she had done to promote swimming in France. They placed a motor car and driver at her disposal so she and Fred could see the sights. She told reporters that she was simply delighted with Paris, her mother's former home, and the people from the city of light. She posed for hundreds of photographs and was invited to give an exhibition of swimming and diving at the Piscine Deligny floating baths, which were moored right in front of the National Assembly.

L'Auto also presented Annette and Fred with their own box at the Théâtre Marigny near the Champs-Élysées.[34] Before long, a French toy manufacturer produced a mechanical miniature of Annette, complete with brief costume and bathing cap. When immersed in water, the toy arms and legs moved just like hers.[35]

Though Annette was still chaperoned everywhere by her father, and had only been in the country for a few days, she had become a sex symbol and one of the most talked about women in France. Three men proposed to her.[36] And there were many other invitations that were even more tempting.

Chapter 13

ON THEIR RETURN TO ENGLAND, Annette and Fred were met with a variety of invitations for her to appear at galas and events staged by many of Britain's leading swimming clubs. They also received a telegram from Arthur Collins of the Drury Lane Theatre, who was most famous for his magnificent Christmas pantomimes. He asked Annette to contact him as soon as possible about performing there.

But Fred's health had taken a critical turn. He was not able to accompany Annette to all of her various swimming galas, waiting anxiously instead at their Russell Square hotel. And with good reason.

In the days after her return from Paris Annette had kept busy giving diving exhibitions. Unfortunately, health and safety standards of 1905 were not best practice, and diving could be a deadly business. Springboards in English swimming pools were inconsistent. No two boards were alike and in some places any old board would be installed just for the occasion of Annette's appearance.[1]

Such was the case when Annette appeared at the spacious baths of the Hornsey Swimming Club in North London on 26 September 1905, two weeks after her Paris swim. It was one of the few events Fred could attend.

There was a big card of events and a large crowd, among them the New Zealand All Blacks rugby union team, who were trampling all before them on a tour of Great Britain in the lead-up to their first ever test match against England, at Crystal Palace in London.

Five of the New Zealanders also beat a team of local swimmers that night in a swimming race,[2] but the feature event saw Australian Barney Kieran win the 220 yards championship of England. Then there was a fine display from members of the Amateur Diving Association,[3] before the most famous female swimmer in the world came out in her brief, figure-hugging costume to make her great leaps of faith.

Annette had her suspicions about the quality of the springboard at Hornsey — it seemed too stiff — but she went ahead nervously with her routine. On only her second dive — a one and a half somersault — the board did not flex enough; instead of touching the bottom of the pool with the palms of her hands, Annette was out with her calculations and crashed into it with her forehead.[4]

She came to the surface with blood streaming down her face. As pool attendants dived in and hauled her out, Fred was frantic.[5]

A doctor stitched the wound in Annette's dressing room. Reporters who visited her hotel the next day said that she was recovering well, though the muscles in the back of her neck were also damaged.

In order to prevent a recurrence of the accident, Annette had her own portable diving board made so she and Fred could take it to all her exhibitions.[6]

The newspaper accounts of Annette's accident reached Alice in Mentone before Annette could send word, and it heightened Alice's desire to reunite her family. In the meantime, Alice could be well pleased with the progress of her children in Melbourne. Maurice, now twenty, and his mother would soon organise the music for the Archbishop of Melbourne's visit to Mentone to lay the foundation stone for the new St Patrick's Church.[7] Maurice was making his way as a violinist and conductor in Melbourne, and also making sweet music on the cricket field, as a star batsman and bowler for St Kilda.[8] However, he told club officials that he wasn't a long-term proposition for them. He was heading to London soon to see Annette and his father. He didn't know how long Fred would last.

ANNETTE HAD TO GET BACK to work, head wound or no head wound. Despite her fame, her standard fee for a swimming and diving exhibition was just three to five guineas, and with the cost of living in London that didn't go far.

She simply could not afford to lose any of the bookings she'd made, but she would later regret that the swimming pools in those days 'were not as hygienic' as they could be.[9]

Just a week after her diving accident, she performed at the Westminster Baths and the Kingston Baths.[10] She had covered her wound with a big sticking plaster and eschewed diving for a display of the trudgen instead, something she repeated a week later at the Wimbledon YMCA pool.[11] Her wound eventually became infected, though, and after it was drained by a doctor she was told she would have a scar on her forehead for the rest of her life.

'Oh well,' Annette said, 'then I'll just wear my hair down the front, that's all.'[12]

She took to wearing a hat or scarf around her head whenever she was photographed.

After giving herself time to heal, Annette and Fred were back in action, booking a tour of England's north and Scotland,[13] and by November 1905, Arthur Collins had booked her, with a lucrative offer, for the London Hippodrome as 'The Champion Lady Swimmer of the World' giving 'An Entertainment of Unexampled Brilliance Twice Daily at 2 p.m. and 8 p.m.'[14] The variety show also featured a German animal trainer with performing lions, tigers and bears, while Annette shared her water tank with an act involving Chinese cormorants catching fish.[15]

Annette had just started at the Hippodrome when Queen Alexandra, the wife of King Edward VII, and her brother, the king of Greece, came to see the show, along with other royals.[16]

They were thrilled with Annette's performance and asked to meet her later. 'Shaking at the knees and trembling with excitement',[17] Annette was ushered in to meet Her Majesty. To Annette's surprise, the Queen was sitting in an armchair calmly nursing Babs,[18] a baby tiger that was part of that night's animal performance.

Annette was now making fifty pounds a week performing at the Hippodrome,[19] and the money – more than ten times the average wage – was just too good to pass up for another immediate challenge at the English Channel, though Annette assured the press that she planned to try again late in 1906.[20]

There were other challenges too. Not only were the best of the Americans throwing down the gauntlet to Annette but, in Melbourne, Beatrice Kerr,[21] a Williamstown teenager who had learnt to swim at the Albert Park Lake and who had won medals at both the Victorian and Australasian championships in 1905, was embarking on a tour of Australia with a view to racing Annette in England.[22] Beatrice had become the biggest name in Australian swimming after the sudden tragic death of Barney Kieren following an attack of appendicitis.

But Annette had more lucrative offers than a race with the latest teen prodigy. She wrote home to her mother early in 1906 to say that she was well booked for a whole year, with a twelve-week contract at fifty pounds a week at the Alhambra in Paris, followed by a season at the Lyceum in London, as many shows as she wanted at the Hippodrome and offers to appear in Vienna and New York.[23] Not only did she now have her own springboard, but she was having her own water tank made in Deptford for shows on the Continent.[24]

Annette gave a long interview on swimming for a new journal based in New York called *The American Magazine*, in which she declared: 'Too much cannot be written in favour of swimming as an exercise. What other form of exercise can you describe to me that gives more general beneficial results? Practice in swimming secures a uniform development of the entire body, it brings every muscle into play, and gives strength to heart and lungs … No medicine physicians can prescribe equals that in toning up the nerves and invigorating the whole system.'[25]

Annette embarked on a walking tour of the Swiss and Italian Alps with Maurice, newly arrived from Melbourne, and she accepted a challenge from Channel swimmer Baroness Isacescu for a long-distance race on the Danube.[26]

She sent a telegram to supporters in London: 'Having fine training, boating, climbing, walking, getting awfully fit.'[27] To friends she wrote: 'Since coming here, I have met the Newcastle United football players. My brother and I accompanied them on several of their walks.'[28]

Then she travelled to Vienna to finalise arrangements for the race with the local aristocrat.

BARONESS ISACESCU WAS a remarkable athlete. The widow of a Romanian nobleman, in 1900 she had swum 32 kilometres in the English Channel when bad weather and salt-water damage to her eyes forced her to give up hopes of matching Captain Webb's feat.[29]

But she was not defeated. 'It is the age for women,' the Baroness declared. 'We have conquered the prejudices, which so long kept us in the background, and we are resolved to show that in feats of endurance, as well as in brain efforts, we are equals of man.'[30]

Even though the Baroness was an aristocrat, her husband's death meant she had to support herself: and she worked as an administrator at a railway station in Vienna.[31] On 3 June 1906, she swam 36 kilometres in the Danube between Tulln and the military swimming school in Vienna.[32] Eight days later, she and Annette lined up to battle it out on the same course.

It was the coldest water Annette had ever experienced, colder even than the Channel, though she was warmed by the fact that not many people, especially women swimmers, had ever swum so far in the beautiful blue river.[33] The Baroness chose not to swim head to head with Annette but instead dived into the water a few minutes after Annette set off.

'The Danube is very treacherous,' Annette recalled. 'Its waters are icy cold and it runs so fast that there are dangerous eddies everywhere. Half the game in swimming that course is knowing your ground.

'Well, we started, swimming far apart. I had not gone far before I found myself sucked into a shallow whirlpool. The water was only about six inches deep and was whirling with great force and speed over a bed of sharp pebbles. Before I could work my way out, my legs were one mass of cuts and bruises.'

Annette was never sure when the rushing currents would meet shallows with rocks.[34] But even though the Baroness knew those waters like the back of her wet hand, she couldn't catch the Australian Mermaid.

'I won the race easily,' Annette recalled, 'by about three-quarters of an hour.'[35]

Fred sent a telegram to the British papers to say Annette had set another record, swimming the course in 3 hours, 11 minutes. 'She was in serious danger at one point through the rapids but finished in great form,' he said.[36]

Annette was paid eighty pounds a week[37] for a two-week series of exhibitions in Vienna, and during her time there saw one of the early productions of *The Merry Widow* in the theatre where it had debuted, with its composer Franz Lehar conducting the orchestra.[38]

ANNETTE AND HER FATHER travelled back to Dover and set up camp with Maurice in a small seaside cottage at nearby Broadstairs[39] to continue training for another Channel attempt. Annette also accepted an invitation to race in the 1906 cross-Paris swim against many of her rivals from the previous year.

In preparation for both events she organised a training swim to the North Goodwin Lightship, a vessel with a booming foghorn that was moored as a warning marker at a sandbank about 13 kilometres into the North Sea.

No one had ever swum to it before.[40] Soon after daybreak on 9 July, Annette set off at a pace that London's chief sporting newspaper described as 'truly astonishing',[41] even though the fog over the waves was so thick she could not see the end of the Broadstairs jetty from the start, and the cliffside Bleak House, made famous by Charles Dickens, was totally blotted from view.

For a time, Fred and Maurice were lost in the fog. Maurice had to row for hours without seeing land, fearful that they might collide with ocean steamers or other craft. Amid the danger and dreary outlook, Annette kept churning through the waves at great speed, guided not by sight but by the booming foghorn in the distance. Occasionally she stopped to eat what she called 'her tucker': some custard handed down to her by Fred.

After covering 8½ miles in 3 hours, 34 minutes and 52½ seconds, she had achieved her goal and climbed aboard the boat, showing little sign of fatigue.[42]

The next week she was in Paris for the 1906 race on the Seine, this time with a greatly expanded entry list of professionals. As well as Annette there had been English, French, Italian, Swiss, Dutch, German, Austrian and Belgian nominations.[43] Baroness Isacescu would be one of the eighteen amateurs to contest a separate race a month later, though she finished at the back of the field.

Annette broke every mould as a sportswoman, and though she never admitted to being deliberately provocative, she could not have failed to realise that she had become a great favourite of the French, not just for her swimming but because of her daring costumes and the form they revealed. With the innocent smile of youth, she could still shock the very foundations of social convention.

At 8 a.m. on 14 July, crowds lined the quays and bridges and shoreline on the Seine for the start of the race.[44]

There were sixteen professional starters, including Annette. They were sent off together in groups of three or four at intervals of 15 to 30 minutes. Annette was still chewing on a chicken wing for breakfast[45] when, with a roar from the great crowd, she took off at 8 a.m. with England's 21-year-old Dora Herxheimer,[46] an art student described in the press as 'a lithe, dark-haired splendidly built little woman' and Rosa Frauendorfer,[47] the muscular Austrian entrant who, like Annette, was just twenty. Annette and Dora wore their long hair loose, but Rosa wore a red bathing cap and a tight-fitting blue costume, similar to Annette's black one-piece.

Rosa had her own unique style of swimming, with a remarkable stroke in which she combined 'the breast, the side, and the over-arm strokes'. Sometimes she would dive under the water and resurface many metres ahead, to raucous cheers when the crowds caught sight of her red cap emerging from the deep.[48]

The battle between the three women was close for a while. Annette took another piece of chicken from her father in the support boat, hoping it would give her wings.

Despite her endurance, though, Annette could not match the speed of the fastest men. The race was eventually won by local hero Albert Bougoin[49] in 3 hours, 6 minutes and 2 seconds, 64 seconds ahead of David Billington, with fellow Englishman Sam Greasley[50] third. The 1905 winner, Emile Paulus, was fourth and big Bill Burgess fifth.

But Billington was furious, punching the river, declaring that the timers had pulled a rort and that the whole thing was 'a put-up job'.[51] He said the winning Frenchman had been towed part of the way by his support boat using an underwater rope.[52]

The sour note left by the men's finish could not overshadow Annette's thrilling battle with Rosa Frauendorfer after their English rival dropped out. Annette and Rosa swam abreast for all 12 kilometres from start to finish, and only centimetres divided them the whole way.

In the end, Annette finished seventh, covering the course in 3 hours, 59 minutes and 30 seconds and beating eighth-placed Rosa by just 1.2 seconds.[53]

Annette once again showed that she had no regard for the staid social conventions of the time. At the finish line the young women embraced in the water, sending the crowd wild as 'they kissed each other fervently'.[54]

Annette was hailed as a thoroughly 'modern mermaid' who was doing so much to advance the cause of women in a society where they were still expected to know their place in a man's world. 'It is the day of feminine achievement,' one Australian newspaper remarked, 'and there is already a proposition in the air to found an academy for young women, where they shall be taught the sports.'[55]

Annette (right) and Rosa Frauendorfer after their neck-and-neck battle along the Seine in 1906. *The Graphic* (London). 21 July 1906, p. 11

ANNETTE WAS NOW EARNING 350 pounds a month from swimming and diving exhibitions, charging as much as seventy pounds for a single appearance.[56]

But she wanted to make history on the Channel, so she travelled back to Broadstairs to continue training. The only thing that could beat her, she said, was seasickness.

It was a continuing theme in interviews, and reporters wondered if the distress she felt swallowing all that salt water on her first attempt in 1905 was now playing on her mind.[57] Annette's pilot devised a new course that he said would give her more favourable tides, and Annette estimated the course to be about 34 miles, which she calculated she could swim in 15 hours.[58]

Owing to diabolical weather, Annette postponed her start from Broadstairs' chalky North Foreland at midnight on Sunday, 5 August 1906, but the weather was more promising the following day.

Annette wanted to start that afternoon, but her father, knowing that the fear of seasickness was 'the weak spot in his daughter's armour' suggested they wait a few more hours until the wind had died away completely.[59]

Fred took her to the Captain Digby Hotel to rest while he kept an eye on the weather. By 1.30 a.m., conditions seemed ideal. There was hardly a breath of wind, the flags at Broadstairs were limp against their poles, and the sea could not have been smoother had it been 'flat ironed'.[60] Cooees rang out from the shore to let the support boat know that Annette was ready.

By lamplight, she donned a blue and white costume and her team smeared her all over with lanoline against the cold. She put on a waterproof wash-leather bathing cap and a celluloid face mask, fastened with elastic.

Accompanied by cheers and more cooees, Annette entered the water at 2.17 a.m. on 7 August. The early morning was beautifully moonlit and hundreds of visitors from Ramsgate and Margate assembled to witness the start. The steamer *Java*, followed her, with Fred and Maurice in a rowboat.[61]

The conditions seemed perfect, but Annette was already seasick before she had been in the water 15 minutes, and soon she had vomited six times. The awful retching that she suffered compelled her to stop swimming and float for a while until she felt better. But she was swallowing large amounts of brine and twice asked for hot water to cleanse her mouth.

After just 45 minutes, Fred asked Annette to get in the boat and try another day, but she replied: 'If I don't do it now, Dad, I never shall'.[62]

She pressed on, but the ordeal was painful even for the spectators, as she was racked with spasms. Considering how sick she was, Annette still made remarkable progress swimming in water illuminated eerily by the beam from the North Foreland Lighthouse.

The Sportsman newspaper reported: 'It was impossible not to admire the pluck with which the Australian girl tried to come round.'[63] After the violent attacks of nausea 'she would for a time lay on the water but then swing over again, and in her characteristic method, forge ahead. But the pluck was to no avail, for she was invariably taken bad again.'[64]

Fred continued to implore Annette to climb onto the tug.

Finally, after 2 hours, 2 minutes in the water, she was convinced to retire. Annette clambered over the side of the *Java*, pale and distressed. Her temperature had gone down fast and her teeth were chattering. She was taken to the stern and wrapped in Turkish towels and dressing gowns. After a little hot soup, which she tolerated far more than the entree of salt water she'd been ingesting all morning, she quickly came round.

Onlookers wondered why Annette had become so seasick so quickly. She had made several long training swims under much worse conditions and performed splendidly, *The Sportsman* explained why in perfectly calm water she was taken ill almost as soon as she dived in.

One expert suggested that Annette was a 'fatalist' and that since she had suffered so much in her 1905 attempt her mind had convinced her that it would happen again.[65]

Annette revealed to her supporters the nature of the ordeal that was a Channel attempt.

> Imagine yourself swimming hour after hour, apparently making no progress. Indeed, sometimes even seeming to be going back rather than forward, while try as you will to prevent it, gallons of salt water seem somehow or other to find their way down your throat. Every swimmer has a boatful of friends ready to hold out a helping hand if the need for assistance arises; but, at the same time, it is very often impossible to see the boat when the relentless waves continually submerge you. Just think for a moment how your arms and legs would ache after travelling for only a short distance when you have to contest every inch with the seething waves. It is far from an enviable task to have to eat and drink while in the water, for as soon as one opens one's mouth the sea is a splendid marksman.[66]

There was some brightness in the failed bid, with a whole new audience having the chance to see Annette perform. She and Fred had negotiated a deal with Charles Urban,[67] a leading figure in Britain's fledgling film industry. A camera team recorded Annette in training at Broadstairs and at other venues,[68] and soon big audiences at the Alhambra Theatre in London's Leicester Square were watching the spectacular dives and powerful strokes of 'the first Australian sportswoman to visit England and Europe with the genuine intention of tackling men and women's records in her sport'.[69]

Before long the short documentary *Miss Annette Kellerman* was being shown around the world, with copies sold for five pounds.[70]

Annette was still only twenty, and reckoned she had all the time in the world to swim the Channel. At the end of August 1906, she swam from Broadstairs to Margate, a distance of more than 10 kilometres.[71] It was good preparation for her, as on 12 September at the Devonshire Park Baths at Eastbourne she broke the world record for the mile in a pool, setting a time of 33 minutes, 21¾ seconds,[72] a minute faster than the record she set in Sydney five years earlier. Beatrice Kerr had just arrived in England for a series of exhibitions and was throwing out constant challenges to Annette,[73] but she would have to cool her heels in the cold British water.

At the end of 1906, Annette was raking in cash touring Scotland with a circus and working on ways she could monetise her fame in America, the entertainment capital of the world.[74]

She went back to performing at the Hippodrome in London in a Christmas spectacular called *A Treasure Ship in Fairy Seas*, with the theatre building a huge round aquarium tank that would hold 15,000 litres. Annette wore a fitted mermaid costume made of actual fish skin.[75] The show featured divers searching the wreck of a treasure ship and the Australian Mermaid fighting off sea monsters who attack them.[76]

It was while performing at the Hippodrome that Annette received an offer that would take her in a completely different direction. It would be a magical journey that would change her life forever.

After arriving in London, as an 18-year-old in 1905 Annette learned that she could not swim before royalty as scheduled with bare legs showing. So she sewed a long pair of stockings onto the racing trunks she favoured giving rise to the famous Annette Kellerman one-piece swim suit that revolutionised fashion.

Chapter 14

FRED KELLERMAN'S health continued to worsen as Annette's prospects became more robust by the day. Fred suspected that he would not have long to share in the extraordinary life that Annette was carving for herself, but he planned to enjoy as much of the ride as he could.

Annette was appearing at the Hippodrome as the Australian Mermaid in her fish-skin suit when she received a telegram from the United States.

It said simply: 'Will you appear at the White City Park, Chicago?'

Would she ever!

The amusement park, which was less than two years old, was the biggest in America.[1] It occupied six hectares on Chicago's South Side and, while modelled on New York's Coney Island, it was twice as large.

Annette was thrilled at the idea of cracking the entertainment industry in America. Then reality hit her like a salty wave from the Channel. She was unsure how she would break this news to her ailing father, whose angina had worsened. Even though Maurice was in England to help, would Fred even be able to stand the excitement of such a trip and all the stresses that came with moving to a whole new world?

Fred soon reassured her. 'Why of course we must go. It's the land of great opportunity.'[2] Fred's unmarried sister, Josephine Kellerman, was living in Colorado and was sure to visit, so they would not be completely alone. Annette agreed to a five-month contract that would involve multiple performances of her diving routine each day.

Fred brought two second-class tickets on the White Star liner *Celtic*. There was considerable publicity leading up to the arrival in America of 'the world's most famous woman swimmer and diver',[3] and much was made of the fact that her mother and some of her grandparents were American-born.

The *Celtic* docked in New York on 30 April 1907 after a delay of thirty-six hours due to thick fog in the harbour. *The New York Times* greeted Annette's arrival by reporting that she found the long delay reaching the dock 'tedious':

> About the time that the stern anchor chain of the ship was being loosened ... she had found out about how far it was to the nearest land, which somebody told her was eighteen miles. She promptly went to the Captain and asked if she might be permitted to swim in. She said that she would venture the trick if the Captain would send a boat with her. The request was refused, and with pouting lips the good-looking swimmer spoke of her chagrin when she had reached the pier. 'Why, I almost swam the English Channel once,' she said, 'and you know what that is.'[4]

Annette was gobsmacked by the New York skyline. When she first gazed at the skyscrapers and the overhead trams she gasped with amazement. There were more motor cars than horse carriages.[5]

All the time in England she had been fascinated by the popular sketches of Charles Dana Gibson, who depicted romanticised views of American life including the pen and ink drawings known as the 'Gibson Girl', the epitome of fashion and decorum. But Annette's ideas that America was built on these 'glamorous foundations' were soon brought back to reality on a walk through the teeming city and across the Brooklyn Bridge.

Annette and American Olympic swimming gold medallist Charlie Daniels.
Library of Congress, Bain News Service, LC-B22- 315-11 [P&P]

'I was expecting to find it a riot of colour and animation with nothing but lovely Gibson Girls parading back and forth across the bridge ... a mixture of the Champs-Élysées and the Pont Neuf on the Seine in Paris. The realisation was a severe setback and heartbreak for me.'[6]

Still, she had only been in the United States for a day when she began laying the foundation for a career as a health and fitness influencer. She posed for photos with America's star swimmer of the time, Charlie Daniels,[7] who had won three gold medals at the 1904 St Louis Olympics and would win another in London the following year.

She told the press that swimming was as necessary as walking, if not more so, and that it should be compulsory for every child to learn, not only for recreation and health, but also to save lives when necessary. Annette said that, for girls, being a good swimmer or athlete was the sure way to beauty and health.

She gave the young women of America some key rules:

Don't overeat, and eat good, wholesome food regularly.

Don't be lazy, and take plenty of good, easy exercise without tiring yourself out.

Go to bed early and regularly and rise early. If you live in the country walk a mile or two before breakfast. If you live in the city walk around the block a few times before sitting down to your meals.

And ...

Be as cheerful as you can. Forget all about your troubles, real or imaginary, and laugh as much as you can. Laughter will take all the bad microbes out of your system and put in their places only the health giving, strength providing germs.[8]

When Annette and Fred arrived in Chicago by train a few days later, she found her image everywhere – photographs, cartoons and artwork that had her posing, swimming, diving and looking innocent and sexy at the same time in her figure-hugging costumes. The press was fascinated by the story of Tom Reece proposing to her during her first attempt at the Channel, and they were transfixed by the shape of this Australian Mermaid, with a syndicated report declaring: 'She is of practically perfect physique, with tapering wrists and ankles, olive complexion and grey eyes which light up a handsome face.'[9]

She wrote syndicated newspaper columns to set the record straight about her life, and to promote the benefits of making a splash in the pool or ocean, telling readers that she believed America would eventually become a nation of great female swimmers.[10]

> Any woman who can walk can learn to swim. She may never become a great swimmer and probably will not if she is out of her twenties, but she can learn to swim sufficiently well to share in the mental and physical delights of the pastime, to say nothing of the healthful features of it ... The best costume is the cheap, ordinary stockinette suit which clings close to the figure, and the closer the better. It should be sleeveless, and there should be no skirts. Skirts carry water and retard the swimmer. They are very pretty and appropriate for the seaside, but not for the swimming pool. Stockings may be worn if they fit tightly, but under no circumstances should shoes be used.[11]

WHITE CITY WAS A FASCINATING workplace, a weird and wonderful kaleidoscope of the thrilling and bizarre. The attractions were staged very much like sideshow alley at an Australian fair, and Fred and Annette took a small enclosure with a high front but no roof on White City's principal thoroughfare.

Some of the press called Annette 'the cooee girl' because of the shout she made before her spectacular high-dives,[12] and her shows were sandwiched between a snake charming act and a display of the Igorot, tribespeople from a remote region in the far north of the Philippines who had been brought to America and paraded at fairs like circus animals.[13]

White City built 'a water palace' for Annette, a specially constructed water tank 14 feet long and 5½ feet deep (4.3 m by 1.7 m), surrounded by seats. Electric lights illuminated the water to startling effect,[14] and posters outside the venue advertised the 'Australian Mermaid'.

Annette was seen as a real curiosity. Swimming was still something of a novelty in America in the early years of the twentieth century. Many people did not know how to swim, and women were often discouraged from taking to the water.

Only three years before Annette's arrival in Chicago,[15] 1021 passengers died trying to save themselves from the burning steamboat *General Slocum* in New York's East River. A large number of the victims died simply because they could not swim. But after her huge publicity build-up, Annette's opening day at the amusement park was not auspicious. May 1907 was the coldest May on record in Chicago. Many reporters came to see Annette's American debut, but when they arrived, they were startled to see snow falling so close to summer.

After what Annette called 'Mother Nature's dirty trick' most of the reporters expected her to postpone the press event, but she told them that the show must go on, and as they huddled together in overcoats with their collars turned up, Annette leapt into the freezing water of the tank. She gave them the very best of her routine and thought they would all go back to their offices and describe the skill, poise and athleticism of the Australian Mermaid. But most of the articles were about her brief costume and her ample figure.

Fred tut-tutted. 'Funny people, these Americans,' he said.[16]

Though she complained about the sexist nature of the reports, Annette knew the sensationalist publicity could only help her career in show business, and she settled down to a lucrative season at White City. Fred charged an admission of ten cents and Annette gave an average of fifty-five short performances a week – five or six on weekdays and anything from twelve to eighteen on Saturdays and Sundays. At each show she performed sixteen dives, backward, forward and sideward, off her elbows and off her head.[17]

Annette wrote home to Alice to say she was making good money steadily, and that the huge sign in front of her theatre proclaiming 'ANNETTE KELLERMAN – The Australian Mermaid' could be seen from just about anywhere in White

City. She would have been happier than at any time in her life except for the fact that her father, just forty-seven, was starting to fade away. Fred spent much of his time in Chicago confined to a wheelchair.

BACK HOME IN AUSTRALIA, Annette's mother was the guest of honour at a soirée for the French residents of Melbourne held in the Independent Hall, Collins Street.[18] Curtains in the French *tricolores* were draped on a stage decorated with palms that reminded Alice of her languid childhood in the South Pacific. Then it was announced that this was, in fact, a farewell concert for Madame Charbonnet-Kellerman.

For thirty years she had adorned Australian music. Now, as she approached her fiftieth birthday, Alice was proud that her daughter was the most famous swimmer in the world. Alice was taking her two youngest children, Mipps and Freddie, to Paris, where the whole family would be reunited within a few months. Annette was helping to fund the voyage from her great success in Chicago.

Many tributes were paid to Alice on the night, and on rising to respond to them, she was greeted by applause that was the equal of anything she had enjoyed in her adopted country.[19] The program concluded with the Marseillaise, played with much spirit by the orchestra and sung by the audience.[20]

There were more concerts, parties and farewells for Alice, until finally, on 18 July 1907, she and her two youngest children, along with their five dogs,[21] sailed for France, where Maurice would meet them on the docks at Cherbourg. Alice would never see Australia again.

Annette wondered if Fred would either.

AT THE SAME TIME THAT Alice and her two children left Melbourne, Fred and Annette met a polite, dark-haired young man selling souvenir programs at White City. His name was Jimmie Sullivan,[22] and he was an enterprising 21-year-old from Minnesota who had the program concession for the amusement park. He was a handsome, charming fellow with 'sparkling brown eyes'[23] and a 'lovely smile',[24] about 5 foot 7 inches (170 cm) tall. He told Fred that he had sat among the freezing reporters when Annette gave her first performance as the snow fell in Chicago. He sold more programs at Annette's performances than anywhere else in the vast amusement park, despite the many other attractions there. Fred and Annette both liked Jimmie's sunny disposition and that nothing ever seemed to faze him in the surreal carnival atmosphere in which they all worked. Jimmie thought the Australians were easy-going, too, and he liked Annette. Very much. Despite her fame, she seemed down-to-earth, and he never heard her swear or saw her get really angry.[25]

Annette often talked to Jimmie about the boys she liked and some of the handsome young men who asked her out after seeing her show. Jimmie was an excellent chaperone, though he always gave Annette's suitors hard looks and told her none of them were good enough. Sometimes he would scare away the really handsome ones by telling them that Annette's father was 'a big whale of an Australian who chewed up fellows like them'.[26]

One night, when Annette and Jimmie were out walking, he tipped his hat to a big bear of a man shaped like a beer barrel on legs. Annette guessed the man was about fifty. He had a gaudy bathrobe draped around his massive shoulders and an impressive handlebar moustache. His name was John L. Sullivan and twenty years earlier he was the heavyweight boxing champion of the world, boasting in bars across America that he could 'lick any sonovabitch in the world'. He and an old foe, Jake Kilrain, were about to reprise their legendary two-hour bareknuckle brawl of 1889 with nightly sparring sessions in a ring at White City, just in front of Annette's water palace.[27]

John L. told Annette that he was a big fan of her diving exhibitions and that it took enormous courage to do what she did. 'How many shows did you do today, little lady?' the big bruiser asked.

Being Sunday, Annette replied: 'I gave eighteen.'

'Jehoshaphat,' John L. said. 'You can stay the rounds too.'[28]

FRED WAS LOSING THE ENERGY to manage Annette's affairs properly, and he asked Jimmie to help her with her appearances and press requests. Annette recalled that the 'kind-hearted, quiet, unassuming man' did everything in his power 'to help the pair from "Down Under".'[29]

Doctors told Fred that he would need someone to look after him constantly, so he sent for his sister Josephine to come over from Colorado. Aunty Jo also kept a close eye on Annette and the university boys from Chicago, who were always chasing after 'the Diving Venus'.[30]

Annette was going through dramatic physical changes. She was experimenting more with vegetarianism and was thinner than the robust, muscular girl who first tackled the English Channel two years earlier. Still, she loved ice cream, and despite protests from her father that it would harm her training, she had Jimmie deliver packages of it to her hotel on the quiet. She would also arrange for Jimmie to escort Aunty Jo on shopping trips and sightseeing excursions – everywhere from the stockyards to countless museums – so that Annette could go out golfing or meet up with one of the handsome young chaps who always seemed to be waiting around her stage door. Jimmie was never happy about it, but he always complied.[31]

These were only diversions, though, for Annette to mask the pain she knew was coming like those rotten tides of the English Channel.

A couple of months into Annette's season at White City, Fred told Annette that he knew he was not long for this world and that he wanted to sail for Paris to see Alice and the other children before it was too late. They had taken a little flat by the Seine and Maurice would come for him and take him there so that he could say his goodbyes.

Fred was now confined to a wheelchair, but Annette remembered that he never lost his good spirits. 'His one thought was to see me well launched on a career and to know that his family had arrived safely in France. When the cable arrived saying mother was in Paris he rallied wonderfully. He had accomplished what he had set out to do.'[32]

'Remember, you can rise above any conditions,' Fred told Annette. 'Never forget you are lucky to have a great artist for a mother. She received her country's award for what she did in Australia for music. You, on the other hand, can do a great deal for the young girls and women by showing them what a healthy life can do.'[33]

Those words coming from a man who was clearly at the end of the line stayed in Annette's mind for the rest of her days. When she said goodbye to her father at the dock in New York, he looked small, reduced, pathetic. Annette told Fred she could never repay him for all that he had done: giving up so much to travel with her to England and America, to give her every opportunity to maximise her talents and realise her potential.

In the two years since they had left Melbourne, Annette had become a major celebrity in England, Continental Europe and the United States, and now at twenty-one she was one of the most admired female athletes in the world and a star attraction at a jewel of American entertainment. She would never forget how her ailing father, sick as he was, went top hat in hand all over London, trying to drum up interest for his daughter among the British newspapers and swimming clubs. Or how, with the threat of angina always with him, he would be in the rowboat in often uncomfortable and sometimes dangerous conditions, helping her in her long ocean and river swims.

Fred had always been a good judge of character and he told her that Jimmie Sullivan was an 'upstanding lad' who would do the right thing by her as her new manager and press agent. He said he trusted Jimmie completely.

As Annette waved goodbye to her father with tears in her eyes and a lump in her throat, she knew that she was seeing him for the last time.

She would find comfort in Jimmie's support.

Jimmie, though, would find Annette a handful. Without her father's guidance, she soon developed a reputation as a wild child, and became embroiled in one scandal after another.[34]

EVEN WITH JIMMIE'S friendly shoulder to cry on, Annette felt lost and afraid in Chicago. Sure, there was admiration and there were accolades everywhere for a feminist icon and trailblazer in women's sport. The prestigious Illinois Athletic Club even elected Annette to its august ranks; the only other woman honorary member among 4000 men[35] was the Empress of Germany.[36]

Newspaper columnists wrote that Annette's 'beauty of face and form' was being 'raved about on three continents',[37] but her father's departure for Paris created an enormous void in her life. Jimmie seemed to take more than a friendly interest in her, but while she thought he was a good colleague, she was his boss and did not consider him 'boyfriend' material.[38]

Instead, she found a soulmate in a prominent Chicago physician, Dr A.N. Dickinson. They met at a dance and Annette often visited his home at Woodlawn, on the shores of Lake Michigan, and spent time aboard his racing yacht.[39] Annette admitted she was 'rather enamoured' with Dr Dickinson,[40] though she noticed Jimmie did not seem at all pleased. The doctor told friends Annette was his 'mermaid sweetheart' and that he was infatuated with her. She had, he confessed, dived straight into his heart as spectacularly as she did into the water.[41]

One night, the charming young doctor waltzed into Annette's dressing room and asked her to marry him. But Annette had already decided that none of the nice Americans she had met quite 'rang the bell'[42] in her affections. She told the good doctor that he was very nice but she'd have to give his proposal a lot of thought.

Later, she asked Jimmie what he thought of Dr Dickinson as husband material.

Jimmie made a sour face. He always did when Annette asked him about male suitors. 'It's none of my business,' he said, 'but he'd never last six months with you. No, make that six weeks.'[43]

Jimmie was so adamant that he took Annette by surprise. 'Maybe you're right,' she said meekly, 'but how do you happen to know so much about it?'

'Listen, I've known you ever since you came over to this country with your dad,' he said. 'What's more, I know you much better than you know yourself.' Jimmie quietly turned on his heel and left the room,[44] leaving Annette to wonder what was eating him.

The Australian Mermaid had always been one to defy social conventions in the way she dressed for her performances, but she now seemed to lose restraint even in situations that were dangerous for others. In addition to Dr Dickinson, she had many other male suitors and pursued an active social life. She would go on outings with the actors and chorus girls from the big shows playing at Chicago theatres, such as *Brewsters Millions, The Yankee Regent* and the *Prince of Pilsen*.[45]

One day during a break from her shows at White City she took a ride on an excursion boat on Lake Michigan with some of the theatrical performers. Annette took a bet with some sailors that if she fell overboard in deep water with all her clothes on, she would have plenty of 'pluck' and be able to save herself.

When the vessel was about 10 kilometres from shore, a cry went up: 'Woman overboard! Woman overboard!' There was a great state of panic on the vessel, but the sailors she'd had the bet with watched on as the boat's purser, fearing one of his passengers was drowning, leapt into the water and swam to Annette. Afraid that Annette's long dress and boots would drag her under, the purser grabbed her by the hair. Another crewman leapt into the water and landed on top of the purser, knocking him unconscious. Then, as the crew lowered the lifeboat, another passenger had to be restrained from diving in to help.

Annette had to pretend she was in distress rather than admit it had all been a ruse.

A lifebuoy was put around the purser's neck and Annette and the two men were hauled into the boat. The ship's doctor had to work on the purser for an hour until he came round.

When the truth of Annette's careless stunt was revealed, *The Chicago Evening American*[46] newspaper devoted a whole page to the event, revealing the scandal to its 300,000 readers and reporting that, when passengers and crew heard of Annette's dangerous trick, they had become exceedingly angry.[47]

The paper reported that Annette had tried to calm everyone on the ship, arguing that what she had done only proved that the men on the steamer were extraordinarily brave and 'ready to face danger in order to save life'.[48] To make up for her recklessness she said she would put on a show immediately for the passengers and 'forthwith she dived from the captain's bridge'.

Not everyone on board was willing to forgive and forget, though. One of the crewmen told the Chicago press that for such carelessness that risked the lives of others, Annette 'ought to be well walloped'.[49]

As it turned out, she was about to receive a far more painful blow.

Chapter 15

THREE MONTHS AFTER Annette said goodbye to her father, Alice sent a telegram from Paris to say that Fred had died.

After he had undergone a heart operation and 'a period of great suffering',[1] Fred had passed away on 8 October 1907, only twelve days after arriving in France. He was just forty-seven.[2] London's *Daily Mirror* was just one of the many papers that paid tribute to a 'very popular'[3] man who had done so much for his daughter's career.[4] Annette called Fred 'a charming, well-educated Australian, a devoted husband and father'. He was buried in the Charbonnet family vault at the Père Lachaise Cemetery.

Annette took the train to New York and boarded the *Adriatic* for Paris on 2 November[5] to attend Fred's memorial service and spend Christmas with her mother and siblings at their apartment at 6 Rue Herschel, bordering the Luxembourg Gardens. She had regularly sent money to help her family.

While Annette was being reunited with them in Paris, newspapers around the world reported that she would marry Dr Dickinson when she returned from Europe in the American spring.[6] It was news to Annette, and Dr Dickenson slowly began to realise his wedding plans were premature and that maybe his 'mermaid sweetheart' just wasn't that into him.

In Paris, Annette's mother had reconnected with many relatives she had not seen for decades, and Annette was delighted to meet them, even under such sad circumstances. There was

Alice's Aunt Valerie, the Contesse d'Auvilliers, and Alice's cousin, the Conte de Bourgade, who for eight years had been secretary of private affairs to the late Pope Leo XIII. Both were frequent visitors to Alice's charming home, along with Alice's old classmate at the Paris Conservatory, Cécile Chaminade, who was now an international music star soon to tour America.[7] Cécile and Annette compared notes on what to expect from audiences there.

Annette also travelled to London to take in West End theatre for a few weeks. She told friends that the money on the American vaudeville scene was a lot better than she could make diving into the cold water of Dover and that she had 'finished altogether with the Channel'.[8] 'I had the endurance,' she said later, 'but not the brute strength that must be coupled with it.'[9]

Annette had been enchanted by a new entertainment fad, 'diabolo tennis', a game that involved a conical double-headed spinning top that was tossed into the air and controlled by sticks held in each hand. Annette had played it with her brothers Maurice and Freddie at the Luxembourg Gardens near her mother's home,[10] and she called it the 'hardest game I ever tackled'. But she figured the diabolo act would be a huge hit along with her high dives when she started a season of appearances at a new amusement park called Wonderland at the holiday resort of Revere Beach, just north of Boston, Massachusetts.[11] The Wonderland program announced Annette as a 'clever, magnetic, beautiful, magnificently formed and modest young woman who comes nearer to being the reincarnated "Daughter of Neptune" than any other creature. When she leaves the springboard she seems to move in space in wondrous curves and suddenly cleaves and glides into the water with the clean smoothness of a lithe oily body.'[12]

Annette said she missed her dad terribly but was heading back to America, not to marry as the press might have said, but to continue on the entertainment path that her father had opened for her.[13] Annette sailed from Liverpool on the White Star liner *Cedric* and arrived in New York on 16 May 1908 after a thrilling voyage that included a spectacular electrical storm when the ship was halfway across the Atlantic. The roaring thunder lasted two hours and the lightning strikes were terrifying as they hit all points of the ship, making it appear as though the huge vessel was ablaze. At one stage Annette looked up to see what seemed like great balls of fire chasing each other down the ship's flagpoles.[14]

Her performances at Wonderland were electrifying too. On her arrival in Boston, Annette was announced in the press as 'a sensational engagement' for Wonderland. 'The Australian Mermaid and champion woman swimmer of the world', the 'Venus Aphrodite',[15] would give 'half-hourly exhibitions in a specially constructed cement basin'.[16]

Huge crowds turned out to see her. She was besieged by admirers, and gave long interviews on the subject of all the love letters she received.[17] They were never-ending. One potential suitor, on discovering that she spoke French, wrote her a letter in that language begging for a rendezvous and telling her to look out for a Panama hat with a red band.

She laughed off all of them over the next few years, and could be frank when doing it.

> 'Chere petite', dear little one – that's me – dear little one – and I'm not little, whatever I am and I'm not his dear or anyone else's either. He thinks I'm adorable, isn't that sweet of him? He wouldn't think so if he knew how much I was laughing at him. Kind of mean too, but he ought to know better.[18]

One admirer even sent Annette a love letter with a case of champagne and a diamond and emerald bracelet. For the first time, Jimmie Sullivan hit the roof, demanding that she at least send the bracelet back. They kept the champagne, though, for a party.[19]

In the absence of Annette's father, Jimmie had become Annette's 'press agent, manager and general factotum'.[20] She was growing to like Jimmie a lot, but her work came first. 'I like to please people,' Annette said. 'I like to give them their money's worth and do all I can to make my act a success. But outside of that I want to enjoy my life like any other girl. And I will. I'm only twenty-two and I don't want to fall in love yet, for if I do I'll be awfully in love.'[21]

Wonderland featured state-of-the-art thrill rides and wonderous exhibitions – even a baby incubator – and there were leading performers from around the world. Annette appeared alongside Pawnee Bill's Wild West Show,[22] a successful rival to another wild west show run by Buffalo Bill Cody.

Pawnee Bill,[23] real name Gordon Lillie, and his wife, May, had spent twenty years building up their travelling show, which featured performances by native Americans and a couple of dozen cowboys and cowgirls. Now it had become a major American attraction. Annette became close with the couple, who told her tales of the Old West and taught her the tricks of rough riding.

While performing at Wonderland, Annette tentatively agreed to a match race over 3 miles in New York's Hudson River against America's own female torpedo, Elaine Golding. But with Jimmie advising her, Annette said she would only take on the American girl for a 1000-dollar cash prize to the winner.[24] It was, after all, the biggest swimming race in the world. No sponsor or promoter was willing to part with that money, though, and Annette knew it. She wasn't about to have her brand tarnished by a potential high-profile defeat.

Instead, she learned of a gruelling swim in Boston, a 12-mile marathon from the Charlestown Bridge across Boston Harbor to a lighthouse known as the Boston Light. It was described by the American press as 'torturous and full of strong crosscurrents because of many small islands'.[25] A year earlier, the course had beaten thirty-two of the best male swimmers from the United States and Canada.[26] In fact, only one person had ever made it, and that was local distance legend Peter McNally, back when Annette was still at the convent school in Sydney. No one believed that a woman could do it.

Annette sought the expert opinion of people who knew the course – 'the whims of the eddies, winds and currents'. She even brought in Peter McNally himself, along with another great Boston swimmer, Sam Mahoney. They helped her map a course, which, due to currents at that time of year, meant she would have to swim a mile or two further than McNally's epic feat.[27]

Annette started doing long-distance swims, going far out into the bay among the waves, and she spent a lot of time riding horses bareback across the sand. She told reporters that she had started dieting and that she was about 20 pounds (about 9 kg) lighter than her first crack at the English Channel three years earlier.[28]

In the week leading up to the swim, Annette and Jimmie went over the course twice in a motor launch. Annette declared that, if the conditions did not turn against her, she had it well covered. She also asked the skippers of the boats that would follow her to give her a wide berth because the gasoline exhaust floated on the water and could distress her.[29]

On 30 July 1908, just before 1 p.m.,[30] Annette dived into the water from the covered bow of the press boat *Marion*. Jimmie accompanied her in a rowboat carrying flasks of cold chicken broth.

It was a fine afternoon[31] and among the crowd of 20,000 lining the shore and watching from bridges was 59-year-old Dr Dudley Sargent,[32] an assistant professor at Harvard University who ran that institution's Hemenway Gymnasium along with other prestigious fitness centres. He had been obsessed with physical fitness and human performance since his days as a high school gymnast in the 1860s.

Supporters in 'scores of yachts and launches',[33] including Peter McNally, followed Annette, cheering her on and singing songs. When Annette joined them in chorus, Jimmie admonished her, saying she was wasting energy. She only laughed and called back: 'Today I feel I could swim to Sydney', though she conceded that a gold bracelet she was wearing above her right elbow was starting to feel very heavy.[34]

As Annette passed the American naval gunboat USS *Gloucester*,[35] two young cadets dived in and followed her for an hour or so, though the pace she set left them gasping, as it did for

Annette's beauty, voluptuousness, boldness and barely-there performance costumes were a constant theme in press articles after her arrival in America. *Billy Rose Theatre Division, The New York Public Library for the Performing Arts, Astor, Lenox and Tilden Foundation*

some artillery men who also took to the water further down the harbour and tried to keep her company.[36]

Still she kept going strongly; Peter McNally called out to her through a megaphone that she had gone further than the best of the previous year's swimmers, Louis Jacot, and was ten minutes ahead of his time.[37]

On she went with no hint of fatigue, though the tide was against her for the last 5 miles of her swim. The sun sank low and grew fat with the colour of burnished copper. Annette was within 800 metres of her goal at the Boston Light when the tide literally turned again and a cross current came up like a concrete barrier.

Annette had covered 12 miles in 6 hours 23 minutes when this unusually swift current pushed her back.

All the swimming experts in the support boats said it was going to be too difficult and dangerous to negotiate the next half mile.

So Annette reluctantly left the water, having gone further than any woman and almost all the men who had ever attempted the course. She was still fresh and told everyone that she was not fatigued in the least.[38] Newspapers reported that all of Boston was 'agog' with her performance,[39] and *The Boston Globe* called it 'one of the greatest feats of skill and endurance ever seen in this part of the country'.[40]

Annette had spent weeks training for the big swim at the northern end of Revere Beach. She rented a suite of three rooms there for herself and Aunty Jo, who was back to help out, as well as a maid. Her landlords were Herbert and Mabelle Pattee, who ran Wonderland's romantic ride, 'Love's Journey', a sort of tunnel of love that Herbert had invented and which operated just a few doors down from Annette's Wonderland show. Herbert was a former Broadway actor. He had been forty and Mabelle seventeen when they had married two years earlier, after he had seen her on Love's Journey with a date. There was trouble in the couple's household, though, as soon as Annette and her entourage put down their luggage. Young Mrs Pattee suspected that her husband took too keen an interest in Annette. The famous Australian was about the same age as Mrs Pattee and her beauty, voluptuousness, boldness and barely-there performance costumes were a constant theme in press articles. The friction in the household would soon explode and Annette and her entourage moved out after three weeks.

Annette had more on her mind than domestic squabbles, though. Watching one of her performances at Wonderland, a stout man with a luxuriant moustache reckoned it was one of the best things he'd seen in his sixty-two years of life and his long career in entertainment. It was certainly more exciting than the first show he'd produced, when he had charged ten cents for patrons to look at a tiny three-month-old baby weighing less than a kilogram who he billed as 'Baby Alice – The Child Wonder'.[41]

The man approached Jimmie and asked to meet 'the mermaid' because he had a business proposition for her. Jimmie had met hundreds of smitten fans just like him, and as her tireless chaperone he demanded that the visitor 'tell me about it first'.

The old showman wasn't used to that sort of response. He handed Jimmie his business card. 'Perhaps this will make my errand clear,' he said as he walked away.

Jimmie looked at the card and almost fainted.[42] The old moustachioed fan was Benjamin Franklin Keith,[43] America's King of Vaudeville, who owned thirty theatres across the United States and Canada.

From his days as a circus boy, Keith had spent all his working life in show business. In 1883 he had opened his first theatre in Boston as an addendum to his curiosity museum. He had found that Americans loved vaudeville shows — variety theatre, comedy, singing, dancing and animal acts — which had become popular in France. Vaudeville was regarded a more polite diversion than the raucous entertainments available in boisterous music hall saloons.

Keith's business had boomed, and to manage the B.F. Keith Circuit, his chain of theatres, he hired a former circus roustabout named Edward Albee.[44] Albee's adoptive grandson, of the same name, became one of America's most famous playwrights.

Keith offered Annette and Jimmie a whopping 300 dollars a week to transfer the Wonderland act to the stage and perform fourteen short shows a week.[45] By October 1908 Annette was doing her diving routines into a glass tank at Keith's theatre opposite the Boston Common. The show also included a display of her skills with the diabolo, some motion picture footage of her long-distance swims, and a dance show involving her ballet skills in front of multiple mirrors that showed off Annette's famous curves from every angle.[46]

Albee knew what he was doing with all those mirrors. He once told a stage manager: 'What we are selling here is backsides, and a hundred backsides are better than one!'[47]

Chapter 16

DESPITE THE OBVIOUS exploitation of Annette's physical attributes and the use of comedians with bawdy acts full of double entendres, vaudeville was promoted as wholesome middle-class family entertainment, and Keith's promotion of Annette quickly made her one of the leading performers in America.

Signs in Keith's theatres asked patrons to be respectful, not to stamp their feet or canes on the floor, to applaud politely and to refrain from 'smoking, spitting, whistling, and crunching peanuts'.[1]

The *Boston Sunday Post* said Annette was one of the greatest entertainment attractions the city had ever seen and that while 'this beautiful young Australian' had made her name swimming and diving, her dancing in front of the mirrors was now winning a whole new audience.[2]

Annette also gave a lecture to hundreds of women in Boston on health and physical fitness, telling them:

> In order to be in good physical condition you must sacrifice little pleasures in the way of eating. It may be interesting to you to know that I seldom eat meat. I'm not a vegetarian by any means, but, regardless of all theories, I maintain that the less meat you eat the more perfect will be your health and strength. The only time I eat meat is before taking a long swim, and this is merely to add weight instead of strength. On rising in the morning the

first thing I do is to take a lemon in a glass of hot water. I never miss a morning without my lemon and hot water. It is without doubt the healthiest drink, far better than breakfast coffee ... If you'll try this, you'll find much to your surprise how refreshing it is, and in a week's time you'll feel like a new woman ... After that I exercise 20 minutes. At noon time I eat my first and best meal of the day. My meal consists of vegetables and sometimes oysters. Of course there may be a lot of women who could not get along without meat, but just try it and after a while you'll see how easy it is to enjoy your meal without meat. In the matter of drinking – time and again I've gone into a restaurant and noticed women drinking beer, wine etc. Of course I do not say that is wrong for a woman to drink, but she should choose her liquor as well as her food. They do not feel the effects until later on then they begin to grow fat, begin to complain, and can't imagine the reason why. That is why I say by sacrificing yourself a little before, you gain so much after.[3]

On 25 November 1908 Annette moved her vaudeville show from Boston to the entertainment capital of America, New York, where Jimmie organised a tank containing more than 100,000 litres of water to be erected on stage at Keith's Fifth Avenue Theatre.

Annette would perform twice a day, afternoon and evening, but each show would last no more than half an hour in a program that included up to twelve other acts.

During her first week in New York Annette appeared on a card that included a Brazilian equestrian team, the leading comedienne Julie Ring, a trained baboon and, in those less racially aware times, 'The Inimitable Black-face Comedians, The Georgia Minstrels'.[4]

Annette's act would generally begin with her wearing a long skirt, which would be quickly torn off to reveal her tight-fitting one-piece bathing suit with a sheer scarf wrapped around it. She would then dance in front of the mirrors and show her skills with the diabolo. Then she would discard the scarf and in her brief bathing suit ascend a ladder to a springboard twelve feet above the water tank to make a series of dives, including front and back somersaults as well as 'neck dives'.

Annette got a great thrill out of the 'splosh', which would always get a laugh as it drenched those sitting closest to the action, often men with opera glasses enjoying a magnified view.[5]

There were always one or two in the audience who ignored Edward Albee's direction to applaud the performers politely and to refrain from wolf whistles. At one of Annette's performances a young man in the front row shouted 'Gee, you're a peach,' which got a laugh and a cheer from those around him.

Annette made it clear that she was nobody's peach. She walked to the end of the diving board and jumped into the water as close as she could to the cocky admirer in the front row, pulling up her knees to her chest and landing with a heavy 'splosh'. A wave of water smacked her target right in his previously smug face. Dripping wet, he promptly left the theatre.

'I think that should teach him better manners,' Annette told the audience. She had also drenched the orchestra conductor, Professor Ward Johnson, but he took it with good grace, shaking the water from his baton and getting back to work.[6]

After five weeks topping the bill at the Fifth Avenue Theatre, Annette wrote to friends in London to say she was having the time of her life. 'I want to tell you that I have said good-bye to long distance swimming and am now a vaudeville artist,' she wrote.

> Well, I was always keen on dancing, as you know and I stuck to it, also my diabolo, which, by the way critics were good enough to describe as the cleverest exhibition ever given in New York. It took me 12 months to reach perfection, as I wished to make a big turn of it. My 'craziness' for the stage has been rewarded. I shall be very busy for the next five years. B.F. Keith, for whom I work the show, spent nearly £700 over the mirror act, and now that it is such a success

Annette shows her skills with the diabolo spinning top before the crowd at a baseball game shortly after arriving in America. *Library of Congress, Bain News Service, LC-B2-842-10 [P&P]*

he is 'tickled to death.' He has a special car for me and has engaged three engineers and 14 men to put up the tank at each place. I have been doing the act for 10 weeks now, and have never seen anything but crowded houses. I am not 'swollen-headed' at all, but must confess that my enthusiasm has carried me away. It all means a fortune for me. I've worked very hard for all this.[7]

Still, it was Annette's body and her risqué performance that attracted the crowds as much as the body of work that made her so proud. Before long she was appearing at more of Keith's venues around America and making headlines everywhere.

One reviewer wrote of a performance in New York: 'The Diving Venus has a good excuse, not to mention a good figure, for dressing as she does. It's a joy to see her spring into the air and then take a header into the tank. Of course, some people might say that she leaves little to the imagination when she gets wet down and trots around in a suit that clings closer than – but oh splash.'[8]

Another remarked on the frantic nature of Annette's work, racing between shows to the Astor Hotel on Times Square[9] for a fund-raising party among wealthy society matrons in their most conservative long dresses. They applauded demurely as Annette, whose costume made her appear all but naked, danced and whirled for them spectacularly – 'a magnificent body ... curve upon curve, firm and splendidly rounded – a chiffon nymph'.[10]

But Annette also knew age and changing tastes would catch up with every performer – even chiffon nymphs who were barely twenty-three. She tried to take out an insurance policy on her routine, but the insurance company reportedly said that with her dives from 'such a height into such a very small tank she was likely at any time to either meet with serious accident or kill herself outright'.[11]

But she could insure herself against patrons ever thinking her act had become old hat. One night, while standing in the wings in her swimming costume waiting to go on, Annette overheard two comedians talking about her. One called her a passing fad and speculated rudely that the novelty would wear off. A performer, he said, had to have much more than a good body to stay in the public eye.

Annette got a sick feeling in the pit of her stomach but knew they were right. Determined to broaden her appeal even more, she located Italian dance teacher Luigi Albertieri, who had arrived in New York from Rome a decade earlier and was now ballet master at the Metropolitan Opera House on Broadway and 39th Street.[12] Annette trained with him for two hours every day, as the love of ballet she had as a child returned to her. She also practised archery and took lessons in fencing from a Cuban master, Professor Ricardo Manrique, who travelled with her entourage when she went on the road to more of Keith's theatres around America.

Every day after the matinee she and the professor would duel with swords. Annette fell in love with gridiron football, too, and went to baseball games and horse races.

ANNETTE KNEW HOW TO work an audience and she knew the value of a good story. She made as much mileage as she could from her provocative image and knew that newspaper reports in the Australian press about 'positively indecent photos of the Australian nymph' would not hurt ticket sales when she returned to her home country.[13]

In the United States, Jimmie fed the press the story that Annette was the daughter of the woman 'who first discovered the wonderful voice of Melba', a diva Annette called 'Nellie' because her 'name was Nellie Mitchell in those days in Australia'.[14] 'Miss Melba', Annette said, was very keen to help Annette develop her own singing career for the stage.

Annette could also stretch the truth when necessary. Decades after she lived in Boston and at a time when she was looking to sell the story of her life to Hollywood, Annette recounted a curious tale of arriving at Revere Beach for her first day of swimming and being astounded by all the old-fashioned swimming costumes women were wearing, complete with shoes, stockings, bloomers, skirts, overdresses with puffy sleeves, sailor collars and, in some cases, even tightly fitted corsets.[15] 'But then, nobody really went swimming,' she wrote. 'Everybody waded in and just bobbed up and down. Those who did swim were so heavily encumbered, they showed no joy in the swimming.'[16]

Annette claimed that when she stripped down to her boy's racing suit to start her training there were shrieks of horror from the crowd and a strapping policeman arrested her for 'indecency'. She said she appeared before a Boston judge the next day and that she lectured him on the stance she was taking for women to wear more comfortable attire in the water to encourage them to take up swimming for vital exercise. She said that the judge agreed with her but declared that she couldn't wear that outfit on a public beach again.[17]

And so, Annette claimed, the incident gave birth to the famous Annette Kellerman bathing suit for women, which she marketed – a tight-fitting jersey knit stockinette which came down to some inches above the knees.

It was a remarkable story, though curiously the press that covered almost every move Annette made in America at the time seems not to have mentioned anything about it. However, they certainly covered another incident that had happened at Revere Beach, causing Annette to break down sobbing in shock.

Chapter 17

ANNETTE WAS IN A LOW mood as she prepared for the evening performance of her vaudeville routine at the Alhambra Theatre in New York's Harlem district on the night of 12 March 1909. She was dealing with all manner of stresses.

Unfortunately, Annette had become embroiled in a high-stakes financial war with B.F. Keith. She had signed a three-year contract with him for 300 dollars a week, but she had walked out on it when a German immigrant named Zelman Moses offered her a 51-week contract paying 1500 dollars a week.[1] Moses had changed his name and set himself up as 'William Morris, Vaudeville Agent', starting a business that would become one of the biggest talent agencies in the world.

The William Morris offer was for Annette to appear at his venues only in the summer. He had no objection to her working for Keith in the winter, so Annette and Jimmie apparently thought that Keith wouldn't mind if, in the summer, they took more money for Annette to perform at Morris's 3500-seat American Music Hall on 42nd Street.

Understandably, Keith wouldn't have a bar of it and said a deal was a deal.

Annette said it was her life and she'd do what she liked.

'See you in court,' Keith replied.

Their relationship descended into a bitter legal war. Keith hired the biggest gun among American attorneys, Henry Waters Taft,[2] the brother and legal counsel of the American president. Annette had started performing at William Morris's American Music Hall before Keith was granted a temporary injunction on her diving. She had been left in the embarrassing position of being able to appear on stage in her one-piece bathing suit but do little except give a talk on physical fitness and watch a replacement diver known as 'Speedy' doing her diving routine.

Things were also not going well between Annette and Jimmie. Annette had been slow to realise that Jimmie was in love with his boss and that he was becoming furious with all the 'Stage Door Johnnies' hanging around the theatre with their chocolates and flowers and their silly brooding looks and their stupid puppy dog eyes on their long idiot faces.

Then reporters had turned up to the Alhambra on 12 March wanting Annette's reaction to her being named, earlier that day, as 'the other woman' in a bitter divorce case taking place in Boston.

Annette's former landlady, young Mabelle Pattee, was suing her much older husband, Herbert, for divorce, and she was painting Annette in a sinister light. Mrs Pattee was described in the press as 'a blonde with great blue eyes and the pinkest of cheeks'.[3] The reporters explained to Annette that, in the hushed Boston courtroom, Mrs Pattee had spoken in a low quiet voice and appeared on the verge of breaking down several times as she detailed two years of what she claimed was abuse from her husband. Her most sensational claims, though, were that Annette had contributed to the breakdown of the marriage by flirting with Mr Pattee during her time as their star boarder. Young Mrs Pattee said Annette had made a habit of 'seating herself in the kitchen, drinking lager beer and munching crackers with her husband'. She said Annette had even taken delight in 'making faces of derision at the young wife'.[4]

When the reporters put this to Annette at the Alhambra, the young woman they called 'the athletic beauty of the Antipodes' immediately broke into a 'fit of hysterical weeping'.[5]

'This is shameful and wicked to say such things about me,' she wailed, tears cascading down her face. 'I hardly knew Mr Pattee. I never liked him even as a passing acquaintance. I would meet him occasionally but only exchanged the most ordinary greetings.'[6]

She sobbed and sobbed, before slowly regaining her composure. 'I never sat in the kitchen with him,' she pleaded. 'I never drank beer with him. I have not tasted a glass of beer since I have been in this country.'[7]

Annette said she only stayed at the house for three weeks and moved out because the Pattees were constantly squabbling.

The reporters' pencils were working overtime as Annette gave them great copy.

Was there anything else she'd like to say? With Jimmie holding her hand, Annette continued: 'It seems cruel and unjust that a girl who has led such a nun-like life as myself, and who has striven to stand as an example [of] a clean, healthful, outdoor woman, should be placed in such an unfair position before the public.'[8]

Annette sobbed some more. What would the mothers of all the girls coming to her lectures think of her now, even if it wasn't true? The news had been cabled to London, too, and Annette knew that her 'poor mother' would read it in Paris. 'She will know it cannot be true of me,' Annette said, 'but it will hurt her so.'[9]

That night the show went on, but it was obvious Annette had red eyes and was smiling through gritted teeth.

In the end, a judge granted Mrs Pattee her divorce and the scandal finally blew over, with Herbert Pattee saying he regretted that such a fine young woman as Annette had been dragged into the turmoil.[10]

As always, Jimmie was there to hold Annette's hand. He was there, too, with a warm hug weeks later, when Judge Ward in New York issued an order restraining Annette from fulfilling her deal with William Morris.[11]

The fight was far from over, and Annette slowly began to realise that she wanted Jimmie to hold her hand for the rest of her life.

Following the ugliness of the Boston divorce case, and as the financial kick from the Morris–Keith battle stung, Annette and Jimmie announced that they were engaged to be married.[12]

IN MAY 1909, WHILE HER legal battles with B.F. Keith continued, Annette was presented with a gleaming, cream-coloured Buick motor car after winning a popularity contest to become Queen of the New York Automobile Carnival.

It had cost a penny to vote in the contest, and of the 100,000 votes cast for 1200 contestants, Annette took more than 51,000 of them, leaving all other female contenders hopelessly flailing in her wake, including Broadway actress Billie Burke, Canadian singer Eva Tanguay, and the star of the Ziegfeld Follies theatrical troupe, Anna Held.[13] Racing car driver Guy Vaughan, who was crowned King of the carnival, received only a fifth of Annette's tally, *The New York Times* attributing the discrepancy to the fact that most of the voters were men and that Annette was what the paper called 'an unusually pretty young woman'.[14]

On 3 May, Annette, wearing her Queen's crown, led a parade of 1000 motor cars as they chugged down Broadway and then along Fifth Avenue in the biggest ever pageant of automobiles seen in New York.[15] Many car manufacturers entered elaborately decorated floats for the parade. The Buick entry featured a huge seashell with dancing girls dressed as mermaids and Annette, seated on a throne wearing her crown and little else above the waistline but beads, her legs enmeshed in a fishtail. It was a cool day and Annette felt like a snow queen surrounded by spectators in fur coats.[16]

The Diving Venus became the Driving Venus,[17] and before long she was making a striking figure as she drove her new open-top Buick tourer automobile through the streets of New York, dressed in a radiant white fur suit and white muff hat.

Just as she had turned the one-piece swimsuit into a revolutionary fashion item, Annette designed her own bold street clothes as well, often improvising. Friends said she could wear a lampshade from her hotel room and make it look good.[18] After buying the white fur suit to go with her car, Annette had wanted a hat to match but couldn't find one. She bought a fur muff instead and put it on her head, telling the surprised sales girl, 'This will do splendidly, thank you.'[19]

Annette advertised for a chauffeur and newspaper reports suggested 'he must have sufficient disrespect for speed laws to be willing to go some. She likes to arrive in a hurry – that's why she likes a driver who will open up on a stretch of good road. "I like to go some myself," declared the young woman ...'[20]

The next day the same paper reported: 'Annette gets him! She picks out a chauffeur who can make a car whizz for biz.'[21] Twenty-four chauffeurs had arrived to apply for the position, but when they were told it was already taken, a policeman had to be called in to calm the situation.

The new driver didn't last long, as Annette started roaring around in the Buick herself, squeezing out every bit of speed she could from its tiny four-cylinder forty-horsepower engine and its narrow tyres, which were more suited to a park bicycle than a flying car.

Annette came to believe there was 'no pleasure in life greater than running your own machine', and that driving in the open air kept her brain alert and stimulated every one of her senses. 'It will be a great day for women,' she declared, 'when the price of an auto is within the reach of everyone.'[22]

When Annette's evening show was finished, instead of going to bars or nightclubs like so many of the other performers, she would wind down by speeding in her Buick out to one of New York's beaches and diving into the dark waves. She would swim far out from shore until she seemed to 'shrink and shrink 'til I was nothing but a flecky bubble and feared that bubble would burst'.[23]

It wasn't long before a policeman, Officer Culbertson, had to chase 'a big touring car ... going at a terrific speed'[24] as Jimmie and Annette rushed to a matinee. Annette pleaded 'piteously' with the arresting officer to let her go. But the policeman took Annette to the Flatbush Station in Brooklyn instead, where for bail she produced 100 dollars from her stocking top as officers looked the other way.[25] She later paid a hefty fine.

Annette had shown an extraordinary degree of fearlessness from her earliest days, leaping into the water from heights at Farmer's Baths and ploughing through murky rivers. Perhaps all the stress over her battles with B.F. Keith had contributed to her recklessness, the thrill of driving fast releasing some of her tension. The heavyweight title fight between the two biggest producers in vaudeville had dragged on for months. Keith had put his lawyer, Henry Taft, on a retainer of 2500 dollars, while Annette's team of lawyers – attorneys George Leventritt, William Guthrie and Benjamin Cardoza – were receiving 1000 dollars each, a huge chunk of the money Annette had earned risking her neck every night on the springboard.

When the injunction period was lifted, in May 1909, Jimmie tried to convince Annette to stick with Morris. This caused a ruckus between them. Jimmie later admitted that there were times when, although Annette would never swear, she would 'haul him over the coals'.[26] Jimmie reckoned his Irish temper was well matched by Annette's fiery 'Frenchisms'.[27]

At her first show at Keith's Fifth Avenue Theatre after winning the Queen of the Automobile Parade, the planks that covered the tank and kept it warm were lifted to reveal an empty pool. Someone had literally pulled the plug on her performance, and William Morris and his men were the obvious suspects.[28]

The tank took forty minutes to refill and heat.

Morris then countersued Annette for breaching the 1500-dollar a week contract she'd signed with him.

The whole legal ruckus painted Annette and Jimmie in a poor light. The entertainment journal *Variety* lambasted Annette as a 'little flopper' and claimed she 'and Mr Sullivan are rapidly becoming known as two people with not a thought in the world worth hanging on to.'[29]

Then, in the United States Circuit Court on 10 May 1909, Judge Charles Hough[30] denied a motion by Morris to prevent Annette performing for Keith. He lambasted Annette, saying that he doubted any of her statements regarding the case, 'even those under oath'.[31] Further, he said he was convinced 'that neither Miss Kellerman nor her fiancé/manager Sullivan has the slightest regard for business honour; indeed they seem incapable of understanding the obligations of a contract, and if their affidavits were important in deciding any matter of fact I should hesitate to accept the statements of either without ample corroboration.'[32]

The ruling was a landmark win for talent managers and promoters, who gained much greater protections over their contracts. Annette was enjoined to fulfil hers with Keith, but *Variety* said Keith first had to 'appease Miss Kellerman's craze for money'[33] to ensure she performed. Annette's pay was eventually boosted to 1250 dollars a week. It was a lot of money but she had to work hard for it and she claimed later that she worked for the next two years across America without a day's vacation.[34]

As Jimmie always told Annette, all publicity is good publicity and, despite the public barbs the couple endured over their attempted cash grab, lucrative offers continued to pour in through Keith's office. One of the first venues at which Annette appeared after the ruling was the open-air Hammerstein's Roof Garden atop the Victoria Theatre on New York's Seventh Avenue. It was built by German-born theatre impresario Oscar Hammerstein, whose grandson of the same name wrote the lyrics for such musicals as *The Sound of Music, Oklahoma!, The King and I, Carousel* and *South Pacific*.

In the broiling New York summer of June 1909, Annette heard that showgirls performing at the Lyric Theatre next door were struggling with the heat during their matinee performances. Annette invited them to come to her theatre and swim in the huge tank, and they splashed about like 'frisky sea lions'. The showgirls came regularly to enjoy Annette's hospitality.[35]

Annette claimed that, at another time when she was performing on the roof at Hammerstein's, a slight English youngster was making people laugh in the downstairs theatre. His name was Charlie Chaplin.

The after-effects of the court case still hurt, but sister Marcelle's arrival in New York for a holiday cheered Annette up. The sisters and Jimmie spent plenty of relaxing summer hours on the city's Brighton Beach. Marcelle also spent several days in August 1909 watching Annette film a short documentary, 'The Diving Venus', for the Vitagraph Company of America. Some of the film was shot in Vitagraph's 50-foot tank in New York and some at the ocean, and the footage would be shown in theatres around the world.[36]

The British cinema magazine *Bioscope* raved about the film, saying that Annette commanded 'one of the highest salaries ever paid a single entertainer' and is regarded 'as one of the most potent box office attractions'.

> In addition to being one of the most perfectly formed women who ever trod a stage, Miss Kellerman is singularly versatile, for she is a champion swimmer, a diver of exceptional ability, one of the best diabolo players in the world and a physical culture expert of note. In this series of views all of her gifts are exploited to greater advantage than they possibly can be shown in the narrow confines of the stage or in the constricted quarters of her stage tank. She opens with physical culture exercises; next she is seen playing at diabolo, that fascinating Parisian fad ...; and the third section of the film is devoted to her short dives and fancy swimming in the huge tank which forms a part of the Vitagraph studio equipment ... The last section of the film is devoted to her famous high dives. These were taken at the seashore and she dives into the ocean instead of into a tank, permitting far greater freedom of movement.[37]

But Vitagraph knew that the paying public wanted to see more than fancy dives and diabolo, and publicity for the film focused on what Annette was wearing, or rather, not wearing.

'Miss Kellerman,' it said, 'is seen to the utmost advantage in the famous black tights upon which the sun glints lovingly as she emerges from the water for a new dive. The dripping silk of the fleshings appears almost iridescent as the angle of reflection is changed with each sinuous move, and in the water the dashes of light as the body is raised above the surface suggests some silver-scaled mermaid disporting herself in her element.'[38]

Chapter 18

ANNETTE WAS BACK at Keith's theatre in Boston in October 1909, performing on the same stage as a teenage comedian with promise named Buster Keaton.[1]

She claimed that Keith's decision not to let her join William Morris ultimately cost Keith's business 25,000 dollars in legal fees and her increased contract. To help defray the expense, the hard-driving impresario made theatres that hosted Annette pay 100 dollars per performance to help with his costs.[2]

Annette flirted with the press, telling them the last few months had been tough and that she would soon be quitting the stage because of her love for Jimmie. 'It's not because I do not like my work,' she said, 'not because the plaudits of the audience are not sweet music to my ears, but simply because there is no ambition higher than the ambition to be a good wife. The man I am going to marry has been my manager for several years, but I expect to manage him quite successfully once he becomes my husband.'[3]

Annette really had no intention of retiring, though, because there was no business like show business.

She had been doing more work with Vitagraph and had appeared in the short films *The Bride of Lammermoor: A Tragedy of Bonnie Scotland* (1909), *Jephtah's Daughter: A Biblical Tragedy* (1909), *The Gift of Youth* (1909), and *Entombed Alive* (1909).[4]

Annette's Vitagraph films and her vaudeville shows were pushed along no end after she and Jimmie were shown the results of studies conducted on Annette's body at Harvard University, just a couple of kilometres across the Charles River from Keith's Boston theatre.

Dr Dudley Sargent, the director of Harvard's Hemenway Gymnasium and other scholarly fitness academies, had seen Annette's great swim in Boston Harbor. He liked what he saw that day and was itching to get his hands and his tape measure on her to quantify her physical proportions.

Dr Sargent had graduated from Yale Medical School in 1878, and after his marriage had broken down in the 1880s, he had devoted himself to his work as an early innovator in physical education and performance testing. The Sargent Test still bears his name, though it is more commonly known now as the vertical jump test.[5] Sargent also invented many kinds of exercise equipment based on pulleys that are still in use in gyms today.[6]

For decades, he had assembled charts plotting physical development. He went to great lengths to research the proportions of the human body, using connections at Harvard, Yale and other academies to collect data, resulting in a huge collection of assessments on more than 10,000 women.[7] He devised a graded series of charts to measure body proportion and symmetry.[8]

Defying the social norms of the time that women were best suited to being in the kitchen or as ornaments for their men, he encouraged women to take up vigorous sports and to have freedom of dress to do it, such as comfortable swimming costumes.

He and Annette were kindred spirits, and when Dr Sargent took his tape measure to Annette he came to realise that he had never seen a woman who so closely fitted his theories of physical perfection, including hip, waist and bust proportions.

Annette stripped down to her bathing suit in the professor's office. He took a tape from his trouser pocket and asked her to stand perfectly still while he took measurements all over her body. He found she was a little shorter than all the press reports had said. Then he placed the tape around her neck, her waist, her shoulders, her upper arms, her forearms, her calves, her bust. He measured the distance between her big toe and her ankle and he asked her to jump on the scales.[9]

Dr Sargent's heart was racing not just due to his proximity to a near naked woman regarded as one of the world's most stunning sex symbols, but because the measurements confirmed his theory. He had been conducting tests on the human body for a quarter of a century and at last he had found what he thought was 'perfection'.

He tested Annette's lungs by making her breathe into a rubber balloon, and he marvelled at the way it filled up almost to bursting.

The professor handed Annette a Navajo rug to wrap around herself as he escorted her into a Harvard lecture room filled with more than 200 students. He led Annette onto a platform as Exhibit A.

'Dr Sargent took off the rug and I was left standing in my little one-piece bathing suit,' she later wrote. He then gave a lesson on 'the female form divine'.

'I want you to carry this figure in your minds,' he told his students, 'and in all your work keep it as an ideal of what a woman's figure should be. Miss Kellerman is a model for all young women to pattern by her beauty of outline and artistic proportions. Miss Kellerman has an appealing calmness and at the same time has an all-round development very superior to any woman I have ever seen. I will say without qualification that Miss Kellerman embodies all the physical attributes that most of us demand in the perfect woman.'[10]

While Annette was still appearing at Keith's Theatre in Boston, a local paper reported that when vaudeville's biggest attraction came out of the water it was easy to understand how 'Professor Sargent of Harvard came to pronounce her the perfect woman'.[11]

Annette laughed off the title of 'Perfect Woman', saying she was '"perfectly healthy", that's all'. She later wrote that she took no great pride in the title; rather, she was glad the Lord had given her a 'homely face' and 'a saving sense of humour'.[12]

She described being labelled 'the Perfect Woman' because of her body as 'the most ghastly thing in the world ... Of course, every other woman said, "I don't see that she's anything".'[13] It diminished her achievements, Annette said, 'and, in any case, my face isn't perfect. There are hundreds prettier than I am and calling me the perfect woman only antagonises other women.'[14]

Not long after Dr Sargent's findings became public, Annette was interviewed by the *Chicago Tribune's* movie critic, Frances Peck Grover, who wrote under the byline Mae Tinee, a play on the word 'matinee'. 'I'd better tell you she looks as good as her pictures,' she told her readers. 'In other words, she has some figure, as a certain languid young man in our office says ... Straight and tall and perfectly rounded. She's no Maxine Elliott [a beautiful actress of the day] when it comes to her face, but it's the kind of face you like. And she has a wide mouth and white teeth and curves in her cheeks when she smiles.'[15]

Despite Annette's public modesty about her looks, she always had a healthy share of vanity. She knew how to work the cameras, too, and looked different in almost every photo. Sometimes she was cool, demure, even ethereal, sometimes tough, severe and strong. She and Jimmie both knew an endorsement from Harvard was a great marketing tool and could help her career no end.

Annette and producers of her shows began using Dr Sargent's statistics as the basis for advertising and publicity campaigns comparing Annette's measurements with the supposed vital statistics of great beauties from antiquity. The 'Perfect Woman' tag went around the world, the public being told regularly that, according to Harvard's Dr Sargent, Annette was 'slightly more beautiful than Cleopatra or the Venus de Milo'.[16]

A lot of guess work was involved in equating Annette with the ancient Greek statue of Venus, a double amputee, or the even more ancient depictions of the Egyptian queen, but some of the statistics published on movie posters and in newspapers were:

KELLERMANN.
Height: 5ft. 4in.
Neck: 12.6in.
Waist: 26.2in.
Hips: 37.8in.
Shoulders: 36.6in.
Upper Arm: 12in.
Forearm: 9.4in.
Chest: 33in.
Foot length: 9in.

CLEOPATRA.
Height: 5ft. 5in.
Neck: 13.7in.
Waist: 29.3in.
Hips: 39.6in.
Shoulders: 40in.
Upper Arm: 12.6in.
Forearm: 9.5in.
Chest: 33.4in.
Foot Length: 9.3in.

VENUS de MILO.
Height: 5ft. 4in.
Neck: 14.8in.
Waist: 31.2in.
Hips: 40.8 in.
Shoulders: 41.1in.
Upper Arm: 13.2in.
Forearm: [n/a – amputee]
Chest: 34in.
Foot Length: 10.4in.[17]

The 'Perfect Woman' was the perfect advertisement to promote swimming, and more people, especially women, began swimming for recreation, casting off their long flowing water dresses for more comfortable attire, the *New York Telegraph* reporting 'a rush of fat folk to the sea'.[18]

Being a bastion of health and fitness became one of Annette's major selling points, not just in vaudeville, but in fashion, public speaking, publishing and, who knows? The Vitagraph film, *The Diving Venus*, showcasing her swimming, diving, and exercising, had proved immensely popular, so maybe there was a future in more films showing off her figure and athletic skills?

Annette became a darling of the popular magazine *Physical Culture*, which not only promoted her views on women and their participation in sport and exercise, but added to Dr Sargent's 'Perfect Woman' tag by inventing a convoluted physical ratio for femininity.

Annette explained the magazine's method was to 'add the measurements of the chest (or bust), the hips, and the thigh, and divide this sum by the sum of the measurements of the neck, waist, wrist, ankle and one-half of the height.

'In my own case,' she said, 'the resulting figure is 113.' Similar calculations from the measurements of a number of women athletes at the time all came close to the figure of 113, and the magazine adopted the number representing the 'ideal ratio of femininity'.[19]

'As for my own measurements,' Annette wrote, 'while I do not claim them to be perfect, I do claim that they show what may be accomplished by full bodily development. In the first place I want you to know that I am not a large-framed woman. As shown by measurements of wrists and ankles I am a woman of less than average size of bone, and had I taken no pains with myself, I doubtless would be considered rather slender and underdeveloped. Again, I would have you note that I am a swimmer, which accounts for the full development of neck, chest, and upper arm, and for the only moderate development of the forearms and calves, since the muscles of these parts are the least used in swimming.'[20]

The huge publicity over Sargent's claims and the endorsement from *Physical Culture* was marketing gold for the new 59-cent

Annette Kellerman bathing suit[21] – a body-hugging one-piece covered with a tunic for modesty – and Annette Kellerman hats, which became all the rage in New York. Annette's celebrity as one of the best-known women in the city only grew with every piece of her merchandise that sold.[22] Her woollen sweater dresses that clung to the figure like a second skin also became hot items.[23]

And of course there was the lucrative lecture circuit. Not long after Annette and Jimmie first started promoting the Harvard endorsement, Annette gave a lecture to an audience of more than 1000 women at the Colonial Theatre in New York.[24] 'The Diving Venus' looked like she had been squeezed into a tight-fitting black velvet gown using corsets. But in startling fashion, and with men barred from the audience, Annette took the gown off, revealing nothing underneath but her swimsuit.

The women were young, middle-aged and elderly, but were united in the common goal of wanting to be as beautiful as they could be. Annette was their high priestess, their fitness guru, their beauty goddess. But she was one of them, and told them her lecture would be 'very informal'.

When one woman piped up to ask whether she should breathe from her thorax, Annette naïvely replied, 'Dear me, I don't know what that is. But I do know that swimming and dancing and systematic exercise and fish, eggs, and vegetables have kept me slim and graceful, and they ought to keep other women that way, too.'[25]

Annette's lectures would eventually take her across the United States, to Canada and around the world. Sometimes she would add a fencing display with her teacher, Ricardo Manrique, to show the female form at its most vibrant. 'These lectures were attended by thousands,' Annette wrote later. 'In fact, I do not believe I have ever lectured but that hundreds were turned away from the doors.'[26]

In her lectures, Annette spoke directly to women as though they were her partners in a shared health and beauty goal. She railed against the fashions of the time and the discomfort so many women experienced being squeezed into whalebone corsets that restricted their breathing and did untold harm to their circulation.

Corsets, she said, were 'fiendish things injurious both to body and health', which caused 'endless harm and misery in the world'. When tightly laced, she said they 'were nothing short of an artificial deformity'.[27] Women often carried smelling salts in case they fainted from lack of oxygen.

Annette harangued female audiences over their hobble skirts and tight waists, and their hats, which so many wore low like blinders that made it impossible to cross a street in a crowded section of the city unless there was a manly policeman 'to pilot you over because your clothes will make you timid'. She said the corset had done more to 'make physical cowards of women than any other thing since slavery. You cannot be brave if your diaphragm is squeezed and you can't breathe properly.'[28]

At another time, she said that women had been 'thoroughly imbued with the idea that it is most unladylike to be possessed of legs or to know what to do with them ... and yet she manages fairly well as a land animal and accommodates her steps to hampering petticoats with a fair degree of skill'.[29]

Annette was receiving as many as 200 letters a day from women wanting to know how to look like her, and in between stage appearances for Keith she was acting as personal trainer to seventy-five wealthy New York ladies who wanted to learn how to swim and dive.

She opened her own office at 1133 Broadway as she and Jimmie began a series of mail-order courses, costing fifteen dollars, which were aimed at providing women with exercises and healthy living advice to increase beauty, health and happiness.

For Annette, this was not just another income stream. Her father had always implored her to remember the example of her mother and the honour the French government had bestowed on her for her work in music in Australia. Fred Kellerman always stressed the principles of giving back to the community, and Annette knew that the focus she was bringing to health and fitness could only help people around the world.

To advertise her course, Annette published a forty-page booklet, *The Body Beautiful,* promising women they could have

> You can have
> **Good Health**
> and
> **A Perfect Figure**
> Under Guarantee
> without drugs, apparatus or appliances
>
> MILLIONS of people have seen in me a living demonstration of what my methods for health and body building will accomplish. The system that has transformed me from a helpless cripple and an incipient consumptive to the woman I now am, will do as much for you, no matter what your present weaknesses or imperfections of figure may be.
> By devoting fifteen minutes daily to my system, for a short time, you can reduce or build up your entire body —or more wonderful still—any part of your body, for the work can be centered upon your hips, waist, limbs—in fact, any part you wish built up or reduced. With my system you can have a figure perfectly proportioned throughout—a full, rounded neck—shapely shoulders, arms and limbs—a firm, well-developed bust—a fine, fresh complexion—a good carriage with bodily poise and grace of movement.
> My system will stimulate and regenerate your vital organs as to successfully guard against weaknesses and disorders. With my system for health and body culture, you can defy time, weakness and ill-health, for it means the complete reorganization of your body.
>
> **My Guarantee**
>
> I have written a new book, "The Body Beautiful," which tells fully how this system is making women more healthy and more beautiful. With this book, which I will send to any one, free upon request, I give full particulars of Guarantee trial plan, whereby you can demonstrate the value of my system in your own case, without risking a penny. Write for my book and "Trial plan," to-day.
>
> **Annette Kellermann**
> Room 704 M   1133 Broadway, New York

An advertisement in the April, 1911 issue of the *Woman's Home Companion* for Annette's health and fitness booklet *The Body Beautiful*.

'Good health and a perfect figure under guarantee without drugs, apparatus or appliances ... If you are too thin, too fleshy, undeveloped or unshapely, if your complexion is sallow, if you are weak, ill, tired or languid, or in any respect not as nature meant you to be, send for my booklet'.[30]

Annette told her fans that her health and exercise routines had taken her from being a 'cripple and an incipient consumptive to the woman I now am' and that she could do the same for anyone willing to devote fifteen minutes daily to her system.[31]

PERFORMING, LECTURING, publishing, and designing her range of swimming suits and hats kept Annette busy, but they didn't keep her out of trouble with the law. When New York decided in March 1910 to temporarily ban her from diving on the Sabbath, she told her audience: 'Ladies and gentlemen, I am sorry that I cannot dive this afternoon. I am as disappointed as you are, for I know you don't care a rap for diabolo. There are two husky policeman just outside and there will be a dungeon for me if I dive.'[32]

A few weeks later, she was fined thirty dollars for roaring down Broadway at what was considered a dangerous 26 miles per hour (42 km/h).[33]

Annette and Jimmie set out on a long tour of the United States, giving diving shows and fitness lectures around the country for Keith and his new business partners, the Orpheum Circuit of Theatres. Annette took her Buick on the train with her so she could motor from town to town on the West Coast.

In Seattle, Annette and Jimmie spent time with visiting Australian sports journalist Bill Corbett,[34] who was on his way home from Reno, Nevada, where he had just covered the 'Fight of the Century' on Independence Day, 4 July 1910, in which the first ever African-American world heavyweight boxing champion, Jack Johnson, all but dismembered the faded former champ, Jim Jeffries, who had been lured out of retirement as the 'Great White Hope' by an American population uncomfortable with a black titleholder.

Corbett had dinner with Jimmie and Annette at the New Washington Hotel in Seattle, and though the young loved-up couple were coy about the matter, the veteran sportswriter suspected that they'd been married in secret.

Corbett described Jimmie to his readers as 'a quiet, shrewd fellow, rather below the middle height'. He thought his accent had something of a southern drawl and he was mightily impressed by the way Jimmie had 'boomed' Annette's profile and career with his clever publicity campaigns.[35]

At every hotel where Annette and Jimmie stayed, there would be a 'Kellerman dish' on the menu, and Corbett was amazed by all the 'Kellerman hats' and 'Kellerman capes' in the windows of the big stores in all the cities he visited.

After a couple of weeks of risky dives and drives in Seattle, Annette and Jimmie roared down to San Francisco, where Jimmie pumped the newspapers as much as he could with 'Perfect

Woman' publicity, while Annette tried unsuccessfully to satisfy her need for speed.

Once again, she was arrested for driving the Buick too fast, this time by Detective James Pearl, and after spending time in the lock-up, she appeared in the San Francisco police court the next morning, 29 July 1910, a few days after what was just her twenty-fourth birthday.

The court was packed with spectators, eager to get an eyeful of the world-famous beauty.

The Oakland Tribune reported:

> Bewitchingly attired in one of the latest Paris creations which served to emphasise her press agent's advance notices that she was the most perfect woman in the world, Annette Kellerman appeared in Judge Conlan's police courts ... on a charge of speeding her auto, and gaily bantered her way to freedom. Incidentally she expressed a knowledge of police regulations and affirmed that she believes she had the number of every crossing officer in town. This may serve as a timely warning to the Oakland squad as Annette is soon to journey across the bay.
>
> 'I thought I knew all the crossing policeman,' said the diving beauty as she benignly glanced up at the court.
>
> 'How could you do that when you've only been in town four days?' inquired his Honour.
>
> 'I make it my business to know as many of them as I can,' she retorted, 'it pays in the long run and it's awfully convenient.'[36]

The case was dismissed. Annette batted her eyelashes at Judge Conlan as she waited to go back to her hotel. 'Why, you're just too nice,' she told the judge. 'You're just like the rest of the San Franciscans I have met.'[37]

Annette was unrepentant, and a few days later appeared in the paper's new motoring section, happily posing at the wheel of the Buick. She told the newspaper that she drove with such zest that her friends wondered 'whether her life would end from a reckless dive into the tank or a smash-up on some boulevard.'[38]

The last time she was in Cleveland, she said, she took her Buick around the speedway there and reached 72 miles per hour (116 km/h), and she had often done the Philadelphia to Atlantic City run at an average of more than 60 miles an hour (97 km/h).

As soon as Annette's appearances at Oakland were finished, she drove Jimmie, who was hanging on for dear life, down to Los Angeles. She told the press that she hoped she might have time to set some more speed records there 'over the more noted road racing courses'.[39]

Jimmie often found Annette's vivacious French temperament hard to understand, but he realised she had seen so much of the world and done so much, which contributed to an untiring energy and ambition. When she made up her mind to undertake something, she really went after it and never let up. She had a vitality second to none.[40]

The vaudeville tour continued right across America, with high dives, lectures that involved cutting off her tight dress to show her curves were real,[41] and more dangerous driving. Finally, she was reduced to a sobbing mess in a courtroom in Atlanta, Georgia, in April 1911 after she was accused of 'burning the wind' as she raced down Peach Street, coming close to running down three women. She was handed a fine of $25.75 and told to grow up.[42]

She would have to. Annette was about to undergo a change that would dramatically affect the rest of her life.

Chapter 19

BY THE END OF 1911, it had been two years since Annette and Jimmie had announced their engagement. Annette liked her freedom and was so busy with all the branches of the Annette Kellerman industry that, she said, there had been no time to make their partnership official.

Jimmie was a brilliant press agent who was notoriously shy when it came to publicising himself, but for a time Annette managed to lure her fiancé onto the stage and incorporate him in her act as a photographer, watching as she approached a set decorated like the beach in Dieppe, France, before stripping off her skirt and starting on her diving routine.

With her contractual obligations to B.F. Keith finally concluded, on 20 November 1911 Annette's career took a new twist when she was able to utilise the ballet skills she had been developing with Luigi Albertieri. She played the title role of *Undine* at the Winter Garden Theatre on Broadway. The prolific composer Manuel Klein had written the score for the pantomime, which was described as 'an idyll of forest and stream', and Annette was playing a water nymph in a role she was made for.[1]

Undine was part of a double-header entertainment that began with an operetta called *Vera Violetta*. It starred a young Al Jolson singing in blackface as an African-American waiter. The cast included nineteen-year-old starlet May West (she later changed her name to Mae West), who became one of Hollywood's enduring sex symbols.

Annette was proud to have the title role in a show with an all-star cast that would also include the French singer and beauty Gaby Deslys, and later the Russian dancer Mikhail Mordkin. Before opening night, Mae West left the cast after a fight with Gaby Deslys,[2] but the show went off without a hitch.

The New York Times review the next day declared:

> Al Jolson in the role of a coloured waiter succeeded in rousing the audience into its first enthusiasm in the early part of the evening, and kept them enthusiastic much of the time afterwards ... *Undine* was a daintily conceived fantasy, mostly ballet. Of course *Undine* exists chiefly for Annette Kellerman and her feats of diving ... Miss Kellerman, the nymph, made her first appearance in white fleshings and did a toe dance with considerable skill ... A change to a black swimming suit, and then Miss Kellerman did her feats of diving that are familiar to most audiences.[3]

The show was a big hit and played for 112 performances[4] before William Morris, now free to use Annette in his productions, decided to take the show to London's West End.

ANNETTE AND JIMMIE arrived in London in May 1912, only a couple of weeks after the *Titanic* sank on her maiden voyage from Southampton to New York.

While the great maritime disaster dominated the news, Annette still made front pages throughout England. She had failed in her quest to swim the English Channel, but she was returning in triumph, with William Morris and Jimmie having made sure that Annette was known as the 'Perfect Woman' throughout England, the British press describing her as the 'most beautifully formed woman of modern times'.[5]

Annette was delighted to be back in London, and the voyage also gave her the chance to see her mother, who was now writing a weekly column on music for a Paris magazine.[6]

The swimming world had changed dramatically since the last time Annette, covered in lanoline and with her father calling out instructions, had set off from Dover for France. The wind and waves had beaten Horace Mew twice more in 1906, and Jabez Wolffe, a glutton for punishment, made an extraordinary twenty-two attempts on the Channel from 1906, until he finally put his quest in the too-hard basket in 1921.

But, on 6 September 1911, on his sixteenth attempt, the big genial Yorkshireman Bill Burgess, who had been so kind to Annette when they swam the Seine together, became the second person to swim the Channel, though he took about an hour longer than Captain Webb thirty-six years earlier.

In Boston, Rose Pitonof,[7] a fifteen-year-old local girl, had become the first female to swim from Charlestown to the Boston Light, going a much longer route than Annette to avoid the shifting currents.[8]

Beatrice Kerr, who had become the toast of Australian swimming after Annette's departure overseas, had given a series of swimming exhibitions in England, but had returned Down Under in October 1911 to gradually fade out of the sport.

Annette's friend from Sydney, Cecil Healy, was preparing to race at the 1912 Olympics in Stockholm, where he and Fanny Durack, Annette's old rival, would both win gold medals.

Annette, though, was done with big-time swimming. As part of the promotion for *Undine*, William Morris hosted a press lunch for her and fifty people at London's Savoy Hotel on 14 May 1912 and 'The Perfect Woman' told the gathering of directors, managers, agents, actors, and pressmen that 'I want you to forget that I was ever a swimmer.'[9] Instead, she wanted to be known as an actor and dancer, and to not be judged on past glories.

Although the pantomime had enjoyed a three-month run on Broadway, Annette was quick to remind the pressmen at the lunch that she was not an American, nor had she become Americanised by her long stay there, a remark which made William Morris laugh loudly.

The correspondent for *The Music Hall and Theatre Review* wrote that before leaving her 'fascinating presence', at the Savoy party 'the fortunate gentlemen' surrounding Annette 'were handed a list of her measurements, whereby her figure compares favourably with those of Venus de Milo and Diana'.[10]

Undine opened at London's Oxford Music Hall on 20 May, with Annette supported by a company of thirty. By July, Annette and *Undine* had moved to the bigger Palace Theatre in the West End, and *The Sporting Life*, which had covered her Channel attempts in great detail, now reported that 'dense crowds' packed in to see her, and that many people were turned away because there were no seats left.[11] Backstage, there were always many male admirers armed with gifts, waiting to congratulate the 'Perfect Woman'.

WHILE *UNDINE* WAS PLAYING at the Palace Theatre, Annette and Jimmie had an almighty row.

Jimmie had arrived at the theatre in a 'tearing rage', something that for him was very much out of the ordinary.

Annette suspected she knew the cause of his anger but was stunned by his fury. 'Jimmie, what's the matter?' she asked.

'Listen,' he said. 'I've played nursemaid for you ever since I came to work for your father. That tramp that's hanging around the stage is just another Stage Door Johnnie. He's no good, and I'm telling him so pronto.'

Annette knew that Jimmie wouldn't hurt a fly. 'You've got a lot of cheek but if you want to know something, he doesn't mean a thing to me. His chocolates and flowers are nice, though.'[12]

Annette had found herself alone at a party given in her honour at a stately English home, where she began to ponder just how 'really grand' Jimmie was. Even though they'd been engaged for two years, she still liked the single life and resisted the idea of being permanently hitched. But she knew she was taking him for granted.

The party hosts were wonderful to her and she was flattered by all their hospitality and attention, but their son was clearly infatuated and gave Annette a 'real rush'.[13]

It made Annette recall all the kind, sweet things Jimmie had done for her: how he'd bitten his lip so many times before they became an item when she'd go off on dates with other men; how he'd wanted her to be happy and thought that confessing his love for her back then would only muck things up for her life. He imagined that one day she'd marry into real money.

Annette had kept putting off a wedding, but now she begged off from the party and rushed back to her fiancé. She was sitting in the dressing room at the Palace Theatre the following night, getting ready for her next show, when Jimmie came in.

There was an awkward silence. Then he asked sheepishly: 'So how was the party? Did you have a good time?'

Annette was just as sheepish about going there alone. 'Yes,' she said softly, looking up at Jimmie with those big eyes, 'but I missed you.'

Jimmie suddenly sparked up. 'Gee, did you?' he blurted out.

Annette rose to her feet and the pair stood there with faintly ridiculous grins. The uncomfortable silence between them broke when the stage manager knocked on Annette's door and told her it was show time.

Annette's feelings for Jimmie were stronger than she'd ever felt for anyone in her life. It terrified her. For a while, Annette ran away from the deep waters of her heart, and so did Jimmie. They constantly dodged the subject of love and only talked business.

But Annette realised how much they were aligned, despite their differences. She loved having a nice quiet person to come home to after doing two shows a day. And later, as she began to experiment with different concepts in her act, Jimmie supported every one of her new-fangled ideas.

Annette started to see how popular Jimmie was with all the other girls and women in the theatre, how they all thought he was so kind, caring and helpful.

The couple sailed for New York on 4 September 1912 aboard the White Star Line's old faithful *Majestic*,[14] which had been brought out of retirement after the company's flagship *Titanic* had sunk in April. Everyone, even those in first class, was nervous on the voyage and alert for icebergs.

With Jimmie still uncertain whether Annette was ever really going to marry him, he often sought solace in the ship's music room, playing nostalgic tunes softly by the hour. Inevitably he would soon have a sea of admirers crowding around, with young ladies hanging off every note.

Jimmie had been in love with Annette almost from the time he saw her diving on that snowy day at White City in Chicago, and Annette knew she couldn't let him get away, but … While she was fêted as a big star wherever she went, Jimmie knew her better than she knew herself – knew all her faults, her foibles.

They were complete opposites, after all. Annette was the face and body of female fitness in America, a world-record holding swimmer who went through her 'physical jerks' every morning and never missed a day practising on the ballet barre. He couldn't swim a stroke and preferred reading to exercise. Though he could be firm, even aggressive, in business dealings, he was a quiet and retiring young man, while she was so often larger than life, one of the boldest, most uncompromising performers on the world stage.

But they also had a lot in common. Both had worked from a young age to support their struggling families. Jimmie, born in the tiny Spring Hill Township in Minnesota a year before Annette, was the oldest son of James Sullivan Snr, an Ohio-born schoolteacher with Irish ancestry, and his wife, Magdalena Oakes, a local woman from a German family. Magdalena taught Jimmie to play the piano well.

Jimmie's father became a salesman but had died of a heart attack and left his wife and children broke. So Jimmie left school to support his family, eventually finding jobs in carnivals and working his way to White City in Chicago, where he met the Kellermans four years later.

Annette loved so much about Jimmie, but was he really right for her? In many ways they were soulmates, and yet they were so different …

Annette and husband Jimmie Sullivan in New Zealand a decade after their wedding. *SLNSW, MLMSS 6270, A2. 104*

As the *Majestic* was nearing New York, jangled emotions and multiple scenarios played out in Annette's heart and mind until, in her words, she 'took the bull by the horns' and asked Jimmie to take a few rounds of the ship's deck.[15]

'Let's take it easy. I hate tramping around the deck,' Jimmie said immediately. He was no athlete, so Annette offered to sit it out in the deckchairs.

'Real life isn't like books, I suppose,' Annette recalled, 'because we just sat there like a couple of dummies trying to make conversation. Finally, I gave up and we started for the lounge door. In desperation I said, "Oh Sweetheart!" Was my face red!

I never saw anyone so flabbergasted. This is the true story of how Jimmie DID NOT propose to me.'[16]

Annette and Jimmie went on a tour of the American east coast with *Undine* almost as soon as they disembarked, and when they reached Danbury, Connecticut, neither could wait any longer.

After what Annette called 'a one-night stand', they went to the City Hall on 26 November 1912 and were married there and then by William A. Leonard, a Justice of the Peace. Two of Annette's supporting cast from the vaudeville show acted as witnesses. There was not much of a honeymoon, as Annette went on stage that night.[17] Mr and Mrs Sullivan tried to keep the marriage a secret and left Danbury the next day, but word leaked out and it was in the newspapers around America within days.[18]

'Perhaps it was not an auspicious beginning for a married life,' Annette wrote. 'It is said that people don't work well together in a theatre. In my case it worked out perfectly. The very fact that neither of us did the same thing was really a boon. It was nice to have a quiet person to get along with after working two shows a day, especially when I started to launch out with new items in my act every tour I made.'[19]

ANNETTE NEEDED JIMMIE'S support more than ever when they returned to New York soon after the wedding. They were now living at a beach house on Sheepshead Bay at the end of Ocean Avenue on Manhattan Beach Park,[20] and Annette was back doing shows for Edward Albee and B.F. Keith.

Annette had received a letter from Albee, who had assumed control of Keith's theatres, to call into his office for an interview. At sixty-seven, Keith had retired from the business and was now living in Palm Beach, Florida. He was about to marry for the second time, to a bride who was forty-one years his junior. Unfortunately, Keith's heart gave out within months of the wedding.

Albee was a hard-nosed, penny-pinching boss who controlled most of America's vaudeville circuits and charged acts a 5 per cent commission on their theatrical bookings. He blacklisted anyone who baulked at the deal and tried to work for rivals such as William Morris. Albee made himself president of the United Bookings Office to oversee the commissions, and Groucho Marx, one of the artists who worked for him many years later, called the organisation 'Albee's Gestapo'.[21] When vaudeville performers tried to form a union, Albee set up the National Vaudeville Artists. Any artist who wanted to step onto his stage had to join *his* union.

Annette had an educated guess at why Albee wanted to see her. She'd been performing her diving routine in America for six years and nothing lasts forever. She was no longer the mysterious young girl in the sheer costume but a married woman of twenty-seven.

Many of her swimming records had been broken, new swimming stars had emerged, and other women around the world were also performing death-defying dives. Even Annette's 'Perfect Woman' tag was under threat from a bevy of pneumatic newcomers armed with tape measures and tight clothes, including Mae West and Zamlock Lowe, the only female law student at the University of California, who was also judged to have 'perfect proportions' by the physical culture department there.[22]

As Annette went through her morning exercises on the ballet barre at home, she was warming up for a stoush with her boss. She told Jimmie to let her do all the talking when the confrontation came.

They arrived at Albee's grand office on the fifth floor of his opulent Palace Theatre on Broadway, facing Times Square.[23] Annette was ready to fight the man she knew had made a fortune from the mirror images of her backside and her death-defying leaps into shallow tanks of water.

After a little preliminary chit-chat about Annette's not-so-secret wedding and her recent tour of the eastern states, Albee cut to the chase. 'Annette, you have been with us for many years now,' he said.

'Yes, I have,' she replied forcefully.

'Well, we think you should know that if you wish any more dates, we will have to make next season's salary less. We will have to cut it from 1500 dollars a week to 750 dollars.'[24]

Annette was seething at what she regarded as a great injustice. Jimmie had never heard her swear, but she went bloody close this

Annette Kellerman as a young ballerina in Sydney. *National Film and Sound Archive (NFSA), 585896*

Annette's swim of more than 10 miles along the Yarra put her on course to attempt the English Channel. *The Weekly Times*, 15 April 1905, p. 12.

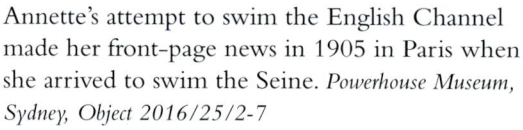

Annette's attempt to swim the English Channel made her front-page news in 1905 in Paris when she arrived to swim the Seine. *Powerhouse Museum, Sydney, Object 2016/25/2-7*

A poster for the 1909 Vitagraph documentary on Annette's performances as 'The Diving Venus'. *NFSA, 1725974*

Annette (back centre) on New York's Brighton Beach in August 1909 with her sister, Mipps, (left) and her future husband, Jimmie Sullivan (right). *State Library of NSW, MLMSS 6270*

6354.   Entrance to Wonderland, Revere Beach, Mass.

Her performances at the Wonderland amusement park at Revere Beach, outside Boston, made Annette one of America's most talked about entertainers.

A Daughter of the Gods was shot on location in Jamaica and had a cast of more than 20,000. With a budget of a million dollars, it was, in 1916, the most expensive movie ever made.

Annette carried her mermaid theme from 1914's *Neptune's Daughter* into the 1918 movie *Queen of the Sea*, shot in the American state of Maine. *NFSA, 585762*

Queen of the Sea was the last of Annette's epic water fantasy movies and the last picture she made with Bill Fox and the Fox Film Corporation.

Annette's nude scenes for *A Daughter of the Gods* in 1916 shocked some conservative Americans but passed the censors. *NFSA, 585711*

Ballet was Annette's first love and her hours of practice every day made her fit for any challenge. *Billy Rose Theatre Collection, The New York Public Library*

A mermaid tail used in Annette's stage shows. *Powerhouse Museum, Sydney, Object 2000/66/4*

One of Annette's favourite photos, from the 1920 film *What Women Love*. *State Library of NSW, MLMSS 6270*

Annette may have been billed as 'The Perfect Woman' but her vaudeville act often included a routine of her impersonating an English gentleman. *State Library of NSW, MLMSS 6270*

At fifty-one, Annette gives some tips on diving to rising young American star Mary Hoeger in Miami in 1937. *Powerhouse Museum, Sydney, Object 2012/91/3*

A hand-tinted image from Annette's 1936 underwater *adagio*. She is dressed in a gold sequinned and feathered dress. *NFSA, 584811*

As a veteran trouper, Annette added the piano accordion to her stage act. *State Library of NSW, MLMSS 6270*

Even well into her 80s, when she was living on Queensland's Gold Coast, Annette remained lithe and supple. *NFSA, 584832*

Annette reflecting on an astonishing career at her Gold Coast home at the age of 88. *TV Times*, 15 February 1975, p. 63

time. She told the former circus roustabout that she had packed out every theatre on his circuit every time she'd played there.

Albee didn't budge. 'This is so,' he said, 'but we don't think you can do it again.'

Annette leapt to her feet as though she was on the 12-foot springboard about to plunge into the deep. 'Well, Mr Albee,' she said, 'it looks as though your circuit owes me nothing. Therefore, I owe it nothing. I won't sign up again. If and whenever I do the circuit again, you will pay me 2500 dollars a week.'[25]

With that Annette and Jimmie said goodbye and turned their backs on the most powerful man in show business.

It was a bold move, but what to do now?

When they were with the journalist Bill Corbett in Seattle, Annette and Jimmie had commissioned him to arrange a season of performances in Australia. Annette had told Corbett that she wanted to see her native land again, and show everyone there the heights reached by the little girl with rickets who was once scared of the water.[26] She told Corbett that she could arrange a special troupe of vaudeville and was prepared to spend 'big money' bringing them Down Under. But, despite Corbett's contacts and his reputation, he'd found it impossible to secure the theatres for her.

Annette and Jimmie were in a quandary. They had expensive tastes that required a sizeable income.

The Vitagraph film showing Annette diving and swimming had proved a big hit around the world and motion pictures were becoming increasingly popular as entertainment and art. Actors such as Lillian Gish, Mabel Normand and Fatty Arbuckle, and directors such as D.W. Griffith and Mack Sennett were becoming household names. They packed out theatres.

Annette had a brainwave. What if she dived headlong into the film business and became a movie star?

Chapter 20

HAVING SLAMMED THE vaudeville door behind her, Annette told Jimmie she wanted to show the world she was much more than just a pretty fish.[1]

For a long time, she had been intrigued by the idea of taking her talents to the silver screen. Now, inspired by the fairy stories she read as a child, she conceived an idea for a water fantasy.

Annette had grown up with a love of pantomime[2] and she told her new husband that she had a wonderful idea for a 'water movie', complete with mermaids, based around the character of King Neptune. All the action on the water, the diving and the obligatory brief costumes would be underpinned by a dramatic love story.

'It's a lovely idea,' Jimmie replied, 'but this is a hard-boiled country. 'Pantomimes and fairytales like they do them in England have never done well over here.'

Annette was not one to give up easily. 'Well, anyway,' she said, 'will you come with me and we'll find out. We'll make the rounds.'

The newlyweds hit the offices of all the big movie identities in New York, where the movie industry was based. They were shown the door every time.

Eventually they ended up in the office of Harry Aitken, who had started life as a Wisconsin farmer but had become a key driver in the distribution of early silent films. He was about to start working with young Charlie Chaplin and would soon invest in the controversial D.W. Griffiths epic, *The Birth of a Nation*. Aitken was also one of the men behind the slapstick antics of the popular Keystone Cops.

The balding, round-faced producer was thirty-six, but looked a lot older. When Annette floated her idea for a marine fantasy, Aitken drew a deep breath and seemed to age before Annette's eyes as he shook his head.

Mary Pickford and her husband, Owen Moore, were about to star in a new production of *Cinderella*, and Aitken said he didn't have high hopes for that, pointing to a picture of Prince Charming and telling Annette and Jimmie a fantasy movie featuring that character was the biggest flop he'd been involved in.

'But Harry,' Annette ventured, 'can't you see a beautiful water scene with mermaids and sirens?'

'No,' said Harry. 'Women always looked like drowned rats to me when they come out of the water.'

So that was that. Annette and Jimmie tried the few remaining movie men on their list, but they always received the same negative reply.

Some of the producers were more than willing to make a picture, even have Annette as the star, so long as it was a comedy with plenty of pratfalls and slapstick.

Annette wanted to go in a different direction. 'There are enough people making comedies now,' she said, 'and my idea is the better one – you just wait and see.'[3]

After their final rejection, Jimmie and Annette ended up at the plush Hotel Astor meeting some friends for dinner. Inside the sumptuous dining room, Annette found herself seated beside a tall, swarthy, debonair Englishman. His name was Leslie T. Peacocke.[4] The middle-aged actor, screenwriter, and budding director, with a luxuriant waxed moustache, was a fascinating dinner companion. Born in Bangalore (now Bengaluru), India, during the time of the British Raj, he was a pukka former captain with the Connaught Rangers, an Irish regiment nicknamed 'The Devil's Own'.

Peacocke was now making a career in silent movies. He had acted in a couple, and had written several well-received short films starring leading actors of the time, including Kathlyn Williams and Owen Moore.

Peacocke and Annette got talking about his work and Annette told him her idea about beautiful mermaids in King Neptune's garden. Peacocke was hooked. Annette regarded the Englishman as 'an idealist' like her, with a love for the fantasy world of fairytales.[5] Peacocke promised to write a scenario. Now Annette had taken the plunge into the movie business.

WITH HIS FINISHED SCRIPT for *Neptune's Daughter* in hand, Peacocke asked Annette to accompany him to the office of German-born Carl Laemmle[6] (pronounced Lem-lee), who had risen from poverty to own a chain of Chicago nickelodeons, small theatres that charged five cents – a nickel – admission. A tiny man barely 150 centimetres tall, Laemmle had become a giant in the young movie industry, and at forty-six he now owned the New Jersey-based Universal Film Manufacturing Company, which would eventually operate under the title Universal Studios.

Laemmle was busy on his plans to open the world's largest motion picture production facility, Universal Studios Hollywood, on almost 100 hectares of a converted farm in the San Fernando Valley outside Los Angeles, where the constant California sunshine was gold for movie makers. He had little time to entertain even the 'Perfect Woman' as Annette, Jimmie and Peacocke sat before his desk, caps in hand.

Laemmle had grown up hungry, in the Jewish quarter of a German town, and was not one for wasting money, but he ruled his movie kingdom with good humour, unusual among the early studio moguls. Most people in the business called Laemmle 'Uncle Carl'.[7] Annette thought he was 'a dear old man',[8] but he was shrewd, too.

He had trouble getting his head around Annette's concept. 'What?' he asked her incredulously. 'A woman fish on the screen?' He peered at the three of them through his round spectacles as though they were mad.

Jimmie piped up. He was a shy and retiring man but the best of the best when it came to selling an idea. 'Listen, Mr Laemmle,'

Jimmie ventured. 'Annette came to this country with a brand-new idea, and she has packed the theatres from coast to coast, time after time.'

Laemmle shifted in his chair.

Jimmie continued with the hard sell: 'She gave the women the modern one-piece suit. She has lectured to thousands of women. Her ideas have always been up to date. Why, if you make this movie, you would be introducing thousands to see her in a new way – and you'd reap the benefit of all this publicity.'[9]

Laemmle knew having the Perfect Woman couldn't hurt audience numbers, and the less she was wearing the more eyeballs there would be. 'So there'll be spectacular diving?'

'Yes,' Annette said.

'You'll show off the figure?'

'Yes,' Annette said.

'And the swimming costume? Brief?'

'Yes,' Annette said.

With a twinkle in his eye, Uncle Carl said, 'I think you have an idea but if this is a failure, heaven help you, Jimmie Sullivan. We can't afford to spend so much money on a picture and maybe lose it.'

Laemmle took out one insurance policy against financial loss by assigning the best director he had, Irish-born Herbert Brenon,[10] to take charge. Brenon was a 34-year-old auteur, a clever young man about Jimmie's height with wavy brown hair. He saw film as high art and he oversaw every facet of a movie's production. Laemmle had concerns that Brenon didn't know what the word 'budget' was all about, but the affable young film maker was already one of the first celebrity directors. Educated at King's College in London, he had come to America at sixteen, working in vaudeville before operating his own small-town nickelodeon.

Brenon had only been directing films for two years, but he had already made more than forty, most of them shorts, though his resume included *Ivanhoe,* a 1913 epic shot in Wales with 4000 cast and crew, and in which Brenon played a leading role.

Annette loved the fact that Brenon had a love of pantomime and could see the beauty of a story involving another world under the sea. Immediately she realised that he was an ambitious young man with a quick mind.[11] Although Brenon was married, his mother, Frances, remained his closest adviser, often sitting next to him as he directed scenes.

Brenon began assembling his team to make sure that *Neptune's Daughter* would be a box office triumph. Veteran stage actor William Shay would play Annette's love interest, and the cast would also include rising star Leah Baird, who had appeared in several films opposite Douglas Fairbanks, one of the young industry's biggest drawcards. Brenon would play the movie's villain, and he began working out ways to make his character's final confrontation with Annette as the daughter of Neptune, King of the Sea, as dramatic as possible.

There were creative differences between the ambitious Brenon and the strutting Peacocke, as the director began reworking the script.[12] But Annette liked Brenon's vision, and loved the fact that they were both young and fearless with their art.

WITH BRENON'S REVISIONS to the script, the final storyline had Annette as a mermaid princess plotting to avenge the death of her sister, who was killed after being caught in a fishing net. She plans to kill the King of the Land. A Sea Witch transforms her into a mortal – though one with superhuman powers – to carry out her revenge quest.

But once on land, Annette meets a humble peasant and falls in love.

Later, at a royal ball where she plans to kill the king, she realises that the humble peasant was really the king in disguise. Her assassination plot is aborted. She returns to the sea but is so miserable that her father demands she go back to the land, become human and be with the man she loves.

While Brenon was busily assembling his cast and crew, Annette made a brief return to Paris to see her mother and siblings and to engage in some diving exhibitions there.[13] Alice was now fifty-five, but her health was patchy.

Annette's advice on beauty and vitality was still playing out around the world and in an Australian newspaper over several weeks she dispensed more advice to her faithful followers on looking taller,[14] the benefits of eight hours' sleep and plenty of sunshine,[15] 'The Importance of Correct Breathing',[16] and how to 'Acquire a Beautiful Neck'.[17]

The trip to Paris also served as a delayed honeymoon for Annette and Jimmie, and was the start of the couple's annual visits there for lavish holidays that told on their finances, despite Annette's celebrity earnings.

Jimmie recalled that the pair mostly lived quietly and simply. 'All invitations to nightclubs were taboo – we just didn't care for them,' he recalled. 'Once, I really was a night owl but found life with Annette and her friends who were outdoor "bugs" much better. Each summer we journeyed to France – Douville, Dinard, and the Riviera. She would pick up her sister and then live on the tennis courts and in the surf.'[18]

The couple returned to New York on 13 November 1913 aboard the *Olympic*, ready to make her movie. Annette posed for photos on the ship's deck as she arrived dressed in a figure-hugging dress of her own design made from velvet with white fox edging along the bottom. She also had a new companion with her, a black pug dog that she called 'Coodles'[19] or 'Cooee' for short.[20]

Annette and Jimmie would never be blessed with children. Annette never elaborated why, whether for physical or personal reasons, but fur babies became her pride and joy.

ANNETTE WAS HOME AT Sheepshead Bay for only a month before she was sailing again, on 13 December 1913, with Jimmie, Coodles, Herbert Brenon and about seventy-five members of his cast and crew. They sailed aboard the Quebec Steamship Company's SS *Bermudian*[21] to shoot *Neptune's Daughter* on the chain of islands that make up the British overseas territory of Bermuda, more than 1000 kilometres east of the United States.

Annette arrives in New York from Paris on board the *Olympic* in November 1913 with her pug dog Cooee. *Library of Congress, LC-USZ62-91616*

The pre-press publicity went around the world, with Jimmie floating a rumour 'but you didn't hear it from me!' that, to promote the movie, Annette would dive off the Brooklyn Bridge into the East River.[22]

After first considering Florida, Brenon had persuaded Annette that the British overseas territory offered some wonderful and mysterious locations for the film, including atmospheric caves and stunning, untouched forests. Since this was long before the age of package holidays and cruise ships, Bermuda remained a largely unknown location to most of the world, only adding to the exotic nature of Annette's tale of a fantasy island.

Annette and Brenon had a shared vision of this movie being the most enchanting, bewitching film ever made, and Annette told the director she would do all her own stunts when they reached

Bermuda because she regarded using a stand-in as cheating the public.[23]

Brenon had arranged for a large glass tank to film his character's underwater showdown with Annette. He also had a glass-bottom boat to film her underwater ballet.[24]

Annette worked closely with Brenon's cameraman, André Barlatier, who had started shooting films for Pathé in Paris before Carl Laemmle lured him to New York with American dollars and the promise of being the cinematographer for Universal's prestige pictures.

Annette made suggestions about the storyline and recalled that she was always on the lookout with Barlatier for locations to make the pictures more captivating. Every time Brenon got stuck for ideas, he would ask Annette, 'What do you think we should do here?'[25]

The movie would eventually have a cast of 1000[26] – mostly local extras – and it was a marvellous vehicle for showing Annette's athleticism and ballet skills as she flitted about in a thin fabric that gave the appearance of being naked while she frolicked.

Decades before Wonder Woman became a comic marvel, Annette was a kickass heroine who beat up the baddest of bad men. In one scene, she was thrown over a cliff with her hands and feet tied. Brenon had Barlatier then shot footage from their glass-bottom boat to capture Annette as she did a 'Houdini' and freed herself to then go on a one-woman search-and-destroy mission against her enemies.

The cliff was about fifty feet high (16 m), but Annette had done so much high diving all her life that it did not seem difficult, though audiences later found it breathtaking.[27]

Brenon was a good swimmer and had volunteered for a scene in which his villainous character wrestles with Annette on a clifftop before they both plunge into the sea together. 'I told him I hoped he was a good swimmer because I didn't want to have to pull him out,' Annette recalled.[28] Herbert said he could handle himself in the action scenes, even though there were no health and safety regulators on the set and there were no rehearsals to iron out any potential dangers.

Both of them were willing to try anything to make it a landmark film, even if they were hurt in the process. And they were.

In the clifftop fall, Brenon's head struck Annette's temple. Jimmie and hundreds of spectators watched on with their hearts in their mouths as both hit the water hard. Annette and Brenon floated to the surface, but while Brenon was a little groggy, Annette was out cold. Jimmie and Lewis Hooper, Brenon's assistant, roared across in a speedboat and hauled Annette to safety.

Concussed or not, Annette was ready for work the next day, 3 February 1914.[29] The show had to go on, and her fight with Brenon's villain was not over. After falling from the cliff, the script called for them to stage a fight to the death underwater. It was very nearly death for both the star and her director.

For the underwater fight scene, Brenon had organised the construction of a cube-shaped concrete tank that could hold 8000 U.S. gallons (30,000 L). It was about 5 metres square with a large pane of glass at the front through which André Barlatier could point his lights and camera to capture the action. Newspaper and magazine reporters from America had been invited over to watch the shooting of the movie's final scenes.

The glass was meant to be 1½ inches (3.7 cm) thick, but the builders had used glass only half that thickness.[30]

Still, what could possibly go wrong? The builders assured everyone that the glass in the tank was safe, but Annette was as nervous as the first time she'd climbed to the top of the diving tower at Farmer's Baths all those years earlier. Her knees were knocking as she paced up and down the beach, waiting for the call to the set.

Brenon gave final directions as the crew rushed about getting ready for the scene, lifting rocks and seaweed into the tank as scenery. Then a large turtle and a variety of fish were dropped in as extras to surround the fight action.

Jimmie and Lewis Hooper had taken the precaution of encasing their hands in hessian bags, and they put themselves on either side of the camera, ready to save Annette and Brenon from the threat of broken glass mixed with raging water.

The director and the star dressed in their costumes, which one magazine described as 'very scanty, exposing much of their naked bodies'. They climbed the ladder to enter the tank. Everyone on the set held their breath as they slowly slid into the water.[31] Then Annette and Brenon wrestled and grappled as Barlatier cranked the camera and the spectators heard it buzz.[32]

There were no problems, though Jimmie remained on alert. Annette and Brenon wrestled and wriggled some more under water. No apparent danger. Calm was restored.

Annette and Brenon were pretty satisfied with the fight scenes, but their enthusiasm to make them perfect drowned out any fears for their own safety or calls from the crew that enough was enough.[33]

They decided to shoot some more. Ever so slightly the glass began to wobble.

Standing beside the cameraman, Jimmie was yelling at Annette: 'Come on out – you've got all the scenes you want.'

She couldn't hear him. The glass wobbled a little more.

'It won't hold much longer,' Jimmie shouted. 'It's too thin for the pressure.'[34]

The onlookers watched as Annette and Brenon resurfaced for a deep breath. Then, despite the calls from Jimmie and the crew to pack it in, they dived back under the water.[35]

They had hardly gone under when there was an almighty 'Boom!' It was 'like the echo of a firing cannon and tons of water rushed through the smashing glass'.[36]

Annette and Brenon suffered horrific cuts as they were hurled through the broken glass, along with the turtle, the fish, the rocks and everything else in the tank. On their way, they knocked over Jimmie, Lewis Hooper, Barlatier and his camera.

Annette and Brenon lay motionless among the wreckage as though dead. Both were covered in blood. Brenon looked as though he had been hacked to pieces with a hatchet. He had suffered shocking cuts to his face and neck, and his left arm had been sliced open from his armpit to his wrist. That wound alone required forty-six stitches.[37]

Annette had been cut badly on the right leg and foot, and she would bear the scars for the rest of her life. But she had been spared the worst of it. With so much experience in swimming underwater she had instinctively crouched and gone with the running water so that her feet took the impact.

Brenon had fought against the surge of water as it sucked him through a jagged hole, and he received wounds to much more of his body. He spent three weeks in hospital.

It was six weeks before Annette could stand properly, because the cut on her foot was too close to the bone for stitches and it wouldn't heal. Annette was grateful her face hadn't been slashed.[38]

WHILE ANNETTE RECOVERED from the shock and pain of her wounds, Fred Cavill, her old mentor from Sydney, suffered even worse agony. His son Arthur had coached Annette before winning the Australian 220 yards professional title. Bill Corbett, the leading Sydney sports writer, had also credited Arthur, and not Alick Wickham, with originating the Australian crawl stroke, while *The Sydney Morning Herald* reported that Arthur was the originator of 'fancy diving' in Australia.[39]

Arthur had become famous in America for daring swims, and on 1 March 1914[40] he had taken up the challenge to swim 3 miles (4.8 km) across the icy waters of Seattle Harbour.

A strong wind was blowing and the cold current took Arthur considerably off course. After an hour and ten minutes in the water, he had swum 4 miles and was less than 500 metres from victory. But, utterly exhausted, he suddenly stopped swimming, grasped the gunwale of the boat accompanying him and fell into unconsciousness.[41]

Arthur could not be revived and the doctor who examined him said he was literally frozen to death, his circulation so retarded by the cold that his heart had stopped beating.

Arthur was eulogised as the first coach of Annette Kellerman.[42]

ANNETTE AND HERBERT BRENON finally limped back to the set to complete *Neptune's Daughter*, but their near-death experiences had already made it the most talked about film of the year. A magazine writer who saw the calamity wrote later that a friend had asked him: 'Do you mean to say that those two people, knowing that the tank would probably break, and that they would be cut to death, dared deliberately to climb in there?'

'Certainly,' the journalist replied. 'It was part of the work and they never even complained.'[43]

In a huge press campaign that built on the publicity from Bermuda, the distributors of the movie sent out tape measures with Annette's vital statistics marked on them, with a blurb that said she had 'measurements that almost surpass belief'.[44]

The 2½-hour, eight-reel movie opened on 25 April 1914 at New York's 'most fashionable playhouse, the Globe Theatre',[45] and even though Annette always preferred the stage to film,[46] she was thrilled that it was a runaway success and the highlight of her professional career to date. It continued the emerging trend of America's biggest playhouses staging motion pictures rather than live theatre, and she called it a 'gem of a picture', the finest work she ever did.[47]

Neptune's Daughter played to capacity houses at the Globe for almost a year. Australian newspapers eventually reported that, 'It sounds almost unbelievable that a picture play could pack a Broadway theatre for 300 nights, but that is the actual record of "Neptune's Daughter" at the Globe Theatre, New York.'[48]

Soon the movie was being called 'a masterpiece', and the 'utmost achievement of the pictorial art'.[49] It set theatre records everywhere it played, running all through the summer at Chicago's Fine Arts Theatre and scoring equal success in Boston, Philadelphia[50] and many other cities. Newspapers declared it 'the sensation of the day, for nothing as beautifully artistic, daringly realistic, or as delightfully thrilling, has ever been flashed on a stage.'[51]

In Chicago, where Annette had started her American career in entertainment seven years earlier, squads of police were needed to control crowds at the Fine Arts Theatre, with moviegoers waiting for hours in double lines around the block in the hope of getting a ticket.[52]

Neptune's Daughter cost 35,000 dollars to make and Universal Studios raked in more than a million dollars in profits.[53]

Annette was on a career high, but all she really wanted to do was see her mother in Paris to show her that the highpoint of her career had come from all her childhood devotion to fairy stories and pantomime.

Annette had no idea that four years of war would soon follow, as the whole world was drawn into the first truly global conflict. Nor did she know that, in Paris, her mother lay dying.

Chapter 21

ANNETTE AND JIMMIE sailed for Paris as the hysteria for *Neptune's Daughter* in America peaked. After a decade of building a career on distance swims and spectacular dives, Annette had finally found fame as an actress, something she had craved since her days as a child playing Lady Macbeth.

She told the press she was tired of 'flopping into tanks' and that 'the trained-seal stuff gets on one's nerves'.[1] At long last, Annette considered herself a true artist, and until the day she died she regarded *Neptune's Daughter* as her greatest work.[2]

Annette sold her stake in the film back to Laemmle for 30,000 dollars and looked for more opportunities as a serious actress and singer. Leslie Peacocke had written a musical called *The Mermaid* and Annette planned to test it in Australia before taking the show to Broadway.[3]

First, though, she contemplated two years in the French capital, staying with her mother and studying with Dame Nellie Melba among others for a career as a stage prima donna.[4] Annette and Jimmie ignored the dark war clouds looming over Europe as the world's powers engaged in an escalating arms race that could have only one outcome.

Neptune's Daughter had not been released in France, but Annette took fifty still photographs from the film to show Alice just what had become of that little girl with rickets who was once afraid of the water. She had bought her mother a three-storey, eighteenth century townhouse at Rueil-Malmaison in the western suburbs of Paris, a picturesque area near Versailles complete with cobblestoned streets, serene public parks and a château that was once home to Napoléon and Josephine Bonaparte.

Annette's older brother, Maurice, was married now[5] and making a career with his violin in New York, but Mipps and little brother Freddie were still living in the house with Alice.

As soon as Annette and Jimmie crossed the large garden and reached the double cedar doors, they knew it would be a temporary arrangement. Mipps, haggard and careworn, met them and exclaimed: 'Mum has suddenly been taken very ill.'

Annette hid her shock at Alice's ravaged condition. She spent the next few days at Alice's bedside, and was thrilled by the joy Alice showed when looking at the stills from the film. Alice smiled weakly when Annette told her that a leading American conductor, Robert Hood Bowers, had composed a beautiful score to accompany the silent movie, and mother and daughter had tears in their eyes as Alice told Annette she was thrilled by her daughter's achievements.

'It was a moment of great pride in my career,' Annette wrote later, 'that I had proved to my mother that I had inherited some of her great artistry.'[6]

ALICE CHARBONNET-KELLERMAN died at her home in Paris on 1 July 1914 and was buried with Fred at the Père Lachaise Cemetery. Among her old friends at the funeral was Cécile Chaminade, the great female composer and former classmate.

A few days earlier, a Bosnian Serb student named Gavrilo Princip had assassinated Archduke Franz Ferdinand, heir to the throne of Austria-Hungary, and his wife, Sophie, in Sarajevo. The killings ignited the powder keg of tensions that had been building for years in Europe, but Annette decided that despite the start of a global conflict, she would stay in Paris for some months, taking singing lessons from Melba, 'quite unmoved by the roar of German guns'[7] as the enemy came within 40 kilometres of the French capital during the First Battle of the Marne.

Annette was still in Paris when, on 1 November 1914, 30,000 Australian and New Zealand troops, the ANZACs, along with 7800 horses, left Albany, Western Australia, in a huge convoy of troop ships heading off to fight as part of a coalition of Britain, France and Russia against an alliance of Germany, Italy and the Austro-Hungarian Empire. The line of ships stretched for 12 kilometres. Eight days later the crew on HMAS *Sydney,* one of the escorts for the fleet, forced the German raider *Emden* to run aground on the North Keeling Island Reef off the Cocos Islands in the first major victory for Australia in what was now the First World War.

On 4 February 1915, Germany declared the waters around Great Britain and Ireland a war zone, and the commanders of their submarines – the U-boats – were told to sink all Allied vessels.

Annette and Jimmie made it back to New York safely, though, and Annette found that, almost a year after its release, *Neptune's Daughter* was still doing a roaring business across America, partly because of all the controversy over Annette's lack of clothing.

V.A. Schriber, the mayor of East Liverpool, Ohio, was appalled by a life-sized, flesh-coloured poster of Annette on a street corner promoting the film, and ordered a policeman to tear it down. The mayor declared it obscene and said it could only corrupt the morals of the town's young boys.[8] Yet in a world that would soon descend deeper into the dark and ugly turmoil of war, Annette's film would be a ray of sunshine, bringing joy and laughter and excitement to millions around the globe.

ON 15 FEBRUARY 1915,[9] ANNETTE made her debut in a musical comedy called *The Model Girl* at the new National Theatre in Washington D.C. The show would be touring for a couple of months, and Annette, travelling with Jimmie and her dog, Cooee, was the star attraction in a cast of sixty supported by a twenty-piece orchestra.[10]

Three weeks after opening in Washington, the show headed 800 kilometres west to the Grand Opera House in Cincinnati,

Ohio. The local press announced Annette as 'one of the best-known women in America' and said that, during the run in Washington she had shown herself to be 'an excellent comedienne, a gifted vocalist and splendid dancer in addition to her athletic and aquatic endowment'.[11]

The tour continued to some of the venues where Annette had starred on the vaudeville stage, including the Detroit Opera House,[12] with Annette driving a new open-top Studebaker car with Jimmie and Cooee by her side.[13]

Half a world away, at the Palace Theatre on Pitt Street, Sydney, the projectionist loaded up the first reel of *Neptune's Daughter* for its Australian premiere on 17 March 1915, a month before the ANZACs stormed onto a cove on Turkey's Gallipoli Peninsula.[14] By the end of June, *Neptune's Daughter* had finished a second record run for attendance in Sydney and was booked to play in the Sydney suburbs. A second copy of the movie was also breaking records in Queensland, while a third was about to open in Melbourne at Tait's Auditorium.[15]

No expense was spared and no exaggeration was deemed too great in promoting the film in Annette's home country. By the time Australian audiences sat down to see Annette on the screen, the 35,000-dollar budget was being reported as 200,000 dollars.[16]

'Never before have the newspapers of the world devoted so much attention or bestowed so much praise on a film production,' one advertising flyer proclaimed. 'Without exception, the metropolitan critics pronounced *Neptune's Daughter* the most wonderful artistic photo-drama ever conceived.'[17]

Interest in the film peaked around the same time that a German U-boat, U-20, torpedoed and sank the British cruise liner *Lusitania*, which had been travelling from New York to Liverpool, England. Of the 1959 men, women, and children on board, 1195 died.[18]

Bizarrely, publicity in Australia likened Annette's movie mermaid to a submarine, and promotional material for the movie included a brochure with some surprising doggerel.

> 'A submarine can swim and dart
> So fast', said Captain Carter,
> 'That if I named the craft' (he laughed),
> 'I'd call it Neptune's Darter.'
> 'The submarine that swims and dives
> Has such a knack of taking lives,
> That by your nomenclature plan
> I'd call it Annette Kill-a-man!'[19]

NEPTUNE'S DAUGHTER had been the talk of the movie world for more than twelve months, and Herbert Brenon felt like the biggest man in movies. He wanted to make an even grander epic than D.W. Griffiths' *The Birth of a Nation*, which had been released in January 1915 and, with the Ku Klux Klan as its heroes, was on its way to being the highest-grossing movie in the short history of motion pictures.[20]

Brenon conceived an extravaganza with a cast of at least 20,000, and a million-dollar budget – ten times the spend on Griffiths' homage to white supremacy.

Annette would feature as another fantasy character from an undersea world. It had to be Annette and no one else, as Brenon told a reporter from *The Cincinnati Herald*:

> When I go to the theatre to see Annette Kellerman's act, I want to sit in the back and imagine her a wonderful, animated bronze, rather than a human being. There was never a figure more inspiring to artist or sculptor than Miss Kellerman's when she is poised on the tip of a springboard just before she leaps into the air. The ancient Greek masterpieces look gross beside her.[21]

Brenon was likely influenced in creating his fantasy film by the hit Broadway play *The Darling of the Gods*, and he stimulated his creative juices by visiting the Metropolitan Museum of Art in New York to gaze at masterpieces such as *The Birth of Venus*.[22]

Following the success of Bermuda as a location for *Neptune's Daughter*, Brenon and Annette decided to shoot their new movie among the coral cays and reefs of another exotic location – Jamaica. Brenon had the idea to build an entire Moorish city from scratch and then burn the whole thing down.

'Uncle' Carl Laemmle baulked at the budget Brenon proposed, so Brenon had Annette and Jimmie accompany him to a meeting with a Hungarian-born producer with the unfortunate name of Wilhelm Fried Fuchs. After one bad pun too many, Fuchs had changed his name to William Fox.[23] Annette always called him 'Bill'.[24] He ran a company called the Fox Film Corporation, with studios at Fort Lee in New Jersey, a short ferry ride across the Hudson River from New York.

Annette remembered that Fox was more businessman than film maker, with a greater interest in the accounts than Brenon's avant-garde art. He had made his money from owning nickelodeons and then building theatres.

Brenon had become Fox's human cash register, directing three hit films for him in 1915 featuring the Fox Film Corporation's sex sirens, Theda Bara and Valeska Suratt.

The Fox publicity machine said Theda had been born in the Sahara Desert under the shadow of the Sphinx and was the daughter of an Arab sheik and a French actress. She was in fact the daughter of a Polish tailor from Cincinnati, and at the height of her fame still lived with her family. She had made her name in another Fox film called *A Fool There Was*, in which she played The Vampire, a notorious woman who sucks money out of men rather than blood. Her image as the original 'vamp' seductress continued throughout her career.

When Annette and Brenon first visited Fox to discuss their concept and the million dollars, Fox treated his visitors like 'imbeciles'.[25] He told them he was only really interested in more Theda Bara movies and the cash receipts they delivered.

But, deep down, Fox saw the livewire Herbert as the man who could take a million-dollar movie and make many millions from it. 'Herbert was Fox's little baby,' Annette recalled. 'Fox would do anything for him.'[26]

A Daughter of the Gods would be the most expensive film in the short history of movies. Money was no object for Brenon because the money wasn't his, and he and Annette began the audition process to find a flotilla of 200 attractive young women who could be taught to swim like mermaids, their tails to move in unison with no splashing.[27]

They arranged to trial a bevy of beauties at Dr Savage's 'natatorium' on West 29th Street, New York. Journalists gathered to watch the eager young hopefuls splash about, as young women of all shapes and sizes crowded the pool – on the water, under the water or languidly basking poolside.

Brenon cast a close eye over their physical contours. Annette would have to spend weeks in Jamaica training them not only to swim well but to do it with their legs tied together and encased in mesh mermaid tails.

A HEATWAVE HAD JUST broken in New York on the bright summer's day of 26 August 1915[28] as Jimmie and Annette, with black pug Cooee, boarded the cargo ship *Carillo* for the 2000-kilometre journey south to Kingston, Jamaica. Shooting for the film would begin immediately, but with war raging in Europe and the sea full of German sharks in their submarines, Annette and the 1000 other people on board the *Carillo* hoped the shooting didn't start before they got there.

Brenon had received special permission from the British government to take his production to Jamaican waters and organised a fleet of four cargo vessels from the United Fruit Company to transport his cast, crew, equipment and costumes on the long journey to the West Indies. A luxury yacht called the *Nemesis* was chartered to ferry Annette and the mermaids through the island sand reefs of Jamaica to film on different locations when they got there.[29]

But as the *Carillo* was being readied to sail, two young women stowaways were discovered trying to join the first troop of 100 water beauties. While a policeman was sought, the stowaways ran to the ship's rail and tried to escape with 'pretty dives' worthy of Annette. The young women were nabbed by longshoremen at the opposite pier, but Brenon, who had watched the performance bemused, declared that the girls 'had proved their merit and would be sent along on the next shipload of mermaids'.[30]

In dark humour peculiar to the era, *The Washington Times* reported: 'If by any chance the United Fruit Company's steamer *Carillo* strays from her course between here and Jamaica and gets into the war zone, it is hardly probable that her passengers will be lost if a submarine sends a torpedo into her. She carries a passenger list of 100 mermaids. Those who do not believe that there is such a being as a mermaid will be convinced when the new Fox spectacle is shown on the motion picture screens a few months from now.'[31]

Along with Annette and Jimmie, there were 1200 people on the Fox payroll on that first boatload heading to Kingston, among them the large cast, Brenon and his assistant directors, seven camera crews and a number of leading set designers. William Shay would again star opposite Annette, and the cinematographers would include André Barlatier, whose images from *Neptune's Daughter* had captivated the world, and Roy Hunt,[32] who would be a leading cameraman in Hollywood for another four decades.

More passengers would follow on the three other cargo ships, along with more than 1000 tons of equipment, chemicals for developing film and costumes worth 200,000 dollars.[33]

The *Carillo* avoided any German hazards that might have been off America's east coast, but when the ship arrived in Kingston, the Jamaican governor, Brigadier General Sir William Manning, threatened to blow the movie out of the water. On the pier to welcome the 'Perfect Woman' and the boy genius director, the veteran soldier took one look at Cooee and said there was no way the dog was getting off the ship.

'The inhabitants of Jamaica fear rabies more than they fear the wrath of God,' he told Annette.

'Well,' she told him, 'there ain't going to be no picture.'[34] If her canine baby couldn't stay, she'd go home too, picture be damned.

A captain from one of the fruit cargo steamers offered to take Cooee to Colon in Panama, where she would be looked after until Annette came to collect her. But then the captain of an oil tanker anchored in the bay offered to take the dog and also provide lodgings for Annette and Jimmie, who decided to abandon their suite at the United Fruit Company's plush Myrtle Bank Hotel[35] for a spartan existence on the oil ship.

'It was a case of Mahomet and the mountain. Since Cooie [sic] might not go to Miss Kellerman, the wondrously formed Annette went to Cooie,' reported the *New York Star*. 'Mr and Mrs James Sullivan's Jamaican address was the malodourous steamship.'[36]

Annette and Jimmie bought a little 'putt-putt' motor boat[37] to travel out to Cooee every night after filming. The dog's little upturned nose and huge affection were a constant source of comfort for Annette as she prepared for another round of death-defying stunts, the memories of the water tank disaster in Bermuda fresh in her mind. Likewise, Annette and Jimmie were a similarly reassuring presence for the little dog all at sea in a foreign land. With her ears pricked, Cooee 'would go crazy' every night when she heard Annette's boat coming across the water.[38]

ONCE THE COOEE standoff had been settled, Herbert Brenon began supervising his enormous production. Sir William Manning handed over much of the island to the movie people to do as they wished, knowing that they would bring money and jobs to Jamaica, even if it meant an economic vacuum when they packed up and left. To Manning's delight, the mangrove swamps around Kingston and Fort Augusta were drained to make the film sets mosquito proof and eliminate the risk of malaria.[39]

Brenon rented a large house for Annette and Jimmie,[40] but most nights they still preferred visiting Cooee on the oil tanker. The director renovated the 250-year-old ruins of Fort Augusta, a few kilometres by sea from Kingston, and inside its grounds erected a gigantic Moorish city costing 350,000 dollars[41] across 20 acres [8 hectares], complete with slave markets, mosques, minarets, bazaars and a sultan's palace with sumptuous interiors.

Herbert Brenon called the shots as a director with ideas and ambition.

One report noted: '... this city was erected in its entirety in a little more than six weeks. Its sidewalks are of bricks and concrete. The walls of the buildings are of stucco on foil lath, braced and built firmly to withstand the ravages of the tropical hurricanes'.[42]

Brenon's divers also built an underwater city in Montego Bay,[43] where Annette and the water nymphs could be filmed with a camera encased in a specially designed diving bell.

Even though he had banned Annette's dog, the Jamaican governor considered the huge amount of money Fox was pouring into the colony and allowed Brenon to create a zoological garden. A South African firm that traded in wild animals shipped in lions, tigers, elephants, panthers, flamingos, swans, baboons and rare species such as birds of paradise. There were seventy-five camels, and even kangaroos.[44]

Property workshops were built that were capable of turning out the most elaborate work, from a 'freak' horror head to a huge and gorgeously realistic elephant that could supplement the real ones. Chemical laboratories, storehouses and printing and developing plants were built for proper care of the negative. An ice plant was installed to ensure the tropical water used in development of the negatives was chilled to the right temperature.

Brenon's workmen also constructed the biggest stage in the world – 170 metres by 65 metres – so that designers could start erecting the huge sets, with as many as six companies working at one time.

Dressing rooms were built for 2000 people. Carpentry shops were established, employing 300 workmen using the latest American tools. Machine shops containing every appliance imaginable were established, along with repair shops for the fleet of ten automobiles needed to convey the companies to various parts of the island. Gasoline store houses and supply stations for oil and tyres were built.

Medical staff headquarters[45] for Dr Edward Reynolds and two assistants[46] were erected.

The cast list was extraordinary, as reporters visiting the set informed their readers:

> In addition to the 1200 actors sent from America, there will appear in the picture 10,000 Hindus interned in Jamaica since the completion of the Panama Canal; 5000 British cavalrymen, the English West Indian squadron of battleships and cruisers, and more than 5000 additional people recruited among the native Jamaicans. With a weekly salary payroll in excess of 20,000 dollars to actors and directors not counting any cost of material, it is quite possible to see for yourself that William Fox is spending one million dollars for a single deluxe feature film.[47]

It wasn't just the staggering sets and extraordinary budget that would stun audiences when *A Daughter of the Gods* was released. This was a movie woven around the almost superhuman powers of its star. Annette Kellerman always delivered for the people who paid to see her perform. In this movie her fans would see her cheat death from on high, and even swim with man-eating crocodiles.

Chapter 22

A DAUGHTER OF THE GODS was unlike anything the movie business had ever seen. Annette played a mysterious, exotic, sensual figure from a mythical kingdom, leading a cast that included near-naked mermaids and dancing girls, a sultan, sheik, prince, pirates, a harem, eunuchs, a wicked witch, a good fairy, slaves and crusaders, a charging army of gnomes, and ravenous crocodiles that turned into white swans.

Brenon's script was based on Middle Eastern folklore, and, given the scale of the sets, the size of the cast, and the money being spent, the making of the film was a tale all of its own, a fantasy within a fantasy. The unprecedented scale of the film challenged Annette to come up with action sequences even more thrilling and dangerous than the near-death experiences that had helped make her reputation.

William Fox came to the set only once before shooting began, but he became increasingly anxious as his accounts department regularly presented him with huge bills on Brenon's tab. Sixteen years earlier, Fox had been a struggling businessman with just 675 dollars[1] to his name, and the expenditure of seven figures on a movie was making him sweat.

The movie's opening credits would announce that, 'In the Land of Happiness, ruled by the Fairy of Good Kindness, there dwelled the Soul of the Song Bird in the form of the Beautiful Anitia, a free, untrammelled girl of the Ocean'.[2]

It would be the first time a major star appeared naked on

screen: Annette – or Anitia in this performance – bathes under a waterfall, her conveniently long dark hair acting as the briefest modesty shield. In another scene, dozens of mermaids dance in diaphanous cloaks, wet with sea water, their bare breasts inviting the audience's attention in scenes unlike anything ever shown by a major motion picture company.

Annette earned 1500 dollars a week, and with the movie taking nine months to shoot she would collect 50,000 dollars, the biggest payday for any movie star until that time.[3]

The money did not come easy, though. Refusing to use stunt doubles, she risked her life many times. Brenon coaxed her into one death-defying shoot after another as her character escapes all manner of close calls and cruel predicaments to eventually achieve immortality as Queen of the Mermaids.

The seven camera crews, totalling 100 men, shot 68 kilometres of film to create the 150-minute epic.[4] Each scene was captured by four cameras,[5] and Brenon employed novel colour tinting techniques to brilliant effect,[6] as well as innovative editing that employed 'almost kaleidoscopic swiftness as scenes piled upon one another'.[7]

Brenon made full use of William Manning's colonial power, and American dollars ruled as the governor effectively made the Fox Film Corporation 'the supreme sovereign',[8] with carte blanche to transform Jamaica's landscape and its economy to his requirements. *Photoplay,* the Chicago-based movie magazine, called Brenon 'The King of Jamaica'.[9] The young director thought of everything to promote loyalty from his cast and crew – it wasn't his money after all – and he had a local band playing on set constantly to keep morale high. He also let cast members keep baby sharks in his hotel bathtub, and put on a concert which raised 3500 dollars for the British Red Cross.[10]

Though Annette was a relative newcomer to the movie business and this was the biggest movie ever made, it was her vehicle. She had a steering hand with the film at every level, even with the Egyptian shipbuilders who came to Jamaica to make replicas of Byzantine vessels.[11]

Annette spent two months training the mermaids – 150 of them made it onto the screen in one scene – and she directed how they were all to look. She sourced just the right silvery cloth for their tails and had 10,000 metres of it shipped from New York. There were 1200 seamstresses, most of them locals, working on the 15,000 costumes that were needed in addition to all those brought from America.[12] The fabric did not last long in sea water and new mermaid tails had to be sewn every ten days. The costume department was under the charge of Irene Lee, whose daughters Jane and Katherine had principal roles in the movie.[13]

Annette remembered the movie fondly as 'a beautiful film' and she described as 'inspiring' the shot taken from a clifftop of 150 women with mermaid tails all swimming in unison.[14]

At the foot of the Roaring River Falls, 'one of the beauties of Jamaica', virgin rainforest was cut down so that 300 local workmen could deposit 100 cartloads of sand and clay. They then constructed an entire 'gnome city' built to scale with hundreds of houses, stores, churches, public squares and winding streets. Brenon organised 1200 local children to play the gnomes,[15] with green costumes like Santa elves, white beards and pointed caps. They referred to Annette as 'the pretty lady' and she called them 'the dearest kiddies I have ever seen'.[16] The children ranged from babes in arms to seven years old, and they earned a shilling a day, and an extra shilling if they brought a donkey.

Annette had huts built to accommodate the parents of the 'gnomes', and paid them to take time off from work to be near their children. When not on underwater assignments the mermaids acted as childminders. The children were taught fairy stories and fables so that behaving like gnomes became second nature.

In between shooting the film and visiting her dog on the oil tanker, Jamaica was a paradise playground for Annette. Fresh from its destruction of the German raider *Emden*, the Australian warship HMAS *Sydney* had been sent to Jamaica as its base to guard neutral ports in the Americas, and it would be joined

Annette's most expensive film *A Daughter of the Gods* in 1916 was also her most controversial, laden with one daring scene after another.

briefly there by HMAS *Melbourne*. Annette loved the company of her fellow Australians, and one day the *Sydney*'s skipper, Captain John Glossop, showed her pieces of the *Emden*'s wreckage that had been turned into ornaments. He gave her a piece of an oar from the wreck that became one of her treasured possessions.[17]

Sometimes Annette sped along white shell roads in a Packard automobile, but more often she cantered around on a stunning black horse called Pluto, threading through the forest amid the luxuriant tropical foliage to Manning's residence, King's House, where she and the principal members of the production were welcome guests. At the tennis courts near Jamaica's Rose Gardens, she held her own against the best players among the visiting naval officers of the British West Indian squadron. Often, she would steer the yacht *Nemesis* or the motorboat *Nerissa* across Kingston Harbour to the new but ancient-looking Moorish city at Fort Augusta.[18]

Jimmie told a magazine reporter that the movie highlighted Annette's place as the world's 'foremost exponent and exemplar of the outdoor life'.[19]

She was in the thick of the action behind the scenes and in front of the cameras for the entire shoot, one reporter remarking: 'Thus, as fencer, horseback fighter, dancer, poseuse, swimmer, diver and actress of the leading role, this extraordinary woman kept up, for three-quarters of a year in a tropical clime, her extraordinary range of activities.'[20]

Annette became such a favourite with the Jamaican children that when the script called for the gnomes to attack her, they were hesitant. 'It took the longest time to make them realise that they must whip me and push me,' Annette said, 'and when they finally decided it was alright, they did so, but with no heart in the task.'[21]

When the script called for her character to be burnt at the stake before a miraculous rescue, she was surrounded by real flames. Even though stage hands off camera surrounded her with fire extinguishers, Annette suffered burns on her right arm and leg and was confined to bed for a week.[22]

Then, clad in a complete suit of armour and mounted on horseback, Annette looked like Joan of Arc charging into battle against the ruler of the Moorish City, leading an army of gnomes behind her on ponies before that army was transformed by magic into crusaders.

'I was very proud of what I did in that picture,' Annette recalled years later. 'I rode at the head of a little army – all these little people – it was beautifully done. We had to come down a gorge to the bottom and when I think of it now I must have been mad. If I'd taken two steps the wrong way I would have been over the precipice. It never struck me that I was doing anything silly. I had no sense of danger, I really didn't.'[23]

At the time, a movie magazine reporter noted: 'Mention must be made of her marvellous scenes in the hall of the sultan's palace, her aerial somersault and dives into the gnome's pool, her marvellous poses in the woods as a child of nature, and her rare sport with the fishtailed maidens out at sea – not forgetting her stunt in swimming under water still clad in the suit of armour wherein she had fought on the city battlements.'[24]

Annette later wrote:

> What I loved best of all in *A Daughter of the Gods* was when I dived off a swing high up, seventy feet over the water. As I swung backwards and forwards over a gorgeous mirror-like lagoon, hundreds of little gnomes watched me from below.
>
> Back and forth I swung until the swing arrived at its highest peak, then I dived from it into the crystal-clear water.[25]

Annette was rarely fazed by what another writer called one 'hair-brained' idea after another.[26] For one escape, Annette had to dive out of a tower window and clear sharp rocks to land in the swirling Caribbean Sea, 103 feet below.[27] Annette was dressed in a long flowing robe of white silk, and as she came through the air she looked 'like some huge white bird'.[28] She claimed she had no fear of heights at all and never used a stunt double for anything she did.[29]

While she had faced most of the deadly challenges, Annette had definite qualms about diving into the waterfall with her hands tied behind her back – even though it was her idea.

She later claimed that Fox had crossed out the scene with a blue pen when Brenon had first shown him the script, but that she had protested by telling the producer: 'That's the way. Somebody's always trying to take the joy out of life.'

According to Annette, Fox told his stenographer to send a cable to Jamaica, ordering engineers to build a 60-foot waterfall.[30]

When it came to filming the scene, Annette eyed the location, the precipice and the rapids below. She told Brenon that she'd risked her neck plenty of times for him but on this one she wasn't so sure. Brenon tried to reassure her that it was perfectly safe. No friend of the canine species, he grabbed a little dog running around nearby and threw it into the torrent. Brenon was nonplussed, not to say shame-faced, when the dog did not resurface. Annette was even less keen to do the scene then, but when the dog was found very much alive and vocal in one of the nearby limestone caves a few minutes later, she reluctantly agreed to go through with the plan.[31]

Brenon wanted to shoot the scene before it got dark, so Annette, her hands having been tied behind her back, took a deep breath and dived into the heart of the rapids.

She survived the perilous cascade down the waterfall, and with her hands still tied behind her back, swam through mountainous waves to a reef, and 'while the waves dashed her upon the rocks', she used the sharp edges to cut the ropes that bound her hands.[32]

Brenon and his film crews finally breathed easy as Annette emerged from the ordeal alive, though covered in blood from her torn-up wrists, lucky that the jagged rocks had not cut an artery.

While William Fox was boiling at Brenon pushing the movie beyond its schedule and over its already huge budget, there was also mounting tension between Annette's director and her husband. Annette and Brenon were kindred spirits in their own way – daring risk takers with a shared passion. The movie was their baby and the pair would trek for miles through the Jamaican countryside looking for the most beautiful locations. Annette recalled that they 'did some beautiful, beautiful things' together.[33] Jimmie was concerned not so much by Annette and Brenon's emotional bond, but by all the close calls she had in making the film. Brenon was willing to push Annette to the most extreme hazards to make his film irresistible to audiences, and Annette was usually only too willing to go with his ideas.

ANNETTE BELIEVED HER most dangerous stunt in Jamaica was in a scene where two eunuchs throw her into a pool full of live crocodiles. It was her idea, she said, and since Jimmie had travelled back to New York on business at the time there was no safety catch on her daring. The American crocodile is one of the largest species of the reptiles, with males sometimes exceeding 6 metres in length and 1000 kilograms in weight. They congregate in the salty river swamps along the Jamaica coast and, according to Annette, the ones brought in for the movie were 'really savage, and fought one another all the time, chewing each other to pieces'.[34]

Jimmie had helped to collect them with Jamaican crocodile experts, believing that, while Brenon would shoot footage of the man-eating beasts, rubber ones would be used for the scenes involving Annette. He underestimated his wife's daring.

Annette could never forget the terror she faced that day to give her audience the best show she could. 'We had to have some rehearsals,' she recalled. 'They had to make it look natural. But one of the men – I don't think he wanted to do it. He kept saying, "No for you missus, no for you!"'[35]

When it came to time to shoot the scene, Brenon was going to throw a dummy crocodile into the water, but Annette said, 'No! I'll do it.' Then she had second thoughts and for a while lost her nerve. She wanted to shriek.[36]

> Finally they brought the crocodiles in. They were the real thing. You'd take a piece of wood to them and they'd snap it in half, just like that … The Sheik let four or five crocs through a sluice gate. It was real melodrama and they looked ferocious when they came through. But when a crocodile is lying with his mouth wide open and looks terrifying, he's actually calm. They let them all settle and they fed them well, and believe me I watched after that! I said, 'I'm ready.' I came down some steps with these eunuchs … Well, just out of line with the camera there was a little ladder you could go up. The idea was one [eunuch] would take my shoulders … and then the other one my feet. And then they'd go one, two, three plunk! and throw me in.[37]

Annette looked at the five ferocious crocodiles with dread. Five men were out of the line of camera to one side so they could go for the crocs if the crocs went for her.

> But what happened was that I looked down at them [the crocodiles] and all of a sudden I saw one fella that looked tremendous. And I said 'Wait a minute! Wait a minute!' I said, 'Stop Herbert! Stop! I don't want to worry you but

that one over there ... I don't like the look of him. He's got a tremendous mouth and it's facing my shoulders.' I said, 'Face my feet to them, so it's not so tempting.'[38]

Annette was bound hand and foot, and as she hit the water one of the crocodiles moved towards her. 'Zowie, it was an awful moment,' she recalled,[39] but she was up that ladder almost in the instant she touched the water.

'I must have been guarded by my Good Fairy,' Annette wrote later, 'because, though these horrible monsters attacked each other, yet when I was thrown in amongst them, they were so taken by surprise, and I was so quick getting out of the water, they did not even try to grab me.'[40]

She told journalist Nixola Greeley-Smith soon after: 'I had to do all the dangerous stunts with the crocodiles last of all, so that if anything happened to me – if by chance one of those brutes took off a leg or an arm – the picture would be released on time just the same.'[41]

When Jimmie returned from New York and heard about Annette diving in among live crocodiles he became so angry at Brenon that Annette thought there would be 'murder'. Confronting Brenon, Jimmie demanded: 'How could you let her do it?!' When Brenon shrugged and replied 'She was all right', Annette thought Jimmie was 'going to shoot him. They had to pull them apart.'[42]

It wasn't all Brenon's fault, Annette told Jimmie later. He was just over-ambitious, she said, and so was she.

'That's the way I was. I'd get carried away on things.'

While the scene would later thrill moviegoers, Annette remembered it as ultimately being 'one of the most horrible episodes of my life'. It gave her frequent nightmares about crocodiles that seemed terrifyingly real, and it brought the trouble in paradise to an explosive head.

The relationship between Jimmie and Brenon would never heal and the angst between them coincided with Fox's fury over what he saw as an enormous waste of money during production.

By the end of shooting in Jamaica, producer and director were waging war over the telephone.

Annette said Brenon's worst enemy was his mother. 'She went everywhere with him and everything that Herbert did was just right. Whether she egged him on to this and that I don't know.' In the end, Annette said, Fox and Brenon were fighting like 'cats and dogs'.[43]

The crocodile scene looked sensational, but to Annette's shock and chagrin, William Fox told everyone that the dummy reptiles Annette used were wonderful. They were so lifelike you'd swear they were the real thing, he said.

Whenever Annette and Jimmie would protest and say 'Bill, they were real crocodiles', Fox would just wave them away with a laugh.[44]

Chapter 23

FILMING IN JAMAICA FINISHED, in May 1916, with the most spectacular scene of all, as Herbert Brenon set fire to the Moorish City. Tens of thousands of people watched 350,000 dollars of Fox's money and nine months of hard work go up in smoke.[1]

The incendiary moment sparked firestorms everywhere. Soon the cast and crew had sailed from Jamaica, taking with them their American dollars and all the jobs the local people had become used to, leaving economic ash in their wake.

Brenon was ready to torch Annette's career, too, after all the heat he had taken from Jimmie over the crocodile stunt. There was no more Irish charm from the director. 'The way he spoke to me!' Annette recalled. 'We were just a few hours out from New York. Herbert said, "Well, as far as I'm concerned, you're not going to do any more pictures."'[2]

Annette was heartbroken. In a sense the pair were soulmates making art for the ages.

Brenon had gone over budget by 100,000 dollars or so. Despite the fact the movie was soon 'the celluloid mint of New York',[3] Fox was so angry about the cost of production and Brenon's insubordination, he fired the director even before the footage had been edited down to ten reels for the final two-and-a-half-hour cut. Fox appointed the experienced script writer and editor Hettie Gray Baker, later a Fox executive and author of books on cats, to re-edit the movie as Fox wanted it.

Fox removed Brenon's name from the credits and banned the director from any publicity events. He forbade him to attend the film's launch or even visit any of the Fox theatres showing *A Daughter of the Gods* across America.

Fox had decided that, as the man who stuffed the pay envelopes, he was entitled to full credit for the movie as author, producer and director.

Brenon immediately filed for a temporary injunction to stop the film being released without his due credit and sued Fox for half a million dollars for damage to his reputation. Brenon said that the sly Fox had promised him almost the entire credit for the film when it was completed.[4]

A New York judge ruled that Brenon's claim was based only on an oral agreement[5] and denied the injunction, but Brenon fought on with more legal moves.[6]

ANNETTE WAS HARDLY off the boat when she realised a lifelong ambition that had started with those ballet lessons in Sydney more than twenty years earlier. She and Jimmie were living temporarily in New York's swish Hotel Netherland, which, at seventeen storeys, was then the tallest hotel in the world.

For years, Annette had been taking ballet lessons from Luigi Albertieri – twenty dollars a lesson with as many as ten lessons a day – so that sometimes she felt like all her salary was going on dance tuition.[7]

After the lessons she would take a brisk walk around the perimeter of Central Park: from her hotel on 59th Street up Fifth Avenue, across the northern end of the park, through 110th Street, down Central Park West and back home.[8] On 16 May 1916,[9] all of Annette's training resulted in a stunning guest performance at New York's Metropolitan Opera House, where Albertieri was the ballet master.

The occasion was the All Star Musical and Novelty Benefit for the Actors' Fund of America.[10] Her invitation to appear came from Broadway producer Daniel Frohman, whose brother Charles, another leading impresario, had died on the *Lusitania* a year earlier. The program featured some of the biggest stars in America, including soprano Geraldine Farrar, baritone Antonio Scotti and violinist Fritz Kreisler. Frohman had hoped to showcase the Italian tenor Enrico Caruso, but he had sailed for Italy to see family, promising to return to New York in six months if he was not called up for the Italian army.[11]

Annette performed *The Dying Swan* solo, a dance created by the Russian ballerina Anna Pavlova, who was also performing in New York at the time. Annette stunned the audience with her performance and *The New York Star* declared: 'Signor Luigi Albertieri is the recipient of many congratulations on the surprise he helped Miss Annette Kellerman put over today at a benefit performance ... no one suspected her of being a Prima Ballerina.'[12]

The show raised 9000 dollars[13] and sparked in Annette a love for charity work that she would carry for the rest of her life. She positively swooned when Frohman exclaimed 'what a versatile and artistic girl you are' following her show-stealing routine.[14]

Annette later wrote: 'I need hardly say that this was the biggest thrill in my whole career – to dance at the Metropolitan Opera House with a 90-piece orchestra.' She only wished that her mother and father were still alive to see it.[15]

There was talk of Annette doing a double act with the Russian ballet star Vaslav Nijinsky,[16] and Annette told the press she would guarantee him 1400 dollars a week, the same as he received from the Russian Ballet at the Metropolitan.[17]

Jimmie believed that Annette's constant ballet training was the secret of her athletic success, giving her the balance, poise, strength and fitness to overcome even the most demanding physical challenges.[18]

After nine months of excitement and death-defying action in Jamaica, life in New York was sedentary by comparison, although, in reality, Annette was rarely still. She had taken up golf and hit the ball so far and straight she thought about playing professionally, but her real love remained the stage.

She and Jimmie were busy building a palatial home together in the north-east corner of Queens, at Douglas Manor, a semirural upmarket housing estate 20 kilometres from the theatres of Broadway. The house had a frontage of 22 metres, with a wing jutting out on either side. One of the wings was reserved for the family bedrooms, while the other was for guests.

At the centre was a great living room with an immense log fireplace, the walls displaying trophies of Annette's athletic exploits.

Across the road was a diving pier for Annette and a yacht dock, with two superb golf courses nearby. Jimmie had joined the Manhasset Yacht Club, and when Annette wasn't performing or attending Albertieri's ballet classes she would be in the waters of Long Island.[19]

As she basked in the success of her appearance at the Metropolitan Opera House, Annette awaited the outcome of the Fox-Brenon battle and the public reaction to her celluloid adventures in the most expensive movie ever made.

ANNETTE'S NAKED AND NEAR-NAKED scenes passed the eighteen censors at America's National Board of Review, who approved the movie 'in its entirety without change or suggested alteration of any sort'.[20] They described Annette's scenes in the surf, in particular, as 'wonderful'.[21]

Years later, Annette claimed that she wasn't really naked in the movie, that she was wearing 'a very thin pair of tights',[22] but millions of people, especially young men, gave her scenes very close inspection and no one believed her, unless the tights were made of air.

The Fox publicists declared that the movie was 'the most daring thing ever done in pictures' and 'a masterpiece of art' with 'the frequent scenes in the nude ... as graceful and free from suggestion as the rarest paintings in the Metropolitan Museum of Art'.[23]

A Daughter of the Gods premiered at New York's Lyric Theatre on 17 October 1916,[24] three months after Annette's thirtieth birthday. Brenon was still banned from attending, but the capacity guest list included not only William Fox, Annette and Jimmie, but

A Daughter of the Gods was a mix of thrilling action and sublime beauty with scenes ranging from Annette's escape from being burnt at the stake to near-naked mermaids reclining on a Jamaican beach.

stars such as Theda Bara, Ethel Barrymore and Norma Talmadge, and the financier Diamond Jim Brady. The movie screened for two and a half hours, with a five-minute intermission, and was accompanied by a Wagnerian score by Robert Hood Bowers. The audience was enthralled. Newspaper magnate William Randolph Hearst was in raptures, declaring it 'a wonderful picture, bigger than the biggest I have ever seen. Nobody should miss seeing it.'[25]

The New York Dramatic News praised the brilliance of the film-making, for which Fox now took all the credit, declaring that 'the actual mechanical perfection of the film has probably never been equalled. Camera effects, dissolves and unique photographic feats abound.'[26]

Photoplay was similarly enthusiastic: 'For sheer material size of spectacle *The Daughter of the Gods* outdoes anything yet seen ... The crowds of citizens and soldiers – countless, almost – which surcharge the great squares beneath Brenon's long shots make one involuntarily applaud the discipline and military technique which made this picture possible.'[27] Fox presented Annette's nudity as high art, although much of the publicity for the movie centred around the body of the 'Perfect Woman'. Life-sized cardboard cutouts of a scantily clad Annette, along with details about her physical measurements, were placed in cinema foyers, and every female patron was given a paper tape measure to see how she compared.

Fox sent out statistics to every media outlet in America detailing the scale of the movie and his brilliance in leadership. Key statistics included: total number of persons appearing in the picture – 21,218; largest number used in a single scene – 19,744; more than 200 mermaids and 300 dancing girls; an entire Caribbean island and all of its population utilised; a special municipality created and governed by William Fox for his thousands of employees.[28]

Fox produced a staggering fifty-two 'big feature' films in 1916, starring 100 'celebrated box office names' but he labelled *A Daughter of the Gods* 'the greatest picture ever made'[29] and sent out forty touring companies to publicise the film and assist theatres in its screening, which was fifteen more than the number of teams sent out for *The Birth of a Nation* and three times as many for another epic, *Quo Vadis*. 'There has never been a film or legitimate production exploited by means of forty companies,' *Motion Picture News* reported. 'The word "company" means a complete organization including a manager, two advance agents, a musical leader and musicians, and a crew to run the stage and the electrical and mechanical effects. For all the big-city productions, one, and some-times two, baggage cars [on trains] will be carried.'[30]

Though there were many serious injuries in shooting the film, Fox boasted that there 'was no loss of human life in the making of even the most hazardous scenes'.[31]

Not that Annette didn't go close. During a time of rampant debate in America over whether women were responsible enough to vote in presidential elections, Annette's superhero antics in *A Daughter of the Gods* went some way to swaying public opinion. One columnist remarked that anyone who believed that women were 'too weak physically to contend with a man at the voting booth and therefore should be denied the franchise, should go to see Annette Kellerman in *A Daughter of the Gods*'.[32] Another wrote that Annette displayed courage that was 'nothing short of divine'. 'If votes were obtained by physical or mental courage, Miss Kellerman would demand a million of them.'[33]

Perhaps the movie in some way encouraged the United States Congress, because before too long it ratified the 19th Amendment to the United States Constitution, giving women equal voting powers to men.[34]

At the Washington D.C. premiere of the movie, held at the Belasco Theatre, President Woodrow Wilson and Edith, the widow he had married a year before, were the special guests. Wilson, a Democrat, was facing calls for American troops to enter World War I and was in the midst of a gruelling re-election campaign, with voting just weeks away. *A Daughter of the Gods* gave Wilson welcome respite from an intensely stressful neck-and-neck race with Republican candidate Evans Hughes in the polls.

Wilson and Edith had seen motion pictures before, but only at the White House or at private entertainments. This was the first time they had ventured to a theatre together and security was tight, given the fate of Abraham Lincoln, who had been assassinated at a nearby Washington theatre half a century earlier. Newspapers around the world reported that 'The President was greatly pleased with the picture and said that *A Daughter of the Gods* was a wonderful and unusually beautiful film.'[35]

Not everyone agreed. 'Of course, *A Daughter of the Gods* does not pretend to be dramatic,' *Motion Picture News* pointed out. '... It's a fairy story, and you can take it or leave it at that. Children always enjoy fairy stories, and they certainly will enjoy *A Daughter of the Gods* ... As for grown-ups, that is quite another proposition. An evening of watching a fairy story minus anything resembling good, strong drama will hardly appeal to the general run of theatregoing and motion picture–going folk. In other words, *The Daughter of the Gods* is a big thing, but it doesn't grip.'[36]

And while the *Boston Transcript* reviewer said the movie was 'worthwhile to see' with all its 'rushing, gesticulating and fighting, galloping crowds ... as a play or a plot or an idea' it was 'drivel ... a meaningless hodgepodge of pseudo-allegorical absurdities as might be developed in a nightmare or conceived in a madhouse'.[37]

However, Fox's publicity team, with plenty of free lunches and free movie merchandise to give away, ensured that the reviews were mostly positive, even gushing, for both the movie magnate and the 'Perfect Woman' around whom the film was based. *The Wilmington Dispatch* called *A Daughter of the Gods* 'William Fox's sublime cinema achievement starring the world's most beautiful woman Annette Kellerman'.[38]

Four months after its premiere, the movie was still playing to packed houses at New York's Lyric Theatre after more than 250 consecutive matinees and evening screenings 'with no end to the engagement in sight'.[39] At the Majestic Theatre in Boston, 'all records for attendance at any theatrical attraction in that city were smashed'.[40]

At the movie's premiere in Pittsburgh, Annette appeared on stage in front of the cinema's blue plush curtains and was showered with flowers of every description, as she bowed, smiled and waved to one of the biggest theatre audiences Pittsburgh had ever seen.[41]

Some of the fawning coverage probably embarrassed Fox and Annette, but they were glad to lap it up.

Writing in the *Chicago Herald*, drama critic Jack Lait asked:

> What have you done, William Fox? You have rifled the storehouse of Fairyland and the Realm of Myths. You have photographed on man-made strips of film the ephemeral fantasies of the dreamers of Greece and the children's poets ... You have taken a woman of bone and blood and brought her back a demi-goddess ... Indeed it is a wonderful thing, this shower of magic you call *A Daughter of the Gods*. And had you combed the seven seas and all the world you could not have aimed your too-seeing camera on one more nearly heavenly, one more beautifully ideal than the exquisite superwoman Annette Kellerman.[42]

When the film opened in London, it was praised as an all-British production, given that it was filmed in a British territory, was directed by a London-educated filmmaker and starred an Australian.[43] The *Pall Mall Gazette*, which had covered Annette's long-distance swims a decade before, called it 'probably the most wonderful film ever produced'.[44]

In Sydney, where it all started for Annette, *A Daughter of the Gods* opened at Wirth's Hippodrome, two days before Christmas 1916, to rave reviews, with *The Daily Telegraph* telling holiday audiences that it was a 'truly remarkable' film that surpassed even the advance publicity because it would be difficult to imagine a more fascinating piece of work.

> The performance throughout of Miss Kellerman as the 'child of the sea' is as skilful as it is graceful and refined. Though she is scantily clad, and at times hardly clad at

all, there is nothing to which objection can be taken, so delicately does she comport herself.[45]

In Perth, the *W.A. Sportsman* newspaper was more blunt, noting that 'Annette Kellerman appears in the nude in several scenes in *A Daughter of the Gods*' and that the number of male patrons at the cinema had gone up 'in leaps'.[46]

In fact, for some male patrons it seemed that one viewing wasn't enough. In Toledo, Ohio, a man named John Watson accused his wife of assaulting him after he attended Annette's movie more than once.

Local reports said he had presented 'a pitiful sight' when he appeared in police court. Bandages covered four deep gashes in his head, inflicted, he told the mayor, by his wife wielding a potato masher.

Mrs Watson pleaded not guilty to the charge but admitted to the court: 'I assaulted him alright but I contend that I had a right to do it.' Shaking her fist at her husband she said, 'That scoundrel went to see that Annette Kellerman movie three times in three days and he'd tell me every night what a pretty form she had.'[47]

HERBERT BRENON WAS not one to sit around. While his lawsuit was pending against Fox, he formed his own company and made two more feature films before the end of 1916.

He had the last laugh. His name was finally restored to the movie's credits and over the next decade he went on to direct major pictures at Paramount, including two celebrated fantasies, *Peter Pan* and *A Kiss for Cinderella*, and the action epic *Beau Geste*. At United Artists he made the critically acclaimed drama *Sorrel and Son*, for which he was nominated for an Academy Award.

Fox recouped the huge investment in *A Daughter of the Gods* and made a 250,000-dollar profit on the 1.1 million dollars the movie eventually cost.[48] Though Fox had banned Brenon from the premier of *A Daughter of the Gods*, a reporter from *Photoplay* magazine wrote that the director was spotted in the second row at the Lyric Theatre on opening night disguised in hand-me-down clothes and a crepe-hair Van Dyke beard.[49]

Brenon never repaired his relationship with Annette and Jimmie, though. Not that they were overly concerned. By the time *A Daughter of the Gods* was breaking box-office records, Annette was perfecting a new vaudeville routine and was about to take the place of Anna Pavlova on stage at the biggest theatre in the world.[50]

She would also soon face the most dramatic moment of her life.

Chapter 24

WITH THE ENORMOUS success of two movies behind Annette, William Fox offered her a five-picture deal, but she told him her first love was the stage and she preferred to make movies one picture at a time.

Annette and Jimmie were now living in their grand home overlooking Long Island Sound, and she began experimenting with new and ever more dangerous tricks to keep audiences enthralled.

Given the fame Annette was generating as a movie actress, Edward Albee was keen to promote her again, and sent word that he wanted to let bygones be bygones and was willing to sweeten their relationship with a large amount of money. Rather than dignify Albee with a personal appearance, Annette and Jimmie sent a theatrical agent to negotiate with him instead, and they secured a deal for 2500 dollars a week for when Annette's show was ready.

Annette completely changed her vaudeville act for a new show, starting a ballet dance she called the 'peacock' in honour of the man who wrote *Neptune's Daughter*. She followed it with a physical culture routine involving stretches and bending her body into a variety of poses while she told jokes. Then, in a landscape setting inspired by the popular artist Maxfield Parrish, Annette changed into a tight scarlet one-piece bathing suit and performed a series of dives into a glass-fronted tank with coloured lights that illuminated her every movement in the water.[1]

Annette also began to experiment with wire walking, after seeing a performance by Bird Millman,[2] Colorado's Queen of the High Wire and the star attraction at Barnum & Bailey's Greatest Show on Earth. Bird had been described as a 'fairy on a cobweb' as the petite young woman from America's west danced and skipped about at death-defying heights – sometimes between skyscrapers – dressed in frilly skirts and waving a parasol as though taking a jaunt down a city boulevard.[3]

Among Annette's friends in show business were a pair of New Zealand wire walkers known as the Dunedins. When Annette asked them if they could teach her the tricks of the high wire, they thought she had gone crazy.

'Well,' Annette said, 'I am a ballet dancer. I have good poise and diving has given me a good sense of balance. There's no reason why I shouldn't become quite an expert at wire walking.'[4]

The Dunedins relented and, with Jimmie watching, heart in mouth, Annette practised every morning in New York's semi-dark Palace Theatre amid acrobats, jugglers, bicycle riders, dancers and animal acts.

Though Jimmie was always nervous about Annette's stunts, she loved the fact that he was always the first to rally around when she had a new idea. All he said when she spoke of starting on the wire was, 'All right, go ahead, but for heaven's sake don't break your neck.'[5]

CHARLES DILLINGHAM,[6] who was on his way to producing more than 200 Broadway shows, offered Annette the chance of a lifetime – to replace Anna Pavlova on stage at the biggest theatre in the world. The 35-year-old Pavlova had started to go off, leaving a sour taste with New York audiences.[7] She and her touring ballet company had performed all over the world and were a central act in Dillingham's 'Big Show' at the 5200-seat New York Hippodrome,[8] billed as the largest theatre in the world.

Dillingham was convinced that 'the little Russian dancer'[9] was no longer a big drawcard and was terminating her contract early on

Annette replaced ballerina Anna Pavlova as the headline act at the cavernous New York Hippodrome in 1917.

13 January 1917 to showcase a bigger star, Annette Kellerman, and her 'water show' featuring a school of mermaids and chorus girls.

Annette told Edward Albee to wait, and she performed her first show for Dillingham at the cavernous theatre on 15 January, with newspapers declaring that 'the new star of the Hippodrome made a great sensation at her debut' and that it appeared likely she would fill 'every single seat at the Hippodrome for every single performance'.[10]

Interviewed at the time by *Motion Picture Classic Magazine*, Annette credited her phenomenal success to 'hard work, the never-say-die spirit, and the singular good fortune of being handled by able managements.'[11]

'Modest, matter-of-fact Annette!' the magazine journalist remarked. 'There isn't an ounce of conceit in her nimble brain or her sinuously beautiful body. As she says, she is always trying. That of itself spells the difference betwixt success and failure.'[12]

Dillingham paid Annette 2000 dollars a week and for the next six months she stunned audiences in an act based around her two hit movies. Her show featured a series of glass-fronted tanks behind the Hippodrome's great sunken pool. The tanks were decorated with paintings of deep-sea coral, rocks and sea plants, and behind these were giant waterfalls as high as the Hippodrome's roof. Ballet dancers played the part of glow worms flitting about behind a screen onto which the images of fish were projected electronically. Annette trained 200 young women to play the part of mermaids and glow worms, just as she had coached the women for *A Daughter of the Gods*. The largest waterfall flowed 13 metres from the ceiling to the huge tank sunk into the stage.

As the Queen of the Mermaids, Annette thrilled audiences when she slid down a long chute and splashed into the main tank.[13] But she saved the best for last. The stage was dark except for the main tank, which was illuminated by a spotlight from above. High above, clad in bright maroon silk that clung tightly to her curves, Annette waited perfectly still on a springboard. As the spectators began to applaud, she leaped backward 13 metres, going over the waterfall and 200 of the cascading mermaids into the water.

Mipps, still in Paris during the war, was in awe when she heard of her big sister's performance, writing:

> Dillingham must have had a fine understanding and confidence in Annette's mental and physical powers, for he let her do all the stage setting etc. money and effort no object or problem. On this great stage she had a huge glass-fronted tank centre stage, then … smaller ones on either side. The setting appeared to be a series of under-water pools with a series of running cascades from above to the different pools, everything moving, waving and colourful.[14]

Annette's 2000 dollars a week seemed like a bargain with the weekly gross for the Big Show sometimes being as much as 45,000 dollars a week.[15]

Life at the Hippodrome was one of the big moments in Annette's career. It was, she said, 'a thriving beehive of star talent',[16] and on a daily basis she would chat with the teenage figure-skating sensation who went by the one name, Charlotte,[17] and the great conductor of marching bands, John Philip Sousa,[18] who wrote the marching song for the U.S. Marines and 'The Stars and Stripes Forever'. He told Annette she was his favourite movie star.[19]

War still raged in Europe, but Dillingham had big plans for Annette and Sousa.

ON 2 APRIL 1917, PRESIDENT Woodrow Wilson appeared before a joint session of Congress to request a declaration of war against Germany, citing the fact that German submarines had recently been sinking American merchant ships, as well as its attempts to entice Mexico into attacking the United States. War against Germany was declared on 6 December, and against the German ally, Austria-Hungary, the following day.

On 12 December, Annette, dressed in a white suit, white boots and wearing a white Panama hat, mounted a pure-white, frisky horse from Ringling Brothers circus as she and Sousa, the man called 'the pied piper of patriotism',[20] led a marching band on Dillingham's flag-waving parade through New York's Times Square.

The parade had been organised to celebrate the Hippodrome's twelfth anniversary, and there were exquisitely decorated floats celebrating the entertainment industry, including one featuring Neptune and his sirens and another depicting a snowy fairyland.[21] But it quickly turned into a recruiting drive, as cheering onlookers waved placards that declared 'Your Country Needs You'.[22]

Men in military uniform, boy scouts and girls clad in khaki all marched behind Annette and Sousa, along with a float with men representing the 'Spirit of 1776', dressed like George Washington's troops from the War of Independence.[23] Other performers from the Hippodrome's Big Show marched as well, including the singer Sophie Barnard, and Jennie Powers, the animal trainer for Ringling Brothers, as well as Chin-Chin the baby elephant, who ambled along in the midst of the marchers, and Monko the chimpanzee, who rode in his own small automobile, wondering what all the fuss was about.[24]

Eventually the United States would mobilize 4.7 million military personnel for the war, overwhelming numbers that hastened an end to the global conflict. All the while the war raged during the darkest period the world had yet known, Annette and other entertainers did their best to boost morale on the home front.

DURING THE MONTHS THAT Annette headlined at the Hippodrome, she practised daily on a high wire stretched 30 metres across the stage. She was working up to the most dangerous stunt of her career. William Fox had seen Annette doing 'a little fox trot on a wire' and thought she could do it in a movie, only much higher.[25] On 24 June 1917,[26] work began on what Fox called Annette's new 'sub-sea' picture that would be even 'more elaborate' than *A Daughter of the Gods*,[27] which continued to pack out theatres in America and Australia and was now being shown in China and Russia.

George Bronson Howard,[28] a leading writer of the time, had penned a script for the new film. The director would be the young but already vastly experienced John G. Adolfi.[29] Annette thought he was 'a funny little chap'[30] but, at the age of twenty-nine, he had already directed a number of successful features.

To make the movie, Fox had secured the assistance of the Smithsonian Institute of Washington, the British Museum and the United States Fisheries Commission. Scenes at the bottom of the ocean would be filmed using a patented submarine apparatus.[31]

Annette had started preparing for her new movie long before Fox announced it to the press. The film would feature a lot of Annette riding a horse at breakneck speed, so she and Jimmie took up residence at the Montauk Inn, 'a grand old-fashioned place',[32] as Annette recalled, high on a hilltop on the eastern end of New York's Long Island, where the views were 'a feast for the eyes'. The inn was surrounded by miles of open moors where Annette could spend hours on the back of her horse, Bonnie, which had a habit of bucking at the most inopportune times.[33]

Annette was not at Montauk long in June 1917[34] when she took off one morning on Bonnie, leaving Jimmie to do some paperwork at the inn. Annette revelled in the energetic ride, racing across rolling hills, marvelling at the power of the horse and the stunning beauty of her surrounds.

She was returning to the stables that afternoon when Bonnie was frightened by a car and bucked. Before Annette could regain her balance, she was flung from the horse's back and crashed into a puddle in which a large rock was submerged. Her spine smashed against the rock and she was knocked unconscious.

As time passed at the inn, Jimmie became increasingly restless, and he was constantly looking out the window and asking other guests if they'd seen his wife that day. Jimmie's anxiety grew until another hotel guest, squinting into the distance, saw a far-off white spot.

Jimmie exclaimed that Annette was wearing a white riding suit. He jumped into the car with another guest and roared across the fields until he found Annette in the puddle, 'begrimed and unconscious'.[35] He and his companion carefully loaded her into the car, drove her back to the inn and called for a doctor. The nearest one was nearly 25 kilometres away in East Hampton and took more than an hour to arrive. By then, Jimmie was in a bad state.

Annette was conscious now, but she couldn't move her legs. After examining her, the doctor told Jimmie that his wife couldn't be moved in case she suffered more spinal damage. Annette and Jimmie endured an anxious night.

The following day, a specialist arrived and the two doctors reported that while no bones were broken they would not be able to tell if Annette had suffered permanent spinal damage for a few more days.

Left with that uncertain diagnosis, Annette lay staring at the ceiling, wondering if she would ever walk or swim again. 'Poor Jimmie, every time he came into the room,' Annette recalled, 'I could tell he had been crying.'[36]

Jimmie arranged for a nurse to travel over from East Hampton, and she regularly brought food to Annette's room. But Annette was so downhearted she refused everything, so that when the two specialists arrived a couple of days later to examine her again, she was terribly weak.

When the doctors sat Annette on the end of the bed, she fainted. Jimmie was stunned, and as they let the patient rest, the doctors took Jimmie to another room to tell him that his wife's swimming and diving days were over. Dancing was a thing of the past, too.[37]

But this was a young woman who had spent her first few years in braces, and she knew what it was to overcome a disability. She decided that nothing would stop her walking.

Annette began a monologue in her head, telling herself that she could move her feet a little and that meant she could walk.

She asked her nurse to bring some soup and chicken, lots of it, because she wanted to muster all the strength she could. Annette then forced herself to wolf down everything. She asked the nurse to let her rest for half an hour, then come back and bring a watch. 'And don't tell Mr Sullivan about any of this!'

When the nurse returned, Annette asked for help to sit on the edge of the bed.

The nurse was horrified. 'Oh no, no, you must wait until the doctors come back,' she said.

'Now listen,' Annette replied. 'Please help me. I know I will be able to sit with your help.'

The nurse did as she was asked.

Annette was in agony, but through gritted teeth she managed to ask the nurse to time her in that position for three minutes.

'I fought against fainting,' Annette recalled, 'and I stuck it out. At the end of the three minutes, I was still conscious. So I said to the nurse, "Now help me to stand up. I am going to walk to the end of the room."'

The nurse watched nervously as Annette walked across the room and back to her bed again. Annette felt terribly weak and 'the pain was heavy', but she wouldn't give up.[38]

She then asked for her robe and said she was going to walk downstairs to 'Mr Sullivan'.

> It took me a long time to get down the hall. Little by little I arrived at the head of the wide old-fashioned staircase that led down to the big living room of the inn. In the corner of the large room, Jimmie was sitting on one of the wall seats and all about him were the guests of the inn. They were all trying to tell him that the doctors' decision was not final and that they were coming for a final test. Suddenly Jimmie looked up and saw me. I'm not exaggerating ... He thought he was seeing a ghost. He rushed towards me – coming fast up the stairs calling 'Sweet! Sweet!' I was so anxious to get down alone that all I said was 'now let me do it by myself'. There were only nine or 10 steps still to go but to me it seemed like many miles.[39]

When Annette reached the bottom of the stairs she almost fell on her face. Jimmie caught her and helped her to a chair, then rushed to a phone to give the doctors the good news.

With Jimmie's help Annette was eventually able to walk back up the stairs to bed.

Annette called the incident the 'most dramatic episode' of her life.[40]

Jimmie would have to aid Annette's recovery for some weeks, as she turned to ballet for therapy. At first, she could not raise her legs more than 15 centimetres as she tried to perform her exercises, but gradually her range of motion returned.

Swimming was out for some time because Annette's spine ached awfully in the cold water, but her painful daily diligence at the ballet barre paid off.

Annette had to work fast. Shooting for her new movie would begin in just a few weeks and she was facing her most dangerous stunt yet.

Chapter 25

ANNETTE WAS STILL limping and stiff, but by mid-August 1917[1] she had recovered from her injuries well enough to travel to the picturesque resort town of Bar Harbour, Maine, about 800 kilometres north-east of New York, near the Canadian border. William Fox brought together a team that included hundreds of girls playing mermaids and water nymphs, for another Annette vehicle, to be called *Queen of the Sea*.

Annette's love interest for the movie would be provided by Hugh Thompson, a descendant of America's sixth president, John Quincy Adams.[2]

The cinematography would be under the supervision of Frank D. Williams[3] and Carl Gregory. Williams had already done a great deal of work with Fatty Arbuckle and Charlie Chaplin, and was the cameraman on *Kid Auto Races at Venice*, the film debut of Chaplin's Tramp character. He was also revolutionising movie making with his patented 'Williams process', which allowed film makers to integrate an actor's movement with previously shot backgrounds.

Bar Harbour is situated on Mount Desert Island and had long been a retreat for some of America's richest families, including the Rockefellers. Annette and Jimmie, along with some of their staff, moved first into lodgings at the Old Russian Tea House, and then into a home on Ocean Drive, where they prepared for three months of filming,[4] much of it on the estate of Herbert Satterlee, America's former Assistant Secretary of the Navy and the son-in-law of financier J.P. Morgan.

Additional scenes for the movie would be shot in California, Florida, Mexico, Jamaica and Bermuda.

Annette had a wire erected about 2 metres off the ground,[5] and despite her back injury she practised wire walking every day.[6]

As soon as the couple arrived at Bar Harbour, fans were competing for the best vantage points on the beach to see the Perfect Woman. Such was the clamour for beachside seats to watch the filming that Annette hit on the idea of charging spectators 50 cents each, with proceeds going to the local hospital and to the Red Cross.[7] Soon after, Annette gave a special four-minute swimming exhibition that raised another 4000 dollars for the hospital.[8]

Among those paying to watch Annette's brief spectacle were Satterlee; John D. Rockefeller Jr; Mrs Kate Pulitzer, widow of the famous newspaper publisher; General Horace Porter, America's former ambassador to France; and Frank Polk, America's Assistant Secretary of State.[9]

Before long, many of the wealthy families on the island were having parties on the beach to watch Annette perform, getting out to the locations early, along with the crews, and setting up on the rocks with caviar and champagne from generously filled automobile hampers.[10] Each day, there would be hundreds of cars parked around the sandy stretch as the Diving Venus acted out her scenes as Merilla, the beautiful mermaid who must save four humans to earn a soul and become human herself. *The New York Telegraph* reported that watching the making of *Queen of the Sea* became high society's diversion at Bar Harbour and that eventually thousands visited the locations at Sun Rocks or at Sand Beach. One journalist estimated that, for one scene, Annette was being watched by families whose wealth added up to 400 million dollars.

Soon Annette and the rest of the cast and crew were being invited to sumptuous beach clambakes, as the mermaids, mermen and millionaires mingled. Some of the richest folks in America waited on the movie people, serving them charred corn cobs, steamed clams and broiled chicken.[11] The hundreds of young ladies in the cast were having such a good time that Adolfi had to impose an 11 p.m. curfew.[12]

Fox promised that *Queen of the Sea* would exceed 'in sumptuousness anything ever seen on stage or screen', even *A Daughter of the Gods*.[13] At one stage the assistant director, Jack Kellette, using fish as his bait, managed to lure 10,000 seagulls to the skies over Sand Beach on the Satterlee estate for an important scene. The ground was white with birds, as though there had been a snowstorm.

Fox said he was spending another million dollars on the film and no expense would be spared. A great Viking ship was built especially for the production, only to be wrecked for one of the most dramatic features of the film. Annette and Adolfi also supervised the building of a 30-metre structure called the Tower of Knives and Swords, which would be a dungeon filled with intricate machinery for the torture of the villain's victims.[14]

Along with plenty of focus on Annette wearing not much, Fox promised that there would be thrills, chills and spills into the ocean from great heights. Annette would be chained in the dungeon and attacked by live ferrets, there would be a life-and-death struggle in the raging surf, moonlight surf scenes, a battle with great balls of fire, and an escape from a bloody death by revolving knives.[15]

Filming conditions for Annette and her cast members were difficult. While Bar Harbour's rugged coastline made for great vistas, the treacherous rocks were as slippery as glass and covered with barnacles that were sharper than a serpent's tooth.[16] Mermaids and mermen often had to spend hours in water that even the ducks found icy. In case anyone was badly hurt, Fox had supplied a 'resuscitation squad' with a nurse, a 'late-model stretcher', a pulmotor artificial respiration device and a good supply of hot tea, coffee and blankets. This was all cold comfort to Annette as she waited nervously in the build-up to her great stunt of the movie, an escape on a steel wire stretched between two towers, and then a dive into the sea when her pursuers cut the wire.

It took Annette weeks to work up the courage to attempt the stunt, and even then, she wished she hadn't suggested the wire be positioned 26 metres high[17] over sharp rocks. Annette was not too proud to admit that for a long time she was 'simply petrified with fear'.[18] It had appeared so easy when she had practised near the ground. Way up high, it now looked well-nigh impossible.[19]

For three weeks Annette prepared herself for the height. She would sit for hours on a ledge atop the Tower of Knives and Swords, looking straight out over the wire. The great hazard she faced was that for the first 4.5 metres of the wire walk there were sharp rocks below and less than a metre of water. This meant that Annette had to walk 4.5 metres out on the wire before reaching the deeper water which would allow a safe dive.

The wind was another critical factor. When Annette was finally ready to perform the scene, there was a week of gusts, the last three days producing terrible, violent gales. Each day, Annette was in costume with full make-up, trying to keep her nerve as the wind blew the wire around like a piece of string.

When it finally subsided, Annette emerged from the tower. She said the first step she took on that swaying wire was the most awful in her life. If she didn't keep her balance for the first part of the stunt, she recalled, 'it was curtains for the Queen of the Sea'.[20]

A reporter for *The Moving Picture World* was among the big crowd of spectators gathered around the rocky Maine coastline in the first week of October to see if Annette would live or die. 'The danger was pointed out to her, but she declined to permit the employment of an expert wire worker,' the reporter noted.

'For more than six months she has been at work mastering this difficult art, having begun when she was appearing at the Hippodrome last spring ... [but] all of her practice on the low wire availed her nothing when it came to do the real stunt. The tempo or time of the wire was different, and Miss Kellerman found that she had to begin all over. The wire had a stretch or span of 150 feet [46 m], and ... it could not be kept taut.

'After waiting a week for a strong wind to subside Miss Kellerman decided to go ahead.'[21]

Annette's spectacular dive from the high wire between two towers in *Queen of the Sea*.

Five cameras were focused on Annette, and US Navy patrol boats circled the area, keeping any other vessels from ruining the shot. It was dangerous enough as it was, without Annette having to repeat the stunt.

Jimmie, John G. Adolfi, the camera crews and all the wealthy onlookers held their breath. Taking a deep breath herself, Annette took her first nervous step onto the wire. Immediately the wire buckled and swayed, and Annette was almost blown over by an icy wind.

From the beginning it was a struggle to keep balanced. Annette's calves and thighs burned as she used every bit of strength in them to stay upright.[22] Twice she stumbled, but she regained her equilibrium and kept tentatively moving forward.

Once she had gone far enough to be over deeper water, she dived off the wire. The gusts were so strong that they turned her in the air before she righted her body and hit the ocean perfectly.[23]

There was raucous cheering from the crowd watching.

'Everything went off all right,' Annette said later, 'but I was glad when it was over.'[24] She was also glad when Adolfi said that one take was enough and he didn't need to shoot the scene again.

Two days after the stunt, 'Skid' Williams, an expert in high explosives, used 250 sticks of dynamite to blow into dust the Tower of Knives and Swords that Annette had escaped. Huge rocks were thrown a great distance for the film's climactic scene.

A week later most of the film crew and cast packed up and headed back to Fox's studios at Fort Lee, New Jersey, to film interior shots and begin the editing process on the first section of the film. Adolfi used many innovative techniques, both in the filming of the underwater sequences and in the editing of a sword fight in the dark, illuminated only by sparks when the blades collided.[25]

Annette and Jimmie stayed on in Maine for some more exterior shots, with Annette directing some of the footage.[26] The water had been so cold in Maine that Annette and some of the cast would head for California to film underwater scenes there,[27] and to capture footage of seals frolicking.[28]

ANNETTE BECAME FRIENDLY with many of the great silent film stars of her age, working closely with some of them at Fort Lee before Fox moved most of his operation to Hollywood the following year. She had known comedy great Buster Keaton since their vaudeville days. He called her 'Ann' and promised they would make a movie together one day. Annette called him 'one of the nicest men she ever met'. Many years later, Annette was saddened that, in her words, Buster 'lost his head and drank and went to the dogs' following his tumultuous marriage to fellow actor Natalie Talmadge. Will Rogers was 'an awfully nice chap' too, and she would often go horse riding with him. She knew

Lon Chaney well, and Douglas Fairbanks, and although she didn't think much of Fairbanks, she thought his tiny second wife, Mary Pickford, was lovely.

Annette wasn't too keen on Cecil B. de Mille, who 'was very much taken up with his girls', hiding his womanising behind a veil of married respectability, but she liked his older brother William, a Broadway playwright and scriptwriter.[29] Annette was also friends with Gloria Swanson, Charlie Chaplin, Erich Von Stroheim and 'The Father of the Western', Thomas Ince, who made more than 800 films.

'At that time, Hollywood was not the Hollywood it became,' Annette recalled. 'Everybody was just scratching for bread and butter. If they were in a Fox film they were lucky. Those were the days before everyone got too high hat and got to the drink. There were no special stars.'[30]

Annette had only just arrived back in New York when she and William Farnum, another Fox star and one of the highest paid actors in Hollywood, led the Grand March through New York for the prestigious College Students' Ball.[31]

Annette started the New Year, 1918, back on stage for Edward Albee at the Palace Theatre on 2500 dollars a week in an act with ten separate parts. Variety described 'The Kellerman Big Show' as a personal triumph for Annette, since she produced it herself. It was a potpourri of vaudeville stunts, with her backing troupe of dancers dressed as flowers for one act and bathing beauties for another.

Annette appeared in a variety of outfits, including a long silver dress with a bodice that fit like a glove, and a peacock dress with blue and green sequins and a huge bunch of real peacock feathers standing out at the back.

Then she changed into a tight gold one-piece outfit to make her fancy dives, accompanied by singing girls in swimsuits.[32]

Eventually Annette would take her show on tour around America and Europe, adding a male impersonation act as an 'English Johnny' as well as more song and dance routines and a fox trot performed on the high wire.[33]

QUEEN OF THE SEA was released in September 1918, fifteen months after filming had begun at Bar Harbour. William Fox was not shy about selling himself or his products, calling his movie 'a masterpiece of film craft' and 'a riot of feminine beauty'.[34]

The Fox publicity teams worked around the clock' hyping it as 'not only one of the costliest photo-plays ever made, but also the most beautiful', with 'magnificent marine scenes, beautiful pictures of the floor of the ocean, mermaids, fairies and gnomes of the deep.'[35]

Fox told the press that more than 1500 people appeared in the movie, including the most 'shapely woman in the world'[36] and 500 other beautiful girls posing as mermaids.

Adolfi had used 50 miles of film.

'Although William Fox, the producer of *Queen of the Sea*, has long been known for the lavish way in which he spends money on his works,' newspapers reported, 'in this production he surpasses anything he has attempted.'[37]

The movie was 'bigger, costlier, more beautiful than even *A Daughter of the Gods*', Fox said, and the famous star was surrounded by 'a great galaxy of ravishing, youthful nymphs'. There was 'desperate combat between mermaids and sirens beneath the waves', and a 'terrific storm at sea, shipwreck, stirring rescues, battles of men and demons of the deep'.[38]

Annette, it seemed, could do just about anything: by November 1918, when the First World War ended, *Queen of the Sea* was reported to have 'scored a sensational success all over the country'.[39]

Her stage show for Albee was also a huge hit.

One evening while Annette was closing her West Coast tour at Albee's Orpheum Theatre in Los Angeles, Charlie Chaplin joined the audience for what he called 'a spectacular act'. Years later Chaplin recalled:

> To celebrate the ending of a long engagement, [Annette] brought on to the stage a four-year-old boy, the son of her [stage] manager, who had been amusing the scene-shifters

with some dance steps he had picked up from his father. That boy was Jackie Coogan. He delighted the jazz-fed patrons of the Orpheum to such a degree that when he had finished his performance ... they could hardly be persuaded to leave the theatre. For me, the incident was even more significant. For years I had wanted to film the story that was eventually called *The Kid* but I had postponed the production time after time because I could not find the right child for the name part. A mere chance had shown me the very boy I needed.[40]

The Kid starring Chaplin and Jackie Coogan became a cinema classic.

Eleven days before Christmas 1918, Annette shared a stage at the Palace Theatre in a benefit show with what was billed as 'the greatest galaxy of stars ever assembled in the world's greatest music hall'.[41] Among the performers were Al Jolson, George M. Cohan and Harry Lauder.[42]

Annette was the biggest name in New York vaudeville, and one of the highest paid movie stars in the world. Now she was starting a new project. She was about to become a best-selling author.

Annette's body had been the subject of scrutiny for many years; now she was about to change the way that women viewed their own bodies, forever.

Chapter 26

TO MOVIEGOERS OF 1918, Annette was beautiful, super-fit and utterly fearless, and she took that same audacious approach when it came to addressing women of the time. However, while she might have been a thoroughly modern daredevil, her ideas on love and marriage were still anchored in the Victorian era.

On matters of health and fitness Annette had been one of the most outspoken and influential women in the world for a decade. She could be just as outspoken when it came to telling women that if they wanted to keep their husbands or boyfriends it was entirely up to them. She told them they needed to work at being or staying beautiful if they were to keep men interested.

Although she and Jimmie were devoted to each other, Annette had seen enough show business philandering to know that there were many men with wandering eyes and hands. So, in 1918, building on her success as the great female action hero of the movies, Annette published two books. She intended them as a wake-up call to declare that a fit, healthy, strong, happy woman was the sexiest being in the world. No doubt her direct, 'no prisoners' approach made some women resent her lack of tact, while other women would have seen a flaw in her logic and argued that women need to care for themselves for themselves and not to please men.

'Our system of marriage,' Annette wrote in *Physical Beauty – How to Keep It*[1] 'is not sufficient to kill the deep instincts of life and love, and not only does the girl who fails to possess beauty of body fail in finding love, but the woman who loses her beauty of body fails to keep that love which she has found.'[2]

> All our religion and all our morality has failed to keep men good – if by goodness we mean for a man to remain faithful in spirit as well as in the flesh to the love of a woman who loses her physical attractiveness. So we find the world filled with unhappy homes from which love has flown with the passing of the fresh complexion and the lithe figure of girlhood, and all because of the popular fallacy that marriage blinds a man forever to feminine charms and obviates the necessity for the wife's remaining attractive ... The more intellectual women of to-day recognise that they can no longer make pretty clothes and nicely powdered noses take the place of genuine bodily beauty ... When women fade at thirty, grow fat at forty, and shrivel up at fifty, no system of morals will save them, for man's love must have feminine beauty as a flower must have water ... men will instinctively turn again and yet again to the fleeting beauty of youth.[3]

When it came to failed marriages, she wrote, 'in seven cases out of ten ... we should find that the wife had lost her physical charm for her husband'.[4]

'The average woman takes it as a matter of course that she shall "settle down" after marriage. And she usually settles with a thump ... As a result we have hundreds of young and middle-aged women, fat, shapeless, loose, engaged in a continuous struggle with their buttons; or scrawny umbrellas of women, with every curve a hollow, and every bone trying to make itself felt and seen.[5]

'Health and the beauty of health light the fires of love and keep them burning,' she declared. 'It is a more potent sermon on "How to Keep Your Husband" than all the issues of *The Homely Ladies' Journal*, which tries to answer that question with a lot of drivel about "tact" and "sympathy" and "warmed slippers" and "attractive dishes from leftovers".'

A woman 'must be beautiful of body to the very core of her being,' she propounded. 'She must have health-beauty, vital radiant health that keeps the bloom upon her cheek, the flash and sparkle in her eye, the snap and vigour in her carriage, grace in her every movement, and last but by no means least, the vivacity of mind that can no more flower in a sick and weakly body than roses can thrive on barren impoverished soil.'[6]

Annette's mail-order courses from a decade earlier often referenced her sporting career, but they were clearly aimed at women less concerned with performing physical feats and more concerned with adhering to the standards of beauty popular at the time.[7]

In those courses she encouraged women to look better for their husbands and prospective husbands, and to use her exercises to build 'a firm, well-developed bust: a fine, fresh complexion, a good carriage with bodily poise and grace of movement'.[8]

She gave advice on exercises women could do around the home, such as picking up papers in pieces from the floor without bending the knees, or reaching high up on the toes as if doing ballet.[9]

Back then, she claimed her system could help women with nervous conditions and that the exercises regenerated their vital organs to guard against ill health.

Exercise was in many ways, according to Annette, 'the one thing' that would enable women to retain their good looks under any and all conditions, and that vitality from proper exercise was 'necessary not only in rendering the body immune from disease but is a necessity to a good personal appearance'.[10] She told her older subscribers that 'freshness and bloom may be restored at least in part to every woman who has begun to fade'.[11]

Annette's 1918 book *Physical Beauty – How to Keep It* was released just before *Queen of the Sea* hit cinemas, and excerpts appeared in the press across America, with images of her displaying what so many regarded as physical perfection. She advised her readers to stand in front of the mirror naked and examine themselves. 'Is your flesh firm or is it loose or wobbly? Now bend over in various attitudes. Are there unsightly wrinkles and rolls of loose flesh?'[12]

She encouraged readers to lie on their backs, then assume a sit-up position and hold the position while grabbing their abdomens: 'If you are thin there will be rolls of skin no bigger than your fingers, if you are moderate there should be a half inch or so depth of fatty tissue as large as a broom handle. But if you are too fat there will be big rolls of loose flesh above the tightened muscles ... Don't think you can eat carelessly and be either healthy or beautiful.'[13]

Never one to mince her words, Annette was hard on her own appearance too, explaining, 'When I say exercise and diet will make a woman healthy and beautiful I don't mean she'll have a classical nose and gorgeous blonde hair. I have about three hairs myself and I don't approve of my nose at all. I mean a woman can acquire vitality, health, magnetism and symmetry.'[14]

She explained that in her opinion: 'The most important means to feminine beauty are muscular development and weight control through diet ... But one must also consider breathing and bathing, and the care of the skin; the care of the nerves by a proper balancing of work and play, rest and sleep; the care of the hair, eyes and teeth; clothing in its relation to health, and the problems of personal hygiene peculiar to women.'[15]

> Pure air, fresh air, cool invigorating air, together with those mystical elements that dwell in sunlight and the great out-of-doors are panaceas for our ailments more valuable than oceans of medicine ... Get out-of-doors and stay out at least two hours a day. Take up some form of outdoor athletics. If swimming, skating, golfing, canoeing and all the other jolly sports are not for you, then walk. Walk in the sunshine and in the wind. I almost said in the rain. Even if I had, your chance of health would be better than if you stayed indoors at all times.[16]

To Annette, swimming was 'the best sport in the world for women'.[17] It was clean and healthy,[18] she said, and had totally revamped her life when she was a child. All the success she

BEAUTY OF CARRIAGE AND GRACE OF MOVEMENT FIND EXPRESSION IN THE HANDS AND FEET.

MODIFIED FORM OF THE DIP AND PUSH-UP EXERCISE.

Annette detailed ways for women to exercise at home in her 1918 book, *Physical Beauty – How to Keep It*.

enjoyed on the world stage was down to the lessons of courage and determination that she learned in the water.

In Annette's second book of 1918, *How to Swim*, she told readers that: 'Swimming is a graceful art, and women can swim more gracefully than men. What is more, they can swim with almost as much strength, and, at least in distance swims, very nearly equal men's records …'

> There are a few men particularly adapted to distance-swimming, who by sheer size and greater brute strength, will always surpass the best records of women, but comparing the average men and women who have had an equal amount of training I believe that the women swimmers will actually show superior endurance. This is illustrated by the fact that in my second swim-through-Paris race, in which I was entered with numbers of men and women swimmers, all of the women completed the course,

whereas over 60 per cent of the male swimmers dropped out along the way. This seems to indicate (and I have observed it elsewhere) that women swimmers know how to husband their strength to better advantage. Men are more inclined to rush in with the riotous energy which they possess, and use themselves up in a short time.

Annette urged her fans to petition local governments in America to provide more public pools, because it would improve health in the community 'from 10 to 17 per cent', by her calculations. She organised an America-wide swim class that she said numbered 750,000 people. She provided members with tips on swimming in her regular newspaper columns.[19]

QUEEN OF THE SEA did not live up to Fox's expectations, with many moviegoers regarding it as a remake of *A Daughter of the Gods*, only with different costumes.

But it certainly made an impact. Fox had suggested theatre managers display large cutouts of a scantily clad Annette in 'a prominent place',[20] though the more conservative members of the public were not too thrilled at having her charms thrust their way. In May 1919, in Buffalo, New York, Captain John Marmon of the local police precinct marched into the lobby of the Family Theatre and ripped down three large pictures of Annette. Although the film had already 'made a tremendous sensation in Boston, New York and Chicago', Captain Marmon declared it was not fit to be exhibited on his watch.

Theatre manager Samuel Carver had the ban overturned, arguing that Annette's film was a 'beautiful fairy tale' which had enjoyed a huge run in New York for three months. The very same posters torn down by the police captain had been shown for weeks in front of a Boston theatre without complaint.[21]

At the time, Annette was in the middle of a cross-American road trip with Jimmie and Cooee, taking in the great wide spaces of her adopted home as she staged what she called 'the first lap of her tour around the world'.[22] Movies were all well and good she said, 'but to sit in the audience and watch yourself on the screen is a poor substitute to anyone who has been on the other side of the footlights'.[23] Vaudeville was terminally ill because of the rapid rise in the popularity of film, but Annette still wanted to wring a few years out of it if she could. In any case, she now feared being typecast, becoming a sort of female Tarzan 'going from tree to tree'.[24]

Instead, Annette went from city to city, playing the Orpheum theatres for Edward Albee across the United States: Kansas City, Missouri,[25] and Omaha, Nebraska, in February;[26] Duluth, Minnesota,[27] in March; and Portland, Oregon, in April.[28]

By May 1919, Annette, Jimmie and Cooee were in California,[29] and they decided to put down roots. They saw it as a golden state of opportunity, not just in entertainment but to further Annette's ambition to be a positive influence on women everywhere.

Chapter 27

ANNETTE AND JIMMIE took a holiday on Catalina Island,[1] off the Californian coast, and then moved into a rented house at Pasadena. Annette went to see Mary Pickford filming *The Hoodlum,* and towered over her tiny friend in some publicity shots: the Queen of the Sea with America's Sweetheart.[2] Mary told Annette she couldn't swim a stroke and Annette promised to teach her, before later explaining that Hollywood was her first stop for a world tour in which she also hoped to make a series of short films showing women how to dance and exercise.[3] She set tongues wagging in downtown Los Angeles when she went shopping in trousers.

At the time, Mipps was still in Paris, helping as a Y.M.C.A. translator for the Australian troops being repatriated back home on the great fleet of ships from France. She had a front row seat among a crowd of hundreds of thousands to watch the victory parade by detachments of all the Allied troops through Paris on 14 July 1919.

Mipps wrote to Annette to say she was going home to Australia at last, after years of stress through the war.

Annette sent an urgent telegram: 'We are going to Australia, so come over here quickly and you can come with us.'[4]

'As usual,' Mipps recalled fifty-five years later, 'she got her way and then she wrote, "Come quickly, as we'll be going soon". So I cancelled my service berth and scrambled over to the U.S.A., rushed through New York, not even taking time to see Niagara.'[5]

Annette told Mipps that they should meet up at Yosemite National Park, about 500 kilometres north of Hollywood, but, as Mipps explained, Annette wasn't there yet, having rushed off to start filming other projects, including an instructional film for women on how to master the game of golf.[6] She kept Mipps waiting for a while, but the scenery was so spectacular Mipps didn't mind.

When Annette finally turned up to Yosemite for a tearful reunion with her little sister, she and Jimmie were driving a car overflowing with cameras, props, reflecting screens and costumes. Jimmie managed to rope in a holidaying magazine journalist, Emma-Lindsay Squier, to write a feature article about Annette on location.

Emma-Lindsay found the action hero sitting on the end of a high-diving board 10 metres above the Camp Yosemite swimming pool, and reluctantly accepted her invitation to come up and join her, all the while hanging on for dear life to the sides of the plank.

Annette was wearing a blue mandarin coat over her bathing suit, and a cap of blue rubberised silk covered her hair.

'Isn't Yosemite the most wonderful place?' Annette said. 'The air is so bracing up here. Yesterday we walked miles to Glacier Point to get some scenic shots, and this morning I went up to the top of Yosemite Falls and back, and I'm not a bit tired.'

'I'm going to dive presently,' she added, leaning over and looking down at the clear green water. 'It's awfully cold – snow water from the mountains, you know.'[7]

Annette said she was tired of the water fantasy movies and thought that, 'despite her gobsmacking stunts', *A Daughter of the Gods* was 'ghastly'.

'I want people to stop thinking of me as a sort of human fish. I made my reputation by diving and swimming, of course, but since then I've done all sorts of things. In vaudeville I combined in my act wire walking, ballet dancing, fencing, swimming and general athletic exercises.'

'People ask me such funny things,' she went on with a quick humorous smile. 'They ask if I can smoke a cigarette under water or eat a banana at the bottom of the tank. I want to make them recognise me as something more dignified than a freak person who can do stunts in the water.'[8]

The writer noted that Jimmie and Annette were a very affectionate couple; he called his wife 'Tootie', and she called her husband 'Hon'.

Annette was in Yosemite filming an educational feature, she explained, showing women how they could have good health and illustrating how her athletic stunts were done.

One of the scenes was what Annette called 'Athletic Housework'. 'I pick up things from the floor without bending my knees,' she explained, 'dust the chandelier with my feet while standing on my head, and use the lamps like dumb bells.

Annette also filmed a wire-walking scene over Vernal Falls. 'Oh yes, I suppose it was dangerous, but I balanced all right, though the wind was so high that I had to throw away my Japanese umbrella and trust to my own devices. Then I drove a golf ball from "Overhanging Rock," and we'll call that "the longest drive in the world," because it's 4000 feet straight down.[9]

'This picture,' Annette continued, 'is for the purpose of showing women that they can have good health if they are willing to work for it. Not only that, but they can learn anything they like with concentration, perseverance and will power. People often say to me that I must have had a great talent for doing the things I do – but I didn't; everything that I have learned came hard.'[10]

Annette said the educational film was being shot 'first with a regular camera registering what I do, then with a slow camera which makes the action appear on the screen eight times slower than it really is, so every movement can be followed accurately.'

She later showed the writer what she meant as Jimmie directed and a cinematographer cranked his camera while Annette brought her arms straight above her head, poised on tiptoe for an instant, then, as lightly as if she had been flicked from the springboard, she went out and down in a graceful arc, cutting the icy green water so cleanly that there was not even a splash.[11]

The motivational film was being financed by a rising star in movies, Sol Lesser,[12] who saw the opportunity to marry Annette's popularity to the rising tide of female empowerment.

At seventeen, Lesser had inherited his family's San Francisco nickelodeon. He became a documentary maker and then a leading film distributor, working closely with Charlie Chaplin. By the age of thirty, Lesser hoped a movie about a thoroughly modern woman, played by Annette, would be the big hit of 1920 – the year that American women were finally given full voting rights. Lesser would spend almost half a million dollars on Annette's film,[13] to be called *What Women Love*, and Annette was to have full control.[14]

Bernard McConville, who had written many scripts for Mary Pickford and Norma Talmadge, was signed to write the screenplay, and Nate Watt directed, after the original choice, Watt's long-time collaborator – Lois Weber, the leading female director in Hollywood – had to pull out.

The message would be that the twentieth-century woman could be anything she wanted to be.

MUCH OF *WHAT WOMEN LOVE* was shot at Laguna Beach and in San Francisco Bay in early 1920, but this would be no water fantasy like Annette's three previous blockbusters. Rather, it was a modern romantic comedy. Annette was a 1920s heroine – an adventurous society girl named Annabel Cotton, whose parading around in scanty bathing suits is a constant irritant to her narrow-minded father, the head of the Purity League. Instead of a mermaid's tail, Annette wore boxing gloves. She was still the greatest female action star in movies – in one scene, she jumped from the wings of a biplane that glided about 13 metres above the sea.[15] In another scene, where she has to escape the villainous advances of a boxer, played by Bull Montana, she climbed up the 45-metre mast of a yacht and dived into the ocean, then beat her pursuer in an underwater fight by kicking him in the stomach.

Diving from the mast was another extremely hazardous stunt and Jimmie had begged Annette to substitute a dummy rather than put her own flesh and blood at risk.[16]

What Women Love featured Annette as a hard-hitting all-action tomboy looking for love.

Mipps, watching on bemused, recalled the one and only attempt with the dummy. 'Pouff! off she went, whirling and twirling around in the breeze. First one arm was gone with the wind and then followed a leg the same way and the remains floated down on the water and sank (and so did we ... in hysterics). Annette promptly got up and said, "Are you satisfied now? I'll do it." She was up that mast and out to the edge in a beautiful dive, away and safe from the intruding baddie.'[17]

Filming wrapped up in April 1920, just as Annette received an offer from Sydney entrepreneur Hugh D. McIntosh to do a ten-week tour of Australia at 5000 dollars a week.[18]

Known by the nickname 'Huge Deal', McIntosh had worked as a farm labourer, engine driver, chorus boy, stagehand, pie seller and waiter before making a fortune from sports promotion. He was the first sponsor of the New South Wales Rugby League and he built the cavernous Sydney Stadium to host world championship boxing before becoming a newspaper baron and politician. By 1920 he had started promoting major theatrical acts, and there was none bigger, in his mind, than the Australian Mermaid.

Annette was now renting a house by the seaside at Santa Monica. She was hoping to return to Australia soon, but McIntosh had a reputation as a hard man to deal with, so she played a waiting game.

'Rest and vacation are going to be my middle names,' she told reporters. 'I have put in sixteen weeks of most strenuous work. Diving from aeroplanes, and making playful leaps from the mastheads of yachts, wrestling with lustful villains, boxing with Bull Montana ... Now I'm going to enjoy myself at my new seaside home while the picture is being cut and titled, so that I will be on all twelve [cylinders] again when Sol Lesser is ready to start the production on a roadshow tour.'[19]

WHAT WOMEN LOVE premiered at the Temple Theatre in Santa Ana, south-east of Los Angeles, on 1 June 1920. *Photoplay* magazine called it 'a fine picture for the Kellerman fans and an entertaining picture for anyone ... a story which seeks to prove that even a goggle-eyed mollycoddle may win a heroine if he will mend his ways and learn how to fight ... What women love is a fighting man.'[20]

Sol Lesser promoted the film as 'a thrilling love romance' featuring the kidnapping of a girl; her imprisonment on a yacht; her battle for honour; the revolt of her crew and thrilling rescue; and the conversion of "a Willie boy" to a regular he-man with a wallop.[21]

He said the movie contained '210 smiles, 76 big laughs, 29 thrills, 16 scares, and 4 big sensations (count them for yourself!).'[22]

To promote the movie and to continue her own stage career, Annette, Jimmie and Mipps prepared to embark on a national tour by car with what she called 'a vaudeville revue deluxe',[23] a show that would incorporate the lifestyle films she had shot in Yosemite and other parts of California.

Annette told reporters that this would be her farewell tour of America as she now wanted to go home first before performing in Europe again.[24] She, Jimmie and Mipps would be travelling with a large cast and crew, including a man who would be paid to play tennis with Annette every day.

Annette had won tennis tournaments as a teenager, and the game had become immensely popular in America after World War I. Frenchwoman Suzanne Lenglen had just won the Wimbledon singles and doubles titles and was training in America for the 1920 Antwerp Olympics. Los Angeles had a huge interest in the game, with local champions Mary Browne and Tom Bundy and his wife, May Sutton, both of whom were leading international players.

Annette had taken lessons from the Sutton family for two or three hours a day, and before long Bundy, the first president of the Los Angeles Tennis Club, was presenting Annette with a trophy as its ladies' champion. Annette wanted to keep her serve and volley game alive, even on the road.

Annette and her entourage travelled east via the Mojave Desert in the direction of New Orleans, Baton Rouge and Memphis; following the Missouri River to Kansas; then on to St. Louis; Madison, Wisconsin; Iowa City; Duluth, Minnesota; and then driving on into Canada; Winnipeg, Calgary, Edmonton and Vancouver, before coming back to her house through Seattle, Oakland, Salt Lake City and Denver.

When Annette finally made it back to Santa Monica, she had only enough time to do some publicity work with her old pal from Sydney, Snowy Baker, who was now making a career in Hollywood, too. Then she and her entourage of twenty-three – Jimmie; Mipps, who was now designing all the costumes for the vaudeville revue;[25] and the cast and crew of her show – boarded the *Ventura* in San Francisco on 3 May 1921 for a twenty-one-day voyage across the Pacific. The long voyage would finally deliver the ever-patient Mipps back home to Australia and take Annette to her rapturous fans on home soil.

Annette was as excited as when she and her father had left Adelaide bound for London, as second-class passengers with first-class dreams.

She was eighteen then. Now she was almost thirty-five, with a public image as a daughter of the gods. But she was also like a little girl again, giddy with excitement when she thought about how far she'd come from her days in braces at Farmer's Baths.

Annette was on top of the world, sailing home as the Queen of the Sea.

Chapter 28

'COOEE!'

The traditional Australian call echoed around Sydney's Circular Quay as the *Ventura* neared the Oceanic Steamship Co.'s wharf. The morning of Tuesday, 24 May 1921,[1] had dawned bright after a gloomy few days of rain.

The newspapers had been full of stories about Annette's imminent arrival. Now, as the ship drew closer, spectators were perplexed by the sight of a darkly clad figure perched 6 metres[2] above the deck on the starboard rigging, right in front of the ship's bridge. Again and again, the figure called 'Cooee! Cooee!'

As the liner drew closer, some spectators realised that the figure calling out was Annette. After more than twenty years in show business, she knew how to make a grand entrance.

As the ship approached land, Annette became more and more excited. To those on the wharf, her position seemed perilous, but she was so sure of herself that, finding one arm was not enough to wave, she lifted a leg and waved that also.

When the ship finally berthed, Annette made her way down the gangplank and looked around the magnificent harbour, which was still awaiting a bridge. Old friends and family greeted her, and Annette gushed to awaiting reporters and a motion picture news crew: 'Oh, boy, isn't it just dandy?'[3]

She had learned to swim in the harbour waters just around the corner from Circular Quay, and her enthusiasm at being back where it all started bubbled over. 'I'm really too excited to say much,' she continued. 'I have been looking forward to this for many and many a year, and aren't I just glad to be here again?'[4]

'I tell you, I saw the moon floating over the harbour mouth just before dawn, and I said, "Is there anything better than that in the world?" Take it from me, there ain't no such animal. And the harbour – I never thought so much of that harbour as I did this morning – why, I felt like taking a header, and swimming ashore at any old place.'[5]

One of the reporters asked Annette about the success she'd been enjoying in America. 'The States? Well, yes, I enjoyed myself greatly there – most of the time in the movies, where I did some stunts which in the swimming and diving line they reckoned were "it".' She started to laugh. 'That's why I wasn't a bit afraid up on that rigging – that was nothing, nothing at all!'

Annette was wearing a black velvet coat trimmed with champagne-coloured satin, a black satin pleated skirt, a fur underskirt, champagne-coloured silk stockings, black shoes, and a chic black French hat trimmed with nasturtiums with a large brown bow on the right side. She kept it quiet, but she almost always wore a hat or headscarf to hide the scars from her crash off the springboard when she hit her head on the bottom of the pool in London decades earlier.

Annette announced that she was just about done with the movies, much preferring the vaudeville stage, where she could interact directly with her audience. She had been invited to perform in Australia by the theatrical company J.C. Williamson, and was to be the grand opening attraction for their remodelled Theatre Royal in Sydney on 4 June.[6] Touring a vaudeville show was hard work, 'but when you love it the difficulties soon become small,' she said.[7]

Annette and Mipps had promised themselves that their first ride back in Sydney would be in a hansom cab,[8] and they took one to the welcome lunch, complete with a brass band, that Williamsons had organised in the Winter Garden at the Hotel Australia.

Annette told the audience that most of the entertainers in her vaudeville troupe had travelled with her through America and Canada, including Stuart Barnes, a 'raconteur and humourist',[9] whose monologue was 'one of the finest in America; Jazz Kline, 'a young and widely known jazz artist'; and Dorothy Summers, 'dancer, vocalist, and cornetist'.

'My own share in the entertainment,' she said, 'will include elaborate ballet dancing, male impersonations, wire-walking, songs at the piano, a little monologue, and a glass-tank act. Altogether I am confident of putting up a thoroughly amusing show of sustained interest, and I hope the support of my friends here will crown my joy in returning to them all.'[10]

Annette stayed at the harbourside mansion Carthona,[11] built eighty years earlier by the explorer Major Thomas Mitchell on a promontory of Darling Point, only a couple of kilometres from Annette's childhood home but a world away in opulence. Soon she leased one of Australia's most expensive houses from beer baron Jack Toohey – Bayard, on Wolseley Road, Point Piper.[12]

About thirty relatives and old friends threw Annette another welcome party at the Winter Garden three days after her arrival, and she dazzled, squeezing the most famous figure in the world into 'a flame-coloured georgette frock of the utmost simplicity'.[13] Annette went joy-riding down George Street, climbing out onto the hood of the car to wave to all her fans. She bought pineapples and other fruit from a stall in Martin Place, and flowers for her grand home.[14]

She fulfilled three long-held wishes: hearing Mass at St Mary's Cathedral and at St Patrick's on Church Hill, and visiting St Vincent's, where she spent her high school years.[15] The New South Wales Ladies' Amateur Swimming Association honoured her as their most famous representative[16] at a reception where Annette said Australia could wipe the floor with any country in the world when it came to sport.[17] She outplayed many of Sydney's top women tennis players while in town and urged women footballers to fight for their own competition.[18] She tipped Jack Dempsey to beat the Frenchman Georges Carpentier in their upcoming fight in Jersey City. She'd met Dempsey when he was making a movie in Hollywood and thought he was 'such a nice man'.[19] Her tip was accurate.

WILLIAMSONS HAD MISCALCULATED the work needed to renovate the Theatre Royal, so the company subcontracted Annette's show to Harry Musgrove,[20] a former test cricketer who ran the Tivoli Theatre in Sydney. And so 'The Lady Versatile, Miss Annette Kellerman (Herself, In Person) and her Big Show of Vaudeville De Luxe'[21] opened at the Tivoli in a matinee at 2.30 p.m. on 6 June 1921.

Annette's stage show coincided with the screening of *What Women Love* in Australia, and the reviews for both were ecstatic. *The Sydney Morning Herald* called Annette's three-hour vaudeville act 'startling ... with the remarkable range of her varied talents.'

> These reached their climax in a crystal tank act, that was all novelty, charm, and daring from first to last ... she proved herself an accomplished dancer of the classic Italian school, her greatest feat being a lightning like pirouette, executed almost within the arms of her partner ... As the Sea Nymph, charming in green and silver, the star was encored for the profusion of steps which marked her progress, and then, in a scarlet cap and a new costume, she chatted with the audience on her way to the bounding wire, the hardest part of which, she explained, was the floor ... Many times the swimmer dived from a high springboard into the glass vessel, and when all had been safely accomplished was cheered to the echo again and again.[22]

The 'house-full' sign was displayed each night long before the curtain rose.[23]

After four weeks of playing to capacity crowds, Annette moved her show to Melbourne, and there were fans galore to welcome her when the Sydney Express pulled in to Spencer Street Station. Annette said she was 'just crazy' to be back where she began her famous long-distance swims down the Yarra.[24] At Melbourne's Tivoli on Bourke Street, 'a large audience' welcomed Annette back to the city on 9 July.

She gave graceful exhibitions of aquatics, which, she said afterwards, reminded her of the 'little, old Aquarium and Princes Court', where she had performed years ago. Although suffering from an injury to the foot, she executed a fox trot on a tightrope and danced several spectacular numbers.[25]

Annette and her troupe spent five weeks in Melbourne before a week-long run at the Theatre Royal on Adelaide's Hindley Street.[26]

Back in Sydney for a second season, Annette relaxed away from the theatre by joining the crew of the 18-foot skiff *Mona* for a thrill ride on Sydney Harbour, getting thoroughly drenched.[27] She enjoyed the experience so much she sponsored the Sydney competition for the Annette Kellerman Cup in subsequent years.

Late in October 1921, she and her troupe crossed Bass Strait for a tour of Tasmania, though it started badly, with Annette and Mipps seasick after being given a box of delicious chocolate gingers and devouring the lot.[28]

Annette performed in Hobart, Launceston, Burnie and Devonport[29] but, together with Jimmie and Mipps, she spent every spare moment sightseeing – Sandy Bay, the coast, the valleys and mountains. After Hobart, the trio drove north to Ulverstone to see some old friends, revelling in the Tasmanian countryside that reminded them of their time in England.

Then Annette crossed the Tasman with her troupe to appear on stage in New Zealand,[30] as the 'Versatile Goddess of Gladness'.[31] She sponsored a ladies' swimming race of 3 miles in Wellington Harbour,[32] and was the guest star in a tennis tournament at Masterton.[33]

As *What Women Love* did a roaring business in New Zealand theatres in February 1922, Annette completed negotiations in Christchurch with Harry Waters, a local theatre owner, to produce a film starring her and featuring some of the stunning New Zealand coastline.[34] Annette and Jimmie decided that

Nelson, on the northern tip of the South Island, had beautiful white sand, and light the equal of Hollywood. The water in the local reservoir was as clear as that in which Annette had been filmed in the West Indies.[35] Soon Annette was being besieged with applications from hundreds of girls to appear on screen.[36]

Jimmie and Annette advertised in Nelson for a furnished house to rent for a few months.[37] They found one that was 'commodious and suitable'.[38] Jimmie organised a surprise thirty-sixth birthday party there for Annette, and the Nelson Silver Band assembled on the lawn to play selections.

MIPPS HAD FALLEN IN LOVE with an Australian soldier she had met in France after the war, and their relationship had blossomed in the four years since, especially since her arrival back in Australia. The couple planned a Sydney wedding, but despite the closeness of the sisters, Annette decided to miss the event, staying in New Zealand to shoot her movie so as not to overshadow the big day. She feared that the appearance of the Diving Venus would capture all the attention.

On 22 July 1922 at an uncle's house in Neutral Bay, Mipps, now thirty-four, married 32-year-old Fred Wooster, a returned serviceman from Widgee, just outside Gympie in southern Queensland.[39]

Annette and Jimmie were celebrating in New Zealand, too. Eight days after the wedding, the Royal Mail Steamer *Tahiti* arrived in Wellington from San Francisco. Among its passengers were Hollywood cameramen Fred Bentley and Fred Frank, who had been hired to shoot Annette's movie, which would be called *Venus of the South Seas*. Bentley and Frank were experts in underwater photography.[40] Also on board was Al Miller, an expert in developing negatives. He had worked on the Rudolph Valentino Hollywood epic, *The Four Horsemen of the Apocalypse*.

The *Tahiti* also carried a diving bell weighing 3000 kilograms, to be used for underwater filming in the movie, as well as more than 15,000 metres of negative film and a huge 300-kilogram arc lamp with the power of ten million candles.[41]

The film would feature mostly local actors, while Annette would play the hero, Shona Royale, who has to escape the clutches of a greedy ship's captain plotting to steal her South Seas pearl business.

The first scenes were shot in Picton Sound in August before moving to the Nelson reservoir for underwater shots.

Filming lasted five months,[42] but the production was dogged by scandal. Donald Raymond Macartney, a dapper 33-year-old Australian and the assistant managing director of the Annette Kellerman Pictures Co.,[43] was sentenced to twelve months' prison with hard labour at the Supreme Court in Wellington for indecent assault on a sixteen-year-old boy.

In sentencing Macartney, Mr Justice Reed said that police reports stated that Macartney had been warned against interfering with boys in Dunedin, and had also acted in a similar manner with a boy in a Sydney theatre.[44]

Annette distanced herself from the whole sordid business, and the finished movie, the most expensive made in New Zealand to that time, was despatched for the American market on 20 February 1923, aboard the *Tahiti*. Despite all the local excitement, Annette's film was an overly melodramatic, low-budget production costing just 23,000 New Zealand pounds.

In March 1923, Annette went home to Sydney for a long holiday,[45] while Jimmie made a quick trip to Hollywood to market the film to the big American distributors.[46]

Four months later, at the Sydney Sports Ground, Annette kicked off for the big rugby league testimonial match honouring Frank Burge, though a crowd of 15,000 saw the South Sydney Rabbitohs outplay Burge's side, Glebe, 10–0.[47] She organised a fundraising pageant for Australia's team for the following year's Olympic Games in Paris,[48] and worked hard to raise money for disabled returned soldiers.[49]

With Jimmie by her side, Annette returned to California in January 1924[50] after having been away for two and a half years.

But she still called Australia home, and she knew she would return.

Chapter 29

WALT DISNEY WAS a struggling young cartoonist who had just arrived in Los Angeles to help his brother Roy's recovery from tuberculosis. He had dreams of directing Hollywood action movies and was invited by the film distributors, the Lee-Bradford Corporation, to watch *Venus of the South Seas* early in 1924, after parts of the negative had been given a colour wash. Years later, after a cartoon mouse and its friends had helped establish the fortune of the Disney brothers, its creator wrote to Annette asking if she remembered him.[1] How could she not?

Venus of the South Seas ran for fifty minutes and was relegated to B-movie status as soon as it was released in February 1924. Annette was almost forty and realised that, while she wasn't 'so young anymore',[2] she could still rely on athleticism and her daring stunts as foundations for her act, even if vaudeville in America was being killed off by the increasing popularity of motion pictures. She began planning a new stage act to take to England and Europe, where vaudeville still thrived. She continued to live in Santa Monica, opened a store selling health foods in San Diego,[3] and enjoyed a busy social life, overseeing the sales of the Annette Kellerman bathing suits and other clothes she designed, and playing competition tennis.[4]

By 1926, Annette was back on tour, first at the Alhambra in Paris and then at the Hippodrome in Brighton, England, in an act that still involved spectacular dives.[5]

In May 1926, her performances came to a standstill during the nine-day General Strike in which 1.7 million British workers downed tools in support of locked-out coal miners. Annette and Mipps spent time in the museums of Kensington and became 'entranced' by a display of Queensland's Great Barrier Reef,[6] more than 2300 kilometres of spectacularly coloured coral. Annette and Mipps began working on a book called *Fairy Tales of the South Seas,* which was partly Annette's biography and partly aquatic fantasy stories based in places like the islands of Queensland's great reef. Annette wrote the text and Mipps drew the illustrations.

For the next five years, Mipps and Fred Wooster went everywhere with Mr and Mrs Sullivan, as they were known on their passports. The childless couples first toured the length and breadth of Great Britain.

In August 1926, Annette congratulated the American Olympic gold medallist Trudy Ederle,[7] who was coached by Jabez Wolffe and later Bill Burgess, on becoming the first woman to swim the English Channel, twenty-one years after Annette's first attempt. Annette told the press that she was 'naturally proud of her sex'. 'It reflects women's new attitude to physical development,' she said, 'which is also revealed in prowess in other sports.'[8]

As Annette wowed audiences in Britain, her brothers Maurice and Freddie were on the move too. Freddie settled in the South of France with his Argentine-born wife, Juliette,[9] while Maurice had pushed music into the background to become a highly respected New York–based cinematographer, taking part in expeditions to the Arctic[10] and Newfoundland[11] and later to the jungles of Guyana (then called British Guiana) in search of diamonds.[12]

By the end of 1926, Annette was performing in London for the first time in thirteen years, headlining that city's 2300-seat Coliseum[13] in a production for Melbourne-born impresario Oswald Stoll.[14] The Coliseum had a revolving stage and Annette called her shows there the finest of her career.

In the crowd one night was the manager of the 3000-seat Scala in Berlin, who invited Annette to appear there. Annette had to learn the language well enough to give a twenty-minute talk on health and fitness as part of her routine.[15] Germany at the time was coming under the spell of a firebrand orator named Adolf Hitler; Annette's talks on physical perfection were hugely successful, though she later regretted giving help to budding Nazis.[16]

In January 1927, American newspapers reported of her first night in Berlin that 'the famous mermaid ... got the biggest hand of the evening from the audience when she announced it was the first time in her life that she had spoken German on the stage and was enjoying her experience.'[17]

Annette followed her German performances with appearances as *The Dying Swan* in Copenhagen alongside Anna Pavlova, and she took lessons in Danish at the Berlitz School. She also got to dance with King Christian X at a Royal Ball.[18] While Annette was in Copenhagen the 'Ziegfeld of Sweden', Ernst Rolf,[19] asked her to perform in Stockholm. 'But you must do your act in Swedish,' he told her, 'And do some comedy with me.' So Annette learned Swedish.[20]

Annette in costume for her role as *The Dying Swan*, a dance made famous by her co-star in Europe, Anna Pavlova. SLNSW, MLMSS 6270

Rolfe provided accommodation for a month on an island with great pine trees that was an ideal retreat. Fred Wooster would row Annette, Jimmie and Mipps for picnics to nearby islands in a canoe that looked like it had been carved by the Vikings.[21]

From Stockholm, Annette and her companions travelled to Norway for performances, then she did shows in Rotterdam, Amsterdam and The Hague, learning Dutch well enough to give her health and fitness talk in that language.

The travelling foursome revelled in Annette's fame and the opportunities it brought them. They travelled by car all over Europe, including to Switzerland in an unforgettable trip that took in every sight and experience on roads, mountain trails and rivers, and up and down the hills on foot. Annette and Jimmie always stayed at the most luxurious hotels with Annette's trunks of clothes and costumes, and they mingled with the great celebrities of the day such as Maurice Chevalier and Coco Chanel at the Hermitage in Deauville. Marcelle and Fred, not wanting to be free-loaders, made a point of staying in cheaper lodgings, telling Annette they preferred the 'common touch'.[22] But they ate together and saw the sights together, whether it was playing lawn bowls by Lake Lucerne, or digging mussels on the beach at low tide on the French coast and making a fire in the sand to cook them.

EVER-PRESENT DANGER made Annette's vaudeville show immensely popular. There was always the chance she would be killed. Back at the London Coliseum late in 1927, she appeared on top of the bill above the ballet dancers Anton Dolin[23] and Vera Nemtchinova.[24]

Annette's high-wire act incorporated metre-high replicas of famous movie stars of the time, such as Buster Keaton, Charlie Chaplin and Mary Pickford. The dolls were hung on an invisible wire attached below the thicker one supporting Annette 4.5-metre above the stage. They danced in unison with her movements above. They also suffered with her when things went wrong. At a matinee performance at the Coliseum in October 1927, the capacity audience was stunned when Annette, wearing an ornate costume of feathers, crashed heavily onto the stage.

A staple securing one of the jacks supporting the wire had become loose, and Annette was pitched heavily on to the boards. Immediately the curtain came down.

'I don't know how I escaped breaking my neck,' Annette said after she got to her feet. 'I suddenly felt the whole thing give way and found myself on my back on the stage with my legs in the air. I was one mass of feathers, which were torn out of my costume, and I looked like an ostrich shaking himself.'[25]

Annette was a trouper, though. As soon as she was up, she dashed through the curtains to the bewildered crowd and called out 'Here we go again!'[26] before taking her bow to thunderous applause. She reappeared on stage for the evening show as if nothing had happened.

Annette told the press the reason she could still survive such falls was her strict fitness and dietary regime. 'She never eats meat, nor drinks tea, coffee, or alcohol,' one report announced. 'She has breakfast early in the day and supper after her show at the theatre. She eats oranges or dates in between two strenuous hours at the theatre, and lives for the rest on salads, fruit, wholemeal bread and vegetables. She thinks that most people over-eat dreadfully and that the reason most of us have no energy is because our bodies are overworked in expelling the poisons of bad food and too much food from the body.'[27]

Two days after Annette's fall, her old pal Al Jolson helped kill off silent movies forever with the release of *The Jazz Singer*, in which his character in black face sings the song 'Mammy' with sound. The 'talkies' had arrived and would stay for good.

IN OCTOBER 1929, the Great Depression arrived. Even though it decimated their funds, Annette and Jimmie still spent long holidays in France with Mipps and Fred. Annette contemplated opening a physical culture school in the French coastal town of Deauville,[28] but instead accepted more offers to perform in

Germany. Her pay packet had dwindled to sixty pounds a week in Leipzig,[29] but they figured there were bigger crowds and opportunities ahead.

The Sullivans and the Woosters were certainly enjoying themselves much more than Annette's old producer William Fox, who lost control of his company during a hostile takeover in 1930. He had started the Fox Film Corporation with a 1600-dollar investment, and by the time he was forced out it was valued at 150 million dollars and had 28,000 employees.[30] Fox films would later merge with 20th Century Pictures, becoming 20th Century Fox, but William Fox no longer had any role in the business that bore his name.

BY 1932, HITLER WAS MAKING his push for Germany's highest office. Annette said the whole country had become 'politics crazy', focused on cost-of-living pressures and fomenting anger and resentment, unwilling to accept that people across Europe were struggling just as badly. She penned a newspaper column explaining that while in Paris and London the theatres and cafés had become empty, the cheaper German cafés and theatres were packed, patrons seemed to have more money and the Germans were 'well shod and clothed, and I might add that clothes are much dearer than in London'.[31]

Annette was invited back to Paris in the winter of 1932 to fire the starter's pistol for the Christmas race along the icy Seine, a quarter of a century after she had starred in the event.[32] The political climate in Europe was darkening rapidly. Just a week after the Seine race, Hitler was appointed the Chancellor of Germany, preaching revenge against his enemies within the country and without. Annette's mind drifted to the images of tropical Queensland she had seen in the London museums, and soon she, Jimmie and the Woosters were heading for Australia again aboard the *Orsova*, with a contract to make a series of short travel documentaries, 'talkies', for the Excella Films Co. of France. Jimmie would be the cameraman, after getting tips on working around coral from Frank Hurley, the great Australian photographer and adventurer. Hurley warned Jimmie that the lime from the coral would often sully the clear water.

The Sullivans and Woosters arrived in Fremantle on 7 March 1933,[33] and a week later reached Sydney, where they gasped in awe at the huge coat-hanger-shaped bridge across the harbour that had been erected since they were last in town. Surrounded by admirers and at almost forty-seven looking even fitter than in her days as a competitive swimmer, Annette recorded an interview in front of the Fox Movietone newsreel cameras. She wore a beret, tight-fitting twin set and checked scarf, and with an accent still more Australian than American she said she was 'awfully glad to be back in Aussie again – it's a real thrill'. She said she was writing a novel but doubted it would ever see the light of day because novels needed sex appeal and she didn't know 'a thing about that'. The punchline was delivered with perfect timing that made all those around her chuckle.[34] There were more raised eyebrows when she said she was off to go camping on an island and would go about without any clothes. Annette told interviewers she did not smoke or drink alcohol and had been a vegetarian for the best part of twenty years.[35] She now weighed 56 kilograms, about 20 less than when she first attempted the Channel three decades earlier.

Annette did the rounds of interviews and radio talks on health and fitness, promoting bran as a cereal[36] and eight glasses of water a day. In June 1933 Annette and Jimmie arrived in Brisbane to finalise details with the Queensland Government Tourist Bureau to make a 'travelogue' of the Great Barrier Reef. She also advised Sister Elizabeth Kenny, of the controversial polio treatments, about the way exercise had reversed the effects of rickets in her childhood.[37]

She was unsettled by events in Germany and said she hoped to retire in Australia but was still busy with her work, having been on the stage for close to thirty years.[38]

The couple stayed with Mipps and Fred on the Wooster family farm at Widgee before they all set off by car up the Great North Coast Road – later named the Bruce Highway – for Mackay, 800 kilometres away. The road was rough and full of horror stretches,[39] and they camped in tents along the way. Annette loved the great outdoors, but Mipps recalled that Jimmie thought the others were 'nuts to enjoy being uncomfortable and doing without the amenities of the cities'.[40]

The landscape changed from temperate to tropical, and the four travellers were caught in a flood at Sarina for a week or so before covering the last 40 kilometres to Mackay, where, in the first week of August 1933, a launch took them out to Lindeman Island in the Whitsundays, 80 kilometres away.[41] At first, Annette and the others stayed at the Nicolson family's resort, but before long they were exploring nearby Cole, Maher and Seaforth Islands. With Fred Wooster as his assistant, Jimmie began filming scenes of Annette swimming underwater with her prosthetic mermaid's tail.

Although they had been married for more than twenty years, Jimmie still had not learned to swim, perhaps as a mark of independence, with such a strong-willed and famous partner. Instead, he used a diving bell and a glass-bottom boat to film the underwater shots.

Sometimes, local Indigenous men armed with spears stood over pools in which Annette was working to ward off sharks, and on two occasions she feared she would drown when strings of her beads became caught in the coral.[42] But she always came up smiling and was determined everyone else on Lindeman had a good time too.

Over the Christmas holidays of 1933, Annette repaid the hospitality of the Nicolsons by performing a series of shows for tourists, and she organised fancy-dress balls on Christmas Day and New Year's Eve.[43]

Annette and Jimmie camped for a while on Seaforth Island, and a travel company based in Mackay organised forty-five tourists to visit them there for a jazz party on the beach.[44] Annette had a diving tower of rough bush timber built over the water to give displays, and she encouraged visitors to have a go too.

Once, they were stranded on Maher Island for two weeks by a cyclone, and although they hadn't brought enough supplies for the duration, Fred and one of the Indigenous guides caught enough fish to keep everyone well fed. At about this time, Annette was offered a half-share in Hayman Island, which she declined. It went on to become a major tourist destination.[45]

In the new year, Annette and Mipps took over the cooking duties at Lindeman when Mrs Nicolson was indisposed, and visitors thought it quite a novelty to have such a celebrity taking their orders and proving to be 'such an excellent cook, especially with the sweets'.[46]

After a farewell trip among the islands in the tourist launch *Cheerio*, Annette and Jimmie ended their nine-month stay on the island in May 1934.[47] As she left, Annette raved about the beauty of the reef.

> You can have your Colorado Canyon, or your Yosemite Valley, which are certainly very beautiful ... but give me the Barrier Reef ... it is stupendous ... the greatest thing in the world, bar nothing. Why Australians do not appreciate it more I cannot understand.[48]

Annette and Jimmie left Australia for France on the *Mongolia* after a cocktail party in their honour at Sydney's Hotel Australia,[49] but Mipps and Fred stayed in tropical Queensland, taking the lease on the 130-hectare Newry Island, about 50 kilometres south-west of Lindeman. It was a sublime setting with stark headlands, picturesque sandstone cliffs and stunning bougainvillea. The Woosters began work to turn it into a tourist getaway.[50]

Back in Paris, Annette promoted her short films on the Barrier Reef, saying it was 'one of the few remaining unfilmed corners of the world' and that she had spent almost a year in a bathing suit going from island to island to get the perfect shots. She said she had once stayed underwater for three minutes, fourteen seconds, which she believed was a world record for a woman.[51]

ANNETTE AND JIMMIE travelled on to Florida, and just south-east of Gainesville, at a place called Silver Springs, they found crystal-clear waters perfect for Jimmie to film Annette performing an underwater *adagio*, or slow ballet.[52] Annette was almost fifty, but in footage that still survives, her graceful movements give some indication of why she was a world famous performer for so long.

Annette sent photos from the *adagio* to newspapers throughout America to promote a huge charity event she was staging, an event in service to others that would typify the rest of her life.

The wealthy committee of the Elk Club in Palm Beach, Florida, had approached Annette to stage a 'marine fantasy show' as a fundraiser for a hospital for disabled children. It would take place at the exclusive Bath and Tennis Club in February 1936. The show was a huge hit, 'a beautiful program in which more than 100 children took part in unique swimming and diving exhibitions'.[53]

In the following year, 1937, the shrewd showman Billy Rose used many of the ideas that Annette had conceived to produce his extraordinary *Aquacade* – a music, dance and swimming show that featured five-time Olympic gold medallist Johnny Weissmuller[54] – for the Great Lakes Exposition in Cleveland. *Aquacade* was performed on a 40-metre-wide floating stage erected over barges and played to rapt audiences in a 5000-seat amphitheatre.

The show later moved to an 11,000-seat theatre for the New York World's Fair, and Rose brought in new artists, such as the English Channel swimmer Trudy Ederle, and another Olympic champion, Buster Crabbe.[55] When the show crossed the country to San Francisco, Rose hired a local swimming sensation and beauty named Esther Williams.

Aquacade made Rose a fortune. Although Annette had pioneered the one-piece swimsuit, water ballet and synchronised swimming, she never publicly expressed bitterness that her pioneering work went unacknowledged.

Annette said she was introduced to President Franklin Delano Roosevelt at a charity event in the spa town of Warm Springs, Georgia.[56] Roosevelt was there to exercise his polio-stricken legs in the famous artesian springs. The President knew of Annette's childhood battle with rickets and they spent an afternoon talking about exercises that might help him.[57] She also formed a friendship with John Harvey Kellogg, inventor of the corn flake, and they had many discussions about the benefits of their vegetarian diets.[58]

She realised that, having turned fifty, the sun was coming down on her days as the Diving Venus. Instead, she organised charity benefits, pageants and water spectaculars in the millionaires' playground of Florida, sometimes with as many as 300 swimmers on show. She also travelled to different cities to lecture on health and fitness, always devoting ten to fifteen minutes at every appearance to talk about the beauties of the Great Barrier Reef. She would play Jimmie's film of her underwater ballet from Silver Springs to show what women could still achieve, even if they'd passed the half-century,[59] and she claimed that by 1939 she had raised 100,000 U.S. dollars to aid hospitals working to treat infantile paralysis.

Not that Annette was always charitable. She told one interviewer that she was sorry she started the fashion of brief swimwear. 'Look at the awful sights you see in one-piece suits today,' she said. 'Big, fat women bulge out of their suits, disfiguring the landscape. And don't think the men aren't as bad. Why, some of those grandfathers in nothing but trunks ought to have screens around them.'[60]

With her fame now being overshadowed by a new generation of swimming and diving stars, Annette became desperately homesick for Australia, particularly the peace and isolation of the Whitsunday Islands. She suggested to Jimmie that they settle on Newry with Mipps and Fred and become a 'couple of beachcombers'.[61]

The couple had a short vacation in London in January 1939, where Annette told reporters the only face cream she used was olive oil and that plenty of hot water was the best tonic for 'purifying the blood stream and toning up the system'.[62]

She and Jimmie returned to Sydney in March 1939 aboard the *Mooltan*,[63] bringing with them twelve trunks of Annette's costumes and beautiful scenery from her shows. 'Gorgeous materials', she called them, 'feathers, spangles etc.'[64]

Annette made appearances at Coogee to present medals at a swimming carnival and travelled down to Bowral to raise money for the local hospital.[65] By June, she and Jimmie were reunited with the Woosters on Newry Island.[66] Fred and Mipps had built a two-storey guesthouse on the eastern side of the island, with a commanding view of the bay and surroundings.[67] There were a few stone huts covered with exotic foliage, but still the island would only accommodate fourteen.[68]

Annette was in paradise. 'It has everything one needs for happiness,' she said, 'a perfect beach, wonderful swimming, palms, pineapples, papaws, fresh, clear water, delicious fish, and the most succulent oysters you ever tasted. And, best of all, peace.'[69]

Before long, locals were talking about Annette braving the shark-infested 5-kilometre channel between Newry and the coastal town of Seaforth to swim ashore for shopping treks – only in the winter, though, because crocodiles and venomous box jellyfish came out there in summer.

Annette had been on Newry only a few weeks when she spied an oyster shell containing a fair-sized and perfectly round pearl.[70] Not long after, though, everyone on Newry listened to the crackle and hum of their wireless as Prime Minister Bob Menzies made a radio address to the nation. Hitler's Nazis had invaded Poland and, as a result, Great Britain had declared war on Germany. Australia was also at war.

Annette immediately volunteered to serve her country.

Chapter 30

FRED WOOSTER BEGAN building a cottage for Annette and Jimmie on a point of Newry Island overlooking Repulse Bay, where Annette liked to swim. She called her time on the island the 'Dream of Her Life'.[1]

Between two swaying palm trees, she erected a high wire to practise every day in preparation for her return to Sydney and an aqua carnival[2] based on the marine life of the Barrier Reef to aid that city's Royal Price Alfred Hospital. This would be the first of her patriotic fundraisers to aid Australian hospitals, the Red Cross and other charities during the Second World War as the usual donations they needed to operate were now being diverted away to the war effort. Her daily practice on Newry also included ballet dancing, and the playing of her piano accordion, a new addition to her repertoire. She was also writing songs, and while future generations might have found the music hall lyrics of 'The Dinkum Diggers' Dip' and 'A.N.Z.A.C.' juvenile, even corny, they had the desired effect of making donors reach deep into their pockets.

Back in Sydney, Annette and Jimmie rented a home on Bradleys Head Road in the harbour-front suburb of Mosman, and Annette began recruiting her cast. The chief requirement was to look good in a swimming suit. Among the swimmers Annette chose were Olympic gold medallist Clare Dennis[3] and her Australian teammate Kitty Hodgson.[4] The show was promoted as Australia's 'first marine pantomime and undersea fantasy' and was set for 3 February 1940 at North Sydney's Olympic pool, which was converted into a theatre on water for a cast numbering 'several hundred'. There would also be a full orchestra[5] and the Mosman Musical Society's chorus of sixty voices.[6]

As stage manager, Jimmie began working on sets, and Annette wrote a sketch called 'The Evolution of the Bathing Costume'. She and Mipps had sifted through Annette's trunks of costumes and remodelled dozens of outfits, using lamé to shimmer underwater. There were fantastic headdresses, multi-coloured fish costumes, mermaids' costumes, seaweed costumes and coral designs.[7] Tickets would be one guinea (one pound, one shilling) each.

The evening show was an unqualified success. The swimmers and divers performed while bounded by the span of the Sydney Harbour Bridge and the lights of Luna Park. Every now and then a train would go thundering over, but this only added to the atmosphere, as though it was roaring surf breaking on some lonely shore 'while the seaweed maidens trailed their silvers, greens, reds, and purples ...'[8]

Sydney's afternoon newspaper *The Sun* reported:

The first Musical Marine Phantasy to be presented in Australia drew about 2500 people to the North Sydney Olympic Pool last night, where 200 well-known swimmers and society girls, who had intensively rehearsed for six weeks, participated in elaborate water ensembles and spectacular diving feats. A floodlit platform, erected on the pool, was the centre for gaily-costumed dance numbers. Five hundred elaborate costumes were brought from America by Miss Kellerman, and many of them could be used only for the one performance. Amongst the most notable was one sewn with 500 pearls, worn by Miss Kellerman ... Glamorous girls in white brassiere costumes laced with glittering silver, [and] white floodlights [that] turned the water to rainbow hues, drew tumultuous applause for 'the glorious Kellerman girls.'[9]

The biggest cheer came when Annette appeared in the water with Olympic stars Fanny Durack and Mina Wylie, her old rivals from

Farmer's Baths at the turn of the century.[10] Because of her tireless work for the fundraiser, Annette had a ward at Royal Prince Alfred's maternity section named in her honour.[11]

But Annette was only getting started. She and Jimmie drove up to Brisbane the long way via Goondiwindi, and started work on producing the *Aussie Review Parisienne*, a vaudeville show at City Hall in aid of the Flying Doctor Service, which was also struggling financially during the war. It included five of her songs and *The Courier-Mail* newspaper called it 'a feast for eyes and ears'.[12]

Annette returned to Newry on 13 June 1940,[13] and she and Mipps and their husbands listened with sadness to a radio broadcast informing them that the Germans had taken Paris, after having failed in World War I. They also listened to Winston Churchill's stirring speeches over the short wave. Annette was convinced that she could devote all of her time and effort, as well as a large slice of the fortune she had made as an entertainer, to help vanquish the Nazis.

She and Jimmie decided to use all their resources and experience to raise money touring Australia for the war effort. In the larger cities, Annette would produce her own revue, *We're All In It*, and in the smaller towns she would show her 'Underwater Films', which Jimmie had shot, and give her 'famous lecture on physical education'.[14]

The show would travel by truck throughout country districts, and would consist of a company of twelve to fourteen girls, with the remaining members of the company engaged locally in the towns visited because of the transport problems caused by petrol rationing.[15]

Annette wrote twenty songs for the revue, and with the help of Mipps and some ladies staying at Newry, and another group on Rabbit Island, seventy new costumes were produced from the satin, silk and lamé Annette had brought from America, along with hundreds of gold and silver spangles that were sewn onto the material.[16]

Her song 'Spanish Dance' was written to be performed by a 24-piece orchestra.

First there was a spectacular water pageant in the rain for 4000 fans in the Lady Gowrie Red Cross Convalescent Home at Gordon in March 1941;[17] then there were beauty contests and beach parades with Annette as a judge to decide *The Sunday Telegraph* Red Cross Beach-Girl of the Year.[18]

Her efforts went into overdrive when Japan destroyed the U.S. Fleet at Pearl Harbour in Hawaii in December 1941 before taking Singapore.

Annette set up the Red Cross Theatrical Unit in Sydney,[19] and began performing up and down Australia's east coast, writing, directing and starring in shows for Australian and American servicemen all the way up to New Guinea. As well as funding the shows, that sometimes had casts of sixty, she and Jimmie also made major cash donations to the Red Cross as well. Their savings dwindled year by year.

Annette found it just as exciting as performing at the New York Hippodrome or London Coliseum. She wrote for *Variety* magazine, too, and encouraged Hollywood stars such as Gary Cooper to come to Australia to help the war effort.[20] Walt Disney sent an original sketch of Bambi on celluloid for Annette to auction.[21] Greer Garson sent a memento of her film, *Mrs. Miniver*, and Bette Davis also donated a gift to be auctioned.[22] Annette made chocolates from potatoes to be served at charity lunches,[23] gave radio lectures on health, and drew the numbers for the New South Wales lottery.[24] She and Jimmie cooked hamburgers and eggs at the American and Australian club for Australian troops; Annette cooked 1200 eggs every Sunday she was there.[25]

Some of the girls in her troupe, recruited from the Mavis Sykes School of Dance in Sydney's Mosman, recalled that Annette enjoyed the star treatment, was often very theatrical when speaking with them and looked a lot like Gloria Swanson did in *Sunset Boulevard*, which would be made a few years later.[26] Annette still wanted to be 'big', even though she was approaching sixty. Working for the Red Cross gave her the adulation and attention that she had enjoyed at the time *A Daughter of the Gods* was made.

The shows featured dozens of amateurs trained by Annette, and though the end product was sometimes rough around the edges, given the inexperience of some of the performers, it was all for a good cause.

By end of the war, Annette had raised 23,000 pounds for the Red Cross.[27] She was immensely proud of this fact, though her joy was tempered by the death of her older brother, Maurice Charbonnet Kellerman, in New York during the war years.

When the Japanese surrender in August 1945 finally brought an end to World War II, the head of Australia's Red Cross appeals, George Macdonald Dash,[28] told Jimmie and Annette that their fundraising had played a 'noticeable part in winning victory for the Allied cause' and that their wholehearted efforts were 'unexcelled' in his long experience as a fundraiser.[29]

Annette was presented with a flag of the American Red Cross and managed to get it signed by friends in high places, including Generals Eisenhower and Macarthur, and President Harry Truman, whom she called 'a dear little man'.[30]

The fundraising had been such a success that Annette and Jimmie were asked to lead a drive to raise 50,000 pounds for the Building Appeal Committee for the Queensland University Women's College, and Annette was recognised for her efforts with the naming of the Annette Kellerman Room.[31]

Annette and Jimmie returned to Newry Island for a few months before they managed to jag a hard-to-come-by berth on a ship returning to America. It was the *Mariposa*,[32] which left Brisbane at dawn on 11 April 1946 heading for San Francisco with 769 dependents[33] of American servicemen. There were about 500 women who had married American soldiers and sailors, and the babies born to them while the servicemen were in Australia.

Most of the women and babies had recently been vaccinated against smallpox, and sore-armed mothers could do little to quieten restless children at the start of the voyage across the Pacific. Some of the women were too sick to care for their babies and the children were instead fed and kept quiet by Red Cross aids and American army nurses.

The house on Newry Island on the Great Barrier Reef where Annette and Jimmie made a home. *SLNSW, MLMSS 6270, A2.209*

Annette was made the entertainment director for this 'bridal voyage' and produced a show called *The Mariposa Merrymakers*. But there was a decided lack of merriment among some of the miserable passengers and Annette called it 'the most god-awful trip of my life'.[34] Some of the women were reluctant to move to America and many tried to jump ship in Fiji, Okinawa, and Hawaii.[35]

There were even more tears when Annette, Jimmie and the shipload of brides arrived in San Francisco two weeks after leaving Brisbane, with forty-five of the brides left sad-eyed, disillusioned and in many cases destitute with children, after receiving telegrams on the ship that their GI husbands did not want them or their children anymore. They had to catch the next ship back to Australia.[36]

Annette, though, was in more demand than ever. It had been almost thirty years since her last Hollywood movie, but the film industry had not forgotten her. In February 1947, Metro-Goldwyn-Mayer announced it was considering making a film biography of Annette Kellerman's extraordinary life. The glamorous former swimming champion Esther Williams was their pick to play the woman they called 'The Australian Mermaid'.[37]

Chapter 31

WHILE ANNETTE HAD been raising money for the Red Cross during the war years, Esther Williams had been establishing herself as the new face and body of women's swimming.

After winning three U.S. national championships in breaststroke and freestyle at age sixteen,[1] she had been recruited for a starring role in Billy Rose's *Aquacade* alongside Johnny Weissmuller, who was already a major movie star from his roles as Tarzan. MGM's head, Louis B. Mayer, then signed Esther to the studio in 1941, as a female sports star to rival 20th Century Fox's figure-skating heroine Sonja Henie.

By 1944, MGM was calling Esther 'The Girl You Will Dream About' in publicity for the movie *Bathing Beauty*, which the studio described as 'the Most Dazzling Color Spectacle Ever Filmed'. It included an 'aqua ballet' of the type Annette had invented decades earlier. Esther followed that hit with a 'water ballet' in *Ziegfeld Follies* featuring Fred Astaire, Lucille Ball, Judy Garland and Red Skelton.

By 1947 Esther, at just twenty-six, was one of the most powerful women in Hollywood, thanks largely to her stunning beauty and the brilliance of her agent Abe Lastfogel,[2] a long-time president of the William Morris Agency.

Esther and Lastfogel began making plans to film the story of Annette's life, Esther describing Annette as a 'wonderful woman' whose silent movies were her mother's favourites.[3]

Annette, who was a major star long before Esther was born, had ideas of playing herself in the film, even though she was now past sixty. She felt that she looked young enough and remained fit enough to do her own stunts.

Esther and Lastfogel had other ideas. Convincing MGM to back the project was going to take work, so Esther kept the idea rolling as she starred in more hits, in 1949 teaming up with Red Skelton again for *Neptune's Daughter*, though the only similarity between their version and Annette's 1914 epic was the title. Esther played a swimwear designer in a romantic comedy and the movie won an Oscar for the song 'Baby, It's Cold Outside', which she sang with Ricardo Montalbán.

Annette was disappointed with the new version of *Neptune's Daughter* and told *The Los Angeles Times* that she 'cried so about it that at the time I never would have agreed to let [Esther] do my life story'.[4]

But she changed her mind when she met Esther and realised 'she really wanted to make' the story of Annette's life. 'I never would have thought of her for the part,' Annette said at the time, 'she's much too pretty.'[5]

Despite their shared love of swimming and movies, there was an awkward silence at their first uncomfortable meeting. Esther remembered that Annette was very quiet and then suddenly pulled up her skirt and said: 'Look at these legs!'

Esther was impressed by the ice-breaker. 'Swimming muscles,' she said. 'I'd know them anywhere.'[6]

With Lastfogel lobbying hard, Esther took Annette to meet the MGM studio executives to pitch the biopic to them. Annette signed a contract on 8 January 1951 with the producers, the theatre chain Lowes Inc., as Mrs James Sullivan. She submitted the outline of her life, with embellishments, called 'My Story',[7] and insisted that the movie stay as close to it as possible.[8]

MGM tossed most of her ideas into the bin. Instead, a leading Hollywood writer, Everett Freeman, was called in to write a script that had minimal resemblance to Annette's life except for the fact she had starred in spectacular diving shows and water ballets. The profound role of Annette's mother in her life and career was ignored.

The movie would have a five-million-dollar budget and be a Technicolor extravaganza full of beautiful women, thrilling stunts and extraordinary choreography in the swimming pool. Arthur Hornblow, who had already received three Oscar nominations for best picture,[9] was assigned to produce the movie. Mervyn LeRoy, who had made *The Wizard of Oz* in 1939, signed on as director, and the celebrated choreographer Busby Berkeley was hired to devise elaborate synchronised swimming scenes involving complex geometric patterns, so that the bathing beauties, clad in shimmering outfits, would produce stunning kaleidoscopic effects.

Annette would be paid 250 dollars a week as a technical adviser, though she was to keep that confidential.[10] The contract called for her to spend two full days a week from the start of 1951 at the MGM lot. The rest of the time she could devote to the new health food shop she and Jimmie had opened at Long Beach, with plans to expand into a chain she hoped would 'stretch clear across the United States'.[11]

Soon after the MGM deal was completed, the syndicated entertainment columnist Louella Parsons reported acidly that while 'for years Annette Kellerman, the first great woman swimmer' had clung to her life story the way her bathing suit once clung to her, MGM was now splashing around telling the world that Esther Williams would star in Annette's life story, to be called *One-Piece Suit*.[12]

While Annette waited for the cameras to roll, she threw open her home at Pacific Palisades in Los Angeles for a fundraiser to aid the work of Sister Kenny in treating polio victims.[13] The home was a magnificent glass temple on 1000 square metres of land looking out to Catalina Island, and with a gorgeous garden of thriving geraniums that Annette nurtured.

'Don't think I'm a retired old lady, because I am not,' she told George McGann, the American correspondent for Sydney's *The Daily Telegraph*. 'I still make most of my public appearances, and always do my physical exercises and acrobatics in a one-piece suit.'

Twice a week she visited the Veterans' Hospital in Los Angeles to put on a ninety-minute show,[14] playing the accordion and singing songs, including 'Waltzing Matilda'[15] and one she wrote herself, 'Lady of the Lamp'. She donated the copyright of that song to the Red Cross.

'I tell the boys stories about famous people I have met when swimming in Germany, France, and other countries, and show them my physical exercises,' she explained. 'They seem to love it. It's just the same sort of show as I did in Australia, touring the hospitals on my last visit home.'[16]

She said that the greatest accomplishment of her life was not her theatrical career, but the reform she achieved in women's beachwear. 'I honestly believe I did a great service for womankind when I took them away from those ridiculous bloomers and put them into one-piece suits,' she said. But while her attire was seen as risqué at the height of her fame, Annette said she was mortified by what bathing costumes had become by 1951. 'Bikini suits are no good to swim in, and don't give the same figure support that a one-piece does,' she said, adding that Australian girls looked better in the modern bathing costumes than Americans. 'American girls are very beautiful, but they all look as though they are five or six pounds underweight. For me, I'll take any good-looking lass off an Australian beach any time. The Australian girl is still the world's ideal girl.'[17]

AS PREPARATIONS FOR filming intensified, Annette hyped the movie, saying she went through 'half a dozen scripts, all of which I rejected because they just wanted to make it a glamorous, typically Hollywood, romance story. I thought they were silly and undignified. I insisted on the right to edit the script, because I didn't want Hollywood making a mess of my story. My life has been a beautiful one, and I didn't want them doing anything that would make it look cheap in any way.'[18]

Academy Award nominee Louis Calhern was set to play Annette's father, but the role went to another nominee, Walter

Pidgeon, one of Annette's favourite actors. She hoped that Glenn Ford would be cast as Jimmie because Ford was 'the nearest thing I can think of to my dear husband – not too glamorous, and he implies the strength and understanding necessary for the part. We have been married thirty-nine years, and are still just as thrilled with each other as ever we were.'[19] When Jimmie got angry, she said, he would tell Annette that 'any other man would have divorced you long ago'. But Annette told reporters, 'Of course he doesn't mean it. He is a dear!'[20]

To Annette's chagrin, Glenn Ford was bypassed and the role went to Victor Mature, who had recently starred in *Samson and Delilah*. He played the understated Jimmie as a slick and shifty carnival hustler, and Annette thought it was a woeful piece of miscasting. Friends teased Jimmie forevermore, giving him the nickname 'Samson'.

Esther Williams was very happy with the choice of Victor Mature, though. She felt a powerful sexual attraction to him. 'I was married,' Esther recalled, 'but all the passion and most of the love in that marriage were gone, or going. Vic, I knew, was entangled in a similar marriage.'[21]

Shooting of the movie began in February 1952, and Annette visited the set to watch some of the rehearsals and pose with the costumed Esther in her head-to-toe shimmering sequined glory.[22]

Annette stood ramrod straight, with her head held high and chin up. 'You need to stand tall when you have to act without clothes on,' she told Esther.[23]

Esther wanted to get out of her clothes as quickly as she could after filming. Many years later in her autobiograhy Esther related that one night, after doing a steamy love scene with Victor that Esther said was more 'than adequate foreplay':

> we went to my dressing room, locked the door, and unleashed our hunger, our passion for each other. Vic was a strong and fulfilling lover. Even better than I had fantasized ... That first night, we made love over and over and into exhaustion.[24]

It didn't take long for the MGM gossip mill to begin rumbling about the affair, and the Hollywood columnists dropped not so subtle hints. Esther said she assumed Vic's wife had learned to endure his affairs and that her second husband, Ben Gage, 'as usual, was oblivious'.

'We were shameless and happy,' Esther recalled. Some days, she stood trembling with excitement, 'waiting for Vic's secret knock on my dressing-room door'. Fictional desire and real desire blended and every movie scene featuring the screen Annette and Jimmie was full of sexual tension. Esther loved the idea of playing Annette on screen, a real person and a real swimmer rather 'than a superficial character' created to give her an excuse to appear in a bathing suit.[25]

A FEW WEEKS INTO FILMING, Annette sat behind the camera of veteran cinematographer George Folsey[26] on a set representing the wings of New York's Hippodrome while Mervin LeRoy directed a scene in which young Annette meets her idol, Anna Pavlova. With her eyes bright with memories, Annette watched Esther and America's first major prima ballerina, Maria Tallchief, reenact the moment. 'Pavlova was a dream of grace and I used to try to emulate her,' Annette told reporters on set. 'The greatest thrill of my life came at a benefit at the Metropolitan Opera House in 1918 when I did Pavlova's famous swan dance.'[27]

The two actors finished the scene and Esther came over to join Annette and the journalists. 'You know,' she said, 'I am copying the swimming strokes Miss Kellerman made famous. They were different than those in use today. The racing backstroke as we know it had not been developed and the crawl was different. The trudgen was popular then and the under arm, over arm.'[28]

Annette told the reporters that she thought Esther was too tall to play her – 5 feet, 8 inches compared with 5 feet, 4¾ inches – and that she was much too beautiful.

'From the neck down I was all right,' Annette said, with a huge smile, 'but from the neck up, well I never looked like Esther. But the one who is really flabbergasted is my husband. Jimmie

Annette and Esther Williams on the MGM set of *Million Dollar Mermaid* in Hollywood in 1952.

Sullivan is such a quiet unassuming man. When he comes on the set and sees himself portrayed by Victor Mature he just can't get used to the idea.'[29]

'How do you feel about me playing your life?' Esther asked Annette.

There was an awkward silence.

'Do you have a problem with that question?' Esther asked.

'It's not that,' Annette finally answered. 'It's just that I wish you were Australian.'

'I'm the only swimmer in the movies, Miss Kellerman,' Esther replied. 'I'm all you've got.'[30]

Esther claimed that Mervyn LeRoy was exhausted before the movie even started, having just finished filming *Quo Vadis* in Rome. His only direction was, 'Let's have a nice little scene,' whether it was a romantic scene or an action sequence.[31] He used MGM's Stage 30 to film the swimming, which the actors called 'Pneumonia Alley'. The water usually had to be warm for swimmers, but hot air rises and the crew up in the scaffolding above the stage were always complaining about the heat waves, humidity and chlorine fumes, which sometimes made them lightheaded or nauseous. Occasionally, one of the guys would pass out and fall into the water. To compensate, the air temperature of the soundstage was kept at 60 degrees Fahrenheit (15.5°C). This meant that the swimmers all caught colds because they were coming out of warm water into the freezing air.

Esther claimed she almost drowned by staying underwater too long in one of Busby Berkeley's elaborate scenes, and that she broke a toe gripping on to a trapeze for dear life like a parrot on a perch, 16 metres above the soundstage, as coloured smoke from exploding pots swirled around her.

More than 100 swimmers appeared in the movie, recreating and even surpassing Annette's extravaganzas. In the finale, streams of brightly coloured red and gold smoke swirled from the water to a height of 20 metres as women in bathing suits carrying lit torches slid into the pool. Then, hundreds of glowing sparklers emerged from the water in a tribute to the woman who had pioneered the great aqua spectaculars.

Esther's costume designers had fitted her with an extraordinary swim costume, 'much like a diver's body suit, only covered, including the soles of the feet, with gold sequins, 50,000 of them like chain mail. Atop a gold turban, which was wrapped around my head, they perched a gold crown.'[32] Almost fifty years after filming finished, Esther wrote in her autobiography that she was wearing the outfit when she dived from the equivalent of a six-story building and that the crown caused her head to snap back in the water, breaking three vertebrae in her neck.[33] But Annette told interviewers many years later that Esther 'couldn't dive higher than that bed'[34] and that she paid a stunt double, Helen Morgan,[35] 1000 dollars a picture to dive for her.[36]

Filming wrapped up after six months. At a preview screening at a theatre in Hollywood in August 1952, fans mobbed Esther, while Annette was able to sneak through the crowd unnoticed.[37]

Esther and Victor Mature were no longer lovers, but Esther had never thought for a second that their affair would last past the making of the movie. 'But I don't regret a minute in his arms,' she wrote. 'Romances with beautiful leading men don't last but don't knock it until you've had one.'[38]

The film opened at Radio City Music Hall in New York City on 4 December 1952. It was visually stunning but Annette was disappointed at the deviations from the truth and considered the final product a 'a silly little yarn'[39] and a 'namby-pamby' attempt to tell her story,[40] without any thrills.[41]

Still, the movie made a profit and George Folsey's cinematography was nominated for an Academy Award. MGM talked about a sequel focusing on Annette's silent movies and work for the Red Cross.[42] The plan went nowhere, but it was likely a hot topic when Annette would lunch with friends such as Lucille Ball, Barbara Stanwyck, Loretta Young, Walter Pidgeon, Grace Kelly and the newspaper columnist Hedda Hopper. At Grace Kelly's pre-wedding shower, just before her marriage to Prince Rainier in April 1956, Annette gave her friend a lace handkerchief given to her by Enrico Caruso. She told Grace it belonged in a palace and Grace agreed, wearing it at her wedding in Monte Carlo.[43]

Million Dollar Mermaid introduced Annette's feats to a new audience, but it was the old brigade who still paid tribute to her. In April 1956 at Pickfair, the mansion Mary Pickford and Douglas Fairbanks had built during their sixteen-year marriage, Annette attended a reunion of 200 silent movie stars. She was accompanied by Buster Keaton and joined the likes of Harold Lloyd, Marion Davis, Ramon Navarro, Zasu Pitts, and Joe E. Brown.[44]

But Tinseltown was losing its lustre for Annette, and the health food store may not have been the big hit she claimed. She said she got terribly homesick for Australia and really missed her 'cobbers'.[45] So, at the end of 1956, Annette and Jimmie said goodbye to his relatives in America, not knowing if they would ever see them again, and headed to Melbourne for the Olympic Games. Annette was now seventy years old and she wanted to spend her final days under the Southern Cross.

Chapter 32

ANNETTE AND JIMMIE retuned to Australia in November 1956. At seventy, Annette remained in great physical shape and could still kick a leg way above her dyed brown hair and hold it there for photographers.[1] Jimmie's passport photo told a different story. He was seventy-one but looked older. His hair colour was now listed as 'white/bald'.

Annette told *The Women's Weekly* magazine that the two great loves of her long life were Jimmie, her husband of forty-four years, and Cooee, the pug dog that had almost broken her heart when she died many years earlier aged seventeen.[2]

At the Melbourne Olympics, Annette met Australia's new world-record breaker, Dawn Fraser, and was introduced to cheering crowds by Prime Minister Bob Menzies.[3] Some of the fans were old enough to remember her swims down the Yarra.

The days of Annette's death-defying stunts were long gone, but she still lived for the stage and she began a series of intimate shows around Australia, telling stories about the good old days of vaudeville and silent movies in 'a program of reminiscences'.[4]

She showed slides of Hollywood's night spots, of her home at Pacific Palisades and of her famous friends, the pioneers of the film industry.

She read out messages of good wishes to Australia collected from movie stars who, she assured her audience, were mostly 'grand and well-behaved people' fond of their homes and families, unlike the 'sinful' reputation Hollywood had obtained.

She gave an exhibition of keep-fit exercises, which showed she was still supple and graceful, and she said it was her mission to show how diet and exercise were the foundations of good health.[5]

Annette and Jimmie based themselves in Marrickville in Sydney for a while. On 8 February 1960 Annette was awarded a star on the Hollywood Walk of Fame at 6608 Hollywood Boulevard and she and Jimmie then spent the winter of 1961 on Queensland's sleepy Gold Coast, about 80 kilometres south of Brisbane. The Kellermans soon made their move to the Gold Coast permanent, joining Mipps and Fred Wooster, who had retired from their Barrier Reef hideaway resort on Newry.

Sixty years ago, the Gold Coast was a very different place to the ocean-front concrete and glass jungle of today. It was mostly modest houses, beach shacks, caravan parks and cheap holiday flats, and Annette and Jimmie settled down to a life far more spartan than they had enjoyed as Hollywood elites. Most of their money had gone on charity donations, especially during World War II, and on living well while not worrying too much about tomorrow.

The days of Sydney harbourside mansions, luxury French Riviera resorts and plush New York hotel suites were gone. The couple now lived in 'a modestly comfortable flat',[6] which they rented[7] in Bayview Street at Labrador, on the northern end of the Gold Coast. It was in a working-class development of fibre-cement and weatherboard bungalows known as Angler's Paradise. Around the corner, the Woosters made their home in a little house at 10 Broadwater Street, now part of the suburb of Runaway Bay. After Mipps became a widow in 1969, she, Annette and Jimmie became even closer as a family unit.

The Gold Coast was an aquatic playground perfect for a human mermaid, with surfers and swimmers everywhere, the dolphin shows of Marineland, Sea World and the Jack Evans' Porpoise Pool and, just off shore, myriads of fish and frolicking whales.[8]

Annette and Jimmie would walk the beach, and each morning Annette would swim laps in the pool at the Chevron Hotel, one of the few upmarket hotels on the Gold Coast at that time. Jimmie took some home movie footage for posterity of Annette, then in

Annette and Jimmie posed for photographer Bob Avery on the Gold Coast as they approached 60 years of marriage. *City of Gold Coast, goldcoaststories.com*

her late seventies, in a bright-red cap and red swimming suit with leggings, doing her morning exercise routine.[9]

While Jimmie was content to retire gracefully, Annette remained a human whirlwind. She hooked up a broom handle firmly in her kitchen, beside her stove, to act as a ballet barre, and she never missed a day of practice.

She didn't eat foolishly, but was partial to a chocolate biscuit now and then.

She introduced herself to all the social clubs and charities of her area and started fundraising drives, including pageants, in which the girls wore swimming costumes from different historical eras. Often, she would lead the pageant in a costume that she had worn on stage in New York or London fifty years earlier. She hosted lunches and dinners for local clubs, nursing homes and charities.

Many of those who attended the events knew her only as the nice little old lady from Labrador, rather than a woman who was once one of the most famous and daring entertainers in the world.[10] To a younger generation she was largely anonymous, and she hated the fact that so many Australians knew American stars but ignored their own.

Annette became a founding member of the Gold Coast Geranium Club and often opened her home for meetings and get-togethers. Her devotion to the exquisite flowers was rewarded when the London Geranium Club named a new dark-red flower in her honour.[11]

The weight of years began to tell heavily on Jimmie, who never did learn to swim. He and Annette had been married for almost sixty years when he became seriously ill with a particularly virulent strain of flu in the early 1970s. After a year of special care for him, Annette wrote to his sister, Cecilia, in Minneapolis using a strong hand, expansive lettering and bold exclamation marks to declare, 'The doctor says his lungs and heart are very good.' Though the stress had weakened Annette, she assured her sister-in-law she still felt well.[12]

Jimmie wrote to his sister to say, 'Annette is always wonderful and keeps me going when I am ready to give up ... I love her so much.' He never wrote to Cecilia again. Instead, Annette sent her sister-in-law a letter in February 1972 to say: 'My darling Jimmie has passed away – he died in his sleep! Thank God! People loved him. As for me! Sixty years together. He was a wonderful husband and help mate. Jim had a very happy life with me. We lived for one another! We were never separated. At present I am a lost soul.'[13]

Jimmie was cremated at the Mount Thompson Crematorium in Brisbane's south on 5 February 1972. Annette struggled to cope after he died, and Mipps, who was making do on a war widow's pension, eventually persuaded her sister to move into her small 'fibro' cottage with linoleum floors so they could keep each other company. They had been best friends for almost nine decades and they consoled each other in their loneliness.

A friend gave Annette a pedigree Siamese cat. She named it Tania and doted on it just as she had doted on Cooee the dog. In the same way she had used exercise to overcome rickets, Annette now performed morning exercises religiously in the hope she could exorcise some of the heartache she felt without Jimmie.

She would rather miss her breakfast than her exercises, Mipps said, but still the pain of Jimmie's passing remained. She had shelved her swimming when she was nursing Jimmie and never really regained her form.[14]

Annette's brother, Fred, who had lived much of his adult life in the south of France, also died in 1972, on a holiday in Genoa, Italy, and Annette and Mipps arranged for his body to be flown back to France for burial beside his late wife in her family's mausoleum at the seaside resort of Arcachon.

It was at Mipps's modest home that Annette was interviewed by Australian film historian Joel Greenberg in 1974 about the great days of the silent era. Annette's memory needed jogging at times and she would call out to Mipps for assistance, as her sister washed the dishes. Annette became confused about the dates and times of some of the great events in her life and told Greenberg that two years on, she had not recovered from Jimmie's death.

'When he died it was awful,' she explained. 'Sixty years is too long really to be married to one person but we got on so well ... he was a wonderful husband.'[15]

Annette told Greenberg that she was so angry that she did not keep copies of her movies which, like many of the silent era films, were lost or destroyed or simply deteriorated over time. Only the least regarded of her films, *Venus of the South Seas*, remained in its entirety.

Money was short for Annette, too. She had 16,000 U.S. dollars earning 5.75 per cent interest at the Bank of America in Long Beach,[16] but the income it produced did not go far.

A woman named Kitch Robinson, who had lived on neighbouring Rabbit Island when Annette and Mipps were on

Newry, offered to sell Annette's obsolete mink coat for her on a 50 per cent commission. Kitch put an advertisement in *The Sydney Morning Herald* classifieds: 'Movie Star, retired to the Gold Coast, no longer has need for mink coat.' The advertisement sparked enormous curiosity and the coat sold for 600 dollars to a woman who wore it to the opening of the new Sydney Opera House.[17]

In April 1974, Annette put down 220 dollars on a 329-dollar OPSM hearing aid and agreed to pay off the balance at 16 dollars a month.[18] Two months later, with faltering steps, she walked into the Southport branch of the Commonwealth Bank and withdrew 15 dollars from her account. She had only sixteen cents left, but from 8 August 1974, her Australian Government age pension was increased to 62 dollars a fortnight.[19]

Annette remained as generous as ever, though, and despite her dwindling resources she donated her Red Cross flag, signed by Eisenhower, Truman, Macarthur and other famous figures, to the Southport R.S.L. Club.[20]

LATE IN 1974, BUCK DAWSON, the executive director of the International Swimming Hall of Fame based in Florida, placed an advertisement in the Sydney press asking if anyone had an address for the 'swimming legend Annette Kellerman'. Someone evidently did because, early in 1975, Annette received a letter from Dawson dated 17 January.

'Dear Annette: AT LAST we found your address!' he wrote. 'We are pleased to inform you that you are being inducted into the International Swimming Hall of Fame on May 16, 1975 in Fort Lauderdale, Florida.'[21]

The Hall of Fame would pay for Annette to attend, and the guest speaker at the induction ceremony would be Senator Barry Goldwater, who had run against Lyndon Johnson for the United States presidency a decade earlier.

Buck Dawson would organise Esther Williams to meet Annette's flight in Los Angeles for some pre-publicity, and he had arranged for Annette to appear as a guest on America's national *Today Show*, where she would be interviewed by the iconic journalist Barbara Walters as the first 'liberated' woman in sport. The *Today Show*, which Dawson said had 'the biggest daytime audience of any TV show in the world', would also play footage from Annette's swimming and diving days, including Jimmie's underwater footage, and show what they could from her movies.

Annette's old friends Mina Wylie and Alick Wickham were also being inducted into the Hall of Fame, and Olympic greats Johnny Weissmuller and Buster Crabbe, whose fame had mushroomed after playing Flash Gordon in the movies, would be in Florida among an audience of 3000 to salute Annette and the other inductees.[22]

'Please, Annette,' Dawson begged, 'don't think you are too old to come! We must have you here in Florida.'[23]

Annette was beside herself with joy and pride at the honour and it put an extra spring in her step as, now four months short of her eighty-ninth birthday, she did another high kick for a *Gold Coast Bulletin* photographer.[24]

'This trip to America is a nice finale for me,' she told the paper, 'and I'll never want to do anything else. I've had a career second to nobody and I was happily married for sixty years. I've finished up a nice old lady living out her life on the wonderful Gold Coast.'[25]

The ABC produced a television program about Annette called *Behind the Legend*,[26] although she blushed a little and said she was embarrassed at being called 'a legend'.

ANNETTE WAS ADAMANT THAT, despite her age, she would fly to America for the Hall of Fame ceremony, even though she confessed she was now too old to swim. She still sunbathed a little and was still well enough to walk on the beach, grow her geraniums and look after her cat.[27] She and Mipps never missed anything on television starring Annette's pal Lucille Ball.

But in April 1975, a month before Annette was due to fly to Fort Lauderdale, she had a bad fall and badly injured her knee.

It was a shock to a nervous system already overloaded from worrying how she was going to cope with the excitement of interviews and receptions in America.[28] Her doctor said there was no way that in her frail state Annette could make the trip. It was a bitter blow for her.

The organisers understood, and sent Annette a plaque honouring her for more than seventy years of work as the 'greatest salesman for swimming ever'.[29] But she was still broken-hearted about missing the festivity.

Television network Channel 7 prepared a script for a *This is Your Life* episode celebrating Annette's career, but it was scuppered because of Annette's increasing ill health.

She began to fret about what would happen to the enormous collection of costumes and memorabilia she had gathered in the days when she was headline news around the world.

Then, sitting together in Mipps' little house, the elderly widowed sisters watched an ABC current affairs program called *This Day Tonight*. It featured a segment on the Sydney Opera House archives, displaying gowns that once belonged to Dame Nellie Melba, their mother's former music student.

Annette turned to Mipps and told her that's where she wanted her collection to go. The Sydney Opera House, after all, was beside the stretch of water where Annette had learned to swim at Farmer's Baths.

Annette turned eighty-nine on 6 July 1975, and two months later, Barbara Firth, the exhibition co-ordinator for the Opera House archives, and her husband, Gordon, visited her on the Gold Coast. Over five days the Firths itemised the full extent of Annette's seven huge trunks and five suitcases full of history, including her bright-yellow movie mermaid tail, racing costumes, posters from her shows around the world and autographed photos from dozens of her Hollywood pals.

Annette was very tired and would often doze off during the inventory, but then a sudden burst of energy would revive her as she thought of her life being celebrated on such a grand scale at such an august building.

The first Exhibition of the Sydney Opera House Archives of Theatrical Memorabilia was scheduled to be opened by New South Wales Premier Tom Lewis on 15 December 1975.

For Annette, though, her job was done. Her story had come full circle, her life's treasures returning to the place where she first became one with the water. Just a few days after newspapers began reporting her donation to the Opera House, Annette was admitted to a public ward at the Southport General Hospital with a high fever. Annette said she wanted to stay in the public ward because she hated to be alone.[30] Doctors feared the onset of pneumonia.[31]

On 17 October, she was moved from Southport General Hospital to a local nursing home[32] but, as weak as she was, she insisted on crawling or falling out of bed to prove that she could still walk.[33] It was only a matter of time until that stopped. Her health worsened and she was taken back to a public ward at the Southport Hospital.

On 4 November, Annette's eyes closed for the last time and she fell into a coma. She died at 7.20 a.m. on 6 November 1975.

'You could say she died of a heart attack,' her doctor said, 'but really, she just ran out of steam in her ninetieth year.'[34]

Four days after Annette's passing, the Gold Coast said a hushed and reverent farewell when eighty people gathered at the Allambe Garden of Memories in Nerang to pay their final tribute. It was a quiet end to a life filled with action and excitement, and as rain began to fall on the crematorium, one of the mourners remarked that it was fitting, since Annette always loved the water.[35]

School children, members of local surf and swimming clubs and charity representatives formed a guard of honour. Six pall bearers from the Southport Surf Club and the charity Legacy carried Annette's coffin, draped in the Australian and American flags, into the chapel for a service conducted by Roman Catholic priest Brian Curran.

ANNETTE HAD LITTLE MONEY when she died, but she left 10,000 dollars to the Queensland Spastic Welfare League, with the rest of her money to be divided between the Legacy Fund of Brisbane and the Gold Coast Garden Settlement for the Aged, which was run by the Methodist Church.

Her final wish was that Mipps, who had been Annette's carer in her last few years, perform one last act of charity. Way back in 1926, when Annette and Mipps first saw the exhibition about the Great Barrier Reef in London, Annette had floated the idea of ending her days amid the blue waves, white sands and spectacular coral of the islands there. As time went on and the sisters lived on Lindeman and Newry Islands, Annette asked Mipps to do what she could to make that happen if Annette was the first of them to pass.

So it was that a week after Annette's death Mipps took a free seat, No. 19D, provided for her by the airline T.A.A., and made a ninety-minute flight from Brisbane to Mackay. She then travelled on to Shute Harbour, where she boarded a small Twin Otter aircraft for a short flight over Lindeman Island and the waters of Kennedy Sound.

Mipps carried a small casket containing all that remained of a sister she revered. Over Kennedy Sound, as the Twin Otter flew low, a porthole on the aircraft was opened and 88-year-old Mipps said a last goodbye to her adored sister, the daredevil, world champion swimmer, and star of stage and screen. Mipps set Annette's ashes free, and, accompanied by a glorious array of flowers, they floated down on the breeze towards the gentle azure waves of the Coral Sea.

Mipps would go to her own rest six years later, satisfied that she had fulfilled Annette's dying wish.[36]

As the Twin Otter flew on over that glorious reef and spectacular coral, Annette Kellerman was at one with the sea again, her wondrous, joyous spirit drifting off across the vast spread of blue water into eternity, forever the Australian Mermaid.

Acknowledgements

ANNETTE KELLERMAN had an unquenchable zest for life and a tireless passion for her work.

For the last thirteen years, among the brilliant, creative people at HarperCollins/ABC Books, I have been surrounded by a team with the same unstinting zeal.

Thanks so much to my publisher Roberta Ivers, and to Jim Demetriou, Lachlan McLaine, Brigitta Doyle, Helen Littleton, Hannah Lynch, Jacqui Furlong, Erin Dunk, Nicolette Houben, Poppy Nwosu, Trudi Webster and Brendon Redmond for their hard work and generous support of my books.

I'm ever grateful to Jude McGee, a marvellous editor whose advice and enthusiasm is precious.

Thanks also to Michelle Zaiter who designed the stunning cover for this book, perfectly capturing Annette at her most radiant and joyful.

I am in debt to Emily Gibson and Barbara Firth for their 2005 book *The Original Million Dollar Mermaid,* and to Peter Cox for his work with Annette's collection at the Powerhouse Museum, to Beth Taylor and James Dyer from the National Film and Sound Archive of Australia, and to Glenda Veitch, and all of her diligent colleagues at the State Library of New South Wales.

Annette Kellerman was an extraordinary character. Thank you to everyone who helped tell the story of the Australian Mermaid.

Bibliography

BOOKS
Susan K. Cahn, *Coming on Strong: Gender and Sexuality in Twentieth-Century Women's Sport,* The Free Press, 1994.
Forbes Carlisle, *Forbes Carlisle on Swimming,* Pelham, 1963.
Andrew L. Erdman, *Blue Vaudeville,* McFarland & Co., 2004
Emily Gibson, Barbara Firth, *The Original Million Dollar Mermaid,* Allen & Unwin, 2005.
Greg Growden, *The Snowy Baker Story,* Random House, 2003.
Philip Hayward, *Tide Lines,* The Music Archive for The Pacific Press, 2001
William Fritz Jackson, *James Jackson et ses fils: notice sur leur vie et sur les établissements qu'ils ont fondés ou dirigés en,* [James Jackson and his sons: notice on their life and on the establishments which they founded or directed in], Chamerot et Renouard, 1893.
Annette Kellerman, *Fairy Tales of the South Seas,* Sampson Low, Marston & Co., 1926.
Annette Kellerman, *How to Swim,* George H. Doran Company, 1918.
Annette Kellerman, *My Story* (unpublished), SLNSW, MLMSS 6270/1.
Annette Kellerman, *Physical Beauty – How to Keep It,* George H. Doran, 1918.
Groucho Marx, *Groucho and Me,* Da Capo Press, 2009
Cyril Pearl, *Australia's Yesterdays,* Reader's Digest Services, 1974.
Charles Samuels, Louise Samuels, *Once Upon a Stage: The Merry World of Vaudeville,* Dodd, Mead & Co., 1974.
Victoria Sherrow, *The Encyclopedia of Women and Sports,* ABC-CLIO, 1996
Anthony Slide, *Encyclopedia of Vaudeville,* University of Mississippi Press, 2012.
Esther Williams, *The Million Dollar Mermaid,* Harcourt, 1999.
Marcelle Wooster, Unpublished memories of her sister Annette and their family, SLNSW, MLMSS 6270/1.

NEWSPAPERS and MAGAZINES

The *Advertiser* (Adelaide)
The *Advocate* (Melbourne)
The *Age* (Melbourne)
The *Albuquerque Journal* (New Mexico, U.S.A.)
American Music Teacher
Anaconda Standard (Anaconda, Montana, U.S.A.)
The *Arena* (Melbourne)
The *Arena-Sun* (Melbourne)
The *Argus* (Melbourne)
Army News (Darwin)
The *Arrow* (Sydney)
The *Ashbourne Telegraph* (Derbyshire, U.K.)
The *Atlanta Georgian and News* (Atlanta, Georgia, U.S.A.)
The *Auckland Star* (New Zealand)
The *Australian Jewish Herald* (Melbourne)
The *Australian Star* (Sydney)
Australian Town and Country Journal (Sydney)
The *Australian Women's Weekly*
The *Ballarat Star*
Barre Daily Times (Barre, Vermont, U.S.A.)
Barrier Miner (Broken Hill, N.S.W.)
The *Bemidji Daily Pioneer* (Minnesota, U.S.A.)
The *Bendigo Independent*
Berkeley Daily Gazette (California, U.S.A.)
The *Bioscope* (London, U.K.)
Birmingham Daily Gazette (U.K.)
Birmingham Weekly Mercury (U.K.)
The *Boston Globe*
The *Boston Post* (U.S.A.)
The *Boston Sunday Post*
The *Bradford Era* (Bradford, Pennsylvania, U.S.A.)
Brighton Southern Cross (Melbourne)
The *Brisbane Courier*
Britannia and Eve (London)
The *Bulletin* (Sydney)
The *Cairns Post* (Qld)
The *Canberra Times*
The *Catholic Press* (Sydney)
The *Caucasian* (Alexandria, Louisiana, U.S.A.)
Chicago Day Book
Chicago Examiner
Chicago Record-Herald
Chronicle (Adelaide)
Cincinnati Herald (Ohio, U.S.A)
Collier's Weekly (New York)
The *Commercial Tribune* (Cincinnati, Ohio, U.S.A.)
The *County Review* (Riverhead, New York State, U.S.A.)
The *Courier-Mail* (Brisbane)
Critic (Adelaide)
The *Critic* (Hobart)
Daily Capital News (Jefferson City, Missouri, U.S.A.)
The *Daily Express* (London, U.K.)
The *Daily Mail* (Brisbane)
The *Daily Mercury* (Mackay, Qld)
The *Daily Mirror* (London, U.K.)
The *Daily Mirror* (Sydney)
The *Daily News* (London, U.K.)
The *Daily News* (Perth)
The *Daily Record* (Glasgow, U.K.)
The *Daily Telegraph* (Sydney)
The *Daily Telegraph & Courier* (London, U.K.)
The *Danville Gazette* (Danville, Indiana, USA)
The *Des Moines News* (Iowa, U.S.A.)
Detroit News
The *Detroit Times*
The *Dover Express*
Dublin Evening Mail
The *Dundee Courier*

Bibliography

The Dundee Evening Telegraph
Dunkirk Evening Observer, (New York, U.S.A.)
The Edinburgh Evening News
The Empire (Sydney)
The Empire News & The Umpire (Manchester, U.K.)
Evening Despatch (Birmingham, U.K.)
The Evening Journal (Adelaide)
The Evening Mail (Fremantle, W.A.)
The Evening Star (Boulder, W.A.)
The Evening Star (Washington D.C., U.S.A.)
The Evening World (New York)
Eustis Lake Region (Florida, U.S.A.)
Exhibitors Herald and Motography (Chicago, Illinois, U.S.A.)
The Express and Telegraph (Adelaide)
The Fitzroy City Press (Melbourne)
The Fort Wayne Daily News (Texas, U.S.A.)
The Frederick News Post (Frederick, Maryland, U.S.A.)
Freeman's Journal (Sydney)
Gadfly (Adelaide)
The Galveston Daily News (Texas, U.S.A.)
The Geelong Advertiser
The Globe (London, U.K.)
Gold Coast Bulletin (Qld)
Gold Coast Mirror (Qld)
Gold Coast News (Qld)
Grimsby News (U.K.)
Guernsey Evening Press and Star
Halifax Daily Guardian (U.K.)
Harrisburg Telegraph (Pennsylvania, (U.S.A.)
The Herald (Melbourne)
The Herald-Republican (Salt Lake City, Utah, U.S.A.)
The Illawarra Mercury (Wollongong)
The Illustrated London News
Illustrated Police News (London, U.K.)

The Illustrated Sydney News
Indianapolis Star
The Indianapolis Sun
Joliet Evening Herald (Illinois, U.S.A.)
Kalgoorlie Miner (W.A.)
Kansas City Times (Missouri)
The Kinematograph Weekly (London, U.K.)
The Kinematograph and Lantern Weekly (London, U.K.)
The Labor World (Duluth, Minnesota, U.S.A.)
Lancashire Evening Post
Las Vegas Daily Optic (Las Vegas, New Mexico, U.S.A.)
The Leader (Melbourne)
The Leader (Orange, N.S.W.)
The Leeds Mercury
The Libertyville Lake County Independent and Waukegan Weekly Sun (Libertyville, Illinois, U.S.A.)
The Lincoln Daily Star (Lincoln, Nebraska, U.S.A.)
The Lincolnshire Echo (U.K.)
Liverpool Evening Express
Logansport Daily Reporter (Logansport, Indiana, U.S.A.)
London Evening Standard
Long Beach Independent (California, U.S.A.)
Long Branch Daily Record (Long Branch, New Jersey, U.S.A.)
Los Angeles Times
The Lowell Sun (Massachusetts, U.S.A.)
The Lyttelton Times (Christchurch, N.Z.)
Madison Capital Times (Wisconsin, U.S.A.)
The Maitland Mercury and Hunter River General Advertiser
The Maitland Weekly Mercury

The Manchester Courier (U.K.)
The Manchester Evening News
Manchester Times
Maryborough Chronicle, Wide Bay and Burnett Advertiser (Qld.)
The Mercury (Hobart)
The Middletown Press (Connecticut, U.S.A.)
The Morning Bulletin (Rockhampton, Qld)
The Morning Leader (London, U.K.)
The Morning Telegraph (New York)
Motion Picture Classic (New York)
Motion Picture Magazine (New York)
Motography (Chicago, Illinois, U.S.A.)
The Moving Picture World (New York)
Music Hall and Theatre Review, (London, U.K.)
The Muswellbrook Chronicle (N.S.W.)
The Nelson Evening Mail (New Zealand)
Newark Star and Newark Advertiser (Newark, New Jersey, U.S.A.)
Newcastle Daily Chronicle (U.K.)
Newcastle Morning Herald and Miners' Advocate (N.S.W.)
The New Castle News (Pennsylvania, U.S.A.)
Newfoundland Weekly (Boston, Massachusetts, U.S.A.)
The News (Adelaide)
The New York Clipper
New York Dramatic News
New York Star
The New York Sun
The New York Telegraph
The New York Times
The New Zealand Times (Wellington)
Northants Evening Post
Northern Star (Lismore)
North Judson News (Indiana, U.S.A.)
Norwich Sun (New York, U.S.A.)
NZ Truth (New Zealand)

Oakland Tribune (Oakland, California, U.S.A.)
The Ogden Daily Standard (Ogden, Utah, U.S.A.)
The Omaha Daily Bee (Nebraska, U.S.A.)
Pall Mall Gazette (London, U.K.)
The Penny Press (Middletown, Connecticut, U.S.A.)
The People (London, U.K.)
The Philadelphia Inquirer
Photoplay (Chicago, Illinois, U.S.A.)
Picture-Play (New York)
The Pittsburgh Leader
Port Arthur News (Texas, U.S.A.)
The Poverty Bay Herald (New Zealand)
The Prahran Telegraph (Melbourne)
The Press (Christchurch, New Zealand)
The Press-Telegram (Long Beach, California, U.S.A.)
Queensland Times, Ipswich Herald and General Advertiser
The Quincy Daily Herald (Illinois, U.S.A.)
Quiz (Adelaide)
The Racine Daily Journal (Wisconsin, U.S.A.)
The Referee (Sydney)
The Register (Adelaide)
San Antonio Light (San Antonio, Texas, U.S.A.)
San Francisco Call
Santa Ana Daily Register (California, U.S.A.)
The Scone Advocate (N.S.W.)
The Scottish Referee (Glasgow)
The Seattle Star (Washington, U.S.A.)
The Sheffield Daily Telegraph
South Coast Times and Wollongong Argus
Sporting Life: Dryblower's Journal (Kalgoorlie, W.A.)

The Sportsman (London)
The Staffordshire Advertiser
The Stage (London, U.K.)
The Star (Christchurch, New Zealand)
The Star (Sydney)
The Sun (Kalgoorlie)
The Sun (New York)
The Sun (Sydney)
The Sunday Oregonian (Portland, Oregon, U.S.A.)
The Sunday Star (Washington D.C., U.S.A.)
The Sunday Telegram (Clarksburg, West Virginia, U.S.A.)
The Sunday Telegraph (Sydney)
Swindon Advertiser and North Wilts Chronicle (U.K.)
The Sunday Times (Perth, W.A.)
The Sunday Times (Sydney)
The Sydney Daily Telegraph
The Sydney Mail and New South Wales Advertiser
The Sydney Morning Herald
The Sydney Sportsman
Table Talk (Melbourne)
The Telegraph (Brisbane)
The Toowoomba Chronicle
The Toowoomba Chronicle and Darling Downs Gazette
The Topeka Daily State Journal (Topeka, Kansas, U.S.A.)
The Townsville Daily Bulletin (Qld)
The Truth (Brisbane)
The Truth (Perth)
Truth (Sydney)
TV Times (Sydney)
The Van Wert Daily Bulletin (Van Wert, Ohio, U.S.A.)
Variety (New York)
Waco Morning News (Texas, U.S.A.)
The Wairarapa Daily Times (New Zealand)
Walkabout (Melbourne)
W.A. Sportsman (Perth)
The Washington Evening Star (Washington D.C., U.S.A.)
The Washington Herald (Washington D.C., U.S.A.)
The Washington Times (Washington D.C., U.S.A.)
The Weekly Times (Melbourne)
The West Australian (Perth)
The Westminster Gazette (U.K.)
The Wilmington Dispatch (Wilmington, North Carolina, U.S.A.)
The Wimbledon News (London, U.K.)
Winthrop Sun and Visitor (Winthrop, Massachusetts, U.S.A.)
Wolverton Express (Buckinghamshire, U.K.)
Woman's Home Companion (Springfield, Ohio)
The Worker (Brisbane)
The Zeehan and Dundas Herald (Tas.)

WEBSITES

Ancestry.com.au
Australian Dictionary of Biography, adb.anu.edu.au
Australian National Maritime Museum, collections.sea.museum
carllaemmlethefilm.com
dictionaryofsydney.org
extremeweatherwatch.com
gw.geneanet.org
goldcoaststories.com.au
Hollywood Walk of Fame, walkoffame.com
Internet Archive
jolson.org
Kingston Local History, localhistory.kingston.vic.gov.au

Library of Congress, loc.gov
Miss Annette Kellerman (1909), imdb.com.
National Film and Sound Archive Australia, nfsa.gov.au
National Library of Australia, library.gov.au
National Portrait Gallery, portrait.gov.au
'Teaching Melba', nelliemelbamuseum.com.au
New York Public Library Digital Collections, digitalcollections.nypl.org
palava.co
playbill.com
playingpasts.co.uk
Powerhouse Museum, collection.powerhouse.com.au
Reserve bank of Australia, rba.gov.au
Smithsonian Institution, smithsonianmag.com
Sport Australia Hall of Fame, sahof.org.au
starkcenter.org
State Library of New South Wales, sl.nsw.gov.au
State Library of Queensland, slq.qld.gov.auState Library of South Australia, slsa.sa.gov.au
State Library of Victoria, slv.vic.gov.au
thelondonwanderer.co.uk
topendsports.com
trove.nla.gov.au
Wikipedia
Women Film Pioneers Project, wfpp.columbia.edu

Endnotes

Prologue
1. *The Evening Star* (Washington D.C., U.S.A.), 7 February 1952, p. 14.
2. Mervyn LeRoy (15 October 1900 – 13 September 1987).
3. Berkeley William Enos, known professionally as Busby Berkeley (29 November 1895 – 14 March 1976).
4. 'Miss Kellerman in Great Form', *The Daily Mirror*, 1 August 1905, p. 5.
5. Annette Kellerman, *How to Swim*, George H. Doran Co., 1918, p. 34.
6. *Ibid.*
7. 'The Diving Venus', *The Danville Gazette* (Danville, Indiana), 16 February 1911, p. 4.
8. *The Evening Journal* (Adelaide), 10 June 1909, p. 1.
9. *Ibid.*
10. *The Atlanta Georgian and News* (U.S.A), 24 March 1911, p. 7.
11. Susan K. Cahn, *Coming on Strong: Gender and Sexuality in Twentieth-Century Women's Sport*, The Free Press, 1994, p. 6.
12. 'Annette Kellerman, Former Swim Star, Hails Successes of Modern Mermaids', *Long Beach Press-Telegram* (California), 11 February 1951, p. 23.
13. Esther Jane Williams (8 August 1921 – 6 June 2013).
14. Esther Williams, *The Million Dollar Mermaid*, Harcourt, 1999, p. 396.
15. *Ibid.*, p. 388.
16. Vincent X. Flaherty (1907–1977).
17. Vincent X. Flaherty 'Annette Kellerman, of Bathing-Suit Fame,' untitled and undated newspaper cutting, SLNSW MLMSS 6270, Box 2.

Chapter 1
1. Annette Marie Sarah Kellermann (6 July 1886 (Darlinghurst, N.S.W.) – 6 November 1975 (Southport, Qld)).
2. In an area that borders the suburb of Potts Point.
3. Alice Ellen Laurentine Charbonnet (12 December 1858 (Cincinnati, Ohio, USA) – 1 July 1914 (Paris, France)).
4. Frederick William Kellermann (23 May 1860 (Harrington St, Sydney) – 8 October 1907 (Paris, France)).
5. 'Family Notices', *The Sydney Morning Herald*, 10 July 1886, p. 1; *The Sydney Mail and New South Wales Advertiser*, 17 July 1886, p. 151.
6. Birth Certificate of Annette Kellermann, NSW Births, Deaths and Marriages, 2360/1886.
7. Annette Kellerman, 'My Story' (unpublished), SLNSW, MLMSS 6270/1.
8. James Jackson (14 March 1771 – 27 April 1829).
9. William Fritz Jackson, *James Jackson et ses fils: notice sur leur vie et sur les établissements qu'ils ont fondés ou dirigés en* [*James Jackson and his sons: notice on their life and on the establishments which they founded or directed in*], Chamerot et Renouard, 1893, p. 4.

10   Death Certificate of Joseph Jackson, N.S.W. Births, Deaths and Marriages, 1891/009179.
11   Ann Ellen Josephine Jackson (4 December, 1837 (London, U.K.) – 20 June 1882 (101 Victoria St, Darlinghurst, Sydney)).
12   Benjamin Amable Charbonnet (13 April 1833 (New Orleans, Louisiana, U.S.A.) – 15 July 1875 (Chicago, Illinois, U.S.A.)).
13   'Madame Charbonnet-Kellermann', *Table Talk* (Melbourne), 22 November 1889, p. 4.
14   'Madame Charbonnet Kellerman', *The Mercury* (Hobart), 2 January 1906, p. 5.
15   Félix Le Couppey (14 April 1811 – 4 July 1887).
16   'Mdlle. Charbonnet', *The Sydney Mail and New South Wales Advertiser*, 13 July 1878, p. 52.
17   Ibid.
18   'New Caledonia', *The Sydney Morning Herald*, 22 July 1867, p. 2.
19   'Advertising', *ibid.*, 3 September 1870, p. 6.
20   Amable Charbonnet to his sister, the Contesse d'Auvilliers, 19 January 1866, SLNSW, MLMSS 6270/1, A2.37b.
21   Amable Charbonnet to his mother, Marie, 21 April 1867, *ibid*, A2.39a.
22   *The Empire* (Sydney), 6 September 1870, p. 2.
23   'Madame Charbonnet-Kellermann', *Table Talk* (Melbourne), 22 November 1889, p. 4.
24   'Clearances', *The Sydney Morning Herald*, 28 July 1870, p. 4.
25   'Charbonnet-Kellerman', *Evening News* (Sydney), 27 October 1894, p. 6.
26   'Festivities to Admiral Roussin and Officers of the *Atalante*', *The Sydney Morning Herald*, 9 August 1873, p. 5.
27   Histoire des Musiques en Nouvelle-Calédonie 1843–2008, Musée de la Ville de Noumea, Exposition, December 2008, p. 44.
28   *Maryborough Chronicle, Wide Bay and Burnett Advertiser*, 30 October 1875, p. 2.
29   Marcelle Wooster, Unpublished memories, SLNSW, MLMSS 6270/1
30   Ibid.
31   26 October 1876.
32   Marie Gabriel Augustin Savard (21 August 1814 – 7 June 1881).
33   Cécile Louise Stéphanie Chaminade (8 August 1857 – 13 April 1944).
34   John Jerrould, 'Piano Music of Cécile Chaminade', *American Music Teacher*, Vol. 37, No. 3, January 1988, pp. 22–23, 46.
35   In September 1877.
36   'Clearances', *The Sydney Morning Herald*, 17 September 1877, p. 4.
37   'Mademoiselle Alice Charbonnet', *The Geelong Advertiser*, 29 May 1879, p. 3.
38   'Advertising', *The Sydney Morning Herald*, 13 April 1878, p. 2.
39   Kellerman, 'My Story', SLNSW, MLMSS 6270/1.
40   Ibid.
41   'Mdlle Charbonnet's Concert', *The Sydney Morning Herald*, 1 May 1878, p. 5.
42   'Sitting Down at the Piano', *Australian Town and Country Journal* (Sydney), 21 September 1878, p. 28.
43   Ibid.
44   *The Sydney Morning Herald*, 13 May 1878, p. 4.
45   'Advertising', *The Sydney Morning Herald*, 3 July 1878, p. 1.
46   'Mademoiselle Alice Charbonnet's Concert', *Freeman's Journal* (Sydney), 6 July 1878, p. 16.
47   'Amusements', *Evening News* (Sydney), 25 July 1878, p. 3.
48   *Freeman's Journal* (Sydney), 31 August 1878, p. 11.
49   'Advertising', *The Sydney Morning Herald*, 5 August 1878, p. 1.
50   'Amusements. Mdlle. Charbonnet's Concert', *The Sydney Morning Herald*, 27 August 1878, p. 5.
51   Wedding certificate for Fred Kellermann and Alice Charbonnet, NSW Registry of Births, Deaths & Marriages, Marriage Certificate, 1953/1882.

52 Emile Maxilien Kellermann (1871–1951).
53 Kellerman, 'My Story', SLNSW, MLMSS 6270/1.
54 *Ibid.*

Chapter 2
1 'Music & Drama', *The Sydney Mail and New South Wales Advertiser,* 26 October 1878, p. 666.
2 'Music and the Drama in New Zealand', *Australian Town and Country Journal* (Sydney), 14 December 1878, p. 13.
3 'Madame Charbonnet-Kellermann', *Table Talk* (Melbourne), 22 November 1889, p. 4.
4 George Augustus Constantine Phipps, 2nd Marquess of Normanby (23 July 1819 – 3 April 1890).
5 'Mdlle. Charbonnet and the "Markiss"', *Evening News* (Sydney), 9 May 1879, p. 4.
6 *Ibid.*
7 *Ibid.*
8 'Theatre Royal', *The Express and Telegraph* (Adelaide), 9 June 1879, p. 3.
9 'Mdlle. Charbonnet and the "Markiss"', *Evening News* (Sydney), 9 May 1879, p. 4.
10 *Ibid.*
11 George Richard Rignold, born Rignall (1839 – 16 December 1912).
12 'The Critic', *Australian Town and Country Journal* (Sydney), 7 June 1879, p. 41.
13 'You Take Your Choice', *Punch* (Melbourne), 4 December 1879, p. 7.
14 'The Metropolitan Liedertafel', *The Argus* (Melbourne), 2 December 1879, p. 7.
15 Camilla Urso (13 June 1840 – 20 January 1902).
16 'Mademoiselle Alice Charbonnet', *The Geelong Advertiser,* 29 May 1879, p. 3.
17 'Advertising', *The Sydney Morning Herald,* 26 November 1879, p. 2.
18 'Advertising', *The Argus* (Melbourne), 20 December 1879, p. 12.
19 George Leavis Allan (1826–1897).
20 'Charbonnet-Kellerman', *Evening News* (Sydney), 27 October 1894, p. 6.
21 Dame Nellie Melba (born Helen Porter Mitchell, 19 May 1861 – 23 February 1931).
22 'New Music', *The Sydney Morning Herald,* 20 February 1880, p. 6.
23 'How to Play the Piano', *The Sydney Morning Herald,* 16 September 1880, p. 5.
24 'Music & Drama', *The Sydney Mail and New South Wales Advertiser,* 4 September 1880, p. 466.
25 Carlotta Patti (30 October 1835 – 27 June 1889).
26 'Music and Drama', *The Sydney Mail and New South Wales Advertiser,* 2 April 1881, p. 553.
27 'Exhibition Notes', *The Argus* (Melbourne), 30 December 1880, p. 7.
28 Alfred Moul (c. 1852 – 18 January 1924).
29 'A Singular Law Case', *The Sydney Morning Herald,* 18 March 1881, p. 6.
30 'You Take Your Choice', *Punch* (Melbourne), 4 December 1879, p. 7.
31 'Music and Drama', *The Sydney Mail and New South Wales Advertiser,* 2 April 1881, p. 554.
32 'A Singular Law Case', *The Sydney Morning Herald,* 18 March 1881, p. 6.
33 *Ibid.*
34 'Family Notices', *The Sydney Daily Telegraph,* 22 June 1882, p. 2.
35 Magdeleine Joséphine Laurentine Jackson nee Bernard (24 February 1817 (Lyon, France) – 30 July 1901 (Sydney, N.S.W.)).
36 Death Certificate of Joseph Jackson, NSW Births, Deaths and Marriages, 1891/009179.
37 'Advertising', *The Sydney Morning Herald,* 8 August 1881, p. 1.
38 *Ibid.*, 26 November 1881, p. 2.
39 Frederick William Kellermann (c. 1822 (Frankfurt, Germany) – 10 February 1898 (St Leonards, N.S.W.)).

40	William Kellermann (c. 1820 (Germany) – 15 June 1891 (Darlinghurst, N.S.W.)).	10	Frederick Joseph Kellerman (13 March 1891 (Marrickville, N.S.W.) – 1972 (Genoa, Italy)).
41	'Shipping Intelligence: Arrivals', *Empire* (Sydney), 9 May 1853. p. 2.	11	NSW, Births Deaths and Marriages, Registration 21380/1891.
42	'Classified Advertising', *The Maitland Mercury and Hunter River General Advertiser*, 11 January 1854, p. 2.	12	'Advertising', *The Sydney Morning Herald*, 2 April 1892, p. 16.
43	*Sydney and New South Wales, Sands Street Index*, 1880 for William Kellermann.	13	'Madame Charbonnet-Kellermann', *Table Talk* (Melbourne), 22 November 1889, p. 4.
44	*Bulletin of Maitland and District Historical Society Inc.*, Vol. 28, no. 2, May 2021, p. 17.	14	*Ibid.*
		15	*Evening News* (Sydney), 4 December 1890, p. 5.
45	'Advertising', *The Sydney Morning Herald*, 29 Jun 1881, p. 2.	16	*The Illustrated Sydney News*, 22 April 1893, p. 7.
46	'Family Notices', *The Sydney Daily Telegraph*, 22 June 1882, p. 2.	17	Kellerman, 'My Story', SLNSW, MLMSS 6270/1.
47	*NSW Government Gazette*, 19 December 1884, p. 8434.	18	*Ibid.*
48	Maurice Charbonnet Kellermann (7 April 1885 (149 Phillip St, Sydney, N.S.W.) – 9 November 1943 (New York City, U.S.A.)).	19	*Ibid.*
		20	Emily Gibson, Barbara Firth, *The Original Million Dollar Mermaid*, Allen & Unwin, 2005, p. 5.
49	Kellerman, 'My Story', SLNSW, MLMSS 6270/1.	21	'The Sydney Orchestral Society', *The Australian Star* (Sydney), 27 April 1892, p. 6.
50	*Ibid.*	22	Kellerman, *How to Swim*, p. 14.
51	*Ibid.*	23	'The 1890s Depression', rba.gov.au.
		24	Marcelle Wooster, Unpublished memories, SLNSW, MLMSS 6270/1.
Chapter 3		25	*Ibid.*
1	Marcelle Marie Alice Wooster nee Kellermann (14 August 1887 (Darlinghurst, N.S.W.) – 22 June 1981 (Southport, Qld)).	26	Kellerman, 'My Story', SLNSW, MLMSS 6270/1.
		27	Annette Kellerman, *Fairy Tales of the South Seas*, Sampson Low, Marston & Co., 1926, p. 11.
2	'At the Passionists' Church', *Freeman's Journal* (Sydney), 27 April 1889, p. 15.	28	Frederick Cavill (10 July 1839 (Kensington, London, U.K.) – 9 February 1927 (Marrickville, N.S.W.)).
3	'Marrickville Burglaries', *Evening News* (Sydney), 2 November 1888, p. 7.		
		29	'Lavender Bay Baths', *Evening News* (Sydney), 2 June 1893, p. 3.
4	Marcelle Wooster, Unpublished memories, SLNSW, MLMSS 6270/1.	30	The natatorium was a landmark for years at Farm Cove and later Woolloomooloo, but in 1909 a storm tore it from its moorings and blew it across the harbour, leaving it smashed on the rocks of a deserted cove. The then seventy-year-old Fred Cavill declared he was too old to build another pool and decided to retire.
5	Kellerman, *How to Swim*, George H. Doran Co., 1918, p. 14.		
6	Kellerman, 'My Story', SLNSW, MLMSS 6270/1.		
7	*Motion Picture Classic* (New York), February 1917, p. 17.		
8	Marcelle Wooster, Unpublished memories, SLNSW, MLMSS 6270/1		
9	Kellerman, 'My Story', SLNSW, MLMSS 6270/1.	31	Gibson, Firth, *The Original Million Dollar Mermaid*, p. 8.

32 Kellerman, *Fairy Tales*, p. 11.
33 Kellerman, *How to Swim*, p. 14.
34 Percy Cavill (1875–1940).
35 Kellerman, 'My Story', SLNSW, MLMSS 6270/1.
36 'An Interview with Miss Kellerman', *The Ballarat Star*, 8 February 1905, p. 1.
37 Arthur Rowland Channel 'Tums' Cavill (1877–1914).
38 'Sporting Notions', *The Bulletin*, 5 May 1904, p. 26.
39 Kellerman, *How to Swim*, p. 15.
40 Marcelle Wooster, Unpublished memories, SLNSW, MLMSS 6270/1.
41 Kellerman, *How to Swim*, p. 15.
42 *Ibid.*

Chapter 4
1 'Juvenile Party', *The Sydney Mail and New South Wales Advertiser*, 4 November 1893, p. 949.
2 'Social Items', *The Illustrated Sydney News*, 4 November 1893, p. 7.
3 'Juvenile Fancy Dress Ball', *The Sydney Mail and New South Wales Advertiser*, 7 July 1894, p. 28.
4 'New Music', *Evening News* (Sydney), 7 March 1898, p. 3.
5 Kellerman, 'My Story', SLNSW, MLMSS 6270/1.
6 'Australian Musical Association', *Truth*, 21 October 1894, p. 2.
7 Marcelle Wooster, Unpublished memories, SLNSW, MLMSS 6270/1.
8 *Ibid.*
9 *Ibid.*
10 'Madame Charbonnet Kellerman', *The Mercury* (Hobart), 2 January 1906, p. 5.
11 'Hotel Australia', dictionaryofsydney.org
12 'A Society Conversazione', *Evening News* (Sydney), 20 November 1894, p. 2.
13 *Ibid.*
14 *Ibid.*
15 Kellerman, *How to Swim*, p. 15.
16 'The Clitherow Soirees', *The Sydney Morning Herald*, 23 November 1895, p. 9.
17 Kellerman, 'My Story', SLNSW, MLMSS 6270/1.
18 'Theatre Royal – "Henry V"', *Evening News* (Sydney), 30 November 1896, p. 3.
19 Marcelle Wooster, Unpublished memories, SLNSW, MLMSS 6270/1.
20 *Ibid.*
21 Emily Soldene (30 September 1838 – 8 April 1912).
22 'Sydney Week by Week', *Evening News*, 3 June 1898, p. 3.
23 Kellerman, 'My Story', SLNSW, MLMSS 6270/1.
24 Marcelle Wooster, Unpublished memories, SLNSW, MLMSS 6270/1.
25 'Miss Annette Kellermann', *Table Talk* (Melbourne), 19 February 1903, p. 14.
26 Kellerman, *Fairy Tales*, p. 12.
27 Kellerman, *How to Swim*, p. 15.
28 Reginald Leslie 'Snowy' Baker (8 February 1884 (Surry Hills, N.S.W.) – 2 December, 1953 (Los Angeles, California, U.S.A.)).
29 Kellerman, *Fairy Tales*, p. 12.
30 Frank Baker (11 October 1892 (Melbourne, Vic.) – 30 December 1980 (Woodland Hills, Los Angeles, California, U.S.A.)).
31 Gibson, Firth, *The Original Million Dollar Mermaid*, p. 11.
32 Greg Growden, *The Snowy Baker Story*, Random House, 2003, pp. 317–318.
33 'Entertainments: Music', *The Weekly Times* (Melbourne), 3 November 1900, p. 15.
34 'Kellermann Comedy Co.', *The Illawarra Mercury* (Wollongong), 15 January 1902, p. 4.
35 'Miss Annette Kellermann', *Table Talk* (Melbourne), 19 February 1903, p. 14.
36 Frederick Claude Vivian Lane (2 February 1880 – 14 May 1969).
37 Marcelle Wooster, Unpublished memories, SLNSW, MLMSS 6270/1.
38 Alick Wickham (1 June 1886 (Gizo, New Georgia, Solomon Islands) – 10 August 1967 (Honiara, Solomon Islands)).

39 John Trudgen (1852–1902).
40 Kellerman, *How to Swim*, p. 17.
41 Forbes Carlisle, *Forbes Carlisle on Swimming*, Pelham, 1963, p. 135.
42 Marcelle Wooster, Unpublished memories, SLNSW, MLMSS 6270/1.
43 Kellerman, 'My Story', SLNSW, MLMSS 6270/1.
44 Ibid.

Chapter 5
1 Kellerman, *How to Swim*, p. 16.
2 'Miss Annette Kellermann', *Table Talk* (Melbourne), 19 February 1903, p. 14.
3 Marcelle Wooster, Unpublished memories, SLNSW, MLMSS 6270/1.
4 Kellerman, 'My Story', SLNSW, MLMSS 6270/1.
5 Ibid.
6 Kellerman, *How to Swim*, pp. 16–17.
7 Sarah Frances 'Fanny' Durack' (27 October 1889 – 20 March 1956).
8 Wilhelmina 'Mina' Wylie (27 June 1891 – 6 July 1984).
9 'Swimming', *Evening News* (Sydney), 9 December 1901, p. 3.
10 Cecil Patrick Healy (28 November 1881 – 29 August 1918).
11 'Swimming', *The Australian Town and Country Journal* (Sydney), 21 December 1901, p. 41.
12 Kellerman, 'My Story', SLNSW, MLMSS 6270/1.
13 *Punch* (Melbourne), 1 May 1902, p. 23.
14 *The Zeehan and Dundas Herald* (Tas.), 25 September 1901, p. 2.
15 'Mentone', *The Argus* (Melbourne), 24 September 1901, p. 7.
16 'Mentone', *Brighton Southern Cross*, 21 September 1901, p. 3.
17 'Society Notes', *The Arena* (Melbourne), 9 January 1902, p. 15.
18 Kellerman, 'My Story', SLNSW, MLMSS 6270/1.
19 Ibid.
20 'A World's Record', *Illawarra Mercury* (Wollongong), 15 January 1902, p. 2.
21 'Kellermann Comedy Co.', *Illawarra Mercury* (Wollongong), 15 January 1902, p. 4.
22 'Nautilus Swimming Club's Carnival', *The Sydney Morning Herald*, 6 January 1902, p. 4.
23 Ibid.
24 Ibid.
25 'Wollongong Swimming Club Carnival', *The Sydney Morning Herald*, 17 February 1902, p. 4.
26 'First Ladies' Swimming Championship', *The Sydney Mail and New South Wales Advertiser*, 5 April 1902, p. 864.
27 'Ladies' Swimming', *The Daily Telegraph* (Sydney), 15 February 1902, p. 12.
28 'First Ladies' Swimming Championship', *The Sydney Mail and New South Wales Advertiser*, 5 April 1902, p. 864.
29 'Swimming', *The Sydney Sportsman*, 2 April 1902, p. 7.
30 Ibid.
31 'Swimming', *The Australian Star* (Sydney), 14 April 1902, p. 7.
32 'The Gun', *The Sydney Mail and New South Wales Advertiser*, 19 April 1902, p. 1012.
33 'Swimming', *The Weekly Times* (Melbourne), 26 April 1902, p. 18.
34 *The Bulletin*, Vol. 23, No. 1158, 26 April 1902, pp. 15, 24.
35 Kellerman, 'My Story', SLNSW, MLMSS 6270/1.
36 Ibid.
37 Ibid.

Chapter 6
1 Leo Gamble, 'Mentone's Million Dollar Mermaid', Kingston Local History, localhistory.kingston.vic.gov.au
2 Kellerman, 'My Story', SLNSW, MLMSS 6270/1.
3 'A Water Nymph', *The Herald* (Melbourne), 24 January 1903, p. 4.
4 'News of the Week', *Brighton Southern Cross* (Melbourne), 17 January 1903, p. 2.
5 'A Swimming Demonstration', *The Age* (Melbourne), 26 January 1903, p. 9.

6. 'Ladies' Letter', *Table Talk*, 29 January 1903, p. 20.
7. 'A Water Nymph', *The Herald* (Melbourne), 24 January 1903, p. 4.
8. 'Ladies' Letter', *Table Talk*, 29 January 1903, p. 20.
9. 'A Water Nymph', *The Herald* (Melbourne), 24 January 1903, p. 4.
10. 'Ladies' Letter', *Table Talk*, 29 January 1903, p. 20.
11. 'A Swimming Demonstration', *The Age* (Melbourne), 26 January 1903, p. 9.
12. *Punch* (Melbourne), 29 January 1903, p. 150.
13. *Ibid.*
14. *Ibid*, p. 142.
15. *Ibid*, 5 February 1903, p. 175.
16. 'A Champion Lady Swimmer', *The Weekly Times* (Melbourne), 31 January 1903, p. 9.
17. 'Miss Annette Kellermann', *Table Talk* (Melbourne), 19 February 1903, p. 14.
18. *Ibid.*
19. *Ibid.*
20. 'Society', *The Arena-Sun* (Melbourne), 12 February 1903, p. 18.
21. 'How to Swim', *The Brisbane Courier*, 16 March 1903, p. 2.
22. 'Miss Annette Kellermann', *Table Talk* (Melbourne), 19 February 1903, p. 14.
23. 'Society', *The Arena-Sun* (Melbourne), 26 March 1903, p. 18.
24. Cyril Pearl, *Australia's Yesterdays*, Reader's Digest Services, 1974, p. 193.
25. *Punch* (Melbourne), 2 April 1903, p. 24.
26. Pearl, *Australia's Yesterdays*, p. 193.
27. *The Bulletin*, Vol. 24, No. 1208, 11 April 1903, p. 21.
28. *Ibid.*
29. Kellerman, 'My Story', SLNSW, MLMSS 6270/1.
30. *Ibid.*
31. 'Miss Annette Kellermann', *Table Talk* (Melbourne), 19 February 1903, p. 14.
32. *Ibid.*
33. 'Australia's Lady Swimming Champion', *The Sydney Mail and New South Wales Advertiser*, 3 June 1903, p. 1373.
34. *Ibid.*
35. *Ibid.*

Chapter 7

1. Joseph Thomas 'Bland' Holt (24 March 1851 (Norwich, England) – 28 June 1942 (East Melbourne)).
2. 'Theatre Royal', *The Argus* (Melbourne), 9 June 1903, p. 6.
3. *The Bulletin*, Vol. 24, No. 1221, 9 July 1903, p. 27.
4. Marcelle Wooster, Unpublished memories, SLNSW, MLMSS 6270/1.
5. Kellerman, *How to Swim*, p. 18.
6. Marcelle Wooster, Unpublished memories, SLNSW, MLMSS 6270/1.
7. *The Age* (Melbourne), 3 October 1903, p. 12.
8. *The Bulletin*, Vol. 24, No. 1211, 2 May 1903, p. 14.
9. *Critic* (Adelaide), 17 February 1904, p. 27.
10. Marcelle Wooster, Unpublished memories, SLNSW, MLMSS 6270/1.
11. 'Great Swimming Feat', *The Herald* (Melbourne), 23 April 1904, p. 6.
12. The official distance was 2 miles and 21 chains.
13. 'A Remarkable Swim', *The Age* (Melbourne), 25 April 1904, p. 5.
14. 'Swimming: A World's Record', *The Weekly Times* (Melbourne), 30 April 1904, p. 18.
15. 'A Remarkable Swim', *The Age* (Melbourne), 25 April 1904, p. 5.
16. 'Diving Accident', *The Daily Telegraph* (Sydney) 9 May 1904, p. 6.
17. 'Diving Accident', *Sunday Times* (Sydney), 8 May 1904, p. 5.
18. Kellerman, *How to Swim*, p. 19.
19. 'Amusements', *The Advertiser* (Adelaide), 2 January 1905, p. 9.
20. 'A Lady Swimmer', *Evening Journal* (Adelaide), 9 December 1904, p. 3.
21. 'The Lady Swimmer', *ibid*, 7 January 1905, p. 7.

22. 'Miss Annette Kellerman', *Barrier Miner* (Broken Hill, N.S.W.), 14 January 1905, p. 5.
23. Kellerman, *How to Swim*, p. 19.
24. *The Evening Star* (Boulder, W.A.), 26 January 1905, p. 2.
25. 'Swimming Carnival at Maryborough', *The Weekly Times* (Melbourne), 28 January 1905, p. 12.
26. Leo Gamble, 'Mentone's Million Dollar Mermaid', Kingston Local History, localhistory.kingston.vic.gov.au
27. 'Miss Annette Kellerman', *The Argus* (Melbourne), 3 February 1905, p. 8.
28. 'Critic', (Adelaide), 8 February 1905, p. 16.
29. 'Miss Annette Kellerman', *The Argus* (Melbourne), 3 February 1905, p. 8.
30. 'Five-Mile Swim', *The Herald* (Melbourne) 2 February 1905, p. 4.
31. Ibid.
32. 'Miss Annette Kellerman', *The Argus* (Melbourne), 3 February 1905, p. 8.
33. 'An Interview With Miss Kellerman', *The Ballarat Star*, 8 February 1905, p. 1.
34. *The Sportsman* (London), 13 March 1905, p. 7.
35. 'An Interview with Miss Kellerman', *The Ballarat Star*, 8 February 1905, p. 1.
36. Ibid.
37. Ibid.
38. 'Theatres And Entertainments', *The Argus* (Melbourne), 13 February 1905, p. 6.
39. Now the site of the Arts Centre, Melbourne.
40. 'Princes Court', *The Herald*, 18 November 1904, p. 8.
41. 'Theatres and Entertainments', *The Argus* (Melbourne), 13 February 1905, p. 6.
42. 'Sporting Notes', *Critic* (Adelaide), 22 March 1905, p. 12.
43. Gibson, Firth, *The Original Million Dollar Mermaid*, p. 19.
44. 'Two Brisbane Ladies Establish a Long-Distance Record', *Queensland Times, Ipswich Herald and General Advertiser*, 14 February 1905, p. 3.
45. 'Miss Annette Kellerman. Another Long Swim. 10¼ Miles In Four Hours 52 Minutes', *The Geelong Advertiser*, 12 April 1905, p. 1.
46. 'Champion Lady Swimmer,' *Kalgoorlie Miner*, 12 April 1905, p. 8.
47. 'Swimming', *The West Australian* (Perth), 2 May 1905, p. 6.
48. 'Way Down East', *The Sun* (Kalgoorlie), 30 April 1905, p. 7.
49. 'Grease Paint', *Sporting Life: Dryblower's Journal* (Kalgoorlie), 22 April 1905, p. 1.
50. 'Way Down East', *The Sun* (Kalgoorlie), 30 April 1905, p. 7.
51. 'Prince's Court', *The Herald* (Melbourne), 20 April 1905, p. 3.
52. 'Miss Annette Kellerman', *The Bendigo Independent*, 20 April 1905, p. 3.
53. Ibid., 22 April 1905, p. 5.
54. Ibid., 25 April 1905, p. 2.
55. 'Miss Annette Kellerman', *The Argus* (Melbourne), 12 April 1905, p. 8.
56. 'A Great Swim: Ten Miles and a Quarter', *The Herald* (Melbourne), 11 April 1905, p. 6.

Chapter 8
1. *The Herald* (Melbourne), 26 April 1905, p. 6.
2. 'Swimming', *The Advertiser* (Adelaide), 18 April 1905, p. 7.
3. Kellerman, 'My Story', SLNSW, MLMSS 6270/1.
4. Ibid.
5. *The Ballarat Star*, 27 April 1905, p. 2.
6. 'Meteorological Notes and Forecasts', *The Express and Telegraph* (Adelaide), 27 April 1905, p. 1.
7. *The Express and Telegraph* (Adelaide), 27 April 1905, p. 1.
8. 'Australia's Champion Lady Swimmer', *Sunday Times* (Sydney), 2 July 1905, p. 5.
9. Frederick William Kershaw (1869–1934).
10. Kellerman, 'My Story', SLNSW, MLMSS 6270/1.
11. 'Swimming', *The West Australian* (Perth), 2 May 1905, p. 6.
12. Kellerman, *Fairy Tales*, p. 12.

Endnotes

13 Kellerman, 'My Story', SLNSW, MLMSS 6270/1.
14 'Sporting Items', *Birmingham Daily Gazette*, 5 June 1905, p. 8.
15 Kellerman, 'My Story', SLNSW, MLMSS 6270/1.
16 *Ibid.*
17 *Ibid.*
18 Kellerman, *How to Swim*, p. 20.
19 Kellerman, 'My Story', SLNSW, MLMSS 6270/1.
20 Kellerman, *How to Swim*, p. 20.
21 Kellerman, 'My Story', SLNSW, MLMSS 6270/1.
22 'Splashes and Spurts', *The Scottish Referee* (Glasgow), 16 June 1905, p. 6.
23 'Aquatic Champions', *The Daily Mirror* (London), 17 June 1905, p. 5.
24 Bernard Bede (Barney) Kieran (6 October 1886 – 22 December 1905).
25 'Miss Annette Kellerman', *The Sportsman* (London), 20 June 1905, p. 4.
26 *The Dundee Courier*, 20 June 1905, p. 5.
27 'Lady Swimmer's Ambitions', *The Daily Mirror* (London, U.K.), 28 June 1905, p. 4.
28 Prince Arthur, Duke of Connaught and Strathearn (1 May 1850 – 16 January 1942).
29 'The Bath Club: Royalty, Murder & Shunned Pastries', thelondonwanderer.co.uk
30 Kellerman, 'My Story', SLNSW, MLMSS 6270/1.
31 *Ibid.*
32 'Lady Swimmer's Fine Record', *The Morning Leader* (London, U.K.), 1 July 1905, p. 5.
33 'A Plucky Lady Swimmer', *Liverpool Evening Express*, 1 July 1905, p. 5.
34 *Ibid.*
35 'Lady Swimmer's Fine Record', *The Morning Leader* (London, U.K.), 1 July 1905, p. 5.
36 Kellerman, *How to Swim*, p. 20.
37 'Lady Swimmer's Fine Record', *The Morning Leader* (London, U.K.), 1 July 1905, p. 5.
38 *Ibid.* In her memoirs (Kellerman, 'My Story', SLNSW, MLMSS 6270/1) Annette quoted the distance incorrectly, saying her swim was 26 miles.
39 'Lady Swimmer's Fine Record', *The Morning Leader* (London, U.K.), 1 July 1905, p. 5.
40 Kellerman, 'My Story', SLNSW, MLMSS 6270/1.
41 Kellerman, *How to Swim*, p. 21.
42 *Ibid.*

Chapter 9

1 Kellerman, *Fairy Tales*, p. 13.
2 Kellerman, 'My Story', SLNSW, MLMSS 6270/1.
3 'Cheltenham', *Brighton Southern Cross*, 1 July 1905, p. 2.
4 Henry Hamilton Fyfe (29 September 1869 – 15 June 1951).
5 Kellerman, 'My Story', SLNSW, MLMSS 6270/1.
6 Alfred Charles William Harmsworth, 1st Viscount Northcliffe (15 July 1865 – 14 August 1922).
7 *The Daily Mirror*, 2 November 1903 (d), p. 3.
8 'Two Years Old Today', *The Daily Mirror*, 2 November 1905, p 7.
9 Kellerman, 'My Story', SLNSW, MLMSS 6270/1.
10 Captain Matthew Webb (1848–1883).
11 Kellerman, 'My Story', SLNSW, MLMSS 6270/1.
12 *Ibid.*
13 *Ibid.*
14 *Ibid.*
15 *Ibid.*
16 *Ibid.*
17 Kellerman, *How to Swim*, p. 21.
18 *Ibid.*, p. 22.
19 Kellerman, 'My Story', SLNSW, MLMSS 6270/1.
20 *Ibid.*
21 *Ibid.*
22 *Ibid.*
23 *Ibid.*
24 Montague Alfred Holbein (11 August 1861 – 1 July 1944).
25 'Miss Kellerman's Plucky Swim', *The Daily Mirror*, 19 July 1905, p. 4.
26 *Ibid.*

27   Ibid.
28   *The Daily Telegraph & Courier* (London, U.K.), 21 July 1905, p. 5.
29   'For the Channel Swim', *The Daily Mirror*, 22 July 1905, p. 4.
30   Jacob Abraham 'Jabez' Wolffe (19 November 1876 – 22 October 1943).
31   'Lady's Record Swim', *The Daily Mirror*, 24 July 1905, p. 3.
32   'Dover to Ramsgate Record', *Sporting Life* (London, U.K.), 29 July 1905, p. 3.
33   Kellerman, *How to Swim,* p. 42.
34   'Lady's Record Swim', *The Daily Mirror*, 24 July 1905, p. 3.
35   'For Women', *The Daily Telegraph* (Sydney) 2 September 1905, p. 15.
36   'Woman v Waves,' *The Daily Mirror*, 27 July 1905, p. 3.
37   Edmund Caunce Nowell 'Ted' Heaton (1872 – 19 September 1937)
38   'Channel Swim', *The Daily Mirror*, 27 July 1905, p. 3.
39   'Miss Kellerman Fails', *Newcastle Morning Herald and Miners' Advocate*, 29 July 1905, p. 5.
40   'Girl Swimmer's Chances', *The Daily Mirror*, 28 July 1905, p. 4.

Chapter 10
1   On 5 September 1900.
2   Walpurga von Isacescu (1852 – 5 May 1925).
3   'An Attempt to Swim the Channel', *London Evening Standard*, 7 September 1900, p. 2.
4   'Miss Kellerman in Great Form', *The Daily Mirror*, 1 August 1905, p. 5.
5   Kellerman, 'My Story', SLNSW, MLMSS 6270/1.
6   'Fine Swim', *The Daily Mirror*, 2 August 1905, p. 4.
7   Ibid.
8   Ibid.
9   Ibid.
10 Kellerman, 'My Story', SLNSW, MLMSS 6270/1.
11 Ibid.
12 Ibid.
13 'Phenomenal Swim', *The Daily Mirror*, 3 August 1905, p. 4.
14 Ibid.
15 Ibid.
16 'Where Tides Meet', *The Daily Mirror*, 18 August 1905, p. 5.
17 'Afraid of the Sea', *ibid.*, 8 August 1905, p. 4.
18 'Fair Amphibian', *ibid.*, 5 August 1905, p. 5.
19 Ibid.
20 'Plucky Mermaid', *ibid.*, 7 August 1905, p. 4.
21 Ibid.
22 'Afraid of the Sea', *ibid.*, 8 August 1905, p. 4.
23 'Channel Swim Today', *ibid.*, 9 August 1905, p. 5.
24 *The Daily Mirror*, 10 August 1905, p. 15.
25 Thomas William Burgess (15 June 1872 – 2 July 1950).
26 'Girl Channel Swimmer at Practice', *The Daily Mirror*, 17 August 1905, p. 11.
27 'Great Swim', *ibid.*, 17 August 1905, p. 4.
28 'Eager Mermaid', *ibid.* 22 August 1905, p. 5.
29 *The Globe* (London, U.K.), 21 August 1905, p. 2.
30 'Aspirant and the Bagpipes', *The Sheffield Daily Telegraph*, 21 August 1905, p. 5.
31 *The Globe* (London, U.K.), 21 August 1905, p. 2.
32 'Storm Swimmer', *The Daily Mirror*, 19 August 1905, p. 4.
33 Ibid.
34 Kellerman, *How to Swim,* pp. 23–24.
35 'Miss Kellerman Quite Ready to Make Her Great Attempt,' *The Daily Mirror*, 21 August 1905, p. 5.
36 'Plucky Attempts to Swim Channel', *The Daily Mirror*, 25 August 1905, p. 3.
37 'Eager Mermaid', *The Daily Mirror*, 22 August 1905, p. 5.
38 Ibid.
39 Tom Reece (12 August 1873 – 16 October 1953).
40 Horace William Mew (1869 – 1927).
41 'The Channel Swim', *Guernsey Evening Press and Star*, 23 August 1905, p. 4.

42 'Eager Mermaid', *The Daily Mirror*, 22 August 1905, p. 5.
43 'To Swim or Not to Swim', *The Daily Mirror*, 25 August 1905, p. 1.
44 *The Daily Mirror*, 25 August 1905, p. 2.
45 *The Westminster Gazette*, 23 August 1905, p. 4.
46 *The Dundee Evening Telegraph*, 22 August 1905, p. 4.
47 'Eager Mermaid', *The Daily Mirror*, 22 August 1905, p. 5.

Chapter 11
1 Kellerman, *How to Swim*, p. 23.
2 *Liverpool Evening Express* (Lancashire, U.K.), 21 August 1905, p. 7.
3 'Eager Mermaid', *The Daily Mirror*, 22 August 1905, p. 5.
4 Kellerman, *How to Swim*, p. 24.
5 *Ibid.*
6 'Channel Swimmers Fail Again', *The Ashbourne Telegraph* (Derbyshire, U.K.), 1 September 1905, p. 4.
7 Kellerman, *How to Swim*, p. 25
8 'Plucky Attempts to Swim Channel', *The Daily Mirror*, 25 August 1905, p. 3.
9 'Wooed In the Water', *The Catholic Press* (Sydney), 17 May 1906, p. 17.
10 *Ibid.*
11 'Plucky Attempts to Swim Channel', *The Daily Mirror*, 25 August 1905, p. 3.
12 'Four Channel Swimmers', *The Edinburgh Evening News*, 25 August 1905, p. 4.
13 'Channel Swimmers Fail Again', *The Ashbourne Telegraph* (Derbyshire, U.K.), 1 September 1905, p. 4.
14 Kellerman, *How to Swim*, p. 25.
15 *Ibid.*, p. 26.
16 'Plucky Attempts to Swim Channel', *The Daily Mirror*, 25 August 1905, p. 3.
17 *Ibid.*
18 'Four Channel Swimmers', *The Edinburgh Evening News*, 25 August 1905, p. 4.
19 *The Advertiser* (Adelaide), 26 September 1905, p. 9.
20 'Plucky Attempts to Swim Channel', *The Daily Mirror*, 25 August 1905, p. 3.
21 *Ibid.*
22 *Ibid.*
23 'Channel Swimmers Fail Again', *The Ashbourne Telegraph* (Derbyshire, U.K.), 1 September 1905, p. 4.
24 'Swimming,' *The Sydney Sportsman*, 30 August 1905, p. 3.
25 'Wooed In the Water', *The Catholic Press* (Sydney), 17 May 1906, p. 17.
26 'Plucky Attempts to Swim Channel', *The Daily Mirror*, 25 August 1905, p. 3.
27 'Magnificent Spirit', *The Daily Mirror*, 26 August 1905, p. 4.
28 Kellerman, *How to Swim*, p. 26.
29 'Magnificent Spirit', *The Daily Mirror*, 26 August 1905, p. 4.

Chapter 12
1 Kellerman, 'My Story', SLNSW, MLMSS 6270/1.
2 *The Manchester Courier*, 8 September 1905, p. 9.
3 Kellerman, 'My Story', SLNSW, MLMSS 6270/1.
4 *Ibid.*
5 Elaine May Golding (5 May 1890 – 13 March 1951).
6 'A Rival to Miss Kellerman', *The Morning Leader* (London, U.K.), 9 September 1905, p. 7.
7 'Channel Champions in the Seine', *Pall Mall Gazette* (London, U.K.), 11 September 1905, p. 9.
8 *The Illustrated London News*, 16 September 1905, p. 390.
9 *The Empire News & The Umpire* (Manchester), 1 October 1905, p. 10.
10 'An Eleventh Hour Announcement', *The Manchester Evening News*, 9 September 1905, p. 4. In her memoirs, written half a century after the event, Annette mistakenly said she raced against seventeen competitors (not seven).
11 Emile Paulus (5 September 1862 (Paris, France) – 27 February 1938 (Saint-Maur-des-Fosses, France)).
12 David Sydney 'Boy' Billington (1885–1955).
13 Joseph Nuttall (31 August 1869 – 1 June 1942).

14 'Channel Champions in the Seine', *Pall Mall Gazette* (London, U.K.), 11 September 1905, p. 9.
15 Ibid.
16 *The Wellington Journal* (Shropshire, U.K.), 16 September 1905, p. 9.
17 'Channel Champions in the Seine', *Pall Mall Gazette* (London, U.K.), 11 September 1905, p. 9.
18 'Miss Kellerman In Paris', *The Advertiser* (Adelaide), 12 September 1905, p. 7.
19 Kellerman, 'My Story', SLNSW, MLMSS 6270/1.
20 Channel Champions in the Seine', *Pall Mall Gazette* (London, U.K.), 11 September 1905, p. 9.
21 'The Swim Through Paris', *The Dover Express*, 15 September 1905, p. 6.
22 *The Staffordshire Advertiser*, 23 September 1905, p. 3.
23 Kellerman, *How to Swim*, pp. 27–28.
24 Kellerman, 'My Story', SLNSW, MLMSS 6270/1.
25 Kellerman, *How to Swim*, p. 28.
26 Kellerman, 'My Story', SLNSW, MLMSS 6270/1.
27 Ibid.
28 'Great Swimming Race in the Seine', *The Lincolnshire Echo*, 11 September 1905, p. 2.
29 On adjusted time Holbein was awarded third place.
30 'Channel Champions in the Seine', *Pall Mall Gazette* (London, U.K.), 11 September 1905, p. 9.
31 Ibid.
32 Kellerman, *How to Swim*, p. 27.
33 Ibid.
34 'Miss Kellerman Feted', *The Daily Record* (Glasgow, U.K.), 14 September 1905, p. 5.
35 'Miss Kellerman, The Newest Fashion as a Paris Toy', *The Express and Telegraph* (Adelaide), 18 November 1905, p. 5.
36 'Swimming', *Liverpool Echo*, 16 September 1905, p. 8.

Chapter 13
1 Kellerman, 'My Story', SLNSW, MLMSS 6270/1.
2 'Accident to Miss Kellerman', *The Lyttelton Times* (Christchurch, N.Z.), 29 September 1905, p. 5.
3 *The Daily Telegraph & Courier* (London, U.K.), 27 September 1905, p. 5.
4 Ibid.
5 *Swindon Advertiser and North Wilts Chronicle*, 29 September 1905, p. 9.
6 'The Accident to Miss Kellerman', *The Sportsman* (London, U.K.), 28 September 1905, p. 4.
7 'New Church at Mentone', *The Advocate* (Melbourne), 18 November 1905, p. 17.
8 'St Kilda', *The Prahran Telegraph* (Melbourne), 14 October 1905, p. 5.
9 Kellerman, 'My Story', SLNSW, MLMSS 6270/1.
10 *The Morning Leader* (London, U.K.), 4 October 1905, p. 6
11 *The Wimbledon News* (London, U.K.), 14 October 1905, p. 8.
12 Kellerman, 'My Story', SLNSW, MLMSS 6270/1.
13 'Australian Mermaid', *Evening Despatch* (Birmingham, U.K.), 14 November 1905, p. 5.
14 *Morning Leader* (London, U.K.), 14 November 1905, p. 4.
15 *Evening News* (Sydney), 28 December 1905, p. 7.
16 *Illustrated Police News* (London, U.K.), 2 December 1905, p. 13.
17 Kellerman, 'My Story', SLNSW, MLMSS 6270/1.
18 *Illustrated Police News* (London, U.K.), 2 December 1905, p. 13.
19 *The Truth* (Brisbane), 4 February 1906, p. 4.
20 *The Truth* (Perth), 27 January 1906, p. 8.
21 Beatrice Maude Kerr (later Williams: 30 November 1887 (Williamstown, Vic.) – 3 August 1971 (Bondi, N.S.W.)).
22 *The Express and Telegraph* (Adelaide), 27 January 1906, p. 3.
23 'Mentone', *Brighton Southern Cross* (Melbourne), 17 March 1906, p. 4.
24 Ibid.

25 'How to Swim', *Manchester Times*, 9 June 1906, p. 7.
26 *Sporting Life* (London, U.K.), 11 May 1906, p. 4.
27 *Grimsby News*, 25 May 1906, p. 2.
28 *Newcastle Daily Chronicle*, 25 May 1906, p. 6.
29 *Sporting Life* (London, U.K.), 6 September 1900, p. 4.
30 *Northants Evening Post*, 9 August 1902, p. 2.
31 Gherardo Bonini, 'The Magnificent Failure of Baroness Walpurga', playingpasts.co.uk.
32 *Ibid.*
33 Kellerman, *Fairy Tales*, p. 14.
34 Marcelle Wooster, Unpublished memories, SLNSW, MLMSS 6270/1.
35 Kellerman, *How to Swim*, p. 29.
36 'Record by Miss Kellerman', *Evening News* (London, U.K.), 12 June 1906, p. 3.
37 *The Worker* (Brisbane), 18 August 1906, p. 10.
38 Marcelle Wooster, Unpublished memories, SLNSW, MLMSS 6270/1.
39 *Sporting Life* (London), 10 July 1906, p. 4.
40 *Ibid.*
41 *Ibid.*
42 *Ibid.*
43 'Swimming Championship of Paris', *Pall Mall Gazette*, 26 July 1906, p. 9.
44 *Dublin Evening Mail*, 16 July 1906, p. 4.
45 'Girls Swim in the Seine', *The Mercury* (Hobart), 1 September 1906, p. 10.
46 Dora Herxheimer (4 August 1884 (London, U.K.) – 2 July 1967 (New York, U.S.A.)).
47 Rosa Frauendorfer, b. 1886.
48 'Lady's Original Style', *Dublin Evening Mail*, 16 July 1906, p. 4.
49 Albert Bougoin (1886–1960).
50 Samuel Wilson Greasley (1867–1926)
51 *The Advertiser* (Adelaide), 23 August 1906, p. 11.
52 'The World's Champion Swimmer', *The Register* (Adelaide), 2 January 1907, p. 5.
53 'Through Paris Race', *Liverpool Evening Express*, 16 July 1906, p. 7.
54 *The Advertiser* (Adelaide), 23 August 1906, p. 11.
55 *The Sunday Times* (Perth, WA), 9 September 1906, p. 8.
56 *Ibid.*, 16 September 1906, p. 6.
57 'A Painful Swim', *The Sportsman* (London, U.K.), 8 August 1906, p. 2.
58 *London Evening Standard*, 4 August 1906, p. 7.
59 'A Painful Swim', *The Sportsman* (London, U.K.), 8 August 1906, p. 2.
60 *Ibid.*
61 *The Leeds Mercury*, 7 August 1906, p. 6.
62 'A Painful Swim', *The Sportsman* (London, U.K.), 8 August 1906, p. 2.
63 *Ibid.*
64 *Ibid.*
65 *Ibid.*
66 'Cross Channel Swim: Causes of Failure', *The Herald* (Melbourne), 30 August 1906, p. 3.
67 Charles Urban (15 April 1867 (Cincinnati, Ohio, U.S.A.) – 29 August 1942 (Brighton, U.K.)).
68 *Music Hall and Theatre Review*, (London, U.K.), 15 February 1907, p. 16.
69 *The Evening Mail* (Fremantle, W.A.), 18 March 1907, p. 3.
70 *Music Hall and Theatre Review*, (London, U.K.), 15 February 1907, p. 16.
71 *Dublin Evening Mail*, 1 September 1906, p. 2.
72 'Miss Kellerman's Record', *Lancashire Evening Post*, 13 September 1906, p. 13.
73 *Halifax Daily Guardian*, 15 September 1906, p. 2.
74 *Quiz* (Adelaide), 7 December 1906, p. 5.
75 'Music and Drama Abroad', *The Referee* (Sydney), 9 January 1907, p. 12.
76 *The Ballarat Star*, 26 January 1907, p. 2.

Chapter 14

1 'White City is Opened', *Chicago Record-Herald*, 27 May 1905, p. 9.

2. Kellerman, 'My Story', SLNSW, MLMSS 6270/1.
3. Annette Kellerman, 'Valuable Hints to Swimming Novices', *Joliet Evening Herald* (Illinois, U.S.A.), 21 May 1907, p. 6.
4. 'Naval Trick Frees Celtic from Fog', *The New York Times*, 1 May 1907, p. 2.
5. Kellerman, *Fairy Tales*, p. 14.
6. Kellerman, 'My Story', SLNSW, MLMSS 6270/1.
7. Charles Meldrum Daniels (24 March 1885 – 9 August 1973).
8. 'Famous Australian Swimmer Arrives in New York With a Little Advice,' *The Philadelphia Inquirer*, 2 May 1907, p. 16.
9. 'A Modern Mermaid,' *The Caucasian* (Alexandria, Louisiana, U.S.A.), 26 May 1907, p. 7
10. Annette Kellerman, 'Valuable Hints to Swimming Novices', *Joliet Evening Herald* (Illinois, U.S.A.), 21 May 1907, p. 6.
11. *Ibid*.
12. 'Theatrical People on Big Excursion', *The Libertyville Lake County Independent and Waukegan Weekly Sun* (Libertyville, Illinois, U.S.A.), 16 August 1907, p, 12.
13. Claire Prentice, 'The Igorrote Tribe Travelled the World for Show and Made These Two Men Rich', smithsonianmag.com, 14 October 2014.
14. *The Australian Star* (Sydney), 10 October 1907, p. 4.
15. On 15 June 1904.
16. Kellerman, 'My Story', SLNSW, MLMSS 6270/1.
17. Kellerman, *How to Swim*, p. 30.
18. *The Age* (Melbourne), 15 June 1907, p. 13.
19. *Ibid*.
20. *The Leader* (Melbourne), 22 June 1907, p. 45.
21. Kellerman, 'My Story', SLNSW, MLMSS 6270/1.
22. James Raymond Louis Sullivan (4 September 1885 (Spring Hills, Minnesota, U.S.A.) – 4 February 1972 (Southport, Qld)).
23. Gibson, Firth, *The Original Million Dollar Mermaid*, p. 107.
24. Kellerman, 'My Story', SLNSW, MLMSS 6270/1.
25. *Ibid*.
26. *Ibid*.
27. *The Racine Daily Journal* (Wisconsin, U.S.A.) 10 July 1907, p. 7.
28. Kellerman, 'My Story', SLNSW, MLMSS 6270/1.
29. *Ibid*.
30. *Ibid*.
31. *Ibid*.
32. *Ibid*.
33. *Ibid*.
34. 'Beautiful Diver Sobs Her Denial in Divorce Suit', *The Philadelphia Inquirer*, 14 March 1909, p. 25.
35. 'Chosen Few', *Gadfly* (Adelaide), 2 January 1908, p. 5.
36. 'Miss Kellerman's Swim', *The Topeka Daily State Journal* (Topeka, Kansas, U.S.A.), 16 July 1908, p. 2.
37. 'His Mermaid Sweetheart Dove Straight into the Doctor's Heart', *The Indianapolis Sun*, 11 November 1907, p. 6.
38. Kellerman, 'My Story', SLNSW, MLMSS 6270/1.
39. 'His Mermaid Sweetheart Dove Straight into the Doctor's Heart', *The Indianapolis Sun*, 11 November 1907, p. 6.
40. Kellerman, 'My Story', SLNSW, MLMSS 6270/1.
41. 'His Mermaid Sweetheart Dove Straight into the Doctor's Heart', *The Indianapolis Sun*, 11 November 1907, p. 6.
42. Kellerman, 'My Story', SLNSW, MLMSS 6270/1.
43. *Ibid*.
44. *Ibid*.
45. 'Theatrical People on Big Excursion', *Libertyville Lake County Independent and Waukegan Weekly Sun* (Libertyville, Illinois, U.S.A.), 16 August 1907, p. 12.
46. 'Miss Kellerman as a Drowning Woman', *The Sydney Morning Herald*, 9 October 1907, p. 10.
47. *Ibid*.

48 Ibid.
49 Ibid.

Chapter 15
1   *The Sunday Times* (Sydney), 17 November 1907, p. 2.
2   Marcelle Wooster, Unpublished memories, SLNSW, MLMSS 6270/1.
3   *Wolverton Express* (Buckinghamshire, U.K.), 25 October 1907, p. 3.
4   'Death of Mr. Kellerman', *The Daily Mirror*, 17 October 1907, p. 9.
5   'Australian Swimmer Sails', *The Topeka Daily State Journal* (Topeka, Kansas), 9 November 1907, p. 10.
6   'Champion Swimmer to Wed Physician', *The Philadelphia Inquirer*, 25 November 1907, p. 14.
7   *The Daily News* (Perth), 5 February 1908, p. 4.
8   *The Sportsman* (London, U.K.), 23 April 1908.
9   Kellerman, *How to Swim*, p. 27.
10 Marcelle Wooster, Unpublished memories, SLNSW, MLMSS 6270/1.
11 'Diabolo Tennis is Coming to Summer at Revere', *The Boston Post*, 18 May 1908, p. 2.
12 Gibson Firth, *The Original Million Dollar Mermaid*, p. 58.
13 *The Sportsman* (London, U.K.), 23 April 1908.
14 'Heavenly Fireworks at Sea', *The New York Times*, 17 May 1908, p. 1.
15 'Wonderland', *Boston Sunday Post*, 31 May 1908, p. 23.
16 Ibid.
17 'Swimming', *Chronicle* (Adelaide), 7 November 1908, p. 20.
18 *The Pittsburgh Leader*, 9 September 1909.
19 Kellerman, 'My Story', SLNSW, MLMSS 6270/1.
20 Ibid.
21 *Indianapolis Star*, 3 January 1909.
22 *Boston Sunday Post*, 17 May 1908, p. 22.
23 Gordon William Lillie (14 February 1860 – 3 February 1942).
24 *Newark Star and Newark Advertiser* (Newark, New Jersey, U.S.A.), 12 August 1908, p. 6.
25 *The Philadelphia Inquirer*, 3 August 1908, p. 8.
26 'Miss Kellerman's Swim', *The Topeka Daily State Journal* (Topeka, Kansas, U.S.A.), 16 July 1908, p. 2.
27 'Miss Kellerman's Great Swim', *Northern Star* (Lismore), 28 October 1908, p. 7 (quoting *Boston Globe*, 31 July 1908).
28 'Miss Kellerman's Swim', *The Topeka Daily State Journal* (Topeka, Kansas, U.S.A.), 16 July 1908, p. 2.
29 'Annette Kellerman to Make Her Daring Swim Tomorrow', *Boston Post*, 29 July 1908, p. 9.
30 'A Record Swim', *Barre Daily Times* (Barre, Vermont, U.S.A.), 31 July 1908, p. 1.
31 'Swimming Feat', *The Critic* (Hobart), 17 October 1908, p. 8.
32 Dudley Allen Sargent (29 September 1849 – 21 July 1924).
33 *The Detroit Times*, 3 August 1908, p. 2.
34 'Miss Kellerman's Great Swim', Northern Star (Lismore), 28 October 1908, p. 7 (quoting *Boston Globe*, 31 July 1908).
35 Built in 1891 as the yacht *Corsair II* for banker J.P. Morgan.
36 'Miss Kellerman's Great Swim', *Northern Star* (Lismore), 28 October 1908, p. 7.
37 Ibid.
38 'A Record Swim', *Barre Daily Times* (Barre, Vermont, U.S.A.), 31 July 1908, p. 1.
39 Ibid.
40 'Miss Kellerman's Great Swim', Northern Star (Lismore), 28 October 1908, p. 7.
41 'Vaudeville to Pay Honors to Keith', *The New York Times*, 30 November 1913, p. 67.
42 Kellerman, 'My Story', SLNSW, MLMSS 6270/1.
43 Benjamin Franklin Keith (26 January 1846 – 26 March 1914).
44 Edward Franklin Albee (8 October 1857 – 11 March 1930).
45 Kellerman, *How to Swim*, p. 30.

46	'Kellerman at Keith's', *Winthrop Sun and Visitor* (Winthrop, Massachusetts, U.S.A.), 24 October 1908, p. 2.	3	'Fair Swimmer Weeps Over Charges', *Oakland Tribune* (Oakland, California, U.S.A.), 14 March 1908, p. 13.
47	Charles Samuels, Louise Samuels, *Once Upon a Stage: The Merry World of Vaudeville*, Dodd, Mead & Co., 1974, p. 40.	4	'Made Faces at Wife', *Boston Post*, 13 March 1909, p. 1.
		5	'Miss Kellerman Denies Charges', *Oakland Tribune*, (Oakland, California, U.S.A,), 14 March 1909, p. 15.

Chapter 16

1	Andrew L. Erdman, *Blue Vaudeville*, McFarland & Co., 2004, p. 12.	6	'Tearfully Denies Drinking Beer with Another's Husband', *Oakland Tribune*, (Oakland, California, U.S.A.), 13 March 1909, p. 13.
2	'Keith's Theatre', *Boston Sunday Post*, 25 October 1908, p. 24.
3	'Dieting and Weight', *San Francisco Call,* 11 January 1909, p. 5.	7	Ibid.
4	*The New York Times*, 29 November 1908, p. 57.	8	'Miss Kellerman Denies Charges', *Oakland Tribune*, (Oakland, California, U.S.A.), 14 March 1909, p. 15.
5	'Annette Kellerman's Audacity', *The Leader* (Orange), 13 December 1910, p. 2.	9	'Beautiful Diver Sobs Her Denial in Divorce Suit', *The Philadelphia Inquirer*, p. 25.
6	*Indianapolis Star,* 3 January 1909.
7	'Miss Kellerman's New Role', *The Sportsman* (London, U.K.), 6 January 1909, p. 3.	10	'Pattee's Statement,' *Oakland Tribune*, (Oakland, California, U.S.A.), 14 March 1909, p. 15.
8	*The Evening World Daily Magazine*, 15 December 1908, p. 17.	11	'Miss Kellerman Enjoined', *The New York Times,* 31 March 1909, p. 5.
9	'Annette Kellerman Shows Charm of Her Figure', *Logansport Daily Reporter* (Logansport, Indiana, U.S.A.), 23 February 1909, p. 3.	12	'Diver, Dancer, and Diabolist', *The Star* (Sydney), 18 May 1909, p. 15.
		13	Kellerman, 'My Story', SLNSW, MLMSS 6270/1.
10	Ibid.
11	*The Morning Telegraph*, New York, 7 March 1910.	14	'King and Queen of Carnival Parade', *The New York Times*, 25 April 1909, p. 32.
12	The Metropolitan Opera House has since been relocated to Lincoln Square.	15	'Automobile Parade Carnival Feature', *The New York Times*, 3 May 1909, p. 8.
13	'The Ladies Page', *The Sunday Times* (Perth), 24 January 1909, p. 6.	16	Kellerman, 'My Story', SLNSW, MLMSS 6270/1.
14	'Swimmer is a Musician', *The Lincoln Daily Star* (Lincoln, Nebraska, U.S.A.), 12 October 1908, p. 6.	17	*San Antonio Light* (San Antonio, Texas, U.S.A.), 23 May 1909, p. 17.
15	Kellerman, 'My Story', SLNSW, MLMSS 6270/1.	18	*Atlanta Georgian*, 25 March 1911.
		19	Kellerman, 'My Story', SLNSW, MLMSS 6270/1.
16	Ibid.
17	Ibid.	20	*New York Telegraph*, 29 June 1909.
		21	*Ibid.*, 30 June 1909.

Chapter 17

		22	Gibson, Firth, *The Original Million Dollar Mermaid*, p. 76.
1	*The Referee* (Sydney), 28 April 1909, p. 12 (quoting *Variety* magazine).
		23	Kellerman, *How to Swim*, p. 36.
2	Henry Waters Taft (27 May 1859 – 1 August 1945).	24	*New York Telegraph*, 30 July 1909.
		25	Gibson, Firth, *The Original Million Dollar Mermaid*, p. 75.

26 Kellerman, 'My Story', SLNSW, MLMSS 6270/1.
27 Marcelle Wooster, Unpublished memories, SLNSW, MLMSS 6270/1.
28 'Our Grandest Little Flopper', *Variety*, 8 May 1909, p. 6.
29 *Ibid.*
30 Charles Merrill Hough (18 May 1858 – 22 April 1927).
31 'What's Next for Kellerman?', *Variety*, 15 May 1909, p. 4.
32 *Ibid.*
33 *Ibid.*
34 Kellerman, *How to Swim*, p. 31.
35 *The New York Sun*, 28 June 1909.
36 *Kinematograph Weekly* (London, U.K.), 2 September 1909, p. 13.
37 'Vitagraph', *The Bioscope*, 30 December 1909, p. 45.
38 Miss Annette Kellerman (1909), imdb.com.

Chapter 18
1 'Keith's Theatre', Winthrop Sun and Visitor (Winthrop, Massachusetts, U.S.A.), 9 October 1909, p. 2.
2 Kellerman, *How to Swim*, p. 31.
3 'Miss Kellerman to Wed', *Chicago Examiner*, 4 October 1909, p. 9.
4 Clarice M. Butkus, 'Annette Kellerman', Women Film Pioneers Project, wfpp.columbia.edu
5 'Dudley Sargent', topendsports.com
6 Carolyn de la Peña, The University of California at Davis, *Dudley Allen Sargent: Health Machines and the Energized Male Body*, Iron Game History, October 2003, starkcenter.org
7 *The Atlanta Georgian and News*, 24 March 1911, p. 7.
8 Lauren Osmer and Jan Todd, 'It is Now Within Your Reach: Annette Kellerman and Feminine Agency in Physical Culture', *Iron Game History*, Summer 2020, p. 8, starkcenter.org
9 Kellerman, 'My Story', SLNSW, MLMSS 6270/1.
10 *Ibid.*
11 'Keith's Theatre', *Winthrop Sun and Visitor*, (Winthrop, Massachusetts, U.S.A.), 9 October 1909, p. 2.
12 Gibson, Firth, *The Original Million Dollar Mermaid*, p. 61.
13 Annette Kellerman interviewed by Joel Greenberg, 1974, Oral History, National Film and Sound Archive Australia, ID: 563992.
14 Kellerman, 'My Story', SLNSW, MLMSS 6270/1.
15 Gibson, Firth, *The Original Million Dollar Mermaid*, p. 77.
16 *The Globe* (London, U.K.), 16 May 1917, p. 3.
17 A 1917 advertisement for the movie 'Daughter of the Gods', National Film and Sound Archive, ID: 383277.
18 Gibson, Firth, *The Original Million Dollar Mermaid*, p. 86.
19 Annette Kellerman, *Physical Beauty – How to Keep It,* George H. Doran, 1918, p. 51.
20 *Ibid.*, p. 50.
21 *Long Branch Daily Record* (Long Branch, New Jersey, U.S.A.), 10 July 1914, p. 16.
22 'Our American Letter', *The Telegraph* (Brisbane), 5 February 1910, p. 9.
23 Kellerman, 'My Story', SLNSW, MLMSS 6270/1. They were released in 1916.
24 'The Curves Are Only Me', *The Chicago Examiner*, 24 November 1909, p. 3.
25 'Annette Kellerman Shows Her Figure', *The Telegraph* (Brisbane), 17 January 1910, p. 12.
26 Kellerman, 'The Body Beautiful', *Collier's Weekly*, 1922, p. 3.
27 Kellerman, *Physical Beauty – How to Keep It*, p. 263.
28 *The New York Evening Journal*, 11 May 1912.
29 Kellerman, *How to Swim,* p. 45.
30 Advertisement for *The Body Beautiful* in the April 1911 issue of the *Woman's Home Companion*.
31 *Ibid.*
32 *The New York Telegraph*, 7 March 1910.
33 *The New York Times*, 18 June 1910, p. 3.
34 William Francis Corbett (1857–1923).

35	'Annette Kellerman', *The Sun* (Sydney), 14 January 1913, p. 1.	16	*Ibid.*
36	'Diving Beauty Charms Judge, Wins Freedom', *Oakland Tribune*, 29 July 1910, p. 8.	17	'Annette Kellerman Takes Life Plunge', *The Penny Press* (Middletown, Connecticut, U.S.A.), 30 November 1912.
37	*Ibid.*	18	'Annette Kellerman: A Secret Wedding', *The Sun* (Sydney), 14 January 1913, p. 1.
38	'Friends Now Wonder if Her Life Will End in Swimming Tank or a Smash-Up', *ibid.*, 31 July 1910, p. 43.	19	Kellerman, 'My Story', SLNSW, MLMSS 6270/1.
39	*Ibid.*	20	Gibson, Firth, *The Original Million Dollar Mermaid*, p. 112.
40	Kellerman, 'My Story', SLNSW, MLMSS 6270/1.	21	Groucho Marx, *Groucho and Me*, Da Capo Press, 2009, p. 137.
41	'Annette Kellerman Not Padded', *The Sun* (Sydney), 9 December 1910, p. 7.	22	'Chinese Beauty Rivals Kellerman', *The Des Moines News* (Iowa, U.S.A.), 18 September 1913, p. 12.
42	'Kellerman cries and pays $25 fine', *The Atlanta Georgian and News*, 1 April 1911, p. 8.	23	Anthony Slide, *Encyclopedia of Vaudeville*, University of Mississippi Press, 2012, p. 386.

Chapter 19

1	'Things Doing in Gotham', *The Herald-Republican* (Salt Lake City, Utah, U.S.A.), 26 November 1911, p. 8.	24	Kellerman, 'My Story', SLNSW, MLMSS 6270/1.
2	'Vera Violetta', jolson.org	25	*Ibid.*
3	'Lively Operetta at Winter Garden', *The New York Times*, 21 November 1911, p. 9.	26	'Annette Kellerman: A Secret Wedding', *The Sun* (Sydney), 14 January 1913, p. 1.
4	'Undine', playbill.com		

Chapter 20

5	'The Perfect Woman', *The Music Hall and Theatre Review* (London, U.K.), 16 May 1912, p. 12.	1	Kellerman, 'My Story', SLNSW, MLMSS 6270/1.
6	'Music', *Punch* (Melbourne), 23 February 1911, p. 30.	2	Annette Kellerman interviewed by Joel Greenberg, 1974, Oral History, National Film and Sound Archive Australia, ID: 563992.
7	Rose Weene, nee Pitonof (19 April 1895 – 15 June 1984).	3	Kellerman, 'My Story', SLNSW, MLMSS 6270/1.
8	'Outdid Miss Kellerman', *The Bradford Era* (Bradford, Pennsylvania, U.S.A.), 8 August 1910, p. 6.	4	Captain Leslie Tufnell Peacocke (9 March 1869 (Bangalore, India) – 5 March 1941 (New York City)).
9	'The Perfect Woman', *The Music Hall and Theatre Review* (London, U.K.), 16 May 1912, p. 12.	5	Annette Kellerman interviewed by Joel Greenberg, 1974, NFSA, ID: 563992.
10	*Ibid.*	6	Born Karl Lämmle (17 January 1867 – 24 September 1939).
11	*The Sporting Life*, 12 July 1912, p. 7.	7	'The film', carllaemmlethefilm.com
12	Kellerman, 'My Story', SLNSW, MLMSS 6270/1.	8	Annette Kellerman interviewed by Joel Greenberg, 1974, NFSA, ID: 563992.
13	*Ibid.*	9	Kellerman, 'My Story', SLNSW, MLMSS 6270/1.
14	'Overseas News', *Football Post*, 7 September 1912, p. 12.	10	Alexander Herbert Reginald St. John Brenon (13 January 1880
15	Kellerman, 'My Story', SLNSW, MLMSS 6270/1.		

(Kingstown, Ireland) – 21 June 1958 (Los Angeles, California, U.S.A.)).
11. Annette Kellerman interviewed by Joel Greenberg, 1974, NFSA, ID: 563992.
12. *Ibid.*
13. *The West Australian* (Perth), 8 December 1913, p. 7.
14. 'Increase Your Height', *The Maitland Weekly Mercury*, 6 September 1913, p. 12.
15. 'How to be Beautiful', *The Fitzroy City Press* (Melbourne), 27 September 1913, p. 5.
16. *The Express and Telegraph* (Adelaide), 25 October 1913, p. 8.
17. *Ibid.*, 1 November 1913, p. 8.
18. Kellerman, 'My Story', SLNSW, MLMSS 6270/1.
19. Annette Kellerman interviewed by Joel Greenberg, 1974, NFSA, ID: 563992.
20. 'Australian Diving Venus Returns from Trip Abroad', *The Galveston Daily News* (Texas, U.S.A.), 23 November 1913, p. 16.
21. *The Ogden Daily Standard* (Ogden, Utah, U.S.A.), 1 January 1914.
22. 'You'll See the Diving Venus at the Movies', *Chicago Day Book* (Chicago, Illinois, U.S.A.), 17 January 1914, p. 24.
23. Annette Kellerman interviewed by Joel Greenberg, 1974, NFSA, ID: 563992.
24. 'Motion Picture News', *The Frederick News Post* (Frederick, Maryland, U.S.A.), 27 December 1913, p. 3.
25. Annette Kellerman interviewed by Joel Greenberg, 1974, NFSA, ID: 563992.
26. Advertisement for *Neptune's Daughter*, *Chicago Examiner* (Illinois, U.S.A.), 16 May 1914, p. 9.
27. Kellerman, *Fairy Tales*, p. 14.
28. Annette Kellerman interviewed by Joel Greenberg, 1974, NFSA, ID: 563992.
29. 'Annette Kellerman Hurt as Swimming Tank Bursts', *Philadelphia Inquirer* (Pennsylvania Illinois, U.S.A.), 4 February 1914, p. 1.
30. Kellerman, *How to Swim*, p.33.
31. *Motion Picture Magazine*, July 1914, p. 60.
32. *Ibid*, p. 61.
33. Kellerman, 'My Story', SLNSW, MLMSS 6270/1.
34. *Ibid.*
35. *Motion Picture Magazine*, July 1914, p. 61.
36. *Ibid.*
37. Kellerman, *How to Swim*, p.33.
38. Annette Kellerman interviewed by Joel Greenberg, 1974, NFSA, ID: 563992.
39. *The Sydney Morning Herald*, 4 March 1914, p. 13.
40. 'Annette Kellerman's Teacher is Drowned', *Chicago Examiner* (Illinois, U.S.A.), 2 March 1914, p. 1.
41. 'Frozen to Death', *The Sun* (Sydney), 3 March 1914, p. 6.
42. *Ibid.*
43. *Motion Picture Magazine*, July 1914, p. 60.
44. 'Neptune's Daughter', imdb.com.
45. 'In the Theatres', *The Joliet Evening Herald* (Illinois, U.S.A.), 30 September 1914, p. 8.
46. Annette Kellerman interviewed by Joel Greenberg, 1974, NFSA, ID: 563992.
47. *Ibid.*
48. 'Annette Kellerman', *The Daily Telegraph* (Sydney), 13 March 1915, p. 8.
49. 'In the Theatres', *The Joliet Evening Herald* (Illinois, U.S.A.), 30 September 1914, p. 8.
50. *Ibid.*
51. *Ibid.*
52. *Chicago Tribune* (Illinois, U.S.A.), 19 May 1914.
53. Kellerman, *How to Swim*, p. 32.

Chapter 21

1. *Detroit News,* 10 May 1914.
2. Annette Kellerman interviewed by Joel Greenberg, 1974, NFSA, ID: 563992.
3. Gibson, Firth, *The Original Million Dollar Mermaid*, p. 125.
4. *Punch* (Melbourne), 30 July 1914, p. 7.

5. He married 21-year-old Germaine Gabrielle Coutures in Paris in 1911.
6. Kellerman, 'My Story', SLNSW, MLMSS 6270/1.
7. *Punch* (Melbourne), 31 December 1914, p. 22.
8. *The Van Wert Daily Bulletin* (Van Wert, Ohio, U.S.A.), 22 January 1915, p. 2.
9. *The Washington Times*, 16 February 1915, p. 8.
10. *The Sunday Star* (Washington D.C., U.S.A.), 7 February 1915, p. 21.
11. *The Commercial Tribune* (Cincinnati, Ohio, U.S.A.), 2 March 1915, p. 3.
12. *Detroit Times* (Michigan, U.S.A.), 12 March 1915, p. 9.
13. *Waco Morning News* (Texas, U.S.A.), 11 April 1915, p. 17.
14. 'Neptune's Daughter', *The Sun* (Sydney), 16 March 1915, p. 8.
15. *Ibid*.
16. Publicity brochure for *Neptune's Daughter*, National Film and Sound Archive, ID: 792364.
17. *Ibid*.
18. On 7 May 1915.
19. Publicity brochure for *Neptune's Daughter*, National Film and Sound Archive, ID: 792364.
20. Annette Kellerman interviewed by Joel Greenberg, 1974, NFSA, ID: 563992.
21. *Cincinnati Herald* (Ohio, U.S.A), 18 May, 1916.
22. The third version by Alexandre Cabanel, painted in 1875.
23. William Fox, born Wilhelm Fried Fuchs (1 January 1879 – 8 May 1952).
24. Annette Kellerman interviewed by Joel Greenberg, 1974, NFSA, ID: 563992.
25. *Ibid*.
26. *Ibid*.
27. 'Mermaid Ballet in Fox Spectacle', *Motography* (Chicago, Illinois, U.S.A.), 8 July 1916, p. 91.
28. 'New York City Weather in 1915', extremeweatherwatch.com
29. 'Gorgeous Film Being Made By Fox', *The Sunday Telegram* (Clarksburg, West Virginia, U.S.A.), 2 January 1916. p. 14.
30. 'Girl Stowaways Prove Mermaids', *The Washington Times* (Washington D.C., U.S.A.), 26 August 1915, p. 1.
31. *Ibid*.
32. J. Roy Hunt (1884–1972).
33. *The Sunday Telegram* (Clarksburg, West Virginia, U.S.A.), 2 January 1916, p. 14.
34. Annette Kellerman interviewed by Joel Greenberg, 1974, NFSA, ID: 563992.
35. Marcelle Wooster, Unpublished memories, SLNSW, MLMSS 6270/1.
36. *The New York Star* (New York State, U.S.A.), 25 November 1916.
37. Marcelle Wooster, Unpublished memories, SLNSW, MLMSS 6270/1.
38. Annette Kellerman interviewed by Joel Greenberg, 1974, NFSA, ID: 563992.
39. 'All of Jamaica in a Movie Film', *The Evening Star* (Washington D.C., U.S.A.), 18 June 1916, p. 2.
40. *Ibid*.
41. *Motion Picture News* (New York, New York State, U.S.A.), 4 November 1916.
42. *The Sunday Telegram* (Clarksburg, West Virginia, U.S.A.), 2 January 1916, p. 14.
43. *Chicago Day Book* (Chicago, Illinois, U.S.A.), 20 October 1915, p. 20.
44. *Anaconda Standard* (Anaconda, Montana, U.S.A.), 2 January 1916, p. 42.
45. *The Sunday Telegram* (Clarksburg, West Virginia, U.S.A.), 2 January 1916, p. 14.
46. *Norwich Sun* (New York, U.S.A.), 24 August 1915, p. 4.
47. *The Sunday Telegram* (Clarksburg, West Virginia, U.S.A.), 2 January 1916, p. 14.

Chapter 22

1. *Dunkirk Evening Observer*, (New York, U.S.A.), 10 July 1918, p. 12.
2. *'Lost Daughter of the Gods'* starring Annette Kellermann, movie reconstruction, Trench Art Productions.

3   Annette Kellerman interviewed by Joel Greenberg, 1974, NFSA, ID: 563992.
4   'Facts of Annette Kellerman Film', *North Judson News* (Indiana, U.S.A.), 11 January 1917, p. 1.
5   'The King of Jamaica', *Photoplay* (Chicago, Illinois, U.S.A.), July 1916, pp. 136–137.
6   *Motion Picture News* (New York, New York State, U.S.A.), 4 November 1916, p. 2861.
7   *New York Dramatic News* (New York State, U.S.A.), 28 October 1916.
8   *Washington Democrat* (Washington, Iowa, U.S.A.), 23 October 1917, p. 4.
9   'The King of Jamaica', *Photoplay* (Chicago, Illinois, U.S.A.), July 1916, p. 135.
10 *Ibid.*, pp. 136–137.
11 *Evening Star* (Washington D.C., U.S.A.), 10 December 1916, p. 30.
12 *Ibid.*
13 *Dunkirk Evening Observer*, (New York, New York State, U.S.A.), 10 July 1918, p. 12.
14 Annette Kellerman interviewed by Joel Greenberg, 1974, NFSA, ID: 563992.
15 *Evening Star* (Washington D.C., U.S.A.), 10 December 1916, p. 30.
16 *The Detroit News* (Michigan, U.S.A.), 17 December 1917.
17 Marcelle Wooster, Unpublished memories, SLNSW, MLMSS 6270/1.
18 *Motion Picture Classic* (New York, New York State, U.S.A.), February 1917, p. 17.
19 *Ibid.*
20 *Ibid.*
21 *The Detroit News* (Michigan, U.S.A.), 17 December 1917.
22 'Perilous Jump of Movie Star', *The Herald-Republican* (Salt Lake City, Utah, U.S.A.) 19 November 1916, p. 41.
23 Annette Kellerman interviewed by Joel Greenberg, 1974, NFSA, ID: 563992.
24 *Motion Picture Classic* (New York, New York State, U.S.A.), February 1917, p. 17.
25 Kellerman, *Fairy Tales*, p. 15.
26 *The Herald-Republican* (Salt Lake City, Utah, U.S.A.), 19 November 1916, p. 41.
27 *Dunkirk Evening Observer*, (New York, New York State, U.S.A.), 10 July 1918, p. 12.
28 Kellerman, *Fairy Tales*, pp. 14–15.
29 Annette Kellerman interviewed by Joel Greenberg, 1974, NFSA, ID: 563992.
30 *Toledo Blade* (Ohio, U.S.A.), 12 January 1917.
31 *Motion Picture Classic* (New York, New York State, U.S.A.), February 1917, p. 17.
32 *The Herald-Republican* (Salt Lake City, Utah, U.S.A.), 19 November 1916, p. 41.
33 Annette Kellerman interviewed by Joel Greenberg, 1974, NFSA, ID: 563992.
34 *Ibid.*
35 *Ibid.*
36 *The Herald-Republican* (Salt Lake City, Utah, U.S.A.), 19 November 1916, p. 41.
37 Annette Kellerman interviewed by Joel Greenberg, 1974, NFSA, ID: 563992.
38 *Ibid.*
39 *The Herald-Republican* (Salt Lake City, Utah, U.S.A.), 19 November 1916, p. 41.
40 Kellerman, *Fairy Tales*, p. 15.
41 *The Herald-Republican* (Salt Lake City, Utah, U.S.A.), 19 November 1916, p. 41.
42 Annette Kellerman interviewed by Joel Greenberg, 1974, NFSA, ID: 563992.
43 *Ibid.*
44 Kellerman, 'My Story', SLNSW, MLMSS 6270/1.

Chapter 23

1   *Motion Picture News* (New York, New York State, U.S.A.), 4 November 1916, p. 2820.
2   Annette Kellerman interviewed by Joel Greenberg, 1974, NFSA, ID: 563992.

3 *Photoplay* (Chicago, Illinois, U.S.A.), February 1917, p. 76.
4 *The Daily Gate City* (Keokuk, Iowa, U.S.A.), 17 August 1916, p. 3.
5 *Photoplay* (Chicago, Illinois, U.S.A.), November 1916, p. 102.
6 'The Brenon-Fox Case', *Deseret Evening News* (Utah, U.S.A.), 7 October 1916, p. 21.
7 Annette Kellerman interviewed by Joel Greenberg, 1974, NFSA, ID: 563992.
8 *Motion Picture Classic* (New York, New York State, U.S.A.), February 1917, p. 17.
9 'All Star Musical and Novelty Benefit Metropolitan Opera House', archives.metopera.org
10 'Singers and Actors' Fund', *The New York Times* (New York State, U.S.A.), 17 May 1916, p. 9.
11 *Logansport Daily Tribune* (Indiana, U.S.A.), 9 May 1916, p. 3.
12 *New York Star* (New York State, U.S.A.), 16 May 1916.
13 *The New York Times* (New York State, U.S.A.), 19 May 1916, p. 10.
14 Kellerman, 'My Story', SLNSW, MLMSS 6270/1.
15 *Ibid.*
16 *Variety* (New York, New York State, U.S.A.), 12 May 1916, p. 4.
17 *Ibid.*, 19 May 1916, p. 4.
18 Kellerman, 'My Story', SLNSW, MLMSS 6270/1.
19 *Motion Picture Classic* (New York, New York State, U.S.A.), February 1917, p. 17.
20 *Motion Picture News* (New York, New York State, U.S.A.), 16 September 1916, p. 1688.
21 *Ibid.*
22 Annette Kellerman interviewed by Joel Greenberg, 1974, NFSA, ID: 563992.
23 *The Bemidji Daily Pioneer*, (Minnesota, U.S.A.), 23 January 1918, p. 4.
24 *Motion Picture News* (New York, New York State, U.S.A.), 4 November 1916, p. 2820.
25 *Ibid.*

26 *New York Dramatic News* (New York State, U.S.A.), 28 October 1916.
27 *Photoplay* (Chicago, Illinois, U.S.A.), August 1916, p. 134.
28 *Dunkirk Evening Observer*, (New York, New York State, U.S.A.), 10 July 1918, p. 12.
29 *The Evening World* (New York, New York State, U.S.A.), 6 January 1917, p. 15.
30 *Motion Picture News* (New York, New York State, U.S.A.), 11 November 1916, p. 3008.
31 *Dunkirk Evening Observer* (New York State, U.S.A.), 10 July 1918, p. 12.
32 Gibson, Firth, *The Original Million Dollar Mermaid*, p. 149, quoting *New York Times Journal*, 19 October 1916.
33 *Ibid.*, quoting *Boston Post*.
34 In 1920.
35 *The Bioscope* (London, U.K.), 18 January 1917, p. 17.
36 *Motion Picture News* (New York, New York State, U.S.A.), 4 November 1916, p. 2861.
37 Gibson, Firth, *The Original Million Dollar Mermaid*, p. 152, quoting *Boston Transcript*, 19 October 1916.
38 *The Wilmington Dispatch* (Wilmington, North Carolina, U.S.A.), 26 February 1917, p. 5.
39 *Ibid.*
40 *Ibid.*
41 *Pittsburgh Leader* (Pennsylvania, U.S.A.), 26 October 1916.
42 *Motography* (Chicago, Illinois, U.S.A.), 13 January 1917, p. 90, quoting *The Chicago Herald*.
43 *The Kinematograph and Lantern Weekly* (London, U.K.), 25 January 1917, p. 4.
44 *Pall Mall Gazette* (London, U.K.), 22 May 1917, p. 3.
45 *The Daily Telegraph* (Sydney), 25 December 1916, p. 6.
46 *W.A. Sportsman* (Perth), 23 March 1917, p. 4.
47 Gibson, Firth, *The Original Million Dollar Mermaid*, p. 148, quoting *The Toledo Blade*.
48 'Big Picture Costs and Road Show Profits', *Variety* (New York, New

York State, U.S.A.), 16 March 1925, p. 27.
49 *Photoplay* (Chicago, Illinois, U.S.A.), January 1917, p. 87.
50 *The New York Clipper* (New York State, U.S.A.), 27 December 1916, p. 1.

Chapter 24
1   Kellerman, 'My Story', SLNSW, MLMSS 6270/1.
2   Bird Millman O'Day, born Jennadean Engleman (20 October 1890 – 5 August 1940).
3   'The Fairy on a Cobweb', palava.co
4   Kellerman, 'My Story', SLNSW, MLMSS 6270/1.
5   *Ibid.*
6   Charles Bancroft Dillingham (30 May 1868 – 30 August 1934).
7   *The New York Clipper* (New York State, U.S.A.), 27 December 1916, p. 1.
8   *The Sunday Oregonian* (Portland, Oregon, U.S.A.), 4 February 1917, p. 3.
9   *The New York Clipper* (New York State, U.S.A.), 27 December 1916, p. 1.
10 *The Sunday Oregonian* (Portland, Oregon, U.S.A.), 4 February 1917, p. 3.
11 *Motion Picture Classic* (New York, New York State, U.S.A.), February 1917, p. 17.
12 *Ibid.*
13 *The New York Times* ((New York State, U.S.A.), 13 March 1917, p. 9.
14 Marcelle Wooster, Unpublished memories, SLNSW, MLMSS 6270/1.
15 *Variety* (New York, New York State, U.S.A.), 9 February 1917, p. 11.
16 Kellerman, 'My Story', SLNSW, MLMSS 6270/1.
17 Charlotte Oelschlägel, aka Charlotte Hayward (14 August 1898 – 14 November 1984).
18 John Philip Sousa (6 November 1854 – 6 March 1932).
19 Kellerman, 'My Story', SLNSW, MLMSS 6270/1.
20 *The Sun* (New York, New York State, U.S.A.), 13 April 1917, p. 5.
21 Kellerman, 'My Story', SLNSW, MLMSS 6270/1.
22 *The Sun* (New York, New York State, U.S.A.), 13 April 1917, p. 5.
23 *Ibid.*
24 *Ibid.*
25 Annette Kellerman interviewed by Joel Greenberg, 1974, NFSA, ID: 563992.
26 *Exhibitors Herald and Motography* (Chicago, Illinois, U.S.A.), 10 August 1918, p. 43.
27 *The Moving Picture World* (New York, New York State, U.S.A.), 14 July 1917, p. 221.
28 George Bronson Howard (7 January 1884 – 20 November 1922).
29 John Gustav Adolfi (9 February 1888 – 11 May 1933).
30 Annette Kellerman interviewed by Joel Greenberg, 1974, NFSA, ID: 563992.
31 *The Moving Picture World* (New York, New York State, U.S.A.), 14 July 1917, p. 221.
32 Kellerman, 'My Story', SLNSW, MLMSS 6270/1.
33 *Ibid.*
34 *The County Review* (Riverhead, New York State, U.S.A.), 22 June 1917, p. 5.
35 Kellerman, 'My Story', SLNSW, MLMSS 6270/1.
36 *Ibid.*
37 *Ibid.*
38 *Ibid.*
39 *Ibid.*
40 *Ibid.*

Chapter 25
1   *The Boston Sunday Globe* (Massachusetts, U.S.A.), 19 August 1917, p. 42.
2   *The Washington Herald* (Washington D.C., U.S.A.), 31 March 1918, p. 16.
3   Frank D. Williams (21 March 1893 – 15 October 1961).
4   *The Moving Picture World* (New York, New York State, U.S.A.), 25 August 1917, p. 1248.
5   Kellerman, *Fairy Tales*, p. 16.

6   'Walks Tight Rope and Dives 85 Feet', *The Moving Picture World* (New York, New York State, U.S.A.), 13 October 1917, p. 221.
7   'Kellerman Film Makers Help Hospital', *ibid.*, 25 August 1917, p. 1248.
8   'Annette Kellerman Raises $4000 for Charity', *ibid.*, 15 September 1917, p. 1806.
9   *The West Virginian* (Fairmont, West Virginia), 17 September 1917, p. 2.
10 'Fox Company Guests of Bar Harbor Society', *Motion Picture News* (New York, New York State, U.S.A.), 1 September 1917, p. 1436.
11 *Ibid.*
12 'Bar Harbor Takes Kindly to Fox's Sirens', *ibid.*, 22 September 1917, p. 1996.
13 'Annette Kellerman in Queen of the Sea', *ibid.*, 1 September 1917, p. 1451.
14 *Exhibitors Herald and Motography* (Chicago, Illinois, U.S.A.), 10 August 1918, p. 43.
15 *Harrisburg Telegraph* (Pennsylvania, (U.S.A.), 10 March 1919, p. 12.
16 'William Fox Provides Resuscitation Squad', *Motion Picture News* (New York, New York State, U.S.A.), 8 September 1917, p. 1631.
17 *The Moving Picture World* (New York, New York State, U.S.A.), 13 October 1917, p. 221.
18 Kellerman, *Fairy Tales*, p. 16.
19 *Ibid.*
20 Kellerman, 'My Story', SLNSW, MLMSS 6270/1.
21 *The Moving Picture World* (New York, New York State, U.S.A.), 13 October 1917, p. 221.
22 Annette Kellerman interviewed by Joel Greenberg, 1974, NFSA, ID: 563992.
23 *The Moving Picture World* (New York, New York State, U.S.A.), 13 October 1917, p. 221.
24 Kellerman, *Fairy Tales*, p. 16.
25 *Exhibitors Herald and Motography* (Chicago, Illinois, U.S.A.), 10 August 1918, p. 43.
26 'New Kellerman Film Well Under Way', *Motion Picture News* (New York, New York State, U.S.A.), 20 October 1917, p. 2729.
27 'Fox Finishes Studio Scenes in Kellermann Film', *Motion Picture News* (New York, New York State, U.S.A.), 27 October 1917, p. 2914.
28 *Exhibitors Herald and Motography* (Chicago, Illinois, U.S.A.), 10 August 1918, p. 43.
29 Annette Kellerman interviewed by Joel Greenberg, 1974, NFSA, ID: 563992.
30 *Ibid.*
31 *Variety* (New York, New York State, U.S.A.), 23 November 1917, p. 48.
32 *Ibid.*, 1 February 1918, p. 20.
33 Kellerman, 'My Story', SLNSW, MLMSS 6270/1.
34 *Exhibitors Herald and Motography* (Chicago, Illinois, U.S.A.), 10 August 1918, p. 43.
35 *The Quincy Daily Herald* (Illinois, U.S.A.), 25 July 1918.
36 *The Moving Picture World* (New York, New York State, U.S.A.), 10 August 1918, p. 798.
37 *The Quincy Daily Herald* (Illinois, U.S.A.), 25 July 1918.
38 *The Moving Picture World* (New York, New York State, U.S.A.), 10 August 1918, p. 798.
39 *Ibid.*, 23 November 1918, p. 843.
40 Charlie Chaplin, 'How I Found Jackie Coogan', *Britannia and Eve* (London), 2 November 1928, p. 31.
41 *The Sun* (New York, New York State, U.S.A.), 13 December 1918, p. 4.
42 *Ibid.*

Chapter 26

1   Kellerman, *Physical Beauty – How to Keep It*, p. 13.
2   *Ibid.*
3   *Ibid.*, pp. 14–15.
4   *Ibid.*
5   *Ibid.*, p. 15.
6   *Ibid.*, p. 16.
7   Lauren Osmer, Jan Todd, *'It is Now Within Your Reach': Annette Kellerman*

Endnotes

      and Feminine Agency in Physical Culture, starkcentre.org
8   Advertisement for *The Body Beautiful* in the April 1911 issue of the *Woman's Home Companion.*
9   Marcelle Wooster, Unpublished memories, SLNSW, MLMSS 6270/1, p. 16.
10   Kellerman, *The Body Beautiful, Collier's Weekly,* 1922, pp. 4, 28.
11   *Ibid.,* p. 6.
12   'Physical Beauty – How to Keep It', *The Boston Globe* (Massachusetts, U.S.A.), 25 August 1918, p. 38.
13   *Ibid.*
14   Gibson, Firth, *The Original Million Dollar Mermaid,* p. 91, quoting *The Pittsburgh Leader.*
15   Kellerman, *Physical Beauty,* p. 28.
16   *Ibid.,* pp. 33–34.
17   Kellerman, *How to Swim,* p. 38.
18   *The Fort Wayne Daily News* (Texas, U.S.A.), 9 August 1916, p. 7.
19   *Ibid.*
20   *The Moving Picture World* (New York, New York State, U.S.A.), 28 June 1919, p. 2006.
21   *Ibid.,* 21 June 1919, p. 437.
22   *The Omaha Daily Bee* (Nebraska, U.S.A.), 16 February 1919, p. 25.
23   Kellerman, *How to Swim,* p. 34.
24   Annette Kellerman interviewed by Joel Greenberg, 1974, NFSA, ID: 563992.
25   *Kansas City Times* (Missouri), 15 February 1919, p. 28.
26   *Omaha Daily Bee* (Nebraska), 16 February 1919, p. 25.
27   *The Labor World* (Duluth, Minnesota, U.S.A.), 22 March 1919, p. 3.
28   *The Portland Morning Oregonian* (Oregon, U.S.A.), 24 April 1919, p. 17.
29   *Berkeley Daily Gazette* (California, U.S.A.), 10 May 1919, p. 3.

Chapter 27
1   *The Moving Picture World* (New York, New York State, U.S.A.), 12 July 1919, p. 209.
2   *Ibid.,* 19 July 1919, p. 422.
3   *Picture-Play* (New York, New York State, U.S.A.), January 1920, p. 67
4   Marcelle Wooster, Unpublished memories, SLNSW, MLMSS 6270/1, p. 38.
5   *Ibid.*
6   'What Every Woman Ought to Know', *Picture-Play* (New York, New York State, U.S.A.), February 1920, pp. 32–33.
7   *Ibid.*
8   *Ibid.,* p. 34.
9   *Ibid.,* p. 92.
10   *Ibid.,* pp. 32–33.
11   *Ibid.*
12   Sol Lesser (17 February 1890 – 19 September 1980).
13   *Santa Ana Daily Register* (California, U.S.A.), 26 May 1920, p. 2.
14   *The Moving Picture World* (New York, New York State, U.S.A.), 27 December 1919, p. 1147.
15   *The Seattle Star* (Washington, U.S.A.), 24 April 1920, p. 3.
16   Marcelle Wooster, Unpublished memories, SLNSW, MLMSS 6270/1, p. 38.
17   *Ibid.*
18   *The Seattle Star* (Washington, U.S.A.), 24 April 1920, p. 3.
19   *Ibid.*
20   *Photoplay* (Chicago, Illinois, U.S.A.), November 1920, p. 86.
21   *The Middletown Press* (Connecticut, U.S.A.), 29 November 1920, p. 8.
22   *Ibid.*
23   *Madison Capital Times* (Wisconsin, U.S.A.), 22 November 1920, p. 7.
24   *Berkeley Daily Gazette* (California, U.S.A.), 5 March 1921, p. 3.
25   *The Sun* (Sydney), 24 May 1921, p. 8.

Chapter 28
1   *Ibid.*
2   *The Daily Telegraph* (Sydney), 26 May 1921, p. 8.
3   *The Sun* (Sydney), 24 May 1921, p. 8.
4   *Ibid.*
5   *The Daily Telegraph* (Sydney), 26 May 1921, p. 8.

6   *The Sun* (Sydney), 22 May 1921, p. 3.
7   *Ibid.*
8   'Celebrated Australian Returns with Her Vaudeville Company', *Table Talk* (Melbourne), 23 June 1921, p. 25.
9   *The Sydney Morning Herald*, 7 June 1921, p. 9.
10 *Ibid.*, 25 May 1921, p. 13.
11 *The Sun* (Sydney), 29 May 1921, p. 17.
12 *Ibid.*, 12 June 1921, p. 17.
13 *Ibid.*, 29 May 1921, p. 15.
14 *Table Talk* (Melbourne), 23 June 1921, p. 25.
15 *The Sun* (Sydney), 29 May 1921, p. 15.
16 *The Sydney Morning Herald*, 13 June 1921, p. 11.
17 *The Toowoomba Chronicle*, 21 June 1921, p. 7.
18 *Evening News* (Sydney), 9 June 1921, p. 7.
19 'The Great Fight', *The Referee* (Sydney), 29 June 1921, p. 5.
20 Henry Alfred Musgrove (27 November 1858 – 2 November 1931).
21 *The Daily Telegraph* (Sydney), 2 June 1921, p. 10.
22 *The Sydney Morning Herald*, 7 June 1921, p. 9.
23 *The Daily Telegraph* (Sydney), 13 June 1921, p. 3.
24 'Miss Kellerman Arrives', *The Herald* (Melbourne), 5 July 1921, p. 10.
25 'Tivoli – Annette Kellerman', *The Age* (Melbourne), 11 July 1921, p. 8.
26 'Annette on Movie Actresses', *Table Talk* (Melbourne), 8 September 1921, p. 42.
27 'Squally Westerley', *The Sun* (Sydney), 16 October 1921, p. 11.
28 Marcelle Wooster, Unpublished memories, SLNSW, MLMSS 6270/1, p. 42.
29 *The Sunday Times* (Perth), 16 October 1921, p. 6.
30 *The Arrow* (Sydney), 16 December 1921, p. 13.
31 *The New Zealand Times*, (Wellington), 15 December 1921, p. 3.
32 *The Daily Mail* (Brisbane), 11 February 1922, p. 3.
33 *The Wairarapa Daily Times* (New Zealand), 6 February 1922, p. 6.
34 'A New Zealand Film', *The Nelson Evening Mail*, 18 February 1922, p. 4.
35 *Nelson Evening Mail*, 22 March 1922, p. 4.
36 *The Poverty Bay Herald* (New Zealand), 23 May 1922, p. 9.
37 *Ibid.*, 10 April 1922, p. 1.
38 *The Star* (Christchurch, New Zealand), 4 May 1922, p. 2.
39 *Truth* (Sydney), 6 August 1922, p. 8.
40 'Filming at Nelson', *The New Zealand Times*, 31 July 1922, p. 3.
41 'The Annette Kellerman Picture', *The Nelson Evening Mail* (New Zealand), 29 July 1922, p. 5.
42 *The Press* (Christchurch, New Zealand), 15 January 1923, p. 11.
43 *NZ Truth* (New Zealand), 7 October 1922, p. 6.
44 *The New Zealand Times* (Wellington), 3 November 1922, p. 4
45 *The Daily Telegraph* (Sydney), 28 March 1923, p. 7.
46 *The Auckland Star* (New Zealand), 31 March 1923, p. 25.
47 *The Sydney Morning Herald*, 23 July 1923, p. 7.
48 *The Daily Telegraph* (Sydney), 9 August 1923, p. 3.
49 *Toowoomba Chronicle and Darling Downs Gazette* (Qld), 1 September 1923, p. 5.
50 *The Daily Telegraph* (Sydney), 26 January 1924, p. 15.

Chapter 29

1   Disney to Kellerman, 12 March 1943, State Library NSW, MLMSS 6270/1, A2. 40.
2   Kellerman, 'My Story', SLNSW, MLMSS 6270/1.
3   Marcelle Wooster, Unpublished memories, SLNSW, MLMSS 6270/1.
4   *The New Castle News* (Pennsylvania, U.S.A.), 2 July 1924, p. 17.
5   *The Stage* (London, U.K.), 29 April 1926, p. 5.

Endnotes

6　Marcelle Wooster, Unpublished memories, SLNSW, MLMSS 6270/1.
7　Gertrude 'Trudy' Caroline Ederle (23 October 1905 – 30 November 2003).
8　'Annette's Comment', *The Daily Mail* (Brisbane), 19 September 1926, p. 5.
9　Julie 'Juliette' Henriette Lafargue (8 January 1890 (Buenos Aires, Argentina)) – 1972 (Monte Carlo, Monaco)).
10　*Daily Capital News* (Jefferson City, Missouri, U.S.A.), 24 September 1926, p. 2.
11　*Newfoundland Weekly* (Boston, Massachusetts, U.S.A.), 27 July 1929, p. 2.
12　*The Australian Women's Weekly*, 21 October 1933, p. 15.
13　*The Daily Express* (London, U.K.), 15 September 1926, p. 6.
14　Sir Oswald Stoll (born as Oswald Gray 1866–1942).
15　Marcelle Wooster, Unpublished memories, SLNSW, MLMSS 6270/1.
16　'Taught Nazis Fitness', *The Courier-Mail* (Brisbane), 9 May 1940, p. 2.
17　*The Albuquerque Journal* (New Mexico, U.S.A.), 30 January 1927, p. 12.
18　State Library of NSW, ML MSS 6270/7 (11).
19　Ernst Ragnar Johansson, professionally known as Ernst Rolf (20 January 1891 – 25 December 1932).
20　Kellerman, 'My Story', SLNSW, MLMSS 6270/1.
21　Marcelle Wooster, Unpublished memories, SLNSW, MLMSS 6270/1, p. 49.
22　*Ibid.*, p. 48.
23　Sir Anton Dolin (27 July 1904 – 25 November 1983).
24　Vera Nemtchinova (10 September 1900 – 28 June 1984). Sometimes spelt as 'Nemchinova'.
25　'Real Stage Fall', *The Daily News* (London, U.K.), 4 October 1927, p. 5.
26　Kellerman, 'My Story', SLNSW, MLMSS 6270/1.
27　*The Sunday Times* (Perth), 30 September 1928, p. 7.
28　*The Scone Advocate* (N.S.W.), 17 August 1928, p. 6.
29　*The Muswellbrook Chronicle* (N.S.W.), 7 October 1930, p. 4.
30　*The Australian Jewish Herald* (Melbourne), 12 June 1930, p. 13.
31　Annette Kellerman, 'A Pen Picture of Life in Germany,' *The Sun* (Sydney), 31 July 1932, p. 19.
32　*The Brisbane Courier*, 27 December 1932, p. 6.
33　*The Daily News* (Perth), 7 March 1933, p. 5.
34　'Annette Kellerman on Sex Appeal', Cinesound Movietone Productions, NFSA ID: 128899.
35　*The Daily News* (Perth), 7 March 1933, p. 5.
36　*The News* (Adelaide), 17 June 1933, p. 6.
37　Kellerman, 'My Story', SLNSW, MLMSS 6270/1.
38　'Barrier Reef Picture', *The Brisbane Courier*, 17 June 1933, p. 14.
39　Marcelle Wooster, Unpublished memories, SLNSW, MLMSS 6270/1, p. 59.
40　*Ibid.*, p. 60.
41　*The Daily Mercury* (Mackay, Qld), 2 August 1933, p. 8.
42　'Give Me the Barrier Reef', *The Telegraph* (Brisbane), 7 May 1934, p. 9.
43　Philip Hayward, *Tide Lines,* The Music Archive for The Pacific Press, 2001, p. 24.
44　*Ibid.*
45　Marcelle Wooster, Unpublished memories, SLNSW, MLMSS 6270/1, p. 62.
46　*The Daily Mercury* (Mackay, Qld), 12 April 1934, p. 2.
47　*Ibid.*, 4 May 1934, p. 8.
48　'Give Me the Barrier Reef', *The Telegraph* (Brisbane), 7 May 1934, p. 9.
49　*The Sydney Morning Herald*, 16 May 1934, p. 7.
50　*Townsville Daily Bulletin* (Qld), 12 December 1934, p. 7.

51 *Birmingham Weekly Mercury* (U.K.), 6 January 1935, p. 7.
52 'Annette's Still in the Swim', *Port Arthur News* (Texas, U.S.A.), 5 February 1936.
53 *Eustis Lake Region* (Florida, U.S.A.), 7 February 1936, p. 6.
54 Johnny Weissmuller, born Johann Peter Weißmüller (2 June 1904 (Freidorf, Austria–Hungary) – 20 January 1984 (Acapulco, Mexico)).
55 Clarence Linden 'Buster' Crabbe II (7 February 1908 – 23 April 1983).
56 *The Herald* (Melbourne), 13 February 1939, p. 13.
57 Marcelle Wooster, Unpublished memories, SLNSW, MLMSS 6270/1, additional note.
58 Photograph, SLNSW ML MSS 6270/7 (11), A2.175.
59 *The West Australian* (Perth), 8 March 1939, p. 6.
60 *The Daily Mirror* (London, U.K.), 25 April 1938, p. 20.
61 Kellerman, 'My Story', SLNSW, MLMSS 6270/1.
62 *The People* (London, U.K.), 29 January 1939, p. 15.
63 *The West Australian* (Perth), 8 March 1939, p. 6.
64 Kellerman, 'My Story', SLNSW, MLMSS 6270/1.
65 *The Sydney Morning Herald*, 27 April 1939, p. 5.
66 *The Courier-Mail* (Brisbane), 27 June 1939, p. 9.
67 *The Daily Mercury* (Mackay, Qld), 26 November 1937, p. 14.
68 *The Courier-Mail* (Brisbane), 10 November 1939, p. 13.
69 *Walkabout* (Melbourne), 1 June 1949.
70 *The Daily Mercury* (Mackay, Qld), 16 August 1939, p. 8.

Chapter 30
1 *The Courier-Mail* (Brisbane), 10 November 1939, p. 13.
2 'Society Throng at Dazzling Pool Show,' *The Sun* (Sydney), 4 February 1940, p. 1.
3 Clara 'Clare' Dennis – later Golding (7 March 1916 – 5 June 1971).
4 Ethel Ellen 'Kitty' Mackay – later Hodgson (5 June 1915 – 25 June 1974).
5 *The Sun* (Sydney), 27 November 1939, p. 9.
6 *The Sydney Morning Herald*, 24 January 1940, p. 2.
7 *Ibid.*, 18 December 1939, p. 6.
8 *The Bulletin*, 7 February 1940, p. 32.
9 *The Sun* (Sydney), 4 February 1940, p. 1.
10 *The Bulletin*, 7 February 1940, p. 32.
11 *The Daily Telegraph* (Sydney), 14 June 1940, p. 12. This was in Royal Prince Alfred's King George V Memorial Hospital for Mothers and Babies.
12 *The Courier-Mail*, 6 June 1940, p. 12.
13 *The Daily Mercury* (Mackay, Qld), 15 June 1940, p. 8.
14 *Ibid.*, 21 September 1940, p. 6.
15 *The Daily Telegraph* (Sydney), 20 February 1941, p. 12.
16 *The Daily Mercury* (Mackay, Qld), 21 September 1940, p. 6.
17 *The Sun* (Sydney), 16 March 1941, p. 23.
18 *The Daily Telegraph* (Sydney), 18 April 1941, p. 8.
19 *Ibid.*, 9 March 1942, p. 7.
20 'Mr. Cooper Goes to Brisbane', slq.qld.gov.au
21 Disney to Kellerman, 12 March 1943, SLNSW, MLMSS 6270/1, A2.40.
22 *Army News* (Darwin), 27 May 1943, p. 3.
23 *The Daily Mirror* (Sydney), 30 June 1943, p. 3.
24 *Ibid.*, 9 February 1944, p. 10.
25 Kellerman, 'My Story', SLNSW, MLMSS 6270/1.
26 Gibson, Firth, *The Original Million Dollar Mermaid*, p. 199.
27 *The Cairns Post* (Qld), 4 September 1945, p. 4.
28 George Macdonald Dash (1886–1959).
29 Dash to J. Sullivan, SLNSW, MLMSS 6270/1.
30 *Gold Coast News* (Qld), 1 September 1974.

Endnotes

31 H. Brotherton, *A College is Built*, Women's College Old Collegians Association, 1973, p. 42.
32 *The Morning Bulletin* (Rockhampton, Qld)), 8 April 1946, p. 5.
33 *The Daily Mirror* (Sydney), 11 April 1946, p. 2.
34 Gibson, Firth, *The Original Million Dollar Mermaid*, p. 204, quoting *Gold Coast Courier* (date unknown).
35 Kellerman, 'My Story', SLNSW, MLMSS 6270/1.
36 *The Daily Mirror* (Sydney), 25 April 1946, p. 8.
37 *The Courier-Mail* (Brisbane), 21 February 1947, p. 6.

Chapter 31

1 Victoria Sherrow, *The Encyclopedia of Women and Sports*, ABC-CLIO, 1996, p. 333.
2 Abraham Isaac Lastfogel (17 May 1898 – 27 August 1984).
3 *The Evening Star* (Washington D.C., U.S.A.), p. A-13.
4 *Los Angeles Times* (California, U.S.A.), 23 March 1952, p. D3.
5 *Ibid.*
6 Esther Williams in documentary *The Original Mermaid*, Hilton Cordell Productions, 2002.
7 Kellerman, 'My Story', SLNSW, MLMSS 6270/1.
8 *Ibid.*
9 He would receive a fourth nomination for *Witness for the Prosecution* in 1957.
10 *The Daily Telegraph* (Sydney), 11 February 1951, p. 13.
11 *Ibid.*
12 *The Lowell Sun* (Massachusetts, U.S.A.), 5 February 1951.
13 *Long Beach Independent* (California, U.S.A.), 2 August 1951, p. 20.
14 *The Daily Telegraph* (Sydney), 11 February 1951, p. 13.
15 'The Girl Who Won't Grow Old', *The Australian Women's Weekly*, 5 December 1956, p. 46.
16 *The Daily Telegraph* (Sydney), 11 February 1951, p. 13.
17 *Ibid.*
18 *Ibid.*
19 *Ibid.*
20 Vincent X. Flaherty, 'Annette Kellerman, of Bathing-Suit Fame,' untitled and undated newspaper cutting, SLNSW MLMSS 6270, Box 2.
21 Williams, *The Million Dollar Mermaid*, p. 390.
22 *The Evening Star* (Washington D.C., U.S.A.), 7 February 1952, p. 14.
23 Esther Williams in documentary *The Original Mermaid*, Hilton Cordell Productions, 2002.
24 Williams, *The Million Dollar Mermaid*, p. 390.
25 *Ibid.*
26 George J. Folsey (1898–1988).
27 *Las Vegas Daily Optic* (Las Vegas, New Mexico, U.S.A.), 15 March 1952, p. 2.
28 *Ibid.*
29 *Ibid.*
30 Williams, *The Million Dollar Mermaid*, p. 393.
31 *Ibid.*, p. 394.
32 *Ibid.*, p. 402.
33 *Ibid.*, p. 405.
34 Annette Kellerman interviewed by Joel Greenberg, 1974, NFSA, ID: 563992.
35 Helen Morgan, nee Crlenkovich (1921–1955).
36 *TV Times*, 15 February 1975, p. 63.
37 *San Antonio Express* (Texas, U.S.A.), 1 August 1952, p. 10.
38 Williams, *The Million Dollar Mermaid*, p. 407.
39 Annette Kellerman interviewed by Joel Greenberg, 1974, NFSA, ID: 563992.
40 Gibson, Firth, *The Original Million Dollar Mermaid*, p. 209, quoting *Gold Coast Weekly*, 1974.
41 *TV Times*, 15 February 1975, p. 63.
42 *South Coast Times and Wollongong Argus*, 2 March 1953, p. 3.
43 *Gold Coast Bulletin*, 7 November 1975, p. 1.
44 *Press-Telegram* (Long Beach, California, U.S.A.), 2 April 1956, p. B-6.

45   *The Daily Telegraph* (Sydney), 11 February 1951, p. 13.

Chapter 32
1. 'The Girl Who Won't Grow Old', *The Australian Women's Weekly*, 5 December 1956, p. 46.
2. *Ibid.*
3. Marcelle Wooster, Unpublished memories, SLNSW, MLMSS 6270/1, p. 67.
4. *The Canberra Times*, 28 February 1959, p. 2.
5. *Ibid.*
6. *Gold Coast Mirror*, 24–30 September 1975, p. 1.
7. *Sunday Telegraph* (Sydney), 16 March 1975, p. 26.
8. Marcelle Wooster, Unpublished memories, SLNSW, MLMSS 6270/1, p. 89.
9. 'Annette Kellerman Home Movie', NFSA-ID: 567.
10. *Gold Coast Bulletin* (Qld), 7 November 1975, p. 2.
11. *Ibid.*, 30 July 1975.
12. Gibson, Firth, *The Original Million Dollar Mermaid*, p. 216.
13. *Ibid.*, p. 217.
14. *Gold Coast Bulletin*, 7 November 1975, p. 1.
15. Annette Kellerman interviewed by Joel Greenberg, 1974, NFSA, ID: 563992.
16. Bank of America statement, SLNSW MLMSS 6270/ 1.
17. Gibson, Firth, *The Original Million Dollar Mermaid*, p. 220.
18. OPSM receipt, SLNSW MLMSS 6270/ 1.
19. CBA passbook, and Department of Social Security notice, *Ibid.*
20. *Gold Coast News,* 1 September 1974.
21. Dawson to Kellerman, 17 January 1975, SLNSW MLMSS 6270/ 1.
22. *Ibid.*, 17 January, 20 January, 7 February, 17 March 1975, SLNSW MLMSS 6270/ 1.
23. *Ibid.*, 17 January 1975.
24. *Gold Coast Bulletin* (Qld), 6 March 1975, p. 4.
25. *Ibid.*
26. *TV Times* (Sydney), 15 February 1975, p. 63.
27. *Sunday Telegraph* (Sydney), 16 March 1975, p. 26.
28. Marcelle Wooster, Unpublished memories, SLNSW, MLMSS 6270/1, p. 93.
29. *Ibid.*, p. 95.
30. *Gold Coast Bulletin* (Qld), 7 November 1975, p. 1.
31. *The Courier-Mail* (Brisbane), 15 October 1975, p. 16.
32. *Ibid.*, 18 October 1975.
33. Marcelle Wooster, Unpublished memories, SLNSW, MLMSS 6270/1, p. 96.
34. *Gold Coast Bulletin* (Qld), 7 November 1975, p. 1.
35. *Ibid.*, 11 November 1975.
36. Marcelle Wooster, Unpublished memories, SLNSW, MLMSS 6270/1, p. 97.